ON HORSEBACK
THROUGH ASIA MINOR

FREDERICK BURNABY

ON HORSEBACK THROUGH ASIA MINOR

ALAN SUTTON · Gloucester
HIPPOCRENE BOOKS, INC. · New York

First Published 1898

Copyright © in this edition 1985
Alan Sutton Publishing Limited

This edition first published in Great Britain 1985
  Alan Sutton Publishing Limited
  30 Brunswick Road
  Gloucester GL1 1JJ

British Library Cataloguing in Publication Data

Burnaby, Frederick
  On horseback through Asia Minor.
  1. Turkey—Description and travel
  I. Title
  915.61'041   DR427

  ISBN 0-86299-231-1

This edition first published in the U.S.A. 1985
  Hippocrene Books, Inc.
  171 Madison Avenue
  New York, N.Y. 10016

  ISBN 0-87052-211-6

Cover picture: detail from The Harem in the Kiosk
by Gérôme. The Fine Art Society, London.

Typesetting and origination by
Alan Sutton Publishing Limited
Photoset Bembo 9/10
Printed in Great Britain
by The Guernsey Press Company Limited,
Guernsey, Channel Islands.

BIOGRAPHICAL NOTE

He lies in silence with the dead,
  So strong, so brave;
In rustling folds above his head
  A flag doth wave.

H. Burrows-Smith

These lines are from the first verse of one of the poems written after his death which prove the popularity and acclaim which Burnaby enjoyed during his lifetime. Today little is known of the strong, ebullient man with Jewish-Italian features who died a hundred years ago, in January 1885, after a brief but exciting life. Frederick Gustavus was born in Bedford on 3 March 1842, the third child and elder son of a fox-hunting vicar and a Squire's daughter; he attended Bedford Grammar, Harrow and Oswestry schools and spent some time in Dresden learning French, German and Italian before passing his army entrance exam in 1859. He had already made an impression on his contemporaries with his intrepid daring, his strength and his physical prowess. It is, therefore, a little surprising that he should have joined the Horse Guards, which at that time played a more social than military role in English society. But the Horse Guards enjoyed at least five months leave a year, and it was this generous allowance of free time that enabled Burnaby to undertake the variety of exciting and daring exploits which earned him his fame.

During his early days in the army he practised boxing, cricket, weight-lifting and fencing. He was six foot four and weighed fifteen stone when he was twenty. Although he suffered from a weak liver, his strength was considerable and sometimes led him into scrapes, as when he was sued for physical assault by a Mr Hooker. Burnaby's letter to *The Times*, defending himself, was his first venture into the world

of letters. His most exciting interest must have been bal-
looning. His first ascent was in a hot-air balloon, in 1864, with
the French aeronaut, Eugene Godard, over Cremorne Gardens. After that he became a founder member of the
Aeronautical Society, and made many ascents with friends and
alone, narrowly escaping death on one occasion, when the
balloon in which he and a French aeronaut were experi-
menting burst, with, as Burnaby delightfully described it, 'a
cracking sound as one hears when an awkward man treads on
a lady's dress.'

Burnaby was interested in political issues, and learnt
Russian to improve his understanding of foreign affairs. He
was a friend of Thomas Gibson (Tommy) Bowles, and with
him founded the fashionable and critical weekly journal,
Vanity Fair. In order to develop his literary ability, as well as
to benefit from the salubrious climate, he persuaded Bowles to
commission a series of articles about Southern Spain and
North Africa, where he spent his leave of 1868–9. In the
following year he made a first brief visit to Russia, but left no
account of his trip. In 1873 and 74 he returned to Spain, the
second time as a war correspondent for *The Times*. (He had
been forbidden by his superiors in the Army from continuing
his association with *Vanity Fair*.) Burnaby had a flexible
personality, and was very popular with foreigners. In 1874 he
joined the headquarters of Don Carlos, and became a life-long
friend of the claimant to the Spanish throne. The following
year, again commissioned by *The Times*, he made a not
uneventful visit to Sudan. He achieved the object of his
mission, an interview with the elusive Gordon, but,
unfortunately, the latter allowed Burnaby to report only on
the nature of the country and the visible improvements
Gordon had made to river communications, so we have no
account of the meeting.

It was on his way back from Sudan that Burnaby happened
to read about the closing of Russian Asia to foreigners. He saw
the information as a challenge to his 'contradictorious spirit',
and immediately decided to go to Khiva, in Turkestan. He
planned a round trip through Russia and Afghanistan to India,
to study the infiltration of Russians towards the Indian border.

He succeeded in reaching Khiva, where he was entertained by the Khan, who expressed regret at the failure of the English to support him against the Russians, who had conquered his nation. Before reaching Afghanistan, however, Burnaby was recalled by the Foreign Office at the request of the Russian government, in order to avoid a political 'situation'. On his return to London, he was much in demand to relate his experiences, and was even invited to dine with the Queen. He related his experiences and warned of the Russian threat in his best-selling book, *A Ride to Khiva*, published in 1876. His fame won him a cartoon appearance in *Vanity Fair*, with a text:

> One of the special characteristics by which 'Fred' is marked out from among the order of young men with whom he might hastily be classed, is that he has never sought to be popular in the Society sense, and that he is no great respecter of persons. With ladies, indeed, he takes an inordinately deferential and mincing tone, yet he is by no means a ladies' man: with men he is blunt, outspoken, and on the defensive always, yet those who know him know that to his friends he is staunch and true as steel, and to all incapable of any mean or ungenerous action . . .

His first book was so successful that Burnaby soon signed a contract with Messrs Sampson Low *et al*, and received £2,500 as an advance on his next book. This was *On Horseback through Asia Minor*, published in 1877, recounting Burnaby's experiences when he travelled the whole breadth of Northern Turkey during the Winter of 1876–77. He wanted to investigate further the Russian threat. He found the Turks mentally and physically ill-equipped to withstand the Russian forces on their doorstep. The Whig government of the time favoured Russia, but Burnaby, a staunch Tory, wanted to point out that the Turks were not all inhuman beasts as the Whigs portrayed them and that the Russians were not incapable of violent and atrocious deeds.

War broke out between Turkey and Russia in 1877 and in the Winter of that year Burnaby returned to Asia for the last time. He joined Baker, a British military advisor to the

Turkish army, and witnessed action in Bulgaria. The conditions were so severe that although Burnaby survived, his servant, Radford, who had accompanied him on both expeditions to Turkey, died on their return to England.

It was six years before another major expedition abroad, but Burnaby did not pass the time uneventfully. In 1879 he made an unsuccessful marriage with Elizabeth Hawkins-Whitshed, who bore him one son before she left England to live permanently in Switzerland because of a lung complaint. Their son remained in England, with his grandmother, while Burnaby himself was in the Midlands, campaigning for a Tory vote in Birmingham in the elections of 1880, but he was defeated by the Whig contingent, Chamberlain and Muntz. In 1882 he became a member of the first council of the Primrose League, a Tory 'support group'. In the same year he made an exciting solo crossing of the Channel by hydrogen balloon. He published an account of his journey, *A Ride Across the Channel and Other Adventures in the Air*, to record his achievement. This was to be his last ascent, however, as: 'Alas, it has been officially intimated to me that the Commander-in-Chief does not approve of my ascending in balloons.'

In 1884, Burnaby, now the Colonel of his regiment, used three months of his leave to visit Sudan and support his old friend, Baker, now in charge of a makeshift Egyptian army, in an unsuccessful attempt to quell Arab rebels. But Burnaby acquitted himself well and was awarded the Sudan medal and clasp and the Khedival Star, which he received from the Khedive of Egypt himself.

His last summer in England was miserable, marred by ill-health, and depression resulting from constant criticism by senior army officers (probably irritated by Burnaby's obstinate independence and his fame outside the army ranks). But he was able to work on *Our Radicals*, a complex novel of passion and politics which he hoped would launch him into the world of creative writers. (The novel was edited and published in 1886.)

In November of the same year the War Office turned down Lord Wolseley's request for the now recovered Burnaby to join his staff in Sudan, in spite of the Colonel's previous experiences in Africa, and once more Burnaby used his leave to join military action abroad, while the Foreign Office tried continually to block his progress. He joined the British Forces on the Nile, who were on their way to relieve Gordon, under seige in Khartoum, and he was killed in action in the battle of Abu Klea on 17 January 1885.

Burnaby was a popular hero in Britain, although he received no official recognition of his bravery and commitment to his country, as his friend Bowles pointed out in *Vanity Fair*:

Fred Burnaby has left a name that will never die; but it will also be cited as one who was treated with quite a remarkable neglect, not to say contempt and disfavour, by his Sovereign, or rather by those who dispense the honours supposed to be awarded by the Sovereign. In spite of exploits as brilliant as those of any Paladin of old, he never once received so much as a word, a ribbon, or a medal, or even the C. B. that is thrown to a Board of Trade clerk when he signs some ridiculous convention. After his Ride to Khiva, and again after his journey through Asia Minor, he gave most full and valuable reports to the Horse Guards; they were received and used and no notice was taken of their author. After the Russo-Turkish war, when he accompanied and assisted Baker Pasha in his masterly retreat across the Rhodope Mountains, and in the various hard-fought battles incidental thereto, he again made the most valuable reports to the Horse Guards; but no notice was taken of their author. In the last year's operations in the Sudan he was severly wounded, was specially thanked in general orders read out before the troops by the General-in-Chief for his services, and was named in despatches; and again no notice was taken, though on the breasts of those engaged at Tel El Kebir crosses were growing like mustard and cress. For the manner in which he commanded the Blues, and the remarkable high state of efficiency and soldier-like smartness to which he brought what had hitherto been regarded as a regiment of loungers, he was repeatedly commended in the highest terms, but from first to last no mark whatever of the Sovereign's favour, not the very least mark, was ever conferred upon him. It is but too true that, like so many more of England's best and bravest sons, Fred Burnaby remained to the day of his death a splendid example of England's ingratitude.

Memorials to Burnaby may today be found in a window of St. Mary's Church, Bedford, and on an obelisk in St. Philip's churchyard in Birmingham. There is also a portrait of the young Burnaby by Tissot in the National Portrait Gallery.

SHEILA MICHELL

PREFACE

It has been said that a man often writes his book first, his preface last. The author of this work is no exception to the general rule. This volume contains an account of a journey on horseback through Asia Minor. I was five months in that country, and traversed a district extending over 2000 miles. My limited leave of absence prevented me from staying more than a few days at the important towns which lay on the route.

Although unable to learn so much as was to be desired of the ways and mode of life of the various inhabitants of Anatolia, I had the opportunity of talking to every class of society with reference to the questions of the day—the Conference, and the impending war with Russia. Pachas, farmers, peasants, all of them had something to say about these subjects.

I met people of many different races : Turks, Armenians, Greeks, Turkomans, Circassians, Kurds, and Persians. They almost invariably received me very hospitably.

The remarks which were made by the Mohammedans about the Christians, and by the Armenians about the Turks and Russians, sometimes interested me. I have thought that they might interest the public.

The impression formed in my own mind as to the probable result of the war between Russia and Turkey was decidedly unfavourable to the latter power. Since this work has been written the soldiers of the Crescent have gallantly withstood their foe. My reasons for arriving at the above-mentioned opinion will be found in this volume. They merely contain a sort of verbal photograph—if the reader will allow me to use the expression—of what I saw and heard during the journey.

A few official reports, referring to the treatment of the members of the United Greek Christians by the Russian authorities will be seen in the Appendices, and amongst other matter a document brought to England by two Circassian Chiefs. It relates to the invasion of Circassia by the Russians. There are also some march routes and descriptions of various districts, taken and translated from different military works.

THE AUTHOR.

SOMERBY HALL, LEICESTERSHIRE.
September, 1877.

INTRODUCTION

IT was the autumn of 1876: I had not as yet determined where to spend my winter leave of absence. There was a great deal of excitement in England; the news of some terrible massacres in Bulgaria had thoroughly aroused the public. The indignation against the perpetrators of these awful crimes became still more violent, when it was remembered that the Turkish Government had repudiated its loans, and that more than a hundred millions sterling had gone for ever from the pockets of the British tax-payer. This was very annoying.

We were on the eve of an important election.[1] Some people declared that our Government might have prevented the massacres in Bulgaria; others, that an ostentatious protection had been shown to Turkey, and that Europe had been wantonly disturbed through the instrumentality of our Ministry.

Illustrious statesmen, who were solacing themselves after the toils of the session, by meandering through the rural districts on bicycles, or by felling timber in sylvan groves, hurried up to town.

Two letters appeared in the columns of the leading journal signed by gentlemen belonging to the Church of England, saying that they had seen Christians impaled by the Turks.

Pamphlets were written and speeches made in which the subjects of the Sultan were held up to universal execration. Several distinguished Russians, who happened at that time to be in England, threw oil on the flames which had been kindled.

Ladies, like Madame de Lievens, of whom the late Duke of Wellington wrote,[2] went from *salon* to *salon* and extolled the Christian motives of the Tzar. This feminine eloquence proved too much for a few of our legislators, who, like Lord Grey in the year 1829, entertained some old opposition opinions of Mr. Fox's, that " the Turks ought to be driven out of Europe."

It was difficult to arrive at the truth amidst all the turmoil which prevailed. Were the Turks such awful scoundrels? Had the

[1] Buckinghamshire.

[2] *Vide* Correspondence of the late Duke of Wellington, letter to the Earl of Aberdeen, *dated* Walmer Castle, July 29th, 1829.

...u gentlemen, to whom I have already alluded, really seen Christians impaled, or were these clergymen under the influence of a hallucination? There was one way to satisfy my own mind as to whether the subjects of the Porte were so cruel as they had been described. I determined to travel in Asia Minor; for there I should be with Turks who are far removed from any European supervision. Should I not behold Christians impaled and wriggling like worms on hooks in every high road of Armenia, or find an Inquisition and a weekly *auto da fé* the amusement of the Mohammedans at Van?

Judging from the pamphlets which were continually being written about the inhuman nature of the Turks, this was not at all improbable. I should also have the opportunity of seeing something of the country between the Russo-Turkish frontier and Scutari.

It was the beginning of November. My leave of absence would commence towards the middle of the month. It was time to make preparations for the journey. On this occasion I determined to take an English servant, a faithful fellow, who had been with me in many parts of the world.

Before leaving London I thought that it might be as well to write to the Turkish Ambassador and ask him if there would be any objection on the part of the authorities in Constantinople to my proposed journey in Asia Minor, at the same time saying that in the event of my obtaining the permission to travel in Anatolia, I should be much obliged to His Excellency if he could supply me with the requisite passport. To this letter I received, by return of post, the most courteous reply. I was informed that every Englishman could travel where he liked in the Turkish Empire, and that nothing was required but the ordinary foreign office passport, one of which His Excellency enclosed.

In the meantime I read all the books I could find which treated of Asia Minor. According to the works of those travellers who have been to Armenia in the winter, the cold would be very great. Indeed Tournefort found the wells in Erzeroum frozen over in July. Milner in his "History of the Turkish Empire," remarks of the mountainous district in Armenia, "Throughout this high region no one thinks, except under most urgent necessity, of travelling for eight months in the year, owing to the snow, ice, and intense cold."

Regimental duty detained me in England during the summer. I could only avail myself of the winter for my journey. I had experienced the cold of the Kirghiz steppes in December and January, 1876, and was of opinion that the clothes which would keep a man alive in the deserts of Tartary would more than protect him against the climate of Kurdistan. For shooting purposes I determined to take a little single Express rifle made by Henry, and a No. 12 smooth-bore. A small stock of medicines was put in my saddlebags in the event of any illness on the road.

My arrangements were completed. I was ready to start.

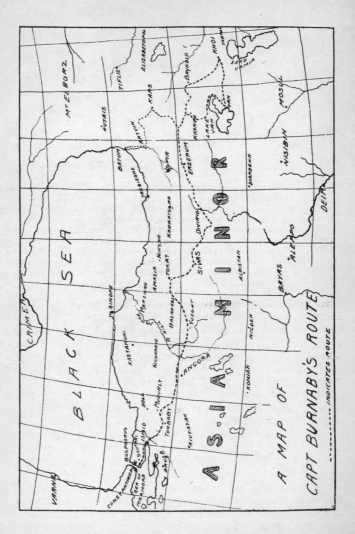

A MAP OF

CAPT BURNABY'S ROUTE

-------- INDICATES ROUTE

CHAPTER I

"Be quick, sir; you have no time to lose!" cried an officious porter in the Charing Cross Station, as he bustled me into a first-class carriage; and I found myself in the same compartment with a Queen's messenger bound for St. Petersburg. Time fled rapidly by, and I had hardly realized to myself that London was left behind, ere I was walking down those very uncomfortable steps which lead to the Calais boat. A rough passage with a number of Gauls, who all talked loud at starting, but whose conversation gradually died away in mournful strains, and we steamed into Calais Harbour; five hours later I was having my luggage examined in the waiting-room in Paris.

"Sir, they ain't found the cartridges, for I took good care to mix them up with the medicine bottles," whispered my servant Radford, as he mounted the box of our fiacre, and I drove away to a hotel, somewhat relieved in my mind, as I was not quite sure whether carrying loaded cartridges is permitted on the Chemin de Fer du Nord. I did not remain long in Paris. The 2000 miles ride which lay before me across Asia Minor would take up every day of my leave.

There was no time to lose, and in a very few hours I was in a railway station taking tickets for Marseilles. The night mail was just about to start. There were none but first-class carriages. The result was that servants and masters had to travel together.

"You will sit in that carriage," said an obese and rubicund Englishman to his groom, pointing to my compartment; "I cannot go with servants;"—and he entered another carriage. Farther on I saw the portly personage in the refreshment-room at Dijon. He was talking to a little Frenchman, and apparently on the best of terms with him. The sound of their voices was mingled with the jingling of glasses and the clinking of knives and forks. Every one was eating as fast as he could. The waiters were serving the different travellers with lightning rapidity, and the proprietor of the buffet was calling out from time to time in a deep bass voice,—

"Ne vous pressez pas, messieurs. Il y a encore 10 minutes avant le départ du train."

"Who is the little man?" I inquired of a talkative Yankee who was sitting by my side during the *table d'hôte*.

"He, sir? He is my cook, and I am taking him with me to Nice."

The obese Englishman heard the remark, and became more rubicund than before.

"I reckon I have collapsed him," muttered the American. "If I have to travel with his darned servant, I don't see why he should not travel with mine."

The train rattled on. Each man in our crowded compartment tried to compose himself to sleep; the red light from the American's cigar gradually died away, and the individual himself, coolly lolling his head on his neighbour's shoulder, sank into semi-unconsciousness.

The morn broke bright and glorious. Winter was left behind; we were in the land of orange-trees and olives.

The steamer for Constantinople started at four o'clock that afternoon, so we drove straight from the station in Marseilles to the harbour. Here I found a splendid vessel belonging to Les Messageries Maritimes, and which was already getting up steam. The captain was bustling about, giving orders. The crew were hauling in the ponderous anchors.

There were not many passengers on board; only a silk-merchant from Lyons, a rabid republican, and a pretty Greek girl,—a friend of Madame Ignatieff, the wife of the Russian ambassador at Constantinople,—who, after paying a visit to some friends in Paris, was again on her way to Constantinople. Our vessel was soon steaming ahead. She ploughed her way splendidly through the waters, and hardly a motion could be perceived inside the spacious saloon which formed the dining-room of the passengers. We were but a small party. The captain, a cheery tar who had been in every part of the world, and knew more stories about the unguardedness of the fair sex than perhaps any other mortal living. The doctor, a somewhat bilious and elderly gentleman, who became easily excited on all religious questions, and gave short dissertations between the courses on the respective merits of medicine and Christianity. The silk-merchant, who cursed the empire, and then informed us that trade had never been so flourishing as under Napoleon's rule. Presently he told me in a whisper that some Frenchmen wished for another Emperor, and he concluded, with an oath, that if there were, he would head a revolution and sacrifice his own life—yes, his own life!— sooner than that the Prince Imperial should sit upon the throne of France.

We steam into the bay of Smyrna; the picturesque and undulating coast is shaded in a framework of azure clouds; the sea, blue as lapis lazuli, is dotted with numerous vessels; flags of almost every nation in the world float in the balmy air; the clean white houses, with their many-coloured wooden shutters, brighten up the glorious landscape; and boatmen, dressed in garbs of many hues and fashions, throng the sides of our vessel.

"I am going on shore," said the silk-merchant, who was surrounded by a crowd of vociferous Greeks. "Our steamer will not start for several hours. Let us dine in a café, and see if the fair sex in this part of Turkey is as beautiful as some travellers would have us believe."

I accepted his proposal, and we walked through the streets of Smyrna. The town, clean as it looked from the harbour, proved to be a hideous deception. The streets were narrow and dirty, and the odour which everywhere met our olfactory nerves was strongly suggestive of typhus. Women were seated in the *patios* or open courts of the houses, and the Greek ladies in Smyrna are evidently not shy. They boldly returned the inquisitive glances of my companion and myself, and appeared rather pleased than otherwise at our curiosity.

"Well, I can't say much for their beauty," observed my

companion. "They have good eyes and hair, but all of them look as if they had not washed their faces for at least a fortnight. Come along and smoke a Nargileh. If there is one thing I love, it is a Nargileh, and when I am inhaling the tobacco I imagine myself to be a Pacha surrounded by my seraglio."

We turned into a café; it was surrounded by a large garden. Some Greek merchants were playing at dominoes; an Italian prima donna, who might have been any age from seventy to a hundred, was singing a popular air; men with game and fish for sale walked up and down, regardless of interrupting the ancient vocalist, and offered their wares to the visitors. Presently my companion moved uneasily in his chair; some drops of perspiration stood on his forehead, and his face was becoming rapidly green under the influence of the Turkish Nargileh.

"I think I have had enough," he remarked. "The room is very hot. *Au revoir.*" And he returned to our vessel.

In the meantime I proceeded to call upon a friend in the town. This gentleman informed me that the Christians and Turks in Smyrna were on the best of terms; however, he added that certain papers, believed to be in Russian pay, were constantly anouncing that there would shortly be a massacre of the Christians; it was said that this was done to excite bad blood between the two sects.

The shrill sound of the steamer's whistle announced that she was getting up steam. Hastily retracing my steps, I arrived on board just as the crew were weighing anchor. The original number of passengers had by this time received a considerable addition. Greeks, Armenians, and Turks were walking about or lying stretched along the deck. Women and children were huddled up in close proximity with the men. A Babel of different languages was going on around me, and an old Greek woman was having an animated squabble with one of the ship's officers, the subject of discussion being as to whether the ancient female had paid the proper fare. The French officer could speak but little Greek, and the shrill-voiced dame no French; in consequence of this it was difficult for them to arrive at any satisfactory solution of the matter.

A Pacha, his son, and the chief of the telegraphs, were the only first-class passengers. However, four ladies, the Pacha's seraglio, had been accommodated on the deck; they were reclining on some cushions in close juxtaposition with their attendant—a negro. The voice of this sable gentleman was pitched in a feminine key; he was busily engaged in arranging some pillows beneath the stoutest of the ladies—a comely dame who would have turned the scale at probably sixteen stone. Two pointer dogs in a large hamper, which was directed to a Bey in Constantinople, added their barking to the general clamour; some horses, bound to Stamboul, were fastened by head-collars to the bulwarks, no horse-boxes being provided. Farther on, and towards the steerage end of the vessel, were 500 recruits, on their way to Servia, in high spirits at the idea of shortly encountering the Russians.

It was a lovely evening; I walked along the deck with the captain, gazing curiously at his motley passengers. The stars shone bright, as became an Eastern clime; a gradually freshening breeze for the moment had cleared the horizon.

"We shall have an easy passage," I remarked.

"Yes, for good sailors," was the reply; "but it will be a little rough for those poor women,"—pointing to the pacha's harem—"and for the half-clad recruits yonder."

The latter did not seem to anticipate the treat that was in store for them. They were scattered in groups about the deck, many of them squatting upon their haunches, and attired for the most part in rags and many-coloured patchwork.

Presently a doleful melody was heard; the dirge which reached our ears told us of the readiness of these embryo warriors to meet the foe and die for the sake of Islam.

"They will die quite soon enough," remarked the captain drily, as the last verse died away. "Look down there," he added, pointing to the ship's hold; "our vessel is laden with 300 tons of lead, and once a week for several months past the steamers belonging to the Messageries Maritimes have been freighted with a similar cargo. This is all going to Odessa. It will be odd if some of the lead does not soon find its way back to the true believers, in the shape of bullets."

"The Russian Government is putting itself to great expense," he continued; "however, there are people so silly as to think that Gortschakoff wishes for peace; and in spite of all his preparations they actually believe in the Conference!"

The captain now left me, but I remained on deck. The freshening gale gradually imparted an oscillating movement to our steamer. The rain fell in large drops. Some of the sailors covered the ladies of the harem with an awning. The horses began to kick, and the dogs in the hamper to bark. A melancholy groan could be heard from that part of the vessel appropriated by the soldiers. The first to succumb was the fat woman ; in despairing tones she called for assistance. The black attendant rushed to the rescue and convulsively grasped the lady's head. It was a funny spectacle—that enormous pumpkin-shaped face supported by two black hands. The now hazy moon cast a shadowy beam on the negro's counten-ance : from black it changed to green ; it assumed a diabolical expression. The vessel lurched ; he lost his balance ; dropping his mistress's head, he fell down upon the pointers. They set up a savage growl. The eunuch started to his feet ; his hair bristled with alarm ; he felt himself all over. However, there was no damage done, and with a sorrowful mien he returned to the side of his mistress.

CHAPTER II

THE following morning my servant awoke me with the an-nouncement that we had arrived in the Bosphorus, and that he had not been able to eat his supper. By this last piece of intelligence he wished to convey to my mind that the storm had been more than usually violent. I was soon dressed, and, going on deck, found it crowded with interpreters from the different hotels. During previous sojourns in Constantinople, I had learnt by experience the discomfort of some of the purely British establishments. I had made up my mind on this occasion to try a French hotel. My hands were filled with cards announcing the merits of the different inns. The commissionnaires were deafening me with their shouts, each man bawling louder than his fellow, when the silk-merchant declared in a loud voice that there was nothing like the Hôtel de Luxembourg, and he added that the *perdrix aux truffes* and the *vol-au-vent à la financière*, as supplied by the chef of that establishment, were something—yes, something; and he kissed the tips of his fingers as he made the last remark, so as to show his appreciation of the exquisiteness of those dishes.

"Perhaps the gentlemen do not wish their luggage examined?" said an officious Greek, the commissionnaire of the Luxembourg. "I will give a baksheesh to the officials in the custom-house, and they will pass the luggage at once. But if we do not give them any money," he added, with a knowing grin, "they will detain you at least an hour, and rumple all the shirts in your portmanteaus."

"Will it be much money?" inquired my companion, who, very reluctant to open his purse-strings, was equally averse to having his shirt-fronts rumpled.

"No, sir, leave it to me," replied the Greek, with an air of great importance.

"I know that this scoundrel will rob us!" ejaculated the silk-merchant. "But we are in his hands. We must pay, whether we like it or not."

We arrived at the custom-house. An elderly official approached the Greek, and, pointing to us, said something in his ear.

"We shall be robbed, I know we shall," muttered my companion excitedly. "If I could only speak the language, I would just give that official a piece of my mind."

The Greek now put some money into the inspector's hand, and the latter, opening and shutting a hat-case, announced that the examination was over. Some porters carried our luggage up the steep hill which led from the port to Pera. We followed in a rickety old carriage. The springs were very weak, and the vehicle rolled from side to side as our horses panted along the wretchedly dirty street. Presently, to the relief of my companion and self, who were neither of us feather weights, the driver pulled up at our destination.

In the evening I went to a Turkish Café Chantant. It was a curious sight. Solemn-looking Turks were seated round the room, each man smoking his Nargileh. Little active-looking Greeks, with cigarettes in their mouths, were eagerly reading the most recent telegrams, and discussing the chances of peace or war. In the interval between the songs a small knot of younger Turks loudly applauded a vocalist. The latter then began to sing about Sultan Abdul Aziz, of all his glory, and how at last pride turned his head. He did foolish things, went mad, and killed himself. "But it was not his fault," continued the singer, in another verse, "it was his kismet. If he had been destined to die a natural death, or on the battle-field, he would have done so. We are all under the influence of destiny. Sultans are like the rest of the world. Great Sultan, rest in peace!"

I had the good fortune to be accompanied by a friend, an old resident in Constantinople. He was a perfect master of Turkish, and he readily translated to me each verse of the song.

"What is your opinion about Abdul Aziz's death?" I inquired of my companion, as the last strains of the melody died away. "Did he really kill himself, as the world would have us believe? or did some one else save him the trouble?"

My companion laughed ironically, paused for a few moments, and then remarked,—

"No one knows the exact facts of the case, but the popular belief is that he was assassinated. Indeed, the Turks say that he had agreed to sell the fleet to Russia, and had consented to allow a Russian force to garrison Constantinople."

"There is no doubt of one thing," continued my friend, "viz. that the late Sultan was thoroughly under Ignatieff's thumb. The ambassador could do what he liked with him. The Softas found it out, and feared the consequences. From these facts the public have jumped to the conclusion that he was assassinated."

"But look," added my companion, pointing to two men in the corner of the room, "there are two of the secret police. If they were not here, we should very likely have had another verse or so, more explicit as to the Sultan's fate. The audience would have been delighted if the singer had given us the popular version of Abdul Aziz's death."

" Are there many secret police ? " I inquired.

" No, there is, if anything, too much liberty in Constantinople ; the papers write what they like, and abuse the Government freely, hardly any of them being suppressed in consequence, whilst some English newspapers which are more bitter against Turkey than even the Russian journals, are sold at every bookstall."

" Do you think that there is any chance of another massacre of Christians ? " I remarked.

" Not the slightest ; that is to say, if Ignatieff does not arrange one for some political purpose. The Turks and Christians get on very well together here, whatever they may do in other parts of the country. However, there is one thing which would be very popular with all classes, and that is, an English army of occupation in Constantinople."

" Why so ? " I inquired.

" Because this would bring some gold into the country. We have now nothing but paper. Your people would spend money, and business would go on better. Why, for the last six months trade has been almost paralyzed. In fact, to tell you the truth, all classes would be very glad to see the English at Constantinople. Not for the sake of your good system of government, as you flatter yourselves in London, or through fear of being massacred by Bashi Bazouks, but simply because you have gold. Unless you bring us some, we shall all soon be ruined."

On the following day I informed the proprietor of the hotel that I wanted a servant who could speak Turkish, to accompany me during my journey. The moment that this became known I was beset by all sorts of individuals, Armenians and Greeks, eager to offer their services. Each man brought his testimonials, and declared that he was the only honest man in Constantinople, and that all the other applicants were thieves, and would certainly rob me. If ever I appeared to have a predilection for one of the candidates, I was immediately informed by the others that the man had been in prison for six months, or else that he was suspected of murder.

In consequence of this I determined to follow the advice of an Englishman who knew Turkey well, and take a Mohammedan servant, who could speak no other language than his own. In that case he would be less likely to have learned any bad habits from the Armenians, and at the same time I should be compelled to speak to him in Turkish, and thus improve my knowledge of that language.

The next morning a Turk came to the hotel, and offered himself for the situation. He was dressed in the Circassian style, and wore a short brown serge jacket, dotted across the breast with empty cartridge cases. His head was covered by a red fez or cap, encircled by a green turban. A loose pair of light blue trousers, fastened at the waist by a crimson sash, and a pair of boots, half-way up the knee, completed his attire. He was a tall, fine-looking fellow, and said that he had previously been coachman to a Pasha, that he was a good groom, and would be faithful to me as an Arab steed to his Arab master. It was a pretty speech, but as I had seen some horses in the desert which invariably kicked whenever their master approached them, it did not produce the effect upon my mind which probably the faithful man desired. However I was in a hurry to get a servant; so I agreed to take the fellow, and give him 4l. per month and his food. In the meantime he said that he knew of some horses for sale, and that he would bring them to the hotel in the course of a few days.

I had previously ascertained that my best plan would be to purchase a stud in Constantinople. In many parts of my proposed journey I should be off the postal track, and then it would be difficult to hire any horses—indeed it would sometimes be impossible, as the natives in certain parts of Kurdistan make use of buffaloes as a means of locomotion. I had once ridden a cow during an African journey. The motion is very uncomfortable; I had no wish to repeat the experiment with a buffalo.

Later on an invitation arrived for me to breakfast with Mr. Schuyler, the distinguished diplomatist, and the author of the highly-interesting volume, "Turkistan." On arriving at his house I found some of the guests already assembled. Amongst others, there were Mr. Gallenga, the *Times'* correspondent, and Mr. White, our consul at Belgrade.

Presently there was a ring at the bell, and who should come in but Mr. Sala, the well-known correspondent of the *Daily Telegraph*. His arrival was quite an unexpected pleasure for our host. Mr. Sala had only reached Constantinople half an hour before, and had come to us straight from the harbour. He had left England about three weeks previously, and first had gone to St. Petersburg. Here he had been introduced to several Russian journalists. He related in a very amusing way their conversation about England's policy towards Turkey, an account of which Mr. Sala had duly posted to the *Daily Telegraph*.

From St. Petersburg he had made his way to Odessa, and had come on *viâ* the Black Sea to Constantinople. He described all the stations along the Russian line as crowded with troops and blocked by military railway carriages ; whilst he laughed incredulously when some of our party gave it as their opinion that the Conference would lead to peace.

Our host opined that the different representatives at the Conference would never agree, and that war would inevitably be the result. He had recently returned from a visit to Philippopolis, where he had been staying with Mr. McGahan, the gentleman who wrote such harrowing accounts of the massacres in Bulgaria to the *Daily News*. Mr. McGahan, it appeared, had made himself very useful to Lady Strangford in assisting her to distribute the funds which had been subscribed for the destitute families in the East, and was immensely popular with the Christians.

Meanwhile the Turkish newspapers, it was said, were very divided in their opinions as to the Conference. The majority of them, however, were inclined to believe that it was a ruse of Russia to gain time for her military preparations, and of England to make Russia unpopular, and to sow discord between her and the other powers.

Later on in the day I met an English officer in the Engineers, who had come to Constantinople during his leave, and was spending his time, in company with some other officers, in surveying a position between the Sea of Marmora and the Black Sea, and which is immediately in front of Constantinople. He was staying at a small village about twenty miles from Constantinople, and asked me to spend a day with him and his friends, when we could ride over the ground which he was surveying. As I was curious to see the country in that neighbourhood, I readily assented to his proposal. It was agreed that I should leave Constantinople by the seven o'clock train on the following morning, and that he should send a horse to meet me at a little station about twenty miles from the city.

Mr. Gallenga had been kind enough to give me an introduction to some influential Armenians in Pera. On returning

to my hotel I found two of these gentlemen awaiting my
arrival. They were very disappointed to hear that I had
engaged a Turkish servant, as they said they could have
procured an honest Armenian, and they kindly volunteered
to provide me with letters of recommendation to the different
Armenian dignitaries in the chief towns which lay in my
route.

It was easy to gather from the conversation of one of these
gentlemen that he was not well-disposed to the idea of possibly
one day becoming a Russian subject.

" What is your opinion of the wish which General Ignatieff
is said to have expressed, about making Bulgaria independent
of the Porte ? " I inquired.

" That would never do," replied one of my visitors. " We
have difficulty enough, as it is, in keeping our people quiet in
Armenia : they will be very indignant if the Christians in
Europe are granted privileges which the Armenians in Asia
are not permitted to share."

" The fact is," observed the other, " that we have no wish
to become Russian subjects. Should this happen, we know
very well what would be the result. We should not be permitted to use our own language, and considerable pressure
would be brought to bear to induce us to change our religion.
We are aware of what has been done to the Catholics in
Poland ; * we have no wish to be treated in the same manner."

" What we require is similar treatment for all sects,"
observed the first speaker, " and that the word of a Christian
when given in a court of law should be looked upon as evidence, and in the same light as a Mohammedan's statement.
If the Caimacans (Deputy Governors) and Cadis of the
different towns in the interior were only compelled to do us
justice in this respect, we should not have much cause to
grumble. However, if the Russians were to go to Van, our
fellow-countrymen would be ten times worse off than they are
at present."

Just then an Armenian priest entered the room. He
stooped, and was apparently on the wrong side of sixty, but
he had a quick, penetrating glance, when he chose to raise his
eyes from the floor, and it was evident that there was plenty
of vigour in his brain, however little there might be in
his body.

* Probably referring to the treatment of the people professing the
United Greek faith. See Appendix A.

" This English gentleman wishes to learn some particulars about the road to Van," observed one of the Armenians ; " I want you to give him all the information in your possession."

" He will find it very difficult to reach Van at this season of the year, on account of the snow, and he will run a considerable risk of being robbed or murdered by the Kurds," replied the priest, without raising his eyes from the ground.

" Have you ever been from Scutari to Van ? " I inquired.

" No, nor hardly any one else. You had better go by the Black Sea to Trebizond, ride from there to Erzeroum, and it is only twelve days from that town to Van ; but you would probably find the road blocked by the snow."

It was clear that this priest could not help me much about my route, so I determined to take a map, Kiepert's Turkey in Asia, and strike a line across country as nearly as possible to Erzeroum. On arriving there I should probably be able to obtain some information about the state of the roads.

In the meantime the priest and his companions had left the hotel—not together, but one by one—as the old man remarked that this would be less likely to attract attention. Indeed subsequently, and throughout my journey, I frequently remarked the same dread of being seen speaking to an European on the part of the Armenian priests. Whether this arises from the fact that they are afraid of being suspected of conspiring against the Turkish Government, or it is the result of a guilty conscience, I cannot say.

Armenian newspapers frequently publish news which cannot be agreeable to the Government, and they are not interfered with by the authorities.

Armenians are not thrown into prison or banished from the capital without this being at once published to the world. Then why so much timidity on the part of the Armenian priests? If they are not engaged in seeking to undermine the Government, one would have thought that they had nothing to fear.

CHAPTER III

The porter at the hotel—A little persuasive force—Trains in Turkey are not very punctual—Two Englishmen—Snipe-shooting—The railroad takes a circuitous course—Krupp guns—The Christians are too much for the Turks in a bargain—Hadem Kui—No horse waiting—The station-master—A lanky, overgrown lad—Buyuk Checkmedge and Kara Bourna—A branch railway required—A station-master's salary—The horse—Attacked by a dog—The defence of Constantinople—A song in which the Turks delighted—Good-looking Hungarian girls—The handsome Italian—"I am not a barrel"—The song about the Turcos—Spontaneous combustion—A special Correspondent—Algeria is not Turkey, but it does not much signify.

I HAD ordered the porter at my hotel to call me early on the following morning, as the train started at seven, and it was quite half an hour's walk to the station. Luckily I awoke myself, and on looking at my watch, found it was about half-past six. Hastily dressing, I hurried downstairs, and found the individual whose business it was to awake me, fast asleep under a billiard table in the café belonging to the hotel. He grumbled at being disturbed, and did not fancy the idea of carrying my box to the station. It was necessary to use a little persuasive force, so, seizing a billiard cue, I gave him a violent poke in the side.

" Get up directly ! I shall miss the train ! "

" Please God you will not," replied the Turk, with a yawn.

I had no time to lose, so, taking the recumbent man by the collar, I lifted him bodily on his legs, put my bag in his hand, and, with another push from the billiard cue, precipitated him down the steps into the street.

" You want me to go to the station, Effendi ! " said the fellow, now thoroughly aroused.

" Yes."

" But the train will be gone."

" Not if we run."

" Run ! " replied the porter, very much astonished, " and what will the Effendi do ? "

" Run too."

And with another thrust from the billiard cue, I started him down Pera.

Fortunately for me, trains in Turkey are not very punctual in starting. On arriving at the railway, about ten minutes past seven, I found that I had time to take my ticket to

Hadem Kui, a small station an hour and a half from Constantinople. There were two Englishmen in the same carriage as myself, one of them an old friend whose acquaintance I had made some years previous in Madrid. They intended to stop at a swamp a few miles from the city, and spend the day snipe-shooting.

Upon my remarking that the railway seemed to take a very circuitous course, my friend smiled.

"Yes," he said, "when the line was about to be constructed, the Government agreed to pay so much per mile,— the result has been that, although the country is level, the line is not quite so straight as it might be."

"Poor Turks!" said his companion, "they are always being abused by the Christians, and yet the latter make a very good thing out of them. Why, only the other day, a quantity of Krupp guns were brought here. The cost price was 150*l.* per gun, but the Turks had to pay 750*l.*"

"The Christians are too much for them in a bargain," he added.

My fellow-travellers now left the train, which had stopped at the side of a wide marsh, and before our engine was again in motion, the report of a gun made me aware that their sport had already commenced.

Half an hour later I arrived at the little station of Hadem Kui. "Is there a horse waiting for me?" I inquired. "No," was the answer of the station-master, a Hungarian. "Can I hire an animal?" "No," was the reply. "How far is it to the village where Colonel H—— is living?" "Seven miles." "What sort of a road?" "No road at all, but deep mud up to the horse's girths." "When does the next train go back to Constantinople?" "Not till seven p.m."

I certainly did not bless my friend H——. To kick my heels about for twelve hours in a station destitute of a waiting-room, and with nothing to occupy my time, was not an agreeable prospect.

"I tell you what you had better do," said the station-master, "send a boy with a note to your friend. There is probably some misunderstanding about the horse, and the boy will be able to get to the village and back again in a few hours."

A lanky, overgrown lad volunteered to take the letter, and, tucking up his ragged trousers till his bare thighs were thoroughly exposed to view, he took off his boots, and started.

In a few minutes I could see him wading through mud at least two feet deep. A heavy M. F. H. would have found himself considerably out of his element if suddenly put down with his field and hounds in that line of country. Imagine layers of the heaviest Bedfordshire plough-fields all heaped one on the top of the other, and then you will fall short in attempting to realize the nature of the soil. If ever an invading army were to make use of the railway from Adrianople for an advance upon Constantinople, and the line between Buyuk Checkmedge on the Sea of Marmora, and Kara Bourna on the Black Sea, be selected by the Turks as a last point from which to defend the capital, the difficulty in transporting heavy guns and baggage to the centre of this position would be enormous. The defenders will have to make a small branch railway in rear of the line of defence, or it will be impossible for them to supply their army.

The station-master now invited me to sit down in his room, and wait till an answer to my note arrived. He was suffering from fever, and complained of the unhealthy nature of the soil. He could not sleep at night, and what most worried him was the incessant click of the telegraph dial. It was a very busy time, and any number of messages were always passing.

"I can read them as they pass, simply by the sound," he continued, "and that incessant click, click, click, all night, is enough to drive a man mad. My brain aches. I toss from side to side. I see devils sitting on the telegraph-box."

"Take my word for it, sir," he added, "there is nothing which breaks a man down so quickly as being a station-master in Turkey."

"What is your salary?" I inquired.

"Only 80*l.* a year. It is not enough to keep a wife," he added. "If I had a wife the life would be easier, but there are no women here. I shall end by hanging myself upon one of my own telegraph-posts—I know I shall if I stay here much longer."

A letter now arrived from Captain F——, a friend of H——'s, to say that, in the absence of the latter, he had opened my letter, and in consequence had sent me a horse. Such a horse as he was too, with no shoulders, and only about thirteen hands high; when I mounted the animal and had let out the stirrups to their last hole they were too short. I had the cramp. When I rode without stirrups my legs were in the mud. It was a choice of evils—the cramp or the mud, and the mud gained the day.

At last I came to the little village where Colonel H—— and his friend were residing. An Armenian servant now informed me that his master was busy surveying, but that he would soon return. The other officer, who had sent me the horse, was also out, but was shortly expected home. In about three hours both of them arrived. H—— had lost his way in the dark. He had been attacked by a dog; the savage brute had bitten his boot, and H—— had only saved himself by using his revolver. He had ordered a man to bring me a horse, but from the officer not being able to speak Turkish his instructions had been misunderstood.

The room was not a large one, and only a few feet square. There was no other, so we shared it between us, I being accommodated on the floor. We were up at daybreak, and rode over the position, a succession of rising slopes, which looked as if nature had made them especially for the defence of Constantinople. The distance from the Sea of Marmora to the Black Sea is twenty-four or twenty-five miles;* but each flank, being covered by lakes and rivers, could be easily watched and secured. The extent of the real fighting-ground would be by these features reduced to nine or ten miles of plain, but with favourable undulations affording a good command over the front. Batteries could be so arranged as to enfilade each other at every point, and should fifty thousand reliable troops ever make a stand at this position, it would be a very difficult one to carry.

This time my friend had mounted me on a different sort of animal to the one which I had ridden on the previous day. He was a stout grey cob, with good shoulders: when I mounted him the first thing which he did was to try and run away. I turned his head towards a neighbouring height, and let him gallop through the deep mud. To my astonishment on arriving at the summit he continued pulling. There was evidently some good stuff in that horse, and I determined to buy him. His owner was not in the village, so I left word that if he would send the cob to Constantinople, I would give £10 for the animal—a very fair price taking into consideration the market price of horses in the capital.

Meantime, after having said good-bye to my hospitable entertainers, I turned my face towards the railway-station.

* See Appendix B., on the defence of Constantinople.

A line of telegraph-posts served me as a guide, and I arrived at the booking-office in time to catch the train.

An acquaintance, a friend of the silk-merchant, called upon me later in the evening. He proposed that we should go together to a café, and hear a song which a French girl sang every night, and one in which the Turks delighted.

The café, or rather music hall, was a fine building, crowded with men of all nationalities. Good-looking Hungarian and Italian girls took the place of waiters, and bustled about, receiving orders from the more than usually excited true believers. Many of the latter, in spite of the Prophet's injunction, were freely partaking of raki. Volumes of smoke from the cigarettes and chibouks of the spectators had created a dense atmosphere in the building. Some of the attendants were remarkably handsome girls. Indeed, as I subsequently learnt, the proprietor of the café would not engage an ugly woman, his idea being that the Turks, his chief customers, came quite as much to look at and talk to his waitresses, as to see the performance. It must have been a hard trial for the digestive organs of the better-looking of these girls. One in particular, a tall and very handsome Italian, with large dark eyes and an innocent expression, which probably her character belied, was in great request, the Turks always inviting her to share the raki or the coffee which she brought them. The performance lasted from eight p.m. till about two in the morning ; it was a wonder that her constitution could stand the trial. I called for a cup of coffee, and when she handed it to me, I asked in Italian what she would like for herself. The girl's eyes sparkled on being addressed in her native tongue.

" Nothing, signore," she said ; " I am not a barrel, although the Turks think I am ; but you are not a Turk. However, I cannot afford to offend them, for the proprietor pays us no wages ; all I have is what the visitors give me. It is a dreadful life, signore. Chocolate, raki, and beer. I only sip, but I have to swallow a little all the same ; then there is lemonade, coffee, mastic, and occasionally, when gentlemen like yourself come here—champagne. It is such a mixture. I have a pain sometimes," she continued, at the same time pointing to the bodice of her dress, " I wish to cry, but I have to run about, smile, wait upon the visitors, and drink with them—it is a dreadful life. Oh, if I could only return to Florence ! "

A Turk seated near me, and who was eagerly gazing at the girl, made a sign to her.

"I must go," she said. "He is a friend of the proprietor—I dare not offend him."

Presently she was sipping some punch from his glass. My friend caught my eye, and laughed.

"Yes," he said, "she is adding punch to the other mixtures. Poor child, it will be a wonder if she does not go off by spontaneous combustion some day. But, hush! the famous singer is just going to give us the song about the Turcos."

A tall and rather stout French girl now came upon the stage. Some long black tresses were hanging down her back. Her dress, which was made of white muslin, was very low in front, and a flaming red sash encircled her waist. The song had reference to the bravery of the Turcos, how they died for France, and how France loved them.

The girl had a good voice. As the last notes died away in the hall, the Turks became greatly excited. Shouts of applause resounded through the building. Close to my table were two Englishmen. One of them appeared to be a correspondent of some newspaper. His pocket-book was open on the table. He was taking notes. "Patriotic song," he remarked to his companion, "capital scene for a graphic letter—sympathy between French and Turks—you see she says France loves the Turks." "Nonsense," said his companion, "she is singing about the Turcos in Algeria, not about the Turks—you have written it all wrong." The Special changed colour for a moment, and then muttered, "Confound it! yes! Algeria is not Turkey, but it does not much signify." And he went on writing.

CHAPTER IV

Osman—Five horses for sale—An industrious man—A cemetery—A wall-eyed Turk—A little black—"He ain't got no shoulders"—A horse with a sore back—A roarer—The blind beggars hear him coming—A Turkish horseshoe—Provisions for the journey—A prince belonging to the Russian Embassy in the hospital—A prince a boot-cleaner—Osman's relatives—The Hotel Royal—A stirrup-cup—Osman's religious scruples—The boat for Scutari—Shipping our horses—Jealous husbands—A Turk's seraglio—Was it a torpedo?—The panels of the Bey's carriage—An explosion of cartridges—Readjusting the luggage—A torrent of expletives.

THE following morning I was awoke by a tap at the door, and who should enter my room but the newly-engaged servant, Osman.

"Effendi," he said, "I have five horses for you to see. They are in a large yard close to the hotel. Splendid horses they are too. I am so industrious," he added, "the Effendi will find this out for himself soon. I am not like other Turks —I like working; I have been running all over Constantinople after the horses, for I heard that the Effendi was in a hurry to start. When will he go and see the animals?"

About half an hour later I accompanied the industrious man to a small plot of ground not far from Pera. It was surrounded by a high wall, and, judging from the number of loose stones which lay about, had once been a cemetery. But cemetery or not it was all the same to Osman, who had not the same reverence for the dead as the rest of his countrymen.

"There are a great many stones," I observed,

"All the better, Effendi," was the reply; "we shall ride over a number of stones on the road to Kars, and a little sooner or later for the horses does not make much difference."

The steeds were now led in, accompanied by their owner, a wall-eyed Turk. They were not much to look at, if one estimated them from an English standard, but I had learnt, in previous travels, that one cannot always judge of Eastern horses by their appearance. I desired my English servant, Radford, to mount the best-looking one of the lot, a little black, about fourteen hands high. He was very thin, and looked as if he had never been given a good feed of corn, but his legs were fine and hard. He put down his feet flat when he walked, and did not go on his toes, which last is a fatal defect to a horse if about to march for many days in succession. Radford eyed the animal from head to foot.

"Lor! sir," he said, "this 'ere horse will never carry me. He ain't got no shoulders!"

"Never mind," I replied. "Jump on him and try."

There was no saddle, and my man had to mount bare back. "Very good," I added, as the animal appeared to carry his burden without any difficulty, "take him round at a hard canter."

The little brute now began to pull hard, and bounded over the rough stones in a way that showed he was well accustomed to such obstacles.

"Does he pull?" I inquired.

"Pull, sir? He pulls my harms off!"

This was enough for me, and I determined to buy the

animal; as a horse that walks well, and will pull with fourteen stone on his back, is not a bad one for a long journey.

The next one produced for my inspection was covered with a rug, the other horses not being provided with any such clothing.

"What is that for ?" I inquired, pointing at the cloth.

"Effendi, I put it on him because I was afraid that he might catch cold," replied the owner.

"Never mind, take it off. When I buy horses I like to see them first."

"He thinks, sir," remarked my faithful servant, "that we buy 'orses as they marry their wives—that is, without looking at them. I should not be surprised, sir, if that 'ere 'orse had a sore back."

The man's remark proved true, and on taking off the cloth a raw place of at least six inches square was exposed to view.

"He has a sore back," I remarked to the owner. "Take him away."

"Sore back ! Yes, he has ; it will soon get well. The Effendi would like this horse though, and he is a great friend of the horse the Effendi has just looked at—they eat out of the same manger. The Effendi had better buy him."

"Get on that little bay," I said to my servant, not paying any attention to the Turk's observation. As my man went past at a trot, I heard a sound which at once made me aware that there was something the matter with the horse's wind.

"He is a roarer," I remarked.

"Effendi, he makes a noise, but he is stout and strong. He would make a capital pack-horse."

The horse was sound in other particulars, and as a roarer for slow marching is as good as any other animal, I determined to buy him—at the same time telling the owner that the fact of the horse's wind not being all right would considerably deteriorate from his value.

"Deteriorate from his value !" said the man, his wall-eye glaring at me ferociously. "No, Effendi, he makes a little noise, but that is nothing ; he is a useful horse, and when I let him out on hire in Constantinople he never runs over the blind beggars. He gives warning of his approach, and they hear him coming."

I had by this time selected two more horses, and now came the knotty point of what price I was to give for the four.

"How much do you want for them?" I inquired.

"How much, Effendi? Sixty liras (Turkish pounds of 18*s.*) I want, and not a piastre less; even then I should be a ruined man."

"Sixty liras! Sixty dogs and sixty sons of dogs!" I replied, attempting to address him in the language easiest understood by a Turkish peasant.

"Ah! Effendi," said the horse-dealer, "you know the value. To you there is much brain, but the Effendi's eyes will show him that sixty liras are nothing for the horses— besides, sixty liras, what are they? Sixty grains from the sand on the seashore to the gold in the Effendi's purse."

I was not going to be bamboozled in that way: taking forty liras from my pocket, I showed him the money.

"There," I said, "that is all I shall give you, and all that your horses are worth."

"Look! forty liras!" The man attempted to impart to his countenance an indignant air, but the sight of the gold was too much for him. "Only forty liras!"

"Yes," I said, "and if you will not sell them, I will buy my horses from another dealer," and I turned to go away.

"No, Effendi, do not stir!" cried the owner hastily. "But *forty* liras—let us say forty-one—one lira more—just one—for a baksheesh."

"Very well," I said, and I handed him the money.

Meantime, Osman, the Turkish servant, led my newly-acquired property to a stable which he had engaged for me in the neighbourhood.

Later on in the afternoon I received a communication from my friend H———, in which he said that he had sent the grey horse to Constantinople by the bearer of the letter, but that the owner of the animal would not take less than sixteen liras for him. As I had thoroughly tried the animal I determined to accept the offer, and my stud was now complete.

The final preparations for the journey were soon made. All the horses were fresh shod, and now I found that a Turkish horseshoe is very different to the one which we use in this country. It consists of a thin circular piece of iron, with a very small hole in the centre, not bigger than a shilling;

almost the entire surface of the hoof being thus protected by the metal.

Two English saddles were bought for myself and Radford, a Turkish saddle was provided for Osman, and two pack-saddles for the baggage-horses. Saddle-bags, corn-sacks, and nose-bags had been also purchased, and a supply of tea and such other necessaries as would be difficult to obtain when once we had quitted the capital.

Everything was now ready for the start, so I hastened to say good-bye to my numerous friends. Whilst visiting one of them—an English lady—a Russian acquaintance called upon her, to solicit subscriptions for a hospital. This building, as it appeared, was being used for all classes of patients, and a prince at the Russian Embassy was at that time occupying one of the wards.

"I went to see him yesterday," said the visitor. "He complains dreadfully of the quietness of the establishment."

"Perhaps he would like a barrel organ in the passage," observed my hostess.

"That is what I said to him," replied the lady. "If he had his own way, he would give a ball there before long."

It would rather astonish English people if they were told that a person holding the position of a Secretary of Embassy was inhabiting a building which in this country is reserved for the impecunious, but no one in Russia thinks anything of such matters; there are so many princes. Not many years ago, a prince could have been seen cleaning the visitors' boots at Dusaux's Hotel in Moscow.

It was Friday, December the 8th, 1876. I have always been a disbeliever in the sailors' superstition about leaving a port on a Friday, and although several of my friends, particularly the Greek, entreated me to postpone my departure till the following day, I determined to run the risk of offending the Fates, and at once to commence my journey.

The street in front of the Hôtel Luxembourg was filled with a crowd of idlers from an early hour. It had been rumoured about that the Giaour was mad enough to wish to go to Kars from Scutari by land, instead of by the Black Sea and Erzeroum, and that he was about to start. The Turk had spread the news. His friends and family had come to see him off. In the meantime, he himself was busily engaged in loading the pack-horses, but occasionally found time to glance superciliously at his admiring and awestruck relatives. At last everything was ready ; giving Osman the little travelling sword, I desired him to strap it round his waist. The crowd of relations were now more excited than before. The by-standers took the liveliest interest in the proceedings. " Osman has got a sword," said one. "He is buckling it on," said another.

Osman's air of importance increased tenfold when I desired him to sling my little sporting-rifle on his shoulder. There was a faint approach to a cheer from a little boy in the crowd. This was instantly suppressed, and in the midst of all the excitement we rode down the streets of Pera.

Several friends of mine were staying at the Hôtel Royal ; as we passed their windows they invited me to take a stirrup-cup, and in addition poured out a bumper for the Turk. How-ever, Osman could not be induced to drink. He was more particular in this respect than many of his fellow-countrymen. He handed the glass to Radford. The latter was not dis-pleased at the Turk's religious scruples, as he thus got two glasses for himself instead of one. He at once tossed off the contents, and smiling benignantly returned the tumbler to his companion. I now shook hands with my friends at the Royal, and we continued our journey towards the port.

" Good-bye, old fellow," cried my hospitable entertainers.

" We shall meet again soon," was my answer.

" Let us hope this side of Hades," said another, and we rode onward towards Galata.

An acquaintance, a Greek gentleman, accompanied me as far as the port. Here I discovered that one boat for Scutari had just started, and that it would be at least three hours before there would be another. This threw out my plans. I had wished to march my horses about five hours that day, but in consequence of the delay, and the shortness of the evenings at this season of the year, night would be on us before we had left Scutari.

The steamer arrived. A wide platform was pushed out from the deck to the shore, and two carriages with some horses, belonging to a Turkish Bey, were taken on board. Then came Radford and Osman, each leading two horses : I followed with the little grey. The carriages and animals belonging to the Bey were placed towards the bow of the vessel, and the other horses near the engines.

The sea was as calm as a duck-pond. In Osman's opinion it was unnecessary to tie up our steeds to the bulwarks. The animals which belonged to the Bey were simply held by their grooms, and stood quietly enough by the carriages. Everything looked *couleur de rose*, and I went up the ladder to a sort of raised deck, which arched over the place reserved for horses, cattle, and other merchandise. Here several Turkish ladies were sitting. They were engaged in sipping glasses full of water. One, who appeared to be the elder of the party, had some sugar in her pocket; producing it, she carefully sugared the tumblers of her companions, and then sugared her own. The faces of these ladies could be clearly seen through the very thin muslin texture which served them as veils. They were not prepossessing, and sadly wanted expression—a defect which I subsequently observed in almost every Turkish woman whose countenance I had the opportunity of seeing. We need not be surprised at this. I have been informed by the Turks themselves that very few women, not one per 1000, can read or write. They amuse themselves with gossip and eating. Their mental faculties become absorbed. They live for the moment, and pine after the coarser and more sensual pleasures. The domestic life in a Turkish family is often not a happy one; the elder and less favoured wives hate to desperation the more attractive and younger additions to the harem. The middle-aged spouse is goaded to madness at being deprived of those favours which the more comely wife is allowed to share. She endeavours to poison her lord's ear with respect to the new arrival. The jealous husband does not know what to believe, his home becomes a pandemonium.

Suddenly a loud report, followed by another, and then another, aroused me from my reflections; a tremendous noise could be heard below our feet, and men's voices expostulating in anger.

What had happened? One of the Turkish ladies let her tumbler fall, the faces of the other passengers became white. Was it a torpedo which General Ignatieff had set to blow up the Mohammedans, or had the engine burst?

I hurried downstairs. The first thing which met my gaze was the black horse, "Obadiah"—I had named him after a favourite old charger—lying stretched out on deck, and my English servant seated on the animal's head. Osman was holding one end of the grey horse's halter, the animal amusing himself meanwhile by lashing out with his heels at the panels of the Bey's carriage. Fortunately the other horses had remained quiet. The Bey's servants, instead of attempting to

save the panels of their master's carriage, vented their wrath
by numerous expletives, and were keeping as far as possible
from the scene of action.

"Well, I'll be d—d!"

This ejaculation, uttered in a strong Celtic accent, attracted
my attention, as I was busily engaged holding up the grey's
foreleg to keep him from doing any more damage to the Bey's
vehicle. The forcible exclamation issued from the lips of an
engineer who happened to be engaged on board the boat.

"What has happened?" I asked.

"Happened, sir! The Lord only knows. We were down
below. There was an explosion on deck. I ran upstairs
and saw smoke coming out of that box. All the horses were
topsy-turvy."

The box in question contained about 500 loaded cartridges,
which I was taking for sporting purposes.

"What does it all mean, Radford?" I inquired.

"Lor, sir, it was that black 'orse Obadiah, as was the
bottom of all the mischief. He is that artful. He stood
quiet enough till we started and the paddles began to turn;
he then began to kick, and frightened the grey. That 'ere
Turk," pointing to Osman, "was a-praying by the side of the
paddle-boxes, and not taking any account of the hanimals,
drat him! Obadiah upset his pack-saddle and then stamped
on the cartridge-box; some of them have gone off. Hosman
left off praying and began to swear, that's all he did; and as
for them there Turks in charge of the other 'orses, they did
nothing. Obadiah slipped up and I sat on his head to keep
him quiet."

Luckily no great damage was done except to the Bey's carriage. We commenced putting the pack-saddle on Obadiah,
but before this operation was completed our vessel arrived at
Scutari. The steamer would only stop a few minutes at the
port. There was no time to properly arrange the baggage.
The greater part of it had to be carried out by hand. A
crowd of idlers stood on the shore; some of them, recognizing
Osman, came to help us in adjusting the saddle, each individual
offering advice as to how the baggage should be strapped to
the saddle; Osman meanwhile talking to his friends about the
awful danger which he had incurred, and how, had it not been
for him, the steamer and all the passengers must inevitably
have gone to the bottom. The Bey's carriage drove past us;
the servants on the box vented their indignation at the

damage done to their master's panels in some strong language. Osman answered them in a torrent of expletives, which, translated into Saxon, would frighten a Billingsgate fishwoman. The bystanders joined in the chorus, and it was some time before we were ready to start.

CHAPTER V

Scutari — The resting-place of departed Turks — A frightened horse— Obadiah—Tea and sugar in the mud—A *rahvan*, or ambler—A runaway steed—Osman always praying whenever there is work to be done—The grave-digger — The Hammall — Radford — Through the swamp—The Khan at Moltape—A *mungo*.

THE shades of evening were falling fast as we rode through the town. Presently, leaving behind the dirty lanes and filthy streets, the main features of Scutari, we emerged upon the open country. The road was in a dreadful state, at least a foot of black mud was piled on the strata below. In order the better to avoid the dirt we rode along a raised path which overhung the highway, Osman and Radford each leading a baggage-horse. In about half an hour we arrived at a place where the highway ascended rapidly for a few hundred yards. The footpath rose yet more abruptly, and here and there large sections of it had fallen into the road below. We were passing by the cemetery at Scutari. Thousands of gravestones which mark the resting-place of departed Turks lay scattered here and there. A deep silence reigned around, and the place appeared a desert, tenanted only by the dead. Suddenly I heard a noise behind me ; a sound of horse's hoofs striking violently against some hard substance. I looked round. The first thing which met my gaze was the horse Obadiah, the source of all our previous difficulties, with his pack-saddle under the girth. In the hurry of resaddling him at Scutari the yarn breastplate and crupper had not been well adjusted, nor had they been properly buckled. The saddle had turned, and Obadiah was amusing himself by a second time kicking at my cartridge-boxes, gun-case, and tins of tea and sugar. Clash went his iron hoof against one of the cases, away flew the white sugar into the black mud. A bang resounded from the gun-case, and that went spinning in another direction. Fortunately the boxes of cartridges had

rolled to a little distance, and were just out of reach of the
now infuriated beast's heels. Osman, in a moment of fear
had released the animal's halter; dismounting from his own
steed, he tried to get to Obadiah's head. This was by no
means an easy task; the path was very narrow, in fact there
was barely room enough for a horse to walk. To reach the
pack animal it was necessary to descend to the road, which
lay some feet below us, and then climb up the steep and
muddy bank.

Whilst this was being done I took charge of Osman's horse,
the roarer, and which he had selected for his own riding,
because, he said, that the animal was a *rahvan* or ambler. He
had rubbed his trousers when he made this remark, and had
grinned complacently: by this gesture he sought to convey to
my mind, that his skin was tender, and that he did not wish
to be galled during the journey.

A noise in front now called my attention to that direction.
The horse that Radford was leading had become alarmed, and
in his struggles to release himself was half way over the bank.

"Let him go!" I cried to my servant, fearing that he
would be dragged over the steep incline.

Down fell the animal on his back, and all the remainder of
my luggage was covered with the slimy clay. The horse was
a little shaken by the fall and did not attempt to rise—he lay
prostrate and helpless in the midst of the havoc which he had
created. Meantime Obadiah, who had been frightened to
death by the luggage which was hanging round his heels,
had kicked away his trammels. Osman approached him from
the bank, and tried to get to his head. It was in vain. The
horse sprang back a yard or so, plunged and kicked, then
slipping like his fellow steed, he rolled down the steep. He
was none the worse for the fall, and bounding on his legs,
dashed headlong along the road—his saddle and everything
he had previously carried lying scattered in every direction.

The sun by this time had long since set. It was nearly
dark. Letting go Osman's horse, I galloped after the runaway, but it was useless; in a moment he disappeared from
view. There was nothing to be done but to return to my
party, and collect the luggage.

"Our fate is a bad one," said Osman. "The horse—curse
his mother—has gone, what shall be done? Praise be to
Allah that the Effendi is not hurt." "I have worked very
hard," he added,

"It is all your fault," I remarked angrily, "It would serve you right if I were to break your head. You ought to have seen that the pack-saddle was properly put on the horse at Scutari."

"Saddle, Effendi? It was all owing to the saddle. It did not fit the horse."

"What does he say, sir?" inquired the English servant.

"Say?—confound him! he says it is the fault of the saddle."

"Saddle, sir! no, it ain't. It is all the fault of his confounded praying. Why, whenever there is any work to be done, he is always down on his knees and a-banging his head against the ground. Real hard work his praying is, sir, and no mistake. I catched him at it this morning in the hotel; then he had another turn on board the steamer—and, look, sir, there he is again. Drat him, he has taken my coat to kneel on!" And rushing up, my servant dragged his property from beneath the prostrate Mohammedan.

We were some distance from Scutari, and about two hours from Moltape, a village in which I intended to pass the night. I determined to send Osman back to the town, and desired him to hire a Hammall, or man with a baggage-horse. In the meantime, Radford and myself could keep guard over our luggage.

The night grew darker and darker. The white grave-stones could be barely discerned. Leaving my English servant to sit upon the luggage in the road, I waded through the mud to a cleaner spot in the cemetery. Sitting down on one of the broken monuments, I awaited Osman's arrival. Presently I heard the sound of steps close behind me. The locality does not bear a good reputation, so grasping my revolver, I prepared for an attack.

"Peace be with you!" was the new comer's salutation, and in a few minutes I discovered that he was the grave-digger, or person in charge of the cemetery. His house, or hovel, was not far off, and he invited me to go there and share his fire. It would not have been safe to have left the luggage, so I declined the offer. Soon afterwards the sound of horses' hoofs in the distance announced the approach of Osman. He was accompanied by a Hammall. The latter, placing the fallen luggage upon his animal, jumped himself on the top of all.

"We had better go back to Scutari, Effendi," said Osman.

"It is late; there will be no village for the next three hours. In Scutari there is good accommodation."

I had no wish to turn back. We had already lost at least half a day through Osman's stupidity; I resolved to continue the march to Moltape, and halt there for the night. Osman could start at daybreak for Scutari, and make inquiries about the lost horse.

"Shall you find him?" I inquired of the Turk.

"Find him, Effendi? of course I shall find him. I will not eat, drink, or sleep till my lord's property is restored;" by way of substantiating this statement, Osman took a piece of bread out of his pocket and began to eat.

"Well," I observed, "you said that you were going to starve till you had found my horse, and you are eating already."

"It is bad for a man with an empty stomach to be exposed to the night air. I shall be all the better able to look for the Effendi's horse to-morrow, and please God I will find him," was the answer.

We continued our journey through the deep mud, the Hammall riding in front as guide. The moon rose and threw her pale shadows on the scene. The Hammall, who was perched up on the top of a pile of luggage, uttered, from time to time, shrill cries. Cracks from his whip resounded from the flanks of his over-taxed steed. Radford rode pensively in rear; the bowl of a short wooden pipe glared with the red-hot ashes of some tobacco. Nothing ever seemed to afflict my English servant. I was going to Kars—well, he must go too; if I had told him that I was going up in a fire balloon, he would have been equally ready to accompany me. I wish we had four hundred thousand men like him in the British army. The soldier who will ask no questions, will go where you like, and die in his place if you tell him to do so, is preferable, in my mind, to the more educated individual who reflects, weighs probabilities, and sometimes runs away.

Now a light appeared in the distance, and then another. The swamp through which we had been riding was gradually replaced by harder soil. A few whitewashed cottages were met with at intervals along our path. Presently we rounded a corner, and a large village was exposed to view. The Hammall rode up to a house which was detached from the rest, and in the centre of the town. He leaped from his horse, and, coming to my side, held the stirrup-leather for me to dismount. We had arrived at a Khan, or resting-place for travellers. On lifting up the latch, or rather pulling at a piece of string which was used as a substitute for a handle, the door opened.

I found myself in a large, low room. So soon as my eyes became accustomed to the dense atmosphere, I discovered that almost all the available space was filled with soldiery. On one side of the room there were a succession of broad wooden shelves, ascending towards the roof, these too were tenanted. It was difficult to put a foot down upon the floor without treading upon the face or body of some follower of the Prophet. The smell which arose from so much humanity was anything but agreeable. A *mudgo*, or circular iron pan on a tripod, was filled with burning charcoal, and placed on a stool so as to be removed from the immediate vicinity of the sleepers. It gave out a blue and sulphurous flame. The charcoal had not been properly burned through previously to being placed in the *mungo*. It added some poisonous fumes to the unhealthy atmosphere.

CHAPTER VI

The proprietor of the establishment—*Lingua franca*—Gold, no paper— Gold a charm to the Greek—No rooms—The Onbashee—His costume —The guard-house—A queer place—"*At gitdi!* the horse has gone!" —The Pacha at Scutari—The corporal's demeanour when offered a tip—A beautiful country—The bay of Ismid—A goose plump as a Georgian woman—A Zaptieh—The chief of the telegraph department in Ismid—A grievance—The appearance of Ismid—Washing-day—The Pacha of Ismid—Mr. Gladstone—"Gladstone is what you call a Liberal, is he not?"—The Turkish debt—Russian agents bring about massacres of Christians.

THE proprietor of the establishment, a Greek, slowly raised himself from a recumbent position. His head was bound up in what appeared to be a red stocking; the toe part of this article of attire hung carelessly over his left shoulder. He was a dirty-looking little fellow, and had a large wen on one side of his forehead. Nature had determined to make him as hideous as possible, and some fellow-mortal had added to her handiwork, for a large scar, barely cicatrized, and apparently inflicted by a knife, extended right across his face. This scar and the wen were, in the daytime, a perpetual resort for blue-bottle flies. These insects, I subsequently observed, had a great affection for the frontispiece of the proprietor.

"What do you want?" he asked in *lingua franca*, that undefined mixture of Italian, French, Greek, and Spanish, which is spoken throughout the Mediterranean.

"I want a place to sleep in."

"Place to sleep in! Sleep here," and he slowly subsided into his original position.

Osman now began to address him, and in a whining tone said that I was his Effendi, a great person with gold, not paper, in my pocket, and that I would pay liberally for accommodation. The allusion to the gold acted like a charm upon the Greek.

"Gold!" he said. "Gold! Let me see it!"

I took out a lira (Turkish pound), and spinning it carelessly in the air, let it fall on an earthenware dish. The coin gave out a metallic ring. The Greek clutched at the fallen lira; but the nimble Osman was too quick for him, and picking it up returned it to me.

"I have no rooms but this," said the proprietor eagerly; "but I have a stable. Why not sleep in the stable? You want a stable for your horses, and I will put down some clean straw for the Effendi."

Our horses were all this time tied up to a post outside. I was on the point of accepting his offer, so as to gain shelter for them as well as for ourselves, when the door opened. A strange figure loomed in sight.

"The Onbashee (corporal)," said the proprietor in a cringing tone, springing to his feet; and seizing several soldiers who were asleep on a bench, he rolled them on to the floor, thus making room for the new arrival. The latter, a dumpy-looking man, with a fez on his head, red regimental trousers, and a short yellow dressing-gown, sat down on the bench, and beckoned to me to sit by his side. The occupants of the room by this time were thoroughly aroused. A small boy, the exact counterpart of the proprietor minus the scar and wen, speedily made some coffee. The fragrant beverage was duly handed first to the Onbashee and myself, and then to Osman and Radford, the head of the latter being in close proximity to the ceiling of the establishment.

I addressed the corporal, and told him that I was an English traveller, who wanted a night's lodging.

"English!" he cried, then springing to his feet he respectfully saluted, and said, "I thought, Effendi, that you were an Italian or a countryman of the Greek here," pointing to the proprietor of the place. "Come along, sir," leaving the building, he led me to a small building, apparently a guard-house, for in the room below there were ten soldiers, some rifles and accoutrements being suspended on a rack on the wall. Ascending a few rickety stairs, I entered a small lobby. It was about ten feet square, and had no furniture save a wooden ledge.

"This is my room," said the Onbashee. "You and the other Englishman can sleep here. I will sleep downstairs with the men." Then bringing two blankets he threw them down on the ledge, saluted in a military fashion, and disappeared.

"Queer place, sir," said Radford, looking round. "However, it is better than the hole downstairs. Shall I sleep here, sir, or in the stable?"

"On the floor," I replied. "Go and look after the horses, and then bring up some rugs."

At daybreak Osman started for Scutari in search of the lost horse. A few hours later I took my gun, and went to see if I could find any snipe in a marsh near the town. About six p.m. Osman returned. It was easy to see from his crest-fallen face that he had heard no news of the lost Obadiah.

"*At Gitdi!* The horse has gone, Effendi," he said. "I have been to every farm-house near here, and no one has seen a black gelding with his tail cut short. Praise be to Allah that I cut all the horses' tails before starting; our animal will be different from the others in the neighbourhood, and will be easily distinguished."

"I went to the Pacha at Scutari," he added, "he has given orders to the police to search for the horse. When he is found, he will be sent after the Effendi by train to Ismid."

Gitdi (it has gone), I began to hate that word. Later on, if our tea had been stolen, Osman invariably greeted me with *gitdi*. It is the first word which a traveller in Turkey hears, he is kept in mind of it during his entire journey. There was nothing to be done but to hire another baggage-horse, and give orders for a start at daybreak.

A few minutes before leaving Moltape, I went to the corporal, and put in his hand a dollar (medjidi), in return for the accommodation he had given me. There were several soldiers present. He declined the present with a grandiose air, adding that his home was mine, and that all strangers were welcome to the abode. However, a few minutes later, when I was alone, he approached, and putting out his hand,

said, "Effendi, no one is looking, I will accept a present."
Human nature in all countries is much the same. The
corporal's demeanour before the soldiers much resembled that
of a railway porter when offered a tip in the presence of a
railway director.

We rode through a beautiful country. Our track lay across
a plain. It was surrounded by undulating hills. Pretty
villas with Venetian windows decked their crests. Vines, fig,
and other fruit trees studded the rising slopes. A few hours
later the path became very bad. We made our way across
deep, half hidden ruts, which compelled us to advance with
the greatest care for fear of breaking the horses' legs.

We ascend a steep incline, and then, far away in the
distance, and across the bay of Ismid, are cone-shaped hills
covered with fleecy snow.

The path turned, we rode along the seashore. The railway
ran along the side of the track, now ascending in tortuous
coils, now disappearing altogether from our view, to appear
once more in the distance, and almost level with the azure
deep. Not a ripple disturbed the surface of the waters;
coloured rocks and stones met our gaze as we glanced into the
abyss below; festoons of variegated sea-weed hung from the
rugged cliffs.

The sun's rays were fierce and scorching. In spite of its
being the month of December, there was a glare as if on a
July day. I was not sorry when, on reaching the crest of an
adjacent hill, Osman dismounted, and suggested a halt for lunch.

"A capital spot, Effendi," he remarked, "there is a spring
of fresh water, a cave, and firewood. I have a beautiful
goose, plump as a Georgian woman, in the saddle-bags. My
brother," pointing to Radford, "shall cook him. Our stomachs
grieve now, but soon they shall be comforted."

He led the way to a sort of cavity in the rock. A fire was
kindled, and the goose, the subject of Osman's admiration,
was shortly simmering on the embers.

Presently the track became worse, if possible, than before.
Several wooden bridges over deep and narrow gullies had to
be crossed. There were no parapets to the bridges. Here
and there holes a foot square let us see the stream below.
Then we traversed lanes of water, in some places up to the
horses' girths. The Hammall went first, and wended his way
with caution. Two ditches skirted the borders of the track;
the rain had fallen heavily, and had one of our horses made a

mistake or floundered, his rider would have found himself in at least six feet of water.

We were nearing Ismid, the Nicomedia of ancient history. Our tired animals seemed aware of its proximity; they quickened their pace. Very shortly afterwards we rode into the town. I had sent forward a messenger to tell the chief of the police that an English traveller was coming to Ismid, and to ask him to provide me with lodgings for the night, there being no hotels in the place.

I was met at the entrance of the town by a Zaptieh, or gendarme. Going before us, he led the way to a house kept by a Greek. Here I found two clean rooms furnished in the European fashion. The Zaptieh, after inquiring if I had any orders to give him, left the room, saying that he would report my safe arrival to the Pacha.

On the morrow I received a visit from the chief of the Telegraph department in Ismid—an Armenian who spoke French. On showing him a letter of introduction which I had received at Constantinople, for the Christian dignitaries in Ismid, he at once became very communicative, and hastened to relate a grievance which, according to him, an Armenian had lately suffered owing to Turkish misrule. It appeared that this man had borrowed money from a Turk, and had given his wife's earrings and necklace as security for the debt. The arrangements for the loan had been made in the presence of my informant. "But now," he continued, " comes the pith of the story. The Turk died. The Armenian, paying the debt to the dead man's heirs, asked for his wife's necklace and earrings. The Turk's family would not give them up. The Armenian appealed to the Cadi. The Cadi would not do justice, because it was the word of a Christian against the testimony of a Turk; and in such instances an Armenian's evidence goes for nothing. However," added the speaker, " I telegraphed to the authorities in Constantinople. An order at once came for justice to be done."

Later on I walked through the town. It is built in the form of a half moon, and is erected on the heights around the shore. Tiers and tiers of houses are perched up in out-of-the-way corners. Here a solitary one stands aloof like an eagle's nest and far above its fellows. No order has been followed in the construction of these houses. Every sort of shape and pattern is to be seen. Many of them are like Swiss chalets. Their wooden walls are bright with an infinite variety of hues.

It was, apparently, a washing-day. The nether garments and shirts of Turks and Christians were suspended from every window-sill. This apparel was of all the colours in the rainbow, and lit up the scene still more. There were a few well-built stone buildings—amongst them the palace of the Pacha. I called upon this official in the afternoon, and found him a tall, fine-looking man, considerably over six feet in height. He was seated in European fashion upon a sofa, and not squatted on the floor like some others of his countrymen who were present at the time of my visit. He spoke French fluently, and also Russian, having spent some years in the Turkish Consulate in Odessa ; his residence there had not inspired him with any affection for the subjects of the Tzar, whom he cordially detested.

"Your minister, Mr. Gladstone, hates us poor Turks quite as much as the Russians do," presently remarked the Pacha.

"Mr. Gladstone is not a minister," I remarked, "he is not by any means omnipotent in England. A great many of my countrymen have already evinced their sympathy for your nation."

"Yes," said the Pacha, "that is true, they have sent medicines to our wounded soldiery. Gladstone is what you call a Liberal, is he not ? "

"He is one of the leaders of the Liberal Party, and was its chief till he was turned out by the actual Government."

"Ah ! I remember," said the Pacha. "He told the people of England that they must not drink after certain hours, and quarrelled with your priests. I read all about it in the newspapers. It struck me as strange conduct in a man who calls himself a 'Liberal.' Has he many friends in Parliament ? "

"Yes, but not so many as formerly ; his conduct about this Eastern question has drawn away some of his most influential supporters."

"Well, at all events if there is war, please God we shall be allies."

"Please God we shall," I replied devoutly.

"You know," he continued, "that we are much stronger than people in Europe believe. We can put an army of 700,000 men into the field."

"Praise be to Allah ! " interrupted an elderly Turk who was squatted on the carpet, at the same time gravely stroking his white beard.

"Why is it that the people in England hate us so much ? " inquired the Pacha.

"Partly on account of the excesses of your irregular soldiers in Bulgaria; but mainly because you repudiated your debt. How should you like to have lent money and then to receive no interest?"

The Pacha laughed.

"Yes, you are right. It was a great mistake. But that is all Russia's fault. Her agents brought about the revolution in the Herzegovina. Her functionaries encouraged Sultan Abdul Aziz in his extravagance, and were the main cause of the debt being repudiated. They thought that this would make us unpopular with England, and they were very right in their conjectures. There is plenty of wealth in Turkey," he continued. "If it were not for the impending war, we could pay some part of our interest now; but Russia will not let us be quiet. She compels us to keep up a large army. Her agents bring about massacres of Christians, and set the whole world against us." *

"If there is a war, I hope that we shall cut the throats of all the Russians," interrupted the old gentleman on the carpet.

"Allah grant that we may!" exclaimed the rest of the assembly.

Coffee and pipes were now handed round, and my interview came to an end. The Pacha having kindly given orders for a telegram to be sent to Scutari, to inquire if anything had been heard of my runaway horse.

CHAPTER VII

An Armenian Bishop—An economical refreshment—Ramazan—Smoking in the streets—The Turkish Government is not so bad—The Koran and a Christian witness—A telegram from the Pacha at Scutari—A post-horse to Sabanja—Two Zaptieh—Turkish swords—A horse lost—Four feet of mud—An ox-cart upset in the mud—Woe-begone drivers—A priest during the Carlist war—Turks and Christians have an extreme dislike to the dread ordeal—Circassian Bashi Bazouks—Women ravished and then butchered by the Russians—Sabanja—Scenery—There was to have been a railway—A mule in difficulties.

IN the evening I called upon an Armenian Bishop. He lived in a quaint old-fashioned house in the Christian quarter of the town, the Turks and Armenians inhabiting different dis-

* These statements of the Pacha are confirmed to some extent by two Official Reports.—*See* Appendices IV. and V.

tricts in Ismid, as in many other Turkish cities. Refreshments were now brought in on a silver tray, and several kinds of jam handed round in little silver dishes. The guest taking a spoonful of jam is expected to swallow it, he then drinks a glass of water. This is an economical refreshment, a very little jam goes a long way in the entertainment.

"How do you like it?" said one of the party.

"Very good," I replied, at the same time having that sort of feeling in my mouth which carried my memory back to boyish days, and to the grey powders which my old nurse used to administer, "very good."

"We always treat our guests in this manner," said an old Armenian pompously. "It is the custom of our nation."

Now the conversation turned upon the Turks in Ismid, and it was pleasant to hear that some of the Turkish officials were well spoken of, even by the Armenians.

"The chief of the police here is a capital fellow," observed one of the company. "During the Ramazan, one of our people was smoking in the streets, a Mohammedan went up to him and struck him with a stick. The chief of the police, who happened to be passing by, saw this. He approached and said, 'Why did you strike that man?' 'Because he was smoking during Ramazan.' 'Did he put his cigarette in your eye?' 'No.' 'Then you had no business to strike him. You shall go to prison and learn to behave better for the future?'"

"Yes," said another of the guests; "the Turkish papers published the story, and highly praised the conduct of the official."

"The Turkish Government is not so bad," observed a third gentleman. "It wishes justice to be carried out impartially throughout the empire, but, so long as the Cadis refuse to take the word of a Christian as evidence, it will be difficult for us to live with any degree of comfort."

"After all," he continued, "this is an abuse which has crept in amidst the Turkish officers. The Koran says that the testimony of a Christian witness is to be taken as evidence, but nowadays many of the Mohammedans have forgotten the Koran."

In the evening a telegram arrived from the Pacha at Scutari. It was to the effect that nothing had been heard of my horse; however, so soon as the animal was found he should be sent after me. This would have been useless.

There was no rail beyond Ismid, and I intended to start the following morning. In consequence of this, I wrote to a friend at the British Embassy, to ask him, in the event of the horse being found, to have the animal sold at the market in Constantinople. Meantime I sent Osman to hire a post-horse to carry my baggage as far as Sabanja, a small village about twenty miles from Ismid, and on the road to Angora. Just as we were leaving Ismid, two Zaptieh or mounted police rode up. They had been ordered by the Pacha to escort me as far as Sabanja. Smart-looking fellows they were, too, with light blue jackets, red trousers, and Hessian boots. Each of them carried a repeating-rifle slung across his shoulder. Revolvers were stuck in the crimson sashes which encircled their waists. Short scimitars, but with no hilt-guards to protect the hand, were slung from their swordbelts.

It is singular that the Turkish military authorities, who have adopted the modern armament in so far as fire-arms are concerned, should be still so backward in the manufacture of swords. A cavalry soldier armed with a Turkish sword without a hilt-guard would have very little chance if engaged in a hand-to-hand encounter with a dragoon supplied with one of our own weapons.

After riding for about half an hour in the direction of Sabanja, Radford—who was leading a pack-horse, remarked to Osman,—

" What have you done with the post-horse ?"

The Turk did not understand the question. When it was interpreted to him, he replied,—

" The animal is in front with the Zaptieh."

As it is always as well to put a Turk's statement to the test, I determined to trot on ahead and look for myself. The Zaptieh had not seen the horse. It appeared that after loading him, Osman had started the animal, much in the same way as an Irishman does a pig, with the object of driving him before our party. We now all dispersed in different directions, and finally, after a two hours' search, discovered the animal tied up by the side of a Khan, an old woman who had observed the horse wandering about having attached him to a post.

The track now became much worse than anything I had previously seen. In many places there were quite four feet of mud. It reached our horses' girths, and with the greatest difficulty we were able to force a passage.

Presently we came to a hollow in the path. Here a cart drawn by four oxen was at a standstill. The bullocks, with only their necks and shoulders out of the mud, gazed plaintively before them. The two drivers had taken off their trousers and under-clothes ; their shirts were tucked up to their armpits ; they waded through the black slime, and goaded the bullocks forward.

A creaking noise was heard from the ponderous wheels. The four bullocks put forth all their strength ; it was a useless effort, one of them pulled the cart a little to one side, the next instant it was upset and half buried in the mire. The two men, with naught on them save little red fez caps and with their tucked-up shirts, presented a doleful picture. They were not burdened with much flesh, and ribs and shoulder bones were prominently thrown into relief by the coating of mud which reached as high as their waists. One poor fellow, wading up to us, asked Osman to give him a light for his pipe. The other one, looking more woe-begotten, if possible, than his fellow, had no pipe, and mournfully asked for a cigarette.

"Effendi," said Osman, "this is a dreadful place. We may be upset. Our horses will not get through. Better go back to Ismid and wait there till the mud becomes hard."

"No ; go on. Horses can march where bullocks cannot."

Osman turned white, he was riding a little in advance of me, and did not at all like being sent forward to experiment upon the depth of the mire.

"He is a poor creature," observed Radford, contemptuously, "Lor, sir, what else can we expect of them ? They don't drink no beer. They turn hup their noses at wine. Hosman's blood ain't no thicker than ditch-water—I will lay a pound it ain't."

Our saddle-bags were covered with mud when we gained a footing on the other side. Osman, riding up to my side, congratulated himself on having guided us through in safety.

"Your face was very white," I observed.

"Yes, Effendi, my blood had turned to milk. It was not for myself, it was for the Effendi. I thought that he might be suffocated. Osman is yours, you can do with him what you like."

All these were very pretty speeches ; however, I had been sufficiently often in the East to know how to appreciate them at their true value. I felt tolerably certain that if Osman's courage was ever put to the test, he would be found to value his existence in this world more than the society of a million beautiful wives in the world to come.

After all, he would have been no exception to mankind in general. I remember during the last Carlist war hearing a story about a priest who, on the eve of an expected battle, addressed the soldiers in his battalion, and informed them that whoever was slain in the morrow's fight should sup with Nuestro Señor in Paradise. The morrow came, the battle raged, and the Carlists were beaten—the priest's battalion being the first to run away, headed by the divine himself, who, tucking up his cassock, ran as fast as his legs could carry him. A soldier touched the reverend gentleman on the shoulder, and said, " You told us, my father, that whoever was slain in to-day's fight should sup in Paradise, but you are running away." " My son," replied the Cura, who was very much out of breath, " I, I—never sup—I suffer from a weak digestion—I only dine." Some people in England believe that a doctrine of predestination makes the Turkish soldiers indifferent to death. This may be true in a few isolated instances ; but, as a rule, both Turks and Christians have an extreme dislike to the dread ordeal.

The track became firmer. We overtook some Bashi Bazouks returning from Bulgaria. They were most of them Circassians, and one could speak Russian. He was very indignant at having been ordered home, and brandishing his long lance, with bright steel point at least twelve inches long, regretted that he had lost the opportunity of transfixing a few giaour Russians.

" Did you kill many women ? " I inquired.

" There were some killed," he replied. " It was a pity. We were sorry for it ; but what would you have our men do ? Some of their own mothers and sisters had been ravished and then butchered by the Russians."

" Have any of your relatives been treated in this way ? " I inquired.

" No," he said, " but in a village not far from Gumri, some horrible cruelties have recently taken place, many women and children were slain, and all because they wished to leave Russia and go to Turkey."

" If my mother or sister had been killed, I should not be particular as to how I avenged her," he continued, " These cowardly Russians set us the example,"

There was no sort of similarity in the attire of the Bashi Bazouks. Each man had dressed himself according to his fancy; the broad sashes around their waists were stuck full of pistols and daggers. The fire-arms, too, were of the most primitive kind; some men had old-fashioned muskets of the Tower pattern, and others were armed with double-barrelled guns, which had been converted from flint to percussion. Their horses looked hard and fit for work, they were as a rule not more than fourteen hands high, and their rough shaggy coats reminded me a little of the Cossack horses which I have seen in the neighbourhood of the Don.

The scenery improves as we approach Sabanja. The flat country previously traversed gives way to rising mountains. They bound our view towards the West. On my bridle-hand is a wide lake. It lies like a mirror almost at our feet. Many coloured grasses and shrubs clothe the slopes which lead down to the limpid water. Acres upon acres of rich grass-land—such as would make the mouth of a Leicestershire farmer water with envy—surround Sabanja on every side. We ride into the village; it consists of about 200 houses, mostly built of dried mud, and with much difficulty I obtain accommodation for the night.

Long before daybreak we were in the saddle. Our road wound through mountain passes. Huge clouds of mist slowly rose from the surface of the lake : they floated away into space, and appeared like icebergs as seen in the horizon. Now we rode by a place where preparations had been made for the construction of a railway. Sleepers were lying by the side of a partly-made embankment. On inquiry, no work had been going on for two years. There was to have been a railway to Angora, but " Para yoke, there is no money," was the answer to my questions on the subject.

Presently we came up to a caravan of mules laden with tea and bound for Angora. The road was very narrow, there was barely room for two horses abreast. One mule, turning his head towards the bank, blocked up the entire path; a blow from our Zaptieh's whip recalled him to consciousness. Backing a few yards he slipped, and rolled with his burden down the slope. The owner cursed, and the other muleteers coming up seemed rather to enjoy his discomfiture.

CHAPTER VIII

THE road became more level. We encountered caravans of camels, the animals not being led by a cord attached to a peg through the nose, but by a halter loosely fastened round the neck.

They were fine beasts and covered with shaggy hair. This, I was informed, is cut off them at certain seasons in the year, and is then converted into a material for tents and rugs. Each caravan was headed by a man riding a donkey, the pace of the latter being if anything a little superior to that of the huge camels behind them.

We continued along the left bank of the river Sakaria, a rapid stream, sixty yards wide and with steep banks; presently we crossed it on a stone bridge, very much out of repair. The centre part had fallen away. This had been replaced by wooden beams covered with loose earth. Presently we came to a large valley abounding with corn, vines, and mulberry-trees, and I halted for the night in the village of Geiweh. The Mudir, a sort of local mayor, came out to meet us, and insisted that I should be his guest. He was a very communicative man, and informed me that Yakoob Khan was about to bring an army of 50,000 men to assist the Sultan.

"How will he come?" I inquired.

"By the sea," remarked my host, his geographical knowledge about Kashgar not being very extensive. He next informed me that Persia was supposed to be very friendly towards Russia, and that the Turks hated the Persians, but liked the Christians, with the exception of the Greeks, whom they believed to be in league with the Tzar.

Shortly after leaving Geiweh, the valley takes a circular form, and is at least three miles in diameter; hills with slopes well adapted for artillery fire surround it on every side. The little stream Kara Su, which is only knee deep, traverses the district, and finds its way a few miles further down into the

Sakaria. The Geiweh valley would be a magnificent position into which to entice a careless general. The exit towards the east is by a steep ravine with precipitous banks, and on the west it is blocked by the Sakaria.

We now reached Terekli, a small town with about 800 houses. Every house was full of soldiers, who were *en route* to the capital. The sun was descending over the mountain tops as we rode through the narrow streets. Hundreds of Bashi Bazouks were performing wild evolutions in the plain below ; some men were firing at a target from horseback at a gallop, others whirling their rifles about to the imminent danger of the bystanders. The many coloured dresses of this guerilla soldiery, and of the lookers-on, lit up the surroundings of the landscape. The wild shouts of the horsemen re-echoed over the mountains. From the distant peaks the bleating of the goats could be faintly heard, as the shepherds were driving them home for shelter. This sound was mingled with the lowing of cattle and the rippling of the stream below. It was a romantic picture. It vividly recalled to my mind some scenes in the Basque provinces during the late Carlist war.

The soldiers started at four the following morning, singing in chorus as they marched through the streets. An hour later we continued our journey through a mountainous district strewed with blocks of granite, and soon afterwards crossed the little river Goonook, another tributary of the Sakaria.* Here the scenery is very wild ; the hills are of all shapes and forms, as if cast down at haphazard by the Titans of old. Now we find a series of natural bastions and ramparts, looking as if they had been chiselled out of the hard white rocks, and then approach a slate mountain, large black stones lying about in endless profusion. Presently we ride along a path bounded on both sides by a precipice. Our track twines like a silver thread amidst the crags which hide the way before us.

We round a corner. A small village is seen below, Torbali is reached, and a Bey, the great man of the place, invites us to share his dwelling.

A little later, a black slave brought me as a present from his master, some small trout and fresh eggs. The slave could talk Arabic. He had been born near Gondokoro, and had been kidnapped from that part of the world by a party of

* For routes which cross the Sakaria, and traverse Asia Minor, see Appendix XIV.

Arabs under Sir Samuel Baker's *bête noir*, Abou Saood. I asked him if he would like to return to his own country.

"Yes," he said, "if the Effendi is going there with Abou Saood. We could then catch plenty of slaves."

"I know where to find them," he added, "we should soon become rich."

There is an old proverb, "Set a thief to catch a thief," but here it seemed equally applicable to slaves. I was struck by the extreme eagerness to kidnap his countrymen which was evinced by this negro gentleman.

"Well," I said, "how are you treated by your master?"

"He is a good man," was the reply, "there is plenty to eat, and not much to do."

"One thing is bad here," he added, "the master does not drink *sharab* (wine). I like *sharab*—lots of *sharab*, it makes one gay. Will the Effendi give me a little *sharab*?"

"I have not any. I do not drink myself."

"And yet you are rich," said the slave. "You have money to buy it, happy man that you are. If I were like you I would drink, drink, drink, all day and all night!"

"But Osman does not drink, he attends to the Prophet's laws."

"Osman is a horse; he does not know what is good," was the reply.

At this moment the voice of the Bey was heard. "*Gell!*" (come) resounded through the building; the negro, leaving me, hurried off to his master.

It was a nine hours' march to Mudurlu, our next halting-place, the route leading through a very mountainous district. The village, or small town, of Mudurlu contains 800 mud houses, which, at the average rate of five people to a family, would give about 4000 inhabitants. The traveller, when journeying in this part of Anatolia, is much struck by the absence of shops. He may pass through village after village, small town after small town, and, unless it be market day, he will be unable to purchase anything.

"Can I buy some meat?" I would inquire of Osman.

"We will see, Effendi. I will run to the Khan, and inquire of the people there."

This was Osman's favourite amusement. Under the pretence of making purchases, he would go to the different Khans, talk for some time to the assembled villagers about his own merits, drink several cups of coffee, and return.

" Well, where is the meat ? "

" Effendi, there is no meat."

" Have you been to look ? "

" Look, Effendi ! My clothes are moist with perspiration. But there are some chickens ; they will do for our dinner."

This was the daily food—chicken. It is not a bad diet if a man is living a sedentary life, and not taking much exercise, but after a nine hours' ride he requires something a little more nourishing. *Toujours perdrix* was too much for a French cardinal ; if the holy gentleman had been riding through Turkey, he would have found *toujours poulet* an equally unsubstantial diet. A crowd assembled to see us depart ; the people in Mudurlu taking as much interest in an Englishman as the inhabitants of London would take in a chimpanzee or newly arrived gorilla. Asiatics have a very high opinion of our skill as manufacturers. English goods can be met with in almost every large town in Anatolia, and the Turks prefer English merchandise to the cheaper but inferior articles sent from Belgium or America.

The Zaptieh who went with me was a magnificent-looking fellow. Picture to yourself a tall, dark Circassian, with large piercing eyes, and carefully trimmed beard—a striking contrast to the huge white turban which surrounded his fez. He was dressed in a green jacket with red facings ; a blue waistcoat peered from beneath it, and a pair of green trousers and red leather boots covered his extremities. He was armed with a sword and revolver, and, when the road permitted, was continually exercising his horse. Now he would break into a gallop, go at headlong speed for fifty yards, then, pulling his steed almost on his haunches, he would start in another direction, and, bending from the saddle-bow, touch the ground. All this was done with the most consummate grace and ease—in fact, as if horse and rider were one.

Soon we left behind us the light sandy soil which admitted of such-like evolutions. A chain of steep heights had to be passed. The mud became at each moment deeper. The baggage animals had great difficulty in ascending with their loads. We were struggling up an almost perpendicular height. At our feet and at least forty yards below yawned a deep abyss. The path itself was in no place more than ten feet wide. The sound of an oath issuing from Osman's lips attracted my attention. One baggage-horse lay on the ground ; he was kicking violently, and his head and shoulders

were over the precipice. Osman had thrown my rifle into
the mud, so as to be able to use his hands more freely, and
was endeavouring to make his way to the fallen animal. The
Turk's high boots came half off each time he lifted his feet,
owing to the sticky nature of the soil. Luckily, perhaps, for
us it was so sticky, the gun-case, which was buried in the
clay, kept the horse from rolling. The Circassian and
Radford had time to reach his head. Pulling off the pack-
saddle, they divided the luggage among the other animals.
We gradually gained the summit of the hill.

CHAPTER IX

IT was quite dark when we reached Nalihan, a village with
about 400 houses, and situated in a corn-growing district. I
halted at the house of the Caimacan. He at once invited me
to take up my abode there for the night. Presently several
visitors appeared—Armenians, Turks, and Circassians—all
eager to question the new arrival. I was seated in the place
of honour, on a rug near the fire; the Caimacan, who was
enveloped in a fur-lined dressing-gown, sat next me. The
rest of the company took precedence according to the amount
of this world's goods which each one possessed—the man who
had 100 cows being seated next to the governor, and the
humble possessor of a mule or a few sheep squatting humbly
by the door.

Asiatics are proverbially reticent. My visitors stared at
each other, and did not say a word. At last the Caimacan
broke the silence. He was wrapped up in a fur dressing-
gown, and looked like an animated bundle. He gave a little
cough, and then said, " Is there any news? if so tell us something." Now the inhabitants of Asia Minor do not talk about

the weather—the state of the roads replaces that topic of conversation so interesting to English people.

"The roads are very bad," I replied.

To this there was no dissent, everbody chorussed the wish for a railway.

"Do you think that one will ever be made?" inquired the Caimacan.

"Probably when you have some money in the exchequer."

"We are very poor; why does not your nation lend us some gold?"

"We have already given you more than a hundred millions: with that money you might have made railways in every part of Anatolia."

"Will there be war?" asked an Imaum (priest).

"I do not know."

"If there is," he added, "I shall go—all the Imaums will go; we will fight by the side of our countrymen. We will kill all the Muscovites."

"Has it not occurred to you," I here remarked, "that perhaps they may kill all the Turks?"

"Impossible! Allah and the Prophet are on our side; they will fight for the faithful."

"What do you think yourself?" now inquired the Caimacan; "will Russia beat us?"

"Certainly—that is, if you have no European allies."

"Why so?"

"Because, if your Government had to put out all its strength to conquer the Servians assisted by only 12,000 Russians, what opposition will it be able to make to an army of 700,000 Muscovites?"

"May their mothers be defiled!" said an old farmer. "They are always interfering with us. All my sons have gone to the war, and I—well, if the Padishah wants me, I will go too."

He was apparently an octogenarian. This announcement on his part was received with great applause by the rest of the company.

"Why do you not give the Armenians arms, and make them assist?" I inquired.

"They are friends with the Russians," said the Imaum. "They would turn against us. Have you Armenians in your country?"

"No."

"But you are a Christian, and they are Christians—you must be the same."

I now had to explain to the company that there is as much difference between an English Protestant and an Armenian Christian, as between a Sunnite and a Shiite.

"And do you hate the Armenians as much as the Shiites hate us?"

"We do not hate anybody. Our religion does not allow us to do so."

"You Christians are a strange people," said the priest; rising, he left the room, followed by the rest of the visitors.

The scenery is very lovely in this neighbourhood, and as we ascended an incline which leads in the direction of Angora, I could not help wishing that I had been born a painter, in order to have placed on canvas a picture of the landscape. A succession of hills, each one loftier than its fellow, broke upon us as we climbed the steep. They were of all forms, shades, and colours, ash-grey, blue, vermilion, robed in imperial purple, and dotted with patches of vegetation. Our road wound amidst these chameleon-like heights. Silvery rivulets streamed down the sides of the many-coloured hills. A rising sun showered its gleaming rays upon the sparkling cascades. They flashed and reflected the tints and shadows. A gurgling sound of many waters arose from the depths below.

We reach the summit of the highest hill. The scene changes. We look down upon a vast plain. It is surrounded on all sides by undulating heights. The white sandy soil of the valley throws still more into relief the many-coloured mountains. Patches of snow deck the more distant peaks. The sun is dispelling the flossy clouds which overhang the loftier crags. The filmy vapour floats away into space; caressing for a few moments the mountains' crests, it is wafted onward, and then disappears from our view.

Now we crossed a rapid stream, about thirty yards wide, and known as the Alatai river. A fragile bridge spans the waters. Soon afterwards we put up for the night at a farmhouse in the village of Tchairhana. The proprietor, a jolly-looking Turk, received us very hospitably. Later on in the evening he brought me a large *yorgan*, or Turkish counterpane, with the remark that possibly the Effendi might feel cold during the night.

The Turkish beds are very primitive; no bedstead being used. One or two mattresses are laid on the floor, the *yorgan* takes the place of sheets or blankets. It consists of a silk quilt, generally lined with linen, and stuffed with feathers. These quilts pass from father to son, and are greatly prized by the Turks. The farmer, to make me appreciate his attention the more highly, remarked that the *yorgan* had been used by his grandfather, as well as by his father on their wedding-nights, and that he himself had employed it on a similar occasion only a few weeks previously.

Osman now interrupted the speaker with the remark that in his family there was also a wonderful *yorgan*—something quite out of the common, it was so beautiful that neither his wife nor himself liked to use it—and that this one was like a furze bush in comparison.

" So you are married, Osman ? " I remarked.

" Yes ; but I have not seen my wife for three years."

" Do you love her very much ? "

" She is a good cook. She makes soup which is more filling than even my brother's here," pointing to Radford.

" Is she pretty ? "

" Effendi, I could not afford to marry a good-looking girl. There was one in our village—such a pretty one, with eyes like a hare and plump as a turkey—but she could not cook, and her father wanted too much for her."

" Well, what did you give for your present wife ? "

" Ten liras (Turkish pounds), but she did not weigh more than forty okas (about 100 lbs.). She was very cheap. However, her eyes are not quite straight, they look in different directions. But that does not signify—she can cook."

" Yes," said the farmer, " a good cook, Effendi, that is what I said to myself when I wanted a wife. Looks don't last, but cooking is an art which the Prophet himself did not despise."

I had no reason to congratulate myself on being the occupant of the farmer's nuptial couch. It was very old and very beautiful, but it was full of fleas, and they gave me no rest.

" You ought to burn that quilt," I observed next morning to the farmer ; " I have not closed my eyes during the entire night."

" What, burn my grandfather's marriage *yorgan*—my father's *yorgan*, and my own *yorgan !* Never, Effendi ! There are fleas, it is true, but they will die, and the quilt will do for my son and his wife, if ever he has one."

The country which we next traversed was entirely uncultivated, although it would have well repaid a farmer. This, however, is the case with millions of acres in Turkey. There are no labourers. The country is depopulated to the last degree, and land which might produce wheat enough for the whole of Great Britain is left fallow.

Presently we came to an old Khan. It had been built by a former sultan, as a refuge for travellers during the winter. At this season of the year the ground is sometimes covered with snow for several weeks in succession, and travelling is very dangerous. Two soldiers were the sole tenants of the building. Whilst I was performing my ablutions in the open air, one of them came to me and asked for a little tea. His comrade was ill, and tea he thought would be good for him. I went to look at the invalid. He was lying on a dirty mattress, and was shivering violently. It was clearly a case of fever, so taking some quinine from my medicine-chest, I administered a dose, and directed his comrade to procure a clean bed for the sufferer. The sick man was very grateful. Eagerly seizing my hand, he kissed it.

"What countryman are you?"

"I am English."

"Your religion is not that of Islam?"

"No."

"What are you?"

"I am a Protestant."

"Protestant," repeated the poor fellow, "I shall remember that."

"A Christian," he continued, "even if he had the medicine, would have let me die like a dog."

It was very clear that the sufferer had not much opinion of the Armenian and Greek Christians. But this was no solitary expressed opinion. Throughout my journey, I found Armenians and Greeks equally despised by the Mohammedans. It is a great pity that the votaries of Christianity in the East should have brought the only pure religion into so great disrepute.

CHAPTER X.

Radford and Osman—The quarrel—Do the Roossians kiss each other ?—
  Bei Bazar—The pig tobacco—Osman's honesty—Forage for five horses
  —It is a good sign in a horse to be always hungry—The Tchechmet
  river—The Mudir at Istanos—The Cadi's mule—The tradition about
  Istanos—Caverns formerly inhabited by marauders—A chasm—The
  entrance to the caverns—A levee of the inhabitants—No newspapers
  in the villages—An Armenian priest—The furniture of the room—Has
  the Conference commenced ?—What is it all about ?—Russia is strong
  and we are weak—The other Powers are afraid of Russia—Will
  England be our ally ?—Are the Christians tortured ?—Here we get on
  very well with the Mussulmans—The pack-saddle.

THERE was something on my English servant's mind that
evening. He did not look happy, and eyed Osman from time
to time with lowering looks.

" My brother is angry with me, Effendi," said the Turk, in
answer to my inquiries. " When he speaks I do not understand, when I speak he does not know what I say."

" What is the matter, Radford ? " I asked.

" Please, sir, I ain't had no dinner. I did not prepare anything for you as the cook in the house was a preparing it.
Well, when you had finished, and Osman had brought out the
dishes, I thought that I should get something to eat. But,
no sir ! for Osman invited a lot of dirty Turks to come and
sit round the victuals. Some of the chaps had just come out
of the stable, and their hands were that dirty. Then they
began a shoving them into the dishes and a licking their
fingers. It turned me hup, that it did. Osman ought to
know better, sir. Whenever I cooks for you I always give
him a tit-bit for himself."

I now explained the matter to Osman, and at the same
time informed him that in future he must look after his
English companion at dinner-time. The difficulty was amicably
arranged, and the two men shook hands together. Osman
wishing to show his affection in a more demonstrative manner,
this, however, was not appreciated by my domestic.

" Lor ! how they kisses each other, just like a lot of great
girls. Do the Roossians kiss each other ? "

" Yes, Radford."

" They must be a poor lot then, sir. I have always heard
that one Englishman could lick two Frenchmen, and I believed
it ; but I'll be blessed if I could not lick half-a-dozen Roossians,
if they have no more in them than these 'ere dirty Turks."

We left Bei Bazar at daybreak. Osman, as usual, did not take the trouble to lead one of the baggage-horses, but drove the animal before him. Presently we passed through a narrow passage. On each side were two walls; the pack-saddle struck against one of them, and Radford's bag, containing the article which he prized perhaps most in the world, some pig tobacco, was torn open.

"I never seed such a fellow as that Osman," exclaimed my indignant servant, "he is always a telling of us as how he is industrious, and if there is a ha'porth of work to do he will borrow a penny and give it to some chap to do the job for him. I believe, sir, as how that fellow is a cheating the horses of their forage. He told me that he fed them in the morning before I was up. He is a liar he is. I was dressed a long time before him, and when he did show himself, he was busy the whole time a praying and a doing something with a little gallipot he carries in his saddle-bags. I don't believe the horses have had a feed of corn this twenty-four hours."

I began myself to be a little sceptical about Osman's honesty. I was paying as much for the forage of the five horses as if I had been in England. The poor brutes were getting thinner every day. I determined to stop at a farm-house and buy some barley. On giving this to the horses, they ate it ravenously, thus confirming my suspicions.

"Osman, you did not feed the horses this morning!" I exclaimed.

"Feed them, Effendi! I fed all of them!"

"But see how hungry they are, they have eaten all the barley you have just given them."

"Yes, sir, they are wonderful horses. They are always hungry. It is a good sign in a horse to be always hungry."

I was not to be taken in by this remark, and so desired Radford in future to see the horses fed. At the same time I resolved to keep a sharp look-out on Osman. It was true that a considerable portion of his time was spent in praying; however, I began to be of my English servant's opinion, that when the Turk was not engaged in prayer, he was either planning or executing a theft, and that all these devotions were performed merely with the view of throwing me off my guard.

We crossed the Tchechmet; it is a tributary of the Sakaria river, and about thirty yards wide. There was a wooden bridge over the stream, but without any parapets; the height from the water being about twelve feet. This river is fordable in many places, the banks are not precipitous, and the bottom is firm.

A messenger, sent forward from the village of Ayash, had informed the Mudir at Istanos, our next station, that an English traveller was on the road. The official, attended by the Cadi and two or three Zaptiehs, came out to meet us. All the party, with the exception of the gendarmes, were clad in long dark blue dressing-gowns, which draggled some distance below the riders' stirrups. The mule which the Cadi rode was not of a quiet disposition; from time to time he kicked as violently as a mule can kick, at his master's robe, the Cadi saving himself by clinging convulsively to the high pommel of his saddle.

Istanos is a little distance from the direct road to Angora. There was no other good halting-place in the neighbourhood, so I determined to make a slight detour and remain there for the night—the more particularly as Istanos is a village of historic fame, the tradition being still extant, that it is the place * where Alexander the Great cut the Gordian knot. The village, which contains 400 houses—half belonging to Armenians, half to Turks—is on the right bank of the river Owas. A lofty rock overhangs the stream, and according to the Mudir, there were several huge caverns which in days long gone by had been inhabited by bands of marauders.

Later on, I procured a guide, and walked to the foot of the rock. A narrow pathway was cut in the solid stone. The track was not more than twelve inches wide, as we ascended it became narrower at every moment. At last we arrived at a spot where the path had given way. There was a chasm about twelve feet wide. The guide hesitated, and no wonder, for if he had essayed the leap and missed it, he must have fallen at least a hundred feet on to the crags below.

"Effendi," he said, "I will try and cross if you like, but if my foot slips I shall be killed. You can see the entrance to the caverns from the place where you are standing."

It was not possible, even if I had wished it, to pass him and try the jump myself. The sun was nearly down, and ere a rope could be brought, night would be upon us. Reluctantly I retraced my steps, having to go backward for some distance owing to the narrowness of the ledge. Should any other

* Opinions are divided about this: some people assuring me that it happened at Ayash, others at Istanos.

traveller chance to visit Istanos, and be able to stay there a day or two, it would be well worth his while to procure a rope and examine these, as far as I can learn, unexplored grottos.

On returning to the Mudir's house, I found a levee of the principal inhabitants, Armenians as well as Turks. I was then informed that they had come to welcome me to their village. The real reason being that they wished to hear the latest news from Constantinople. No newspapers find their way to these out-of-the-way villages. The inhabitants can only learn what is going on in the capital through the arrival of a traveller.

An old Armenian priest was one of the visitors. He sat by the side of the Mudir, on a raised platform in the centre of the room. The legs of these two gentlemen were entirely hid from view, and although the room was very chilly where I was sitting, the rest of the party did not seem to feel the low temperature. I now discovered that there was a hole in the platform. A pan of live charcoal had been placed in the recess. The natives, enveloped in furs, and with their feet over the embers, were able to withstand the cold. The platform was partly covered with a Persian rug. A divan alongside the walls made up the furniture of the room. In the background and near the door stood the servants of the Mudir, and the less important inhabitants. It was not considered etiquette for them to sit in the presence of their superiors. They remained with arms folded and eyes bent down in token of humility. When the Mudir thought that they had humbled themselves sufficiently, he made a sign to them. They all squatted down on their haunches.

"Has the Conference commenced?" inquired the Mudir.

"Yes."

"What is it all about?" said another old Turk, the Cadi.

"It is to see if arrangements can be made so as to prevent war," I replied.

"But we do not want to go to war with any one," said the Mudir. "Russia wishes to go to war with us."

"Why is the Conference not held at St. Petersburg?" asked another of the visitors.

"Because Russia is strong and we are weak—the other powers are afraid of Russia," said the Cadi.

"Do Englishmen like Russia?" inquired the Mudir.

"Some do, and some do not," I replied.

" Do you ? "

" I like the people, but do not like the government."

" Why ? "

"Because it is a despotic form of government, and in my opinion all despotisms are bad."

" I like to hear that," said the Mudir.

" So do I," said each one of the assembled guests, taking the cue from the governor.

" Will England be our ally in the case of war ? " asked the Cadi.

" I do not know, but I hope so."

Some one now entered and spoke a few words to the Mudir. The latter left the room : he was followed by the rest of the visitors, with the exception of the Armenian priest.

" How do you like the Turks ? " I asked.

" Very well," replied the old man, at the same time blowing his nose in his dressing-gown, pocket handkerchiefs being apparently unknown in this part of Turkey. " Here," he added, " the population is half Armenian and half Turk, this makes a considerable difference. In other villages, where the Mohammedans outnumber the Christians, the latter sometimes suffer."

" What do you mean by suffer ? Are they tortured ? "

" No, never," replied the priest, " but if a Turk were to strike an Armenian, and the latter were to hit him back, all the Turks in the neighbourhood would set upon the Christian. Then, if the Christian should complain to the Mudir, the Turk would bring witnesses to say that the Armenian called him the grandson or great-grandson of a dog. The Christian's word would not be taken as evidence. But things are much better than they used to be, and here we get on well with the Mussulmans."

My English servant was very much excited that evening. At dinner-time he put down my plate with a bang on the table, and every now and then looked at Osman with an air of supreme contempt.

" What has happened ? " I at last inquired. " Have you and Osman been fighting, or are you both in love with the same woman ? "

" No, sir, but that Hosman he ain't taken the pack-saddle off our horse's back since we left Scutari. Every night I tells him about it, and he takes no notice of me whatever. I expect that our 'oss has an awful back—a nasty unfeeling brute is

Hosman, sir. How would he like a saddle on his own back night and day for fourteen days?"

"Well," I said, "go to the stable, take off the saddle, and tell me in the morning if the horse's back is sore or not."

I did not share the apprehensions of my English servant. The Turkish pack-saddle is admirably suited for a long journey. During previous expeditions in the East, I had seen some Tartars who kept their horses saddled for weeks and even months together, and all this without in any way injuring the animals. The two English riding-saddles which I had brought from Constantinople had already proved a source of annoyance to me. Our steeds had lost a great deal of flesh, owing to the long and frequent marches, and the panels required fresh stuffing. The grey horse which I rode had been slightly rubbed. In consequence of this I had changed saddles with Osman, who was much lighter than myself. The Turkish saddle not having a panel, is better adapted for long marches. Unfortunately it is an uncomfortable one for the horseman : my own experience being that the English saddle galls the steed, but the Turkish one the rider.

CHAPTER XI

"WELL, how is the animal's back?" I inquired of Radford, when he awoke me the next morning.

"I can't make it out, sir. I took the saddle off, and our horse ain't touched at all. Osman came in when I was a looking at him. He laughed and said ' Eyi ' (good), and I said

' Eyi' too. But, sir, it is a wonder to me that the horse ain't
got an awful back."

"How are you getting on with your Turkish?" I inquired.

"Capital, sir; I often have a talk with Osman, though I
can't say as how we understand each other much. The fellow,
he knows more about horses than I thought he did; one lives
and learns, even from Turks."

We were escorted out of Istanos * by the Mudir and his
two sons, lads of from twelve to fifteen, who had got up at
daybreak to speed the Frank on his way. The Armenian
priest also came to the door. In spite of the early hour, a
great many inhabitants had assembled on the house-tops to
have a look at the Englishman and his party.

"They like your nation," said the Mudir, as the people
saluted us.

"Why so?"

"They remember the Crimean war, and think that you have
come to help us against the Russians."

"I wish I had," was my answer; "but I am here only as a
' traveller.' "

We retraced our steps along the route of the previous day,
marching for some time by the bank of the river. Presently
I came to a well-built stone bridge. It spans the stream,
which is here about forty yards wide, besides being very rapid
and deep. Soon afterwards the path traversed a spacious
plain, formerly the battle field of Tamerlane. At one end of
this plain, and on a hill, or rather ridge of hills, is Angora.
Its ruined battlements and lofty minarets stand out conspicuously. The town itself lies rather in the background
and on a slope. A Zaptieh met us as we were entering a
narrow street, and said that a Turkish gentlemen had sent
him to escort me to his house.

On we rode, through many dirty lanes, until I finally entered
a wide yard. This court was overlooked by a large and handsome building.

"Suleiman Effendi lives here," said the Zaptieh.

The gentleman to whom he alluded now appeared descending some stone steps which gave access to the courtyard. He
approached us, and aided me to dismount; then, taking my
hand, he led me into a large room furnished with chairs, as
well as with a divan, and carpeted with rich Persian rugs.

* For military importance of this district, see Appendix XIV.

Advancing to the place of honour, in the centre of the divan, he asked me to be seated, and sat down by my side. Several of his friends being accommodated on the floor.

Suleiman Effendi was dressed in European fashion, with the exception of his fez. He had a very fair knowledge of Arabic; I soon found that he was well posted in European politics.

"I heard that an Englishman was on his way to Angora," he said, "and determined that you should be my guest. We received the news about you from Ismid."

"Are there any other Englishmen here?" I inquired.

"Only one—the Vice-Consul, a merchant : but I will send and let him know that you have arrived. In the meantime have a glass of raki." Proceeding to a cabinet in the wall, Suleiman carefully unlocked it, and produced a decanter with some glasses.

"Thanks, I do not drink spirits."

"No more do I," replied Suleiman, laughing; "only medicinally, you know;" and he drank off a bumper.

In a few minutes the English Vice-Consul arrived. He was dressed in his official uniform, and was accompanied by a young Bulgarian, who was a merchant in the same business as himself.

Mr. —— was very surprised to see an Englishman in Angora, no one of our nation having visited that town for several years past; and he informed me that a telegram had just been received from Constantinople with reference to the proclamation of a Constitution. In consequence of this the town of Angora was to be illuminated on the following evening ; cannon would be fired, and the Pacha would read the telegram to the populace in the courtyard of the palace.

"What does it—the Constitution—mean?" I inquired.

"Mean?" replied the Bulgarian, who spoke English perfectly ; "it means a quantity of promises which the Government will never fulfil."

"It probably means a Parliament in Constantinople," said the Consul; "but we have no particulars as yet." And, making an appointment for me to call upon him in the morning, he left the room, accompanied by the Bulgarian.

I was very much surprised at this intelligence. A Parliament in Constantinople ! How would the members be chosen ? and who would choose them ? If universal suffrage prevailed, only one in about every 300 of the electors would be able to read or write; all of them would be ignorant of everything beyond the interests of their immediate neighbourhood.

"Is a Parliament possible here?" I inquired of my host.

"It is possible in theory, but impossible in practice," * was the reply. "We require more liberty, but this must be a question of time. We must educate the people, and teach both the Christians and Mohammedans that a difference of opinion on religious matters is not a subject about which men should quarrel. Religion has been the cause of more wars than anything else in history."

"I tell you what it is," he continued, "I believe that in another hundred years there will be either no religion at all, or else that every religion will be merged into one creed."

"The Christian," I observed.

"Who knows?" continued my host. "We live in strange times; even we Turks, the more particularly those who live in Constantinople, begin to argue about such matters. However, there is one thing I cannot understand about you Christians—you appear to me to have so many roads to heaven. For instance, in Anatolia there are American Protestant missionaries, Italian Catholic missionaries, and then there are the Armenians, who profess the Armenian faith."

"Well," I remarked, "what of it?"

"Wait a moment," said my host. "An Armenian, who is of the Armenian faith, is half-way up his staircase to heaven. An American missionary calls after him, 'Where are you going?' 'I am going to heaven.' 'No you are not; that is not the road to heaven. You are going in the wrong direction. Come down immediately, and I will show you the way.' The Armenian descends the steps, and begins ascending the road the missionary points out to him. Presently another voice is heard. It comes from the mouth of an Italian missionary. 'Where are you going?' 'I am going to heaven.' 'No you are not; come down immediately. You are on the road to hell.'"

"The result is," continued Suleiman, "that the poor Armenian does not know which way to turn. He is perpetually going up, or coming down the steps, and he never reaches his destination."

"Stop," I said, "you Mohammedans are also split up into

* This is refuted by an Official despatch recently received from H.M.'s Ambassador at Constantinople, see Appendix IV.

sects. There are the Sunnites and the Shiites, and you both hate each other."

"Alas! it is true," replied my companion, "but if we have two sects, you, according to what I have read, number at least a hundred, and the members of many of the sects think that every one else besides themselves must be damned. A very charitable doctrine that, is it not?" he added.

"Who was the Bulgarian with our Vice-Consul?" I inquired.

"He is in business with the Vice-Consul, and, I am sorry to say, does not love us Turks."

"Why?"

"Because his brother was one of the victims in the late Bulgarian rebellion."

"People in England blame us for the massacres," continued Suleiman. "What could we do? Our regular troops were employed elsewhere. This was owing to the intrigues of Russia; we were obliged to employ Circassians. The Circassians hate the Russians, and indeed they have reason to hate them. Those whose own mothers and sisters have been ravished and butchered, cannot be expected to love their oppressors. The Circassians looked upon the Bulgarians as Russians, hence the bloodshed. A few days ago I read an extract from an English paper, which had been translated into Turkish. It was to the effect that an English priest had seen people impaled by our Bashi Bazouks. Have you heard of this?"

"Yes, but the story has been contradicted."

"It is a pity when Christian priests or Mohammedan Imaums mix themselves up in politics," remarked another Turk; "their place is to calm men's passions, not to rouse them."

They left me; my host having previously asked at what time I should like to dine, with the observation that his hour was mine. Three servants were also placed at my disposal, with orders to supply me with anything I might require.

The following morning I called upon the Vice-Consul, and found him at home with his wife—a delicate-looking lady, who had braved all the hardships of the journey from Ismid in order to be at her husband's side.

Their house was furnished with every English comfort. It was difficult to believe that we were so many days from a railroad.

"That piano cost us a great deal of trouble," said the Vice-Consul. "It was brought here in two parts, and on mules."

"It is wonderful how it could have survived the journey," said the lady. Going to the instrument, she sounded the notes, which were very fairly in tune. "The Turkish ladies are so astonished with the piano," she continued. "They will sit for hours and listen to me playing."

I now started with the Consul to pay a visit to the Pacha. We arrived in a large courtyard, which was badly paved with loose stones. At one end there were some steps which led to the official residence. The courtyard was thronged with people who had been summoned to hear the telegram read about the new Constitution ; men in uniform, beggars, people with petitions in their hands, all swearing and jostling each other, as my companion and myself with difficulty made our way up the stairs. We were at once admitted into the audience-room. I found the Pacha, a tall, good-looking man of middle age, engaged in placing his seal upon a number of documents which an official was handing to him. He received us courteously, and proposed that we should accompany him to the court below, and listen to the proclamation of the Sultan's telegram.

The Pacha then introduced me to his son, a young man about twenty ; he spoke French fluently and without any perceptible accent, having been educated by a French tutor.

"We have only one cannon in Angora," he remarked, "and it is to be fired 101 times. We are a little afraid that it may not be able to stand the ordeal."

"Yes," said his father, "we have only one cannon, but we have sent 25,000 men to the war. We do not require any cannons," he added. "Our own people are quiet enough. The Russians will not find it a very easy matter to reach Angora."

We descended the steps ; on reaching the courtyard, the clerk—a wonderful old gentleman in a green dressing-gown, and with a wheezy voice—called for silence.

The Pacha then announced that the Sultan had been pleased to grant more liberties to his people, and that the present autocratic form of government was to be replaced by a Constitution. The Imaum, or priest, here said "Amin," equivalent to our Amen ; and the Vice-Consul put on his cap with the gilt peak, which he had taken off during the ceremony.

The Pacha's son now invited me to visit his rooms, which were a suite of apartments separate from those occupied by his father. I found his book-shelves well stored with scientific French works, and, to my surprise, discovered that the young Bey was not only remarkably well educated for a Turk, but was much better informed than nine Englishmen out of ten who have been to a public school, and have taken their degree at the university.

"Well, what do you think will be the result of the new Constitution?" I inquired.

"We are what you would call in England a very conservative nation. This sudden change has almost taken away our breath. We have not yet received the document which contains all the clauses of the new Constitution, and only know of them by telegram; if we are to attempt a form of Government such as you have in England, in my opinion we shall fail."

"Why so?" I asked.

"Because not only the electing class, but the men who will probably be chosen to sit in Parliament are only half educated. We shall have ignorant legislators legislating for an equally ignorant nation. We want time," he continued; "we require roads and railways. If there were means of communication, the people would travel and see that there is a good deal to be learnt away from home, and even from you Christians. Give us roads and railways, they will be worth fifty Constitutions, for the latter, in my opinion, will soon be found impracticable."

"It will never be carried out," said the Vice-Consul, who was sitting next to him. "It has been drawn up merely as a sop for the plenipotentiaries at the Conference."

"Well, whatever they do in other places," said the Bey, "we shall carry it out in its integrity here."

As he said these words the boom of the cannon resounded from below, the windows of the room began to rattle, the sound of a mob cheering, rapidly followed the report.

"A great deal of noise and a great deal of smoke: *voilà la Constitution*," said the Consul, and he prepared to leave the room.

"Stop," said the Bey, "you must not walk, I will send my carriage with you. It is almost the only carriage in Angora," he added, "and I have a compatriot of yours as a coachman; he has been with me three years."

CHAPTER XII

The Pacha's carriage—The coachman an Irishman—Christmas day in
Angora—The celebrities of the town—A society of thieves—Fire in
Sivrisa—The Turks and the Armenians—So-called fanaticism—Ten
Pachas in Angora in four years—Cases of litigation—Arrears—The
firman of November, 1875—The famine in Angora—Deaths during
the famine—The goats died—A Mohammedan divine—The Russian
Ambassador and the secret societies—The English newspapers and the
Bulgarian atrocities—A Turk values his nose quite as much as a
Christian—Suleiman Effendi's wife—The Turkish law about property
—A dinner with a Turkish gentleman—A mixture of nationalities—
My host and his digestion—Spirits refresh the stomach—The Prophet
and the old woman in Mecca—There are no old women in heaven.

THE Pacha's carriage was a funny-looking old vehicle. It
gave me the idea of a broken-down four-wheeler, which had
been taken to pieces and converted into an Irish car. There
were no springs. My bones were nearly dislocated as we drove
down the main street, to the Consul's house.

The coachman turned out to be not an Englishman, but
an Irishman. He had lost all signs of the native drollery.
Four years spent in Turkey seemed to have taken the life out
of him. He had been sent home to Ireland during the
previous summer, to buy some carriage-horses for his master.
On returning with his purchases, a storm arose in the Bay
of Biscay. The captain of the vessel had been obliged to
order the crew to throw the horses overboard. This, and the
absence of all female society, had weighed upon Paddy's mind.
He only brightened up for one moment when the Consul,
giving him a glass of whisky, desired him to drink it in honour
of Ould Ireland and of Christmas Day. For it was Christmas
Day in Angora, and the Consul's good wife was busily engaged
in all the mysteries of the *cuisine*.

"You are going to dine with us to-night?" said the hospitable gentleman. "Nay, you must," he added. "We are to
have a turkey stuffed with chestnuts, and my wife is busy
teaching the Turkish servants how to make a plum-pudding.
You will also meet some of the celebrities of Angora."

At dinner one of the guests—if I remember right, an
Armenian—did not seem to share the opinions which the
Pacha had expressed that morning with reference to the quiet
and good order in the city.

It appeared, according to this person, that there is a vaga

bond society, a society of thieves, in Angora, which preys upon Turks and Christians. The members of this society go at night to different houses, and, knocking at the door, order the proprietors, under threat of assassination, to draw the bolts. The inhabitants, who are frightened to death, frequently open the door. The thieves, entering, eat what they find in the house, and afterwards make the proprietor give them a sum of money.

"Yes," remarked another guest, "the worst of it is that several of the chief people in the town are said to be mixed up in this society."

A great fire had taken place in Sivrisa, a short time before. Damage had been done to the Christian inhabitants to the amount of thirty million piastres. The Turks did not willingly receive the Armenians into their houses, but when they did so, subsequently threw their mattresses out of the window, saying that they had been defiled by the contact of a *yiaour's* body. This was mentioned to show the fanaticism of the Turks.

However, during my subsequent travels in Armenia, the impression gradually dawned upon my mind that the Turks were, first of all, very wise not to wish to receive the Armenians into their houses ; and, secondly, if they had been good-natured enough to do so, to destroy the mattresses after the departure of their guests. The Armenians in their habits of body are filthy to the last degree. Their houses and clothes are infested with vermin. The Turks, on the contrary, are much cleaner, and are most particular about the use of the bath. An Englishman would not be pleased if his house became filled with what it is not here necessary to mention. If he did under such circumstances admit strangers, he would probably destroy their bedding the moment that they departed.

One of the visitors now remarked that there had been ten Pachas in four years in Angora, and that this frequent removal of officials was one of the causes which had led to the decadence of the country.

"Yes," said another, " a Pacha never feels sure of his place. Another evil here is the delay in settling cases of litigation. The arrears are enormous, and although in November, 1875, a firman from the sultan called attention to this matter, and ordered all law cases to be settled at once, nothing has been done to carry the edict into execution. If when the

Authorities find that they have a good man as a Pacha, they would leave him for say ten years in office, we should advance much more rapidly than at present."

I next heard that Angora had not recovered from the effects of the famine which had devastated the neighbourhood in 1873–74, the amount of taxes owing by the inhabitants to the Government amounting to more than a million and a half Turkish pounds.   The arrears of taxes owing previous to 1872 had been cancelled, some being as much as ten, twelve, and twenty years due.   Previous to cancelling the arrears, the Government had put up to auction the right of collecting the entire sum ; but, as many of the inhabitants had emigrated, no one ventured to bid.

There were 18,000 deaths in the neighbourhood of the town during the famine, and 25,000 people died subsequently in consequence of its effect.   The chief trade of the district is in goats' hair, 60 per cent. of the goats, sheep, and cattle had perished.   Children had been deserted and left in the streets ; some instances of babies being eaten by their parents were brought to light.

The following morning I received a visit from a relative of my host, Hadji Taifik Effendi.   It is said that he will one day be the head of the Mussulman faith.   I found this Mohammedan divine excessively bellicose in his ideas; he eagerly desired war.

" Why so ? " I inquired.

" Because an open enemy is better than a poisoner in your house.   Because war must come some day, and it is better to get rid of a cancer by sacrificing a limb.*   Russian agents have been doing their best to sow discord amongst the inhabitants of our provinces ; this they did during peace time and whilst a Russian ambassador was at Constantinople."

" Yes," said my host, " and an ambassador who is himself a prime mover in the secret societies which are agitating Europe.   The Russian Government pretends to be alarmed at the secret societies, but it is the hot-bed of all the secret societies in the world.*   You may depend upon it," he continued, " that the massacres which occurred in Bulgaria had been planned long before the outbreak.   Our regular troops had been purposely sent to other parts of the empire.   The Russian authorities were well aware of what was about to

* This is authenticated to a great extent by an Official Despatch. See Appendix V.

take place, and were delighted at the effect which it had upon public opinion in England. One thing, however, I cannot understand, and this is why your newspapers always published the accounts of the Bulgarian women and children who were slaughtered, and never went into any particulars about the Turkish women who were massacred by the Bulgarians, or about our soldiers whose noses were cut off, and who were mutilated by the insurgents in the Herzegovina. A Turk values his nose quite as much as a Christian," he added.

I now learned that Hadji Taifik Effendi had five wives, but that Suleïman Effendi only possessed one. She was the widow of a rich inhabitant of the town, and one day seeing Suleïman pass her windows, was struck by his appearance. She sent an old woman, as intermediary, to him. The marriage was arranged ; the lady bringing all her late husband's fortune to her new spouse.

The Turkish law about the distribution of property after a man's death is rather curious. If a man dies leaving a daughter, but if at the same time he has a brother, the daughter and his brother divide the property. Should he leave two daughters and a brother, each girl takes a quarter, his brother the half ; if he has one son and a brother, the brother is left out altogether, and the son takes everything.

That evening I received an invitation to dine with a Turkish gentleman. My host was one of the guests ; we went together to the place of entertainment. There was a strange mixture of nationalities, comprising Turks, Armenians, an Italian doctor, a certain M. Gasparini, who had been for some years in Angora, and was a great favourite with the inhabitants ; Greeks, a Bulgarian, and our Consul, who is a Scotchman. We passed through a courtyard which surrounded the house. It was illuminated with paper lanterns of various patterns. Presently I found myself in a room surrounded by divans. The guests were all assembled. In the centre of the apartment was a table. On it were placed bottles of red and white wine of Armenian manufacture, raki, mastic, brandy, and liqueurs, whilst biscuits, nuts and filberts, with sardines, were on little dishes interspersed amidst the decanters. My host, who was a stout and very dark man, pouring out a bumper, insisted upon all the company joining him in his libations, then, turning to M. Gasparini, he complained about the state of his digestion.

"Well, if you will drink so much," said the doctor, "you ought not to expect to feel well."

"Spirits," said the fat Turk ; "I like spirits—they refresh my stomach, and I become cheerful.   Send me some medicine," he added.

"There is no good treating these Turks," said the doctor to me, in Italian.   "They mix up everything together, wine, spirits, physic, &c., and then expect to get well.   If they would only carry out their prophet's injunctions, and leave off drinking wine, they would enjoy much better health."

"Did you ever hear the story of the prophet and the old women in Mecca ? " said one of the guests who was listening to the conversation.

" No, what is it ? "

" Well," observed the visitor, " there is a tradition that one day an old woman came to the Prophet and said, 'Oh ! only true Prophet of God, when I die, to which particular heaven shall I be sent ? '   The Prophet, who was continually being bothered by similar questions, and " (aside to the doctor) " whose digestion on that particular occasion was very likely out of order, replied gruffly, 'Go away, go away !   There are no old women in heaven.'   Upon this the aged dame left the house crying.   In a short time the Prophet's domicile was surrounded by all the ancient females in Mecca.   Their cries became so loud that they attracted Mahomet's attention ; he went out to them.   'Oh, holy Prophet ! holy Prophet !' they cried.   'Well, what do you want ? '   'You have said that there are no old women in heaven.   Whatever shall we do ? '   The Prophet was not in the least nonplussed for an answer. 'Quite true,' said Mahomet, ' quite true, I said so.   There are no old women in heaven ; they all become young so soon as they arrive there ! ' "

CHAPTER XIII

The band—Turkish melodies—Turkish music like a Turkish dinner, it is a series of surprises—Turkish etiquette at dinner—The pack-horse is lame—The people ask for many liras—The Postmaster is in bed—The chief of the police—Horse-copers in Aleppo—The fair sex in that city—A test for lovers—We burn our fingers soon enough after marriage—Domestic life in the harems in Angora—The immorality in Yuzgat—Mr. Gasparini—Turkish hospitality—Armenians dress like Turks—Christian women—Great harmony between Turks and Christians—Armenian testimony doubtful—The prison at Sivas—He new evidence—A Turkish veterinary surgeon—Horse-dealers—Two pounds ffered for the horse—History of the Ottoman Empire—The Bey's present—Generosity of the Turks—The devil is not so black as he is painted.

By this time the guests had consumed many cigarettes, smoked numerous Nargilehs, and drank freely of the liqueurs. The host, rising, proposed that we should adjourn to the dining-room. There we found three musicians with instruments much resembling banjos.

"We are to have some music," said the Bey, the Pacha's son, who was one of the guests. "I am afraid that it will not be much to your taste. Our melodies are very different to those which you are accustomed to hear in Europe."

He was quite right; Turkish melodies are very different. There is a wildness and pathos about many of them which strikes the stranger accustomed to the more regular measure which distinguishes European music. Now they resounded so plaintively that the guests involuntarily ceased talking. Another instant the instruments, bursting forth with a startling crash, half deafened us with the clamour.

The performers swung their heads from side to side, and kept time with the quickening air; the strains went faster and faster. The guests were inspired with the musicians' enthusiasm. All the heads began to swing, we Europeans involuntarily marking the time with our feet on the floor. The musicians panted with their exertions. Suddenly the melody left off abruptly, and one of the performers commenced a doleful dirge. This did not last long, and when he was in the most pathetic part, another crash from the orchestra interrupted him in the middle of a verse.

"Turkish music is exactly like a Turkish dinner," observed one of the guests; "it is a series of surprises; the leader of the orchestra goes from *andante* to a racing pace without any *crescendo* whatsoever ; the cook in the same manner—he first gives us a dish as sweet as honey, and then astonishes our stomachs with a sauce as acid as vinegar. Now we are eating fish, another instant blanc-mange. A vegetable is next placed before us, and our stomachs have scarcely recovered from their astonishment, when a sweet soup is served up with some savoury pastry."

The servants, who were much more numerous than the guests, vied with each other in serving the different dishes. Twenty attendant domestics were arranged in Indian file. So soon as the host made a sign to the leading domestic, each kind of food was replaced by another, and number-two servant was prepared with fresh viands, while number one, who had hurried to the kitchen, returned with another dish.

The table was a raised one, chairs were placed round it. This was done in honour of the European visitors. We all ate with our fingers, each man helping himself according to his rank or social position. It was not etiquette for a Cadi to seize a piece of meat before the Bey put his fingers in the dish, a captain had to be careful not to offend the susceptibilities of a colonel.

To eat blanc-mange *à la Turque* requires some practice; however, the Consul and the Italian doctor had been for some time in the East, and used their fingers as readily as a knife and fork.

At last our dinner was over. Fruit, mincemeat, dishes of vegetables, sweets and raisins, salads and creams, concluding with a huge bowl of boiled rice, had been disposed of, the whole having been washed down by tumblers of red country wine very like Burgundy.

" Praise be to God ! " said our host, rising ; his example was followed by the rest of the guests.

A servant poured water over the hands of the visitors, beginning with each man according to his rank. We adjourned into another room. Here coffee, *tchibouks,* and *nargilehs* were handed round to the company.

A servant now approached, and said that Osman was waiting outside, and wished to speak to me.

" What is the matter ? " I inquired. " Have you come to tell me how very industrious you are, or do you want some more money ? " I had previously observed that when Osman wished to speak to me, these two topics were almost invariably the subject of his conversation.

" No, Effendi, but the horse——"

" Which horse ? "

" The bay that makes a noise."

" Well, what of him ? "

" He is lame. My brother has seen him. I have seen him. He will not be able to carry his pack to-morrow."

" Hire two horses instead of one, and lead the roarer."

" Yes, Effendi, that is what I have been trying to do ; but the people ask for many liras ; their hearts are stony at the sight of our difficulties, they open wide their purses for the Effendi's gold."

" Have you been to the post ? "

"Yes, but the postmaster has ten horses, and only one man to look after them. The postmaster says if you hire two baggage animals that you must pay for ten."

" Wait here, Osman," I said ; returning to my host, I informed him of my difficulties.

" Oh ! the dog ! " exclaimed the Bey. " He is trying to cheat you ! "

Tearing a piece of paper from an old letter in his pocket, he wrote a note to the chief of the police, desiring him to bring the postmaster immediately before us.

" The postmaster is in bed," said Osman, who had entered the room.

" In bed or out of bed, he shall be brought here," said the young Bey, stamping the piece of paper with his seal, he gave it to a servant. Presently a noise was heard. The postmaster arrived, followed by the chief of the police.

" You must give this English gentleman two horses at once."

" Yes, Bey Effendi."

" But why did you not do so before ? "

" Because I did not know that it was the Bey's pleasure— the will of the son of our Pacha is my will. Upon my head be it ; the horses shall come."

" Good horses," I remarked, " stout and strong."

" Have I not said so ? " replied the man, and it was agreed that I was to hire two horses as far as Yuzgat, paying the regular tariff of three piastres for each horse per hour.

" People in Turkey who deal in horses are great rogues," said the Bey ; " are they the same in your country ? A horse-dealer near Kars would try and get the best of his dearest friend in a bargain."

" They are much the same in England," I replied ; and the

young Bey began to tell us some stories of horse-copers in Aleppo, where he had passed some years, and in which town the fair sex was more than usually frail.

" The young men in that city have a curious way of showing their affection to the lady of their choice," continued the speaker. " A girl has, say, three lovers—a small allowance for a lady in that part of the world—she does not know which to select, each one of the suitors is eager to display his gallantry."

" What does she do?" asked one of the party. " Accept them all ? "

" No, she takes three bits of live charcoal from out of the fire ; giving each of her lovers a piece, she tells them to place it in the palms of their hands. The fire burns through the skin, the tendons are laid bare; sometimes the amorous gentlemen will resist till the flesh has been burnt to the bone. Here one or two of them generally succumb to the torture ; the man who resists the longest, wins the lady."

" But if they are all equally indifferent to pain, and the charcoal burns out, what happens then ? " I inquired.

" The lady takes three more pieces of charcoal, and begins again with the other hand," replied the Bey. " The more they resist, the better the girl likes them, because it is a proof to her mind that they value her more than their own torture."

" Did you ever try it ? "

" No," said the Bey, laughing. " I can get a wife without any trouble, so I do not care about burning my fingers. We burn our fingers quite soon enough after marriage, as it is."

" Yes," said the doctor, and he began to give me a long account of the domestic life in some of the harems in Angora.

According to the doctor's experiences there was a great deal of immorality amidst the fair sex in the city, although nothing to what existed in Yuzgat, another town which I should pass by on the way to Kars. In Angora, although the women are very unfaithful to their husbands, yet everything is kept more or less concealed. In Yuzgat it was very different, and there you could actually see the dance of the Turkish gipsy women, although in Angora it was strictly prohibited.

M. Gasparini was doing a large practice. He had been established for ten years in Angora and its neighbourhood. From his position as a medical man he had the opportunity of knowing more about the domestic life of the inhabitants than the other European residents.

"Well, although the women may be immoral, the men are very hospitable," said the Consul. "Wherever a stranger may go he is always received with the greatest hospitality. A few years ago a friend of mine, Mr. Thompson, was travelling from the Black Sea to Angora. He arrived at a village. The Khan was full, every room was occupied. However, he was an old traveller, and could easily accommodate himself to circumstances. Taking his cloak, he lay down in the yard and prepared to pass the night in the open air. Presently he was awakened by a tap on the shoulder. On looking up, he found an old Turk bending over him.

"Why are you sleeping here?" inquired the Mohammedan.

"Because there is no room in the Khan."

"This is not right. A stranger, and outside the gate. Come with me."

Taking Mr. Thompson by the hand, the Turk led him to his house, gave him a clean bed and his breakfast, waited himself upon his guest, and would not receive any remuneration.

"Now," added the Consul, "the Turk was a Mohammedan, and Mr. Thompson a Christian; if the Turk had been in England, and had found himself placed in a similar predicament to Mr. Thompson, do you think that there are many Englishmen who would have behaved so generously to an utter stranger?"

The following day I called upon some Armenian gentlemen, and found their houses furnished like my host's, with thick carpets, divans, and pipes, the walls being bare and white-washed. Pictures and looking-glasses were seldom to be seen, the latter being a very costly luxury, owing to the difficulty of carriage.

The Armenians dressed in a similar manner to the Turks. The Christian women were closely veiled whenever they left the house. In many instances, an Armenian was not per-mitted to see his wife* before marriage, and had to take her, as the Yankees say, "on spec."

Great harmony existed between the Turks and Christians. Whenever I dined with an Armenian there were always Mohammedans present. When I visited a Turk's house, I generally found Armenians amongst the visitors. On inquiring whether this state of things prevailed elsewhere, I was in-formed by the Armenians that in other parts of Anatolia, and

* The Armenian women have more liberty in Angora than in many other towns in Asia Minor.

more particularly in Sivas, the Christians were ill-treated by the Turks, and that the prisons were filled with Armenians.

During my stay at Ismid I had heard precisely the same story of the sufferings of the Christians at Angora. I had been told that the Armenians were cruelly oppressed, and that justice was never shown to them. However, in Angora the two religions did not seem to clash. The Mohammedans and Christians were on the best of terms. I began to be a little sceptical as to the truth of the statement about Sivas, and determined not to form any opinion on the matter from mere hearsay evidence, but to see with my own eyes if the prisons were so full of Christians as the Armenians in Angora would have had me believe.

Later on in the day, Radford suggested that it would be as well for me to sell the lame horse and buy another; he was doubtful whether, even without his pack, the animal would be able to march to Yuzgat. The poor beast was very lame, the frog of his foot was much swollen. Whilst we were talking, a Turkish veterinary surgeon arrived : taking out his knife, he made a slight incision in the swollen place.

Meantime several horse-dealers, learning that I wanted to buy a horse, brought me some animals for inspection, at the same time offering me the liberal price of £2 sterling for my own animal.

"Well," said one man, extracting some silver from what appeared to be an old stocking, "I will give twelve medjidis."

"Your heart is very hard, brother, soften it a little," said Osman. " Our horse shall not go for less than forty silver pieces. You love your money, but we love our horse still more."

Nobody would give this sum, and as I thought that possibly the operation performed by the Turkish veterinary surgeon might benefit the animal, I determined to wait another day in Angora. This would also give me an opportunity of inspecting more closely the old Augustin monument, one of the curiosities in the town.

To my great delight the operation proved successful; in the evening the horse could walk without much pain. He would be able to march on the following morning, and so I gave orders for an early start. Just before leaving, a servant arrived from the Pacha's palace. The young Bey, who had observed that I much admired a work entitled the "History of the Ottoman Empire," and which was in his library, had

sent it to me as a present, and hoped that I would do him the
honour of accepting the book as a memento of my visit to
Angora.   There were about ten volumes, the weight would
have been at least twenty pounds, and a considerable addition
to the baggage.   Much to my regret, I was obliged to decline
the kind offer.   The hospitality of the Turkish nation is proverbial.   The generosity of the Turks is equally great.   In
fact, they carry this virtue to excess.   Sometimes after having
admired a horse, I have been surprised to find that the steed
has been sent to my stable, with a note from the owner,
entreating my acceptance of the animal.

I often experienced great difficulty in finding excuses for
not accepting the presents so generously offered to me by my
entertainers.   " I cannot take any more luggage," I would
say, if the present were at all cumbersome.   However, if it
were a horse, I could only decline the gift and say that I had
not sufficient servants to look after the animals.

" But I have plenty of servants, take one of mine ; he will
accompany you throughout your journey, and then will return
to me," would be the answer.

People in this country who abuse the Turkish nation, and
accuse them of every vice under the sun, would do well to
leave off writing pamphlets and travel a little in Anatolia.
There is an old saying that " the devil is not so black as he is
painted," and in many things writers who call themselves
Christians might well take a lesson from the Turks in Asia
Minor.

CHAPTER XIV

My host was up at daybreak to see me off.

" Come and see me in England," I said.

" If Allah pleases, I will," was my friend's reply, and I only
hope that I may have the opportunity of returning Suleiman
Effendi's hospitality.

The road was hard and good for a few miles, we rode for
some time by the Ayash river.

After marching for about five hours, we came to a small farm-house. It was on the opposite bank of the river to ourselves; but there was a ford, and as there was no wood on our side of the stream, I determined to cross and halt an hour for lunch. The house belonged to an Armenian. It was filthily dirty. Vermin could be seen crawling in all directions on the rugs. In consequence of this, I resolved to make our fire outside, and lunch in the open air. There were some turkeys in the farm-yard, and the proprietor coming up, I desired Osman to purchase one of the birds.

"The Effendi wants a turkey," said Osman to the farmer.

This announcement at once created a great commotion among the female portion of the Armenian household—the turkeys being looked upon by the women in the establishment as their own particular property.

"What for?" said an elderly dame, whose face was bound up in what appeared to be a dish-cloth.

"To eat."

"Have you any money?" asked the woman suspiciously.

"Money?" said Osman indignantly; "much money. We can afford to eat turkey every day! Now, then, how much for this one?" pointing to an old bird, apparently the paterfamilias of the brood.

"Osman is an ass, sir," here interfered Radford. "That is a very old cock. Osman has his eye on him because he is the biggest, he thinks that we can chew leather, that he do." And pursuing the brood, my English servant succeeded in catching a young pullet, which he brought triumphantly to the woman.

"How much?" I inquired.

"Twelve piastres" (about eighteenpence), replied the woman.

"Twelve piastres," said Osman; "it is a great deal of money—we could not afford to eat turkey at that rate; say ten, and have done with it."

"The bird is a hen, and will have eggs," observed the farmer.

"She may die and have no eggs, and then you would have lost ten piastres," said Osman. "Come, be quick," he added, "pick the turkey!" And giving the woman the money, the old dame retired to a little distance to prepare the bird for the pot.

When Radford had finished his cooking, and had helped me

to some of the turkey, he put the remainder in my washing-basin, and handed it to Osman, for himself and the man with the pack-horses.

"Why do you not give them the cooking-pot, and let them eat out of it?" I inquired. "Perhaps they will not like eating out of my washing-basin."

"I thought of that, sir; but the pot is that hot that they would burn their fingers a-shoving them into it. Nasty, dirty fellows they are too; preferring dirty fingers to nice clean forks! But Osman, sir, he ain't that nice. He is the greediest feeder I ever see, he would eat out of a coal-scuttle sooner than not fill himself. See there, sir, he has got that turkey's leg. I knew he would have it! It was on the baggage man's side of the basin, and Osman had eaten already one drumstick : the other ought to have gone to the chap with the horses. But Osman ain't got no conscience about eating, whatever he may have when he is flopping himself down on my coat and pretending to say his prayers."

After luncheon the two Turks were so long in loading the pack-horse that I determined to ride forward with Radford, and let the other men follow with the luggage. We had continued the journey for about an hour when, after ascending a hill, I turned round to see if there were any signs of my followers. Nothing was in sight except an Armenian woman, who was on horseback, she was riding cross-legged, and carried a baby in a handkerchief which was slung from her neck.

"Had she seen Osman?" I inquired.

"No," was the answer.

Desiring Radford to remain where he was, I galloped back in the direction of the farm-house. On arriving by the riverside a singular picture met my gaze. A pack-horse was dripping from head to foot, and was without his saddle. All the baggage was wet through. My cartridges, tea, sugar, and coffee were spoiled; Radford's bag, containing his pig tobacco, lay dripping wet by the side of the river. Osman was swearing violently at the man in charge of the pack-horses, and from time to time was administering to him a blow with a stick across the shoulders. The chastised individual was sobbing violently. On seeing me he threw himself down on the ground and began to embrace my knees.

"What has happened?" I inquired.

They both commenced speaking together.

"Stop! One at a time," I remarked.

"Yes, you dog!" said Osman to his fellow-countryman, "How dare you speak? He did not lead the horse, Effendi, he drove the animal before him, and the horse lay down in the river. Everything is spoiled! Oh! you refuse of a diseased sheep,"—this to the culprit. "And the Effendi's cartridges, he will not be able to replace them; and my brother, what will he say about his tobacco? he will be angry—he may beat me! I knew your mother, your grandmother, and great-grandmother—they were all most improper characters—and you, you hound, you are the worst of the family!" As he said these words, Osman began to flog the delinquent most unmercifully.

I was obliged to interfere, taking my servant by the collar, I ordered him to desist, and at once to load the baggage animal.

This accident delayed us considerably on the road. Some time after sunset, on looking at my watch, I found that we had only placed an eight hours' march between ourselves and Angora. We were on a large plain, which was surrounded by hills; our path wound round the slopes of the adjacent height, presently the village of Asra Yuzgat appeared in sight. It is built on the side of a hill. We were soon riding on the tops of the houses, and had to be very careful lest our horses should suddenly come upon an open chimney. Some of the roofs had fallen in. The moon shining on the white rafters gave a ghastly appearance to the scene.

The people in this part of Anatolia have a very economical way of building their habitations. The man who is old enough to take unto himself a helpmate, and who is about to leave his father's roof, marks a piece of ground, generally of an oblong shape and on the side of a hill. He next digs out the earth to the depth of about seven feet. Then, hewing down some trees, he cuts six posts, each about ten feet high, and drives them three feet into the ground, three posts being on one side of the oblong and three on the other. Cross-beams are fastened to the tops of these uprights, and branches of trees plastered down with clay cover all. A few planks, with a hole made in them to serve as a doorway, enclose the outer side of the building, and a broad heavy plank closes the entrance, hinges being replaced by strips of cowhide. A wooden railing divides the room into two parts; one of them is tenanted by the sheep, oxen, camels, and cows of the proprietor, the other by himself and family. No partition-wall separates the cattle from their master; and the smell which arises at night from the confined air and from the ammonia in the building is excessively disagreeable to a European. In cold weather a hole in the roof, which serves as a ventilator, is stopped by a large stone. Fuel, often made from cows' dung, first dried and then mixed with chopped straw, is thrown on the fire. The inmates, sometimes consisting of twelve or more people, lie huddled together on the floor. This last in the poorer houses is covered by rugs made of camel's hair, and in the wealthier establishments by thick Persian carpets.

The barking of the dogs, which swarmed around us, speedily awoke the inhabitants, and a middle-aged Turk, clad in a thick brown mantle, approaching me, said that he was the Caimacan or governor, and that he hoped I would stay at his house that night.

It appeared that my friend the Bey at Angora had written to him about my journey, and had said that I should reach Asra Yuzgat at sunset. The Caimacan knew nothing of our accident on the road: as we had not arrived by one hour after nightfall, he had gone to bed.

His house was not a large one. It consisted of two rooms, a kitchen and a reception-room. The latter apartment was used for all purposes. The owner remarked that he was going on a shooting expedition the following morning; he proposed that I should join his party. There were, according to him, a great many partridges and hares in the neighbourhood. However, my cartridges had been probably all of them spoiled in the river, so I was obliged to decline the invitation.

I was rather tired, and wished to go to bed. On expressing a wish to this effect, a mattress was produced, and put down in one corner, and a second the other side of the room for the Caimacan. Three or four servants were present. No one seemed to have any intention to retire. I took off my clothes, lay down on the mattress, and drew over myself a marvellous thing in the way of *yorgans*, a silk counterpane of as many colours as Joseph's coat, and lined with feathers.

"Are you warm?" said the Caimacan.

"Yes."

"Every one is warm with that *yorgan*," he continued. "It is light, and there are no fleas in it. You will sleep well."

He now prepared to go to bed. The four servants assisted him. First they drew off his boots, and then his nether garments; the Caimacan glancing from time to time at me out of the corner of his eye, probably wishing to see what impression the fact of his having four servants to put him to bed had produced on my mind. He had been astonished when I undressed myself, and had remarked,—

"Why, you have two servants, and you take off your own clothes! What is the good of having servants if you do not make them useful?"

By this time he was in bed. His attendants lay down by his side; Radford and Osman in another corner. The one tallow dip which lit the room was carefully extinguished; soon nought could be heard save the snoring of the slumberers.

I arose at daybreak, and unpacked the wet cartridges, then, taking my gun, I tried some of them; snap—snap—they would not explode. It was no use stopping for the shooting party; so desiring Osman to commence loading the horses, I took leave of my host.

CHAPTER XV

WE rode across a low ridge of mountains, rocks which looked like iron ore lying about in all directions, and presently arrived at the Kizil Ermak, a broad and rapid stream which runs into the Black Sea, about fifty miles S.E. of Sinope. The distance across the river was at least one hundred yards, the left bank being very precipitous. The depth of the water, owing to the recent rains, was not less than seven feet. There is no bridge in the neighbourhood, the nearest being twenty-four miles higher up the river; I was curious to learn how we should reach the other shore. The guide soon solved the problem. Riding about half a mile along the bank, he put two fingers in his mouth and whistled. In a few minutes the sound was answered from the opposite side of the river. Six men appeared in sight. Descending the bank, they dragged a triangular-shaped barge from some rushes, and, getting into it, began to pull with all their might in our direction. The current was very swift, the starting-point was nearly half a mile beyond us; but notwithstanding this, the oarsmen overshot their mark. We had to lead our horses some little distance before we reached the boat.

It was a queer sort of a craft, certainly not more than twenty-five feet long, and about sixteen in its widest part. Its sides were two feet above the water: the men could not approach the bank nearer than twenty yards. The bottom was muddy. Our horses would have to walk through the mud to the boat, and then jump over the bulwarks.

There were altogether eight horses, my own four, three belonging to the post, and the animal the guide rode, a brute which kicked, and already had slightly lamed my grey.

"I shall be drowned," said Osman plaintively, "I know I shall! Can my brother swim?" pointing to Radford.

"What does he say, sir?" inquired my English servant.

"He wants to know if you can save him if he falls into the water."

"Save him? no, sir. I cannot swim a stroke. I wonder what our engineers at Aldershot would say if they had to get us over in such a craft as this? It is wuss than a poontoon!"

The boatmen wanted to take four horses across at a time; a veto was put upon this proposal on account of the guide's horse; it was determined that he should go alone. Taking the saddle off my own animal, I led him into the water; on reaching the boat I climbed into it, and tried to make the horse follow. This was by no means an easy task, he had sunk at least a foot into the mud, and evidently did not fancy the leap into the bark. Three of the boatmen now got into the river. One of them, seizing my horse's tail, twisted it violently, the others poked him from behind with their oars. Osman all this time was expostulating with the animal from the bank.

"Dear horse, jump in! You shall have as much barley as you can eat this evening."

This argument not having any effect upon the horse,

Osman's language waxed stronger, and he heaped numerous curses upon the animal's ancestry.

"Drat you!" said Radford at last; "you are always a-talking when there is something to do. Go and help, can't you?" Suiting the action to the word, he gave a push to the noisy Turk, which nearly upset him into the water.

At length, and by the exertions of all our party, my horse was persuaded to make an effort. Rearing himself up, he placed his two fore-feet in the boat. A chorus of oaths and ejaculations—the hind-legs followed. Once safely in, I bandaged his eyes. The other horses, seeing that one of their number was embarked, followed without much difficulty.

We floated down the stream for some distance, and at a great speed, before the boatmen could get any command over their craft, which whirled round as if in a whirlpool. Fortunately the horses were all blindfolded, and could not see the water. At last we reached the opposite bank, having descended the stream for more than a mile from our starting-point. So much time was lost in getting the other horses over, that night was upon us before we reached our destination, Yakshagan, a large village with two hundred houses. It was only fourteen miles from Asra Yuzgat, though, owing to the river, we had employed from sunrise to sunset in the journey.

At Yakshagan it was necessary to hire fresh post-horses. The official at the station was very uncivil, and declared that he would not supply me with any unless I paid for three horses from Angora. I had only engaged two, however, the man with them had chosen to bring a third animal, instead of riding on one of the baggage horses. At last the difficulty was settled by the guide, who was known to the postmaster, saying that he would be responsible for the amount; whilst I agreed to refer the matter to the authorities at Yuzgat, and abide by their decision.

I started rather late, in consequence of the altercation. After a five hours' ride along a good road and through a beautiful country, we arrived at Madeh. Here there are several silver-mines which, till very lately, have been worked by the Turks. I was informed that water has recently found its way into the pits. In consequence of this the miners had abandoned them.

"It is a great pity," said an old Turk, an inhabitant of the village. "With proper machinery it would be easy to pump out the water, and these mines abound in silver."

"We have got nothing but paper money in Anatolia," he added sorrowfully, "all this rich metal lies buried beneath our feet."

It surprises a traveller to find that the Turks make so little use of their mines. In the course of my ride from Angora I had passed through a country apparently abounding in iron, and with many traces of coal. At Madeh there is silver, whilst copper is also found in the immediate neighbourhood. With intelligent engineers to explore the mineral wealth of Anatolia, Turkey would be able not only to pay the interest of her debt, but would speedily become one of the richest countries in the world.

From Madeh we continued the march to Kowakoli. The country on each side of the road is covered with vines. The grapes in this part of Turkey are very large. The inhabitants preserve the fruit throughout the winter by hanging it up in cellars. The atmosphere is dry; unless the temperature falls much below zero, and the grapes freeze, they can be kept till the early spring. There is no wine made in the neighbourhood. The Armenians, who in other parts of Anatolia make large sums of money by distilling spirits, here neglect this branch of industry. The grapes are either eaten, or the unfermented juice is kept to sweeten pastry, for sugar is very dear, and costs more than a shilling the pound. This price is beyond the means of not only the poorer, but even of the wealthier inhabitants of the district. In consequence of this they drink their coffee without sweetening it, and look upon a present of a few pounds of sugar as a donation worthy of a sultan's generosity.

I was hospitably entertained by an old farmer. He bewailed the disasters caused by the Angora famine, which had been felt throughout all this district. The road from Angora had been blocked by snow for three months and a half. His cattle all died from starvation, his goats had also perished. The late Sultan, Abdul Aziz, had sent large sums of money and food to the suffering people; but the roads were impassable, and the provisions could not reach their destination. Many poor people had died of hunger with cart-loads of corn and barley only a few miles from their doors.

My host had one son, a lad about sixteen years of age. The boy regretted that he was not old enough to join the sultan's forces.

"Your time will come soon enough," observed his parent.

"He does not know what war is like," added the farmer sorrowfully. "A great many men have gone to Servia from this neighbourhood, and several have been killed. God grant, if my boy should have to go, that he may return to his old father."

"Is there much enthusiasm here for the war?" I inquired.

"Immense," replied the farmer; "the people feel that it is a question not only of religion but also of property. We landlords should not like to have Russian assessors grinding us down to the last piastre. We do not wish to be tortured to change our religion, and we do not want to be made soldiers against our will."

"But you are all soldiers now," I remarked.

"Yes, because it is the time of war, and it is a struggle for our very existence. When the fighting is over, our young men will return to their homesteads, and gladden their families once more."

"Do you think that you shall be able to withstand your foe?"

"Allah is always on the side of justice, and He will give us the victory," rejoined the old man proudly. "Our land shall drink our blood ere we give up one foot of soil to the invader."

We now rode towards Sekili, a village about twenty-seven miles from our sleeping quarters.

Presently my grey horse began to walk lame. He had been kicked by the guide's animal on the previous day. My weight was too much for the poor little brute. I resolved to change horses with Osman, who was much lighter than myself. Calling the Turk to my side, I desired him to dismount, and then mounted the ambling steed. The pace of a Rahvan, or ambling horse, is an easy one for the rider; and the animal can get over the ground at the rate of about five miles an hour; the ordinary walk of the small Turkish horses being not much above three.

We passed by some hovels. Their walls were built of marble; the roofs were made of beams covered with mud; the pure white rock presenting a striking contrast to its filthy surroundings. Marble abounds in this neighbourhood. Large blocks were lying on all sides of us, and along our path. Some ruins in the vicinity showed that hundreds of years ago the inhabitants of this part of Anatolia were able to utilize their quarries.

Poor Turkey, she has descended the steps of civilization, and not ascended them like European nations.

However, though mud hovels have replaced the marble palaces of the Turk's ancestors, the Turks themselves remain unchanged. Hospitality—their great virtue—is as rife in 1877 as in the days of Mohammed II. No matter where an Englishman may ask for shelter, he will never find a Mohammedan who will deny him admittance.

We left behind us some mountains of slate, and rode over rich soil, which had been left fallow for miles around.

" There are not inhabitants enough to cultivate the land," was the guide's answer to a question from me about the subject.

He was doubtless right. Asia Minor, like Spain, needs a threefold population to develop her natural wealth. Let foreign settlers go to Anatolia. Let them make railways throughout the country, it could supply the whole of Great Britain with corn, and the mines of coal and of other minerals would prove a source of immense wealth to the inhabitants.

Later in the day we passed a Kurdish encampment. The Kurds all lived in circular black tents, and some women, with unveiled faces, rushed outside the dwellings to see the strangers pass.

The Turkish authorities have great difficulty in collecting the taxes from this nomad race. Whenever the Kurds expect a visit from the tax-collector, they pack up their chattels and migrate to the mountains. Here they can place the Turkish officer at defiance, and only return to the plains when their spies have announced the enemy's departure. A few years ago the wealth of the Kurdish sheiks was very considerable ; many of them owned twenty, and even thirty thousand sheep, besides large droves of horses, and numerous herds of cattle. The famine, however, which devastated the province, was as disastrous for the Kurds as for the Turks. It has left them in a wretched state of poverty.

The Delidsche Ermak, a tributary of the Kizil Ermak, crossed our path. There was no bridge, and we had some difficulty in finding a ford. At last the marks of some horses' hoofs showed our guide the exact spot : riding into the stream —here about fifty yards wide—and with the water up to his horse's girths, he piloted us over in safety. The bottom of the river is firm. I was informed that the stream becomes very shallow during the summer months; the inhabitants can then cross it with their ox-carts.

The village of Sekili is made up of twenty mud hovels. Our accommodation for the night was not of a luxurious kind. But after a long and tiring march a man speedily reconciles himself to circumstances. A fire was lit. Two old hens were stewing in the pot. A kettle full of tea simmered on the fire; and with a pipe after dinner, things looked a little brighter than at first. We next traversed a district abounding with salt. The soil sparkled in the sun. The crystal substance was visible for a considerable distance. Presently some Turkoman girls, with high, picturesque head-dresses, rode by us at a gallop: their merry laughter rang in the air as they passed. Soon afterward we came to their village, the habitations being nothing more or less than a few holes in the side of a hill. The Turkomans pronounce Turkish rather differently to the Turks. At first I had some little difficulty in making myself understood. Indeed, a man must be a polyglot to know all the languages spoken in Anatolia. Armenian, Greek, Circassian, Kurdish, Tartar, Persian, Georgian, and Arabic, besides Turkish, are heard within a radius of one hundred miles. The different sounds in these languages are very puzzling to a stranger who is trying to perfect himself in Turkish.

Some Turkomans, dressed in white tunics, broad red trousers, and with grey sashes round their waists, were sitting idly at the entrance to their burrows. A woman, in a crimson dressing-gown, and a few girls, with naught on save long white shifts, and caps, were busily engaged in drawing water from a neighbouring well. Some goats, which had descended the hill, were feeding on the roofs of the houses.

We entered one of the dwellings, but so many fleas were hopping about that I determined to eat my lunch in the open air. The proprietor of the hovel was very much surprised at our preferring the cold outside to the shelter of his domicile.

"My Effendi does not like fleas," said Osman.

"There are not many here!" said the proprietor. "It does not do to be particular. In Sekili," he continued, "fleas abound, the Effendi ought to be accustomed to them by this time."

"What does he say, sir?" asked Radford, as Osman gradually explained the Turkoman's remarks to me.

"Say! He says that you ought to be accustomed to fleas by this time."

"Accustomed, sir? No, but they are getting accustomed to me. Haldershot is a joke to this here Turkey so far as fleas are concerned."

Presently my servant continued,—

"These Turks, sir, ain't got no decent tobacco, why a pipeful of cavendish, or good bird's hi, is worth all the hay they smoke. No wonder people in England abuse the Turks—and quite right too. Men who might grow shag tobacco, and prefer growing hay tobacco, can't be of much account."

CHAPTER XVI

A victim to the famine—Daili—A conversation with some Turkomans— The massacre of the Teke Turkomans by the Russians—Women violated—Little boys and girls abused and murdered—The Muscovite is a beast—Should not you like to cut the throats of all the Russians? —What is the best way to get rid of a wasp's nest?—A war of extermination—Yuzgat—A cavalcade of horsemen—Mr. Vankovitch— The telegram—Our reception—Old friends of the Crimea—Some visitors—Things have altered for the better—The Christians at Yuzgat —Armenians and Turks dine together—Mr. Vankovitch's experiences —The Polish insurrection—General Muravieff—Brutality to the women at Vilna.

On the track once more; and now we came to a large stone, in the middle of the path. This marked the resting-place of a victim to the recent famine. The poor fellow had fallen down from exhaustion, and had died on this spot. It was too much trouble for the survivors to move his corpse, they had made a hole and buried him where he lay.

My grey horse, which Osman was riding, still went very lame; so I limited our march to six hours, and stopped at the little village of Daili. Here there were only fifteen houses. Many camels and herds of cattle were grazing in the neighbourhood, and the ground appeared to have been cultivated for a considerable distance. On this occasion the fortune of travellers gave us better quarters. The house in which we were lodged was clean. A raised dais of wood was set apart for the servants. Mattresses with cushions were reserved for the proprietor and his guests.

There were some Turkomans in the village, and when the

news was spread that an Englishman had arrived, several of them came to see me.

"We are so glad to see an Englishman," said an old man, the spokesman for their party.

Osman now interrupted him.

"Effendi, they want to tell you that they hate the Muscovites, and that they hope England will not allow the Tzar's soldiers to massacre them like they (the Russians) massacred the Teke Turkomans."

"Were many women and children belonging to the Teke Turkomans killed by the Russians?"

The old man shook his head.

"Many! many!" he replied. "The women were violated by the soldiers. The little boys and girls were abused and then murdered. The men took pleasure in these awful crimes. The Muscovite is a beast! He is worse than a hyena; the hyena sucks the blood of his victim, but the Russian satisfies his lust first, and then tears to pieces the object of his pleasure."

"We hear," he continued, "you have as Padishah, a lady. What does she think of this way of treating the Turkoman's little ones?" *

"And what do you think yourself?" he added. "Should not you like to cut the throats of all the Russians?"

This was rather a strong way of dealing with the question. However, if I had been a Turkoman, and my own sisters had been treated by the Russians in the way the Turkoman women have been, I should have looked upon the matter from a Turkoman point of view.

"They are not all equally guilty," I replied.

"Equally guilty! Yes they are. From the Tzar upon his throne to the soldiers who do his bidding they are a nation of assassins? What is the best way to get rid of a wasp's nest?" he now inquired.

"Smoke it, and destroy the young ones," I replied.

"Well, that," said the Turkoman, "is what we must do with the Russians. We must kill them all. And Allah will be with us; for He knows who began the butchery."

"Have many men gone from this village to the army?" I asked.

"Every able-bodied man is serving, and we are now, all of

* For treatment of the Turkomans by the Russian soldiers, I refer the reader to Mr. Schuyler's highly interesting work, "Turkistan.'

us, going to the front; greybeards as well as boys. We feel
that it is a war of extermination. If we do not defend our
homesteads, woe betide us!"

On leaving Daili the track was firm and good for the first
three hours; it then became very precipitous, and led down
steep declivities, and over a succession of boulders. At last
we came to a large circular plain; it was surrounded by hills;
on one side of this vast natural basin, and on a slope, lay
Yuzgat.

As we were nearing the walls a cavalcade of horsemen
appeared in sight. One of them advancing saluted us by
touching his fez, and then addressed me in excellent French.
He was a Pole, Vankovitch by name, and was employed as
chief engineer in the district. He had received a telegram
from the Italian doctor, M. Gasparini, of Angora, to say that
I was on the road, and had ridden out with some Armenian
gentlemen to welcome us to the town.

An Armenian now asked me to take up my quarters in his
house. I had been lodged beneath a Turkish roof at Angora,
and was curious to see the difference between the Christian
and Mussulman mode of living. I gladly accepted the offer.

Many more horsemen, Turks and Armenians, joined us ere
we entered the city. I now learnt that my kind friend, the
Bey at Angora, had telegraphed to some of his acquaintances,
asking them to do what they could to make my stay at Yuzgat
pleasant.

The news of the approach of an Englishman had already
been spread through the town. The inhabitants had all
turned out to have a look at the stranger.

"An Englishman in Yuzgat is indeed a surprise for the
inhabitants," said a young Turk who was riding by my side.
"I do not believe that one of your nation has been here for
the last twenty years. We Turks are not ungrateful," he
continued, with a smile. "We have not forgotten our old
friends of the Crimea, and what you did for us then."

"Please God you will do as much now!" said another
horseman. "Anyhow your arrival has created an immense
excitement; there was not so great a crowd to see the Pasha
of Angora, when he paid us a visit."

"Sir," observed Radford, who, surprised at the tremendous
ovation I was receiving from the crowd, had gradually sidled
up to my horse, "this reminds me of our riding after Don
Carlos in Spain. Only in Spain, all the people came to look

at Don Carlos, and here they have come to look at us. Just, sir, for all the world as if we were a Lord Mayor with his men in harmour riding in state by the Horse Guards. There have been a lot of dirty Turks kissing Osman already, so pleased they seem to see him; and two or three men were slobbering over my boots as we rode up the hill!"

We entered a courtyard: dismounting, I ascended some steps which led to my host's house. The room placed at my disposal was furnished in a similar fashion to the one which I had inhabited in Angora. Several servants hastened to pull off my riding-boots, and the proprietor said that some Armenians were waiting outside, they wished to speak to me. "Would I see them?"

"By all means," I replied; "show them in."

Several men entered; they were dressed in various costumes, the dressing-gown pattern being evidently a favourite amidst the inhabitants of Yuzgat. The visitors ranged themselves against the wall in order, according to their social positions, and then salaamed me. On my returning the salute, the gentlemen squatted down upon the floor, and the salaaming ceremony was repeated.

"They have come to ask whether you will honour them by inspecting the Armenian school," said my host, who, of higher rank than the visitors, had not squatted down on the floor, but was seated with his legs tucked under him on the divan.

"We are all Christians," said an old, and very dirty Armenian, who looked as if water and he had long been strangers to each other.

"It is a pleasure to see a Christian," he added. "It does me good."

"We are all delighted!" said the rest of the company. Whereupon we salaamed again.

"How do you like the Turks?" I now inquired.

"They get on very well together," observed the Pole, who had accompanied me home, "and the law is carried out very fairly for all classes. I will give you an instance. The chief of the telegraphs in Yuzgat is an Armenian. One day he saw a few Turkish boys teazing some Armenian children, and calling them giaours. He beat the Turkish children. Some Turks, coming up, took the part of the Mohammedan lads, and struck the telegraph-man. The latter complained to the authorities; the Turks who had beaten him were at once imprisoned."

"Twenty years ago this would not have happened," said another of the visitors; "but here things have altered for the better."

"However, at Sivas," he continued, "you will find that the Christians are horribly ill-treated by their Pacha. The prison is full of Christians. There is no sort of justice in that city. The Pacha takes away Christian little boys and girls from their parents, and shuts them up in his seraglio."

"Is this true?" I inquired of Mr. Vankovitch.

"They say so. But you must remember that you are in the East," was the Pole's reply.

"Personally," he added, "I make a rule to believe nothing except what I see myself. You are going to Sivas?"

"Yes."

"Well, you will be able to judge for yourself. At all events, the Christians in this town are not oppressed in any way. You see Armenians and Turks dining together at the same table, and so far as justice is concerned, the Christians obtain quite as much of it as the Mohammedans."

The Armenians, who by this time had finished their coffee, now left the room; and Mr. Vankovitch remaining behind, began to tell me of his experiences in Asia Minor, and of the cause which had induced him to leave his own country.

He had been educated in the Military College at St. Petersburg, and had passed his examination for the engineers just before the Polish insurrection. He had joined the rebels, and taking command of a large band which had assembled near Vilna, had fought against the Russians for more than two years. General Muravieff, known to history by his brutality to the women of Vilna, published four proclamations offering rewards for Vankovitch's head. Fortune favoured the young Pole, who was able to escape his foes. When the rebellion was suppressed, he succeeded in reaching Odessa, and made his way on board a Greek ship bound for Constantinople. After being two days at sea, the vessel, owing to bad weather, was obliged to put back into harbour. The captain then said, that as some Russian officers would be certain to come on board, it would be better for Vankovitch to remain concealed in a friend's house, until the ship could sail. He took the advice; but left all his clothes and other effects in the cabin.

The vessel started that night; he did not receive any warning, and the captain, carrying off his luggage, robbed him of everything he had in the world. The Polish committee in

Odessa raised a little money for their brother in misfortune: after paying for his passage in another steamer, he arrived at Constantinople with barely five pounds in his pocket. This was soon spent, and then in order to earn his bread, he obtained employment as a road-maker. The engineer who superintended the work discovered that the navvy knew as much about road-making as he did himself. He promoted him to be assistant-engineer.

Vankovitch complained that he was unable to write to his father, a gentleman who resided near Vilna. The engineer had sent two or three letters; but on each occasion the envelopes were opened by the Russian police, and the parent had been heavily fined, simply because Vankovitch had dared to write to him.

CHAPTER XVII

M. Perrot—Armenian customs—Man and wife—We keep our wives for ourselves—My host's niece—Law about divorce—Shutting up the wives—Turkish husbands—How to get a divorce—Marrying a divorced woman—Population of Yuzgat—Crime—Mines in the neighbourhood Tax paid in lieu of military service—The Circassians—Their promise to the Turkish Government—Tax on land ; on house-property ; on corn ; cattle—Collectors of taxes—Jealousy about religious matters— Dissensions amongst Christians — American Missionaries — A loyal address—The market—A bazaar two stories high—A walk through the town—Gipsy women—An elderly dame—Obstreperous young ladies—The old woman dances.

My host now returned, and informed me that M. Perrot, a French author who wrote a book about Asia Minor, had resided beneath this roof. On turning over the leaves of the work, which had found its way to Yuzgat, I came to a page in which M. Perrot observes that "one day I inquired of my host why he did not introduce me to the lady of the house ?"

"It is our custom," was the reply. "And I find it a wise one. What good does it do me if other men see my wife ? I took her for myself ; she is my property. I have heard that you Europeans spoil your wives; mine is educated properly. When I enter my harem, she comes to kiss my hand, then she stands upright before me in a respectful attitude, and she only opens her mouth when I address her."

On showing my host the paragraph, he observed, " When M. Perrot was here, my father owned this house. I remember the circumstance well. I was in the room when M. Perrot asked my father to introduce him to my mother. I suppose my parent was under the impression that in Europe you keep your wives for your guests; but anyhow we keep our wives for ourselves."

"What!" I inquired, "would you not introduce me to your sisters or mother?"

"No, certainly not."

Mr. Vankovitch here interposed with the remark that on the following day my host's niece was to be affianced to her future husband; that the bridegroom had not set eyes upon the face of his intended, and no one in Yuzgat, save her own immediate relatives, had ever seen the young lady.

"Well," I inquired, "and if the wife of an Armenian is unfaithful to him, can he obtain a divorce?"

"No," replied my host; "our religion does not allow of such a step; he does not even see his wife's face before marriage."

"Then he has no opportunity of studying her character, and she has no opportuity of studying his?"

"No."

"They are a set of fools," said Vankovitch to me in Russian, this language not being understood by the proprietor. "They think that by shutting up their wives, they can keep them out of mischief, but the husbands are very much mistaken."

"We need not be surprised at it," he continued; "an Armenian lady is in no way educated. She is confined in a harem. She is the slave of her husband, and has to do all sorts of menial work for him—wash his feet, rub them dry, and wait at table. From her earliest childhood a girl is brought up to consider herself as a slave in her father's house; until the Armenians abandon these barbarous customs, their so-called Christianity will not do them much good. A Turkish husband has no difficulty in obtaining a divorce—in fact he is not even put to the expense of going to a court of law. All he has to do is to say, in the presence of a witness, 'I renounce you,' and he is at once freed from his wife, who is at liberty to go where she likes, and marry whomsoever she pleases."

"If a Turk," added Mr. Vankovitch, "once renounces his wife before a witness, he cannot withdraw his renunciation. There is a story that a woman, who wished to be divorced from her husband, dressed up one of her female slaves in man's clothes and provided her with false whiskers and beard,

On entering the harem late at night the husband found this disguised figure lying by the side of his wife. He was furious, and at once renounced the, as he thought, faithless lady. There is a curious law about marrying a divorced woman which is not generally known by Europeans," continued the speaker. "If a Turk has divorced his wife, but she wishes to return to him and he to take her, the lady first of all must be married to some other man, and the rites in their entirety be accomplished; the new spouse then divorces her. After this process she can return to her former husband.

"A husband who wishes to take to himself again his divorced wife, generally chooses some beggar, almost always a very old man; he then offers this elderly individual a sum of money to marry the lady and afterwards renounce her. Sometimes, however, there are difficulties in carrying out these arrangements. The lady takes a fancy to the beggar, and the beggar to the lady. The pauper will not divorce her, and the original husband is laughed at by the rest of the community."

There were 10,000 inhabitants in Yuzgat, but there was very little crime. Only one execution had taken place during the last fifteen years, and this had been for murder.

The town itself is, comparatively speaking, of recent date, its construction dating back 130 years. The neighbourhood abounds with mines, and I was assured that iron, silver, and coal had been found near the city.

The Armenians did not serve in the army as soldiers; but in lieu of military service, paid the Ottoman Government twenty-eight piastres thirty-two paras every year for each male child, from his birth to his death.

The Circassians, of whom there are a great many in this part of Turkey, are not compelled to join the army; but they have promised the Government that every able-bodied man amongst them shall turn out as an irregular horse or foot soldier, should his services be required.

The people in the province of Angora are taxed as follows :— If ground is cultivated, the proprietor gives the Sultan the tithe of the crop.

The owner of a house pays 4*l*. per 1000*l*. of the estimated value of his abode, that is to say, if he is living in it himself. If on the contrary he lets it, he must pay 40*l*. per 1000*l*. The tax for people engaged in trade or commerce, is 30 per cent. on their profits. If a merchant sells corn in a town, he has to pay a duty of two paras for every twenty okas of grain purchased from him, and should he dispose of a horse, sheep, or ox, in the market-place, he must give the Government $2\frac{1}{2}$ per cent. of the proceeds of the sale. A farmer has to pay the Government four piastres a year if he is the owner of a goat, and three for each sheep he possesses. The collectors of taxes in almost every instance were Mohammedans ; many of the Christians grumbled at the way they were assessed.

If an Armenian girl expresses a wish to become a Mohammedan, this gives rise to great jealousy between the Turks and Christians. At the same time the Armenians who profess the Armenian faith detest any member of their community who has accepted the Roman Catholic or Protestant doctrines. The Christians being much more intolerant towards the dissenters from their respective creeds than the Turks are to the Christians.

There has hardly ever been an instance of a Turk accepting Christianity, but the American missionaries in Asia Minor were said to have converted many Armenians to Protestantism.

The Roman Catholic missionaries have not been idle. A number of Armenians no longer reverence the Patriarch in Constantinople, but look upon the Pope as the Head of their Church.

The Turks laugh in their sleeves at the discord in the ranks of the Christian community. They cannot understand why so much hatred and ill-feeling should exist between people who worship the same Messias.

This difference of opinion amongst the Christians is by no means displeasing to the Turkish authorities ; it renders any union between the Armenians and Russia exceedingly difficult.

The following morning a servant brought a paper to my host for his signature. It was a loyal address from the principal people in Yuzgat thanking the Sultan for the Constitution. None of the Armenians believed in the reform. Most of them held the same opinion as the inhabitants of Angora, namely, that the projected Constitution was thrown out as a bait to catch some of the plenipotentiaries at the Conference, and that when the Conference was forgotten the Constitution would be numbered with the past.

Vankovitch now called. I walked with him to the market which he was constructing for the townspeople. It was not a large building, being about eighty yards long by thirty wide ;

the houses were each of them two stories high, built of hewn stone and with glass windows; the latter a great luxury for the natives, glass having to be brought all the way from Samsoun, a port on the Black Sea. The difficulties of transport were very great, half the glass arrived in a fractured state; this, and the extreme difficulty of carriage, added enormously to its cost price.

In the market there was literally nothing which would have attracted an observer's attention. Some of the Armenians sold dye, wood, and goats' hair; others traded in cotton stuffs and calicos, one or two American lamps to burn petroleum were in the window of a small shop which was kept by a Greek.

The engineer had experienced considerable difficulty in persuading the townspeople to let him construct a bazaar two stories high. "Our fathers have always been satisfied with one story," remarked the tradesmen, "then why should not we?"

In spite of the opposition, Vankovitch, with the Caimacan's assistance, had managed to carry the day. The people who had grumbled the loudest about the new order of things were the first to take apartments in the two-storied building.

We continued our walk through narrow lanes, and by the side of tumble-down hovels, till we arrived on the summit of a hill, the outskirts of the town. Some good-looking gipsy women with brown complexions, large dark eyes, and long black hair, were standing at the door of one of these habitations.

"These are the dancers," said Vankovitch; "Dr. Gasparini telegraphed from Angora to ask me to arrange a gipsy dance for you. Let us go and talk to one of the old women, and choose the girls who are to perform."

An elderly dame recognized my companion; she advanced, and invited us to enter her house. When our errand was known, great excitement ensued amidst the younger damsels of the gipsy community. Each one trusted that her good looks and skill in the Terpsichorean art would influence my companion in his choice.

"Be quiet!" said the old woman indignantly to some of the more obstreperous of her young ladies, who, to show my companion their agility, were performing a sort of cancan step, very different from those dances which I had hitherto seen in the East.

"Now, then, Effendi," to my companion, "how many girls do you require?"

"Three."

"Well, three you shall have. The most beautiful and gazelle-like of our tribe. I will come myself," continued the old lady, "and I too will dance, if only to show the Frank Effendi what our dance is like.

It was as much as I could do to keep my countenance; the old woman was very fat; some of the girls, catching my eye, went off into fits of laughter.

"Ah! you may laugh, children," said the old woman indignantly, but none of you can dance like I can. They are not supple like I am, Effendi. They cannot move their hips. They cannot sway the lower part of their bodies. Look here!"

And straightening her aged limbs, the old woman commenced wriggling her different joints, the girls applauding her, and beating time with their hands to each movement of the dancer's body.

"Very good," said Vankovitch, as she sank down on a divan, with a force which would have smashed any less strong piece of furniture. "Very good. You dance like a stag. You shall come too."

"Thank heavens," he remarked in French, "that she did not throw herself on to my lap, for this is the custom of these wild dancers; if she had done so, there would not have been much left of me. But come along, let us return; it is very stuffy here."

After making an appointment with the old lady for the dancers to come to us on the following evening, we descended the hill and walked towards the principal mosque in the town.

CHAPTER XVIII

The Mosque—The interior of the building—The lamps of different-coloured
  crystal—The Turks engaged in prayer—Comparison between Christians
  and Mussulmans — Daravish Bey—A wonderful shot—*Djerrid*—A
  strange request—The chase—A Bosnian lady—Her costume—A side-
  saddle—Even their women go out hunting—Daravish Bey dressed for
  the chase—A long shot—The price of a horse's forage—Most servants
  rob their masters—A Russian officer—The Armenian schools—The
  girls' school—Perhaps you would like to ask the boys some questions ?—
  An amateur setter of questions—Mr. Marillier of Harrow school—A
  sum—The schoolboys of Yuzgat—A half-holiday.

ON taking off our shoes at the entrance, we were at once
admitted into a large building constructed in the form of a
dome. Two vast circular halls, leading the one into the
other, were beneath the lofty ceiling. Stained glass windows,
with infinitesimally small panes, allowed but little light to
penetrate to the interior, which was carpeted with rich
Persian rugs of many hues and fashions. Chains, descending
from the centre of the building, supported a huge circular
hoop of iron. From this were suspended a hundred lamps
of different-coloured crystal. Two enormous wax candles,
each as thick as a man's leg, and about seven feet high, were
fixed in a corner of the building. They had been made to
last a year, and had cost " tchok para "—a great many paras.

The attendant evidently thought that he should impress
my mind with this announcement, and he uttered the word
" tchok " in a way which no Englishman could imitate save
when he is in the extreme agonies of sea-sickness. Forty
or fifty Turks were lying on the floor, and seemed to be in
no way disturbed by the entrance of Mr. Vankovitch and
myself.

" Are there always as many people here ? " I inquired.

" There are very few to-day," was the reply ; " but at
whatever hour you may enter, the faithful will be found
praying to the All-powerful One who rules the Universe."

This, indeed, I subsequently discovered to be the case.
No matter how early or late I might enter a mosque, there
were always some men on their knees, praying to the
Almighty ; and whenever a service was going on, the mosques
were invariably crowded.

" They pray more than Europeans do," said my companion,
the engineer, as we quitted the mosque. " With us," he

added, "the women throng the churches, the men are conspicuous by their absence; in Turkey you will hardly ever meet a man who is in the habit of absenting himself from his mosque. Indeed, a Mohammedan's superstitious feelings would not allow him to do so, even if he felt inclined; he would think that the Divine vengeance would at once pursue him to his destruction."

We now called upon a Turkish gentleman, Daravish Bey. Presently he left the room, and, returning, brought an old flint gun, marked "London, 1802." He next suggested that we should join him in a shooting excursion, and, calling a servant, desired the man to bring in a falcon. This, Daravish Bey said, would be very useful, as, if we missed the partridges, the hawk would catch them for us.

"We shall then have some game to show when we return," he continued, "and the people will not be able to laugh at our beards."

"Vancovitch is a wonderful shot," said another Turk. "He shoots partridges flying! Only think! flying in the air! In the name of heaven, is it not wonderful? Can you hit a partridge, except when he is quite still?"

"Sometimes," I said; "but, unfortunately, most of my cartridges are wet; any how, I will try and find a few dry ones, and will go with you to-morrow."

"There is another thing which you must see before you leave Yuzgat," observed Daravish Bey, "and that is our national game, Djerrid I have already spoken about it," he continued; "the day after to-morrow all the best riders in the neighbourhood will assemble on the plain outside the town. In the meantime, I hope that you will dine with me this evening."

"But I am staying with an Armenian gentleman, and he will expect me to dine at home."

"Bring him with you. Nay, do not disappoint me," he added. "It is many years since an Englishman has been at Yuzgat, and we do not know how to honour one sufficiently when he is here. England and Turkey are old allies, and God grant that they may remain so!"

I returned to my quarters, and found the Caimacan, who had come to pay me a visit. He was very busy, as he had to arrange for some rediff soldiers who were to be despatched at once to Constantinople. After a few compliments and a cup of coffee, he arose and took his departure.

My host now observed,—

" Effendi, will you do me a favour ? "

" What is it ? " I inquired.

" Mr. Vancovitch has discharged one of his under officers, an Armenian. The man is a friend of mine—will you ask Mr. Vankovitch to pardon my friend and reinstate him in his situation ? "

" The officer is a thief," said the engineer ; " for that reason I got rid of him. But this remark of our host will show you what sort of people these Armenians are. He is well aware that the fellow is a rogue. He knows that I do not wish to take him back ; to try and make me do so, he asks you, who are ignorant of the circumstances, to intercede in the matter."

" You will intercede ? " said the host.

" How can I ? Mr. Vankovitch must know the man's character better than I do."

" But Mr. Vankovitch would do it if you asked him."

" I certainly shall not give him the opportunity of refusing," I replied. And seeing that I was obdurate, my host left off pressing me for the moment, but only to return to the attack on the following day.

The next morning, and soon after daybreak, we assembled for the chase. The engineer had mounted me on a magnificent coal-black Arab. He himself rode a little bay, with good shoulders and fine action ; whilst his wife, a Bosnian lady, who was attired in a light blue riding-habit, a hat with a peacock's feather, and who wore on her boot a long cavalry spur, was mounted on a chestnut.

Vankovitch had slung his gun across his shoulders. His double-breasted shooting-coat was dotted with cartridge cases in the Circassian style. He was an object of great interest to a crowd of bystanders, and was evidently the chasseur par excellence of Yuzgat. Some Turkish women, wrapped up in long white sheets, stared through the corners of their veils at Mrs. Vankovitch, and were very much astonished at the proceedings, for the lady was on a side-saddle, which the engineer had lately received from Constantinople. It was only the first or second time that it had been seen in Yuzgat. The giaour woman balanced on a peg on the side of the saddle was a source of considerable wonder to the assembled crowd.

" How odd these giaours are ! " said a Turk to his neighbour. " Why, even their women go out hunting ? What a thing to ride on ! Look, she has only one foot in the stirrup, and her other leg is across a peg in the saddle."

" How could you sit cross-legged if you had on that very thin, long dressing-gown which she is wearing ?" said another bystander. " But here come Daravish Bey and his brother. They are actually going with the Frank to the chase ! "

The attention of the crowd was now taken up by the new arrivals.

The two Turkish gentlemen were both dressed alike in black cloaks lined with fur, and which descended to their heels. Gold necklaces passing through diamond rings encircled each man's neck. Red waistcoats, buttoned up high in front, exposed to view an inch or two of limp, unstarched shirt-front ; loose black trousers covered their legs, and a blue and white shabrach their highly-gilded saddles.

An attendant on a pony bore a falcon on his arm. Some pointers and a greyhound brought up the rear of the procession. Radford carried my double-barrelled gun, and a few cartridges, which on careful inspection seemed not to have been damaged by the wetting in the river. He was also a source of wonder to the crowd. It was whispered about that the gun which he carried was like the Pole's firearm, and that it would sometimes shoot partridges on the wing.

We rode over a mountain, covered with pebbles. Presently one of the pointers began to sniff. Vankovitch thought that there was some game close at hand. He dismounted from his horse, accompanied by Daravish Bey, who was armed with the old English flint-gun. A crowd of men and urchins, who had followed us on foot from Yuzgat, watched the proceedings with the greatest interest. Suddenly a covey of partridges rose about a hundred and fifty yards from the Pole. Two reports sounded in rapid succession, the birds flew away untouched. The attendant released the falcon, and in a few seconds a partridge was in its claws.

A hare broke from behind an adjacent rock. In a moment we were in headlong pursuit, the Bosnian lady riding foremost of the flight, her horse taking the boulders and loose rocks which strewed the path in a way that showed he was well accustomed to this style of hunting.

A well-known sound made me turn my head. To my surprise I saw a young Turk galloping after me on Osman's horse —the roarer. I had given orders that the animal was to be left in the stable, so that he might recover from the effect of our forced marches the week before.

" What are you doing with that horse ? "

" Effendi, I am galloping him," was the quiet reply. " Osman lent him to me, and said that he was his property. Have I done wrong in riding him ? "

" Yes," I said, " take him back at once."

" Sir," interrupted Radford, " that is just like Osman's himpudence, a-lending things which don't belong to him, and he is not that particular in returning them either. He is always asking me to lend him some tobacco, and very little I ever see of it again, except in the smoke which comes out of his mouth."

" How much are you paying for the forage of your horses ? " now inquired Vankovitch, who had returned with the hare in his hand.

" About seven shillings a day."

The Pole began to laugh.

" Seven shillings ! Do you know, my dear sir, that your Turkish servant is robbing you ? "

". Very likely," I replied. " Most servants rob their masters. But what is the price of a horse's forage for a day ? "

" About one-and-a-half piastres, or at the present rate of exchange about twopence of your money. And chickens," continued Vankovitch, " what has he made you pay for them in the different villages on your route ? "

" A shilling a piece."

" He is a thief," said the Pole, you have been awfully cheated ! why the price in the town is only three halfpence for a fat chicken ! When we return to Yuzgat, send for your man, and let me ask him a few questions. You shall not be robbed any more if I can help it. It is a bad thing for other European travellers, and it gives the inhabitants a lesson in robbery. There was a Russian officer here a few years ago. He had been paying as much as a medjidi a day for each of his horses. However, he was a Russian, and it did not so much matter."

The following day I went to see the Armenian schools. In one of them I found 200 girls who, for Turkey, were receiving a fair education. Most of them could read and write. A class for learning embroidery was well attended, some of the elder girls' work being very neatly finished. There were two Mohammedan children in a sewing class. I was informed that many of the Mussulmans had expressed a wish to send their children to the school.

"Perhaps you would like to ask the boys some questions," said a priest who accompanied me through the building.

Now if there is one thing I dislike it is being turned into an examiner. There is always a chance of the boys knowing a great deal more than the amateur setter of questions. But, as the clergyman pressed me, I tried to remember some of the sums which I had once learned under the tuition of my highly esteemed old master, Mr. Marillier of Harrow.

The herring and a half sum would have been too easy; I bethought myself of another.

"Well," said the priest, a little impatiently, "they are waiting for you."

There was a dead pause, and I gave the worthy divine the following question : "If one man can mow a field in three days, and another man in four, how long will they be doing the work, if they are both mowing it together?"

"Come," said the divine, "you have set them a very easy sum," and he duly translated it into Armenian.

"It is hardly worth doing," said one of the schoolmasters, "for of course the answer is three days and a half."

"Of course, three and a half," said the priest.

"No," I replied.

The engineer began to laugh, and we soon afterwards left the school, neither masters nor pupils being at all certain in their minds as to how they ought to set about doing the sum.

I breathed more freely on arriving in the open air, and blessed my old master, who had once set me this catch question, for my reputation as a profound mathematician is established for ever amidst this generation of schoolboys in Yuzgat. After saying good-bye to the senior pedagogue who had accompanied me to the steps of the threshold, I asked him to give the lads a half-holiday. He very kindly acceded to my request; and a cheer from the boys inside, when the good news was imparted to them, made me aware that they, if not their masters, were in no way dissatisfied by my visit.

CHAPTER XIX

I CALLED upon a Greek who had paid me a visit on the day
of my arrival. Several of his compatriots were with him.
They at once commenced conversing about what they suffered
under the Turkish administration.

" We are very badly treated," said one.

" Very badly indeed," said another.

" Are the Christians here ever tortured ? " I inquired.

" No."

" Have you ever heard of any of them being impaled ? "

The company began to laugh.

" No such things go on in Turkey," said my host ; " but
the law is bad, that is what we mean. Just before you
arrived, we were talking about a Turk who had borrowed
some money from one of our countrymen and had given a gun
as security for the debt. The Turk died, and the Christian,
not being paid what he was owed, sold the gun to a friend.
Ten years afterwards a son of the deceased Turk came and
claimed the weapon, which he said was his father's property,
and consequently his own. There were no papers or witnesses
to prove that the gun had been pledged, and the Cadi decided
for the Mohammedan."

"If a Turk had been in the Greek's place, would the same
decision have been given ? " I inquired.

" Yes," was the answer ; " the law is equally bad for Turks
and Christians."

There is one peculiarity about the Armenians and Greeks
in Yuzgat which attracts the attention of the traveller, and
this is that many of them cannot write their own language,
although they employ its characters. Their conversation is
almost invariably in Turkish. In corresponding with a friend

both Armenians and Greeks will write in Turkish, but with the Armenian or Greek letters. The schools, which are encouraged by the Mohammedan authorities are improving the Christians in this respect. The present generation of children can most of them speak, as well as write, in the language of their ancestors.

Later on in the day I mounted my horse, and accompanied the engineer and his wife to the outskirts of the town. Here there is a vast natural basin formed by a circular chain of steep heights. Yuzgat,* which is built on the side of a hill, and with its houses towering above the plain looks down upon the enormous arena. An immense crowd was assembled. Horsemen were present of all nationalities, and clad in every kind of costume. Turks, Persians, Armenians, Greeks, Circassians, Tartars, Kurds, Turkomans, Georgians, were grouped together in little clusters, and talking to their fellow-countrymen. Hundreds of women, clad in long white sheets, had retired a short distance, and from a slight elevation were gazing down upon the assembled multitude.

Presently the horsemen divided into two sides. Each man carried a djerrid or short stick, about four feet long, not quite so thick as a man's wrist, and weighted a little at one end. The right hand of the cavaliers grasped the middle of the djerrid. The two bands of mounted men, reining their horses back, halted facing each other, and about eighty yards apart.

Now, at a signal from the leader of one side, a horseman dashed forward at the opposing band. Brandishing his djerrid in the air, and shouting wildly to Allah, he hurled it at one of his opponents. The latter, who was on his guard, turned his horse on his haunches, and galloped away in the same direction as the missile was coming. Reaching backward, the rider caught the stick, and was greeted by the applause of the bystanders.

Meanwhile the horseman who had first attacked, hastened to regain his party. He was pursued in headlong career by one of the other side, who in his turn hurled the djerrid. The game requires considerable skill in horsemanship, and great nerve. The stick is thrown with all the rider's strength, augmented by the velocity with which his steed is galloping. If the missile be not caught or parried, but strike a man's body, the effect is often serious ; bones are fractured,

* For importance of Yuzgat from a military point of view, see Appendix XIV.

Death sometimes ensues. The horses too have to be highly trained, so as to be able to halt when at full speed, and, turning, to start off in a contrary direction.

" We rode better in our time," said an old man, attired in a crimson dressing gown, and who was eagerly watching the proceedings, to a companion by his side; "but what is that which is coming in this direction?"

In the distance a marriage procession could be seen winding amidst the hills. A bride was being carried in a cart drawn by oxen to her bridegroom's house. A band playing discordant music marched in front. Several women enveloped in sheets of white muslin rode behind the vehicle. They were mounted on donkeys, and sat astride them like men. The position is a curious one, particularly when the lady wears a short dress.

As the procession passed by the crowd, some of the donkeys began to trot. The motion became very disagreeable to the fair equestrians. The robes began to rise, and the husbands running forward, held down their wives' attire. This would have provoked the laughter of a European crowd, but in Turkey women are looked upon as beings to be shut off from the public gaze. The Mohammedan husband as a rule does not like anyone to see him walking with his own wife. The children too look upon their father as a being far superior to themselves. The Turkish parent walks first along the road, the children next some fifty yards behind their father. Last of all comes the wife, alone and neglected. She accepts this lot with resignation—her mother was a slave before her, and she will remain one till death or divorce dissolve the marriage-tie.

I now called upon the head of the Mohammedan religion at Yuzgat. He received me very courteously, and we conversed for some time upon the respective merits of the Mussulman and Christian faith. It appeared that very recently a house belonging to the Imaum (priest) had been burned to the ground.

" I hope you did not lose much property," I remarked.

" Everything I had was burned," said the old man. " But it did not signify. Allah was kind. The inhabitants raised a subscription for me. My house will soon be restored," he continued. " Allah is very good to all the true believers. If a house belonging to one of your Christian Mollahs (priests) be burned down, what does he do?" inquired the old Mohammedan.

" His house is generally insured," I replied. " He pays a

little money every year to a company, and then, if the edifice is destroyed by fire, it is built up again for him."

" Does he pay much money ? "

" Yes, if the house is a good one, he has to pay a large sum every year."

" What is the good of paying at all ? " said the Moham-medan. " Why does he not trust in Allah ? That is what I have done. My new house will cost me nothing. God is great. There is but one God ! And Mahomet, he is the Prophet of God," added the old man piously.

" But I thought that you believed in Kismet—destiny, I remarked.

" Destiny is great, but Allah is greater. He created destiny," was the reply.

" Do you think that Allah can change His mind ? "

" He is All powerful ; He can do what He likes," observed the Imaum excitedly.

Later in the day I walked into an Armenian church. This was a large building, with red carpets, and rather reminded me of a mosque. It must sometimes have been bitterly cold inside, for there were no stoves in the building. I was informed that the upper classes who came to pray all wore furs. As the lower orders are not able to pay for any such warm garments, they must occasionally be half frozen when listening to their priest's oration.

A raised platform at one end of the church was enclosed by trellis-work. It was so constructed that the occupants of the gallery could see the clergyman without their attention being occupied by the congregation.

" This gallery is for our women," said an Armenian, who showed me over the building ; " and the trellis-work is to prevent them from staring at the men."

" Or rather to prevent the men from staring at them ! "

My companion laughed at the remark.

" It answers both purposes ! " he exclaimed. " But if you look at the screen you will see that it is broken in several places ; three or four of the holes in the trellis-partition have been made into one. The women have done this to obtain a better view."

" Do you not separate the women from the men in your churches ? " he inquired.

" No."

" Then if the ladies are as pretty as they are said to be,

your clergyman must find it rather difficult to keep the attention of his flock."

It was getting dusk. I went straight from the church to the Pole's house. There was hardly any furniture in it. This he explained by saying that he was only temporarily employed at Yuzgat; so soon as he had finished building the new bazaar he would have to return to Angora. A few divans, as in the Turkish houses, surrounded the walls. The two-barrelled gun, which sometimes "shot partridges flying," the wonder of the other sportsmen in Yuzgat, was lying in a corner.

After dinner, which was washed down by some very fair red wine, manufactured by the Christians in the town, a little boy, about twelve years of age, entered the room. Coming up to my host, he whispered something in his ear.

"The gipsies have arrived," said Vankovitch. Turning to the lad, he desired him to lay down some carpets at the other end of the apartment.

"That boy does not cost me much," said my host, pointing to his servant. "I found him starving in the streets a few years ago, during the famine. His mother had turned him out of doors. The child had nothing to eat. I took pity on the poor little fellow, and he has been with me ever since. He does more work than all the rest of the servants together; whilst, if I wish to punish him, all I have to do is to point to the door."

CHAPTER XX

The gipsies—A fearful instrument—The musicians—The dancers—The chief of the gipsy women—Her attire—Vankovitch's wife—A glass of raki—The fat woman—The man with the bagpipes—The dance—The two girls—The old lady accompanies them—The castanets—What is the good of dancing?—The Lord Chamberlain, who is he?—The marriage festivals in a harem—The old woman dances a *pas seul*— Osman's interview with Vankovitch—Oh, Osman! thou descendant of a line of thieves!—What is the meaning of this?—The Effendi's horses—The people at the Khans—An undulating country—Mostaphas —Unwillingness to fight their country's battles—Several inhabitants killed in Servia—Industrious insects—A country like the Saxon Switzerland—A district abounding with pine forests—The telegraph wire to Sivas—Sawmills—Gogderi Soo—A house with two rooms—The stable—The fire—The harem—My host and his wives—Two shots in the air—The ladies—Their legs—The discomfort of the proprietor.

SOME gipsy men now entered, and, squatting down on the carpet, began to tune their lutes. One of their party carried a fearful instrument. It was rather like the bagpipes. He

at once commenced a wild and discordant blast. The
musicians were followed by the dancers.

The chief of the gipsy women was provided with a
tambourine. She was attired in a blue jacket; underneath
this was a purple waistcoat, slashed with gold embroidery, a
pair of very loose, yellow trousers covered her extremities.
Massive gold earrings had stretched the lobes of her ears; they
reached nearly to the shoulders, and, by way of making
herself thoroughly beautiful and doing fit honour to the
occasion, she had stained her teeth and finger-nails with some
red dye. Her eyebrows had been made to meet by a line
drawn with a piece of charcoal. Gold spangles were fastened
to her black locks. Massive brass rings encircled her ankles,
the metal jingling as she walked, or, rather, waddled round
the room.

The two girls who accompanied her were in similar
costumes, but without the gold spangles for their hair, which
hung in long tresses below their waists. The girls, advancing,
took the hand of Vankovitch's wife, and placed it on their
heads as a sort of deferential salute. The Pole poured out a
glass of raki for the fat woman, who, though a Mohammedan,
was not adverse to alcohol. She smacked her lips loudly. The
man with the bagpipes gave vent to his feelings in a more
awful sound than before; the lutes struck up in different keys,
and the ball began.

The two girls whirled round each other, first slowly, and
then increased their pace till their long black tresses stood out
at right angles from their bodies. The perspiration poured
down their cheeks. The old lady, who was seated on a divan,
now uncrossed her legs; beating her brass ankle-rings the one
against the other, she added yet another noise to the din
which prevailed. The girls snapped their castanets and
commenced wriggling their bodies around each other with
such velocity that it was impossible to recognize the one from
the other. All of a sudden the music stopped. The pant-
ing dancers threw themselves down on the laps of the
musicians.

"What do you think of the performance?" said Vankovitch
to me, as he poured out another glass of raki for the dancers.
"It is real hard work, is it not?" Then, without waiting for
an answer, he continued: "The Mohammedans who read of
European balls, and who have never been out of Turkey,
cannot understand people taking any pleasure in dancing.

What is the good of it when I can hire some one else to dance for me?" is the remark.

"They are not very wrong," I here observed; "that is, if they form an idea of European dances from their own. Our Lord Chamberlain would soon put a stop to these sort of performances in England."

"The Lord Chamberlain, who is he?" inquired an Armenian who was present, and who spoke French.

"He is an official who looks after public morals."

"And do you mean to say that he would object to this sort of a dance?"

"Yes."

"But this is nothing," said Vancovitch. "When there is a marriage festival in a harem, the women arrange their costumes so that one article of attire may fall off after another during the dance. The performers are finally left in very much the same garb as our first parents before the fall. We shall be spared this spectacle, for my wife is here. The gipsies will respect her presence, because they know that she is a European."

Now the girls, calling upon the old woman, insisted that she too should dance. The raki had mounted into the old dame's head. Nothing loath, she acceded to their request; rising to her feet, she commenced a *pas seul* in front of the engineer. First shrugging her shoulders, and then wriggling from head to toe, as if she were suffering from St. Vitus's dance, she finally concluded by kneeling before my hostess, and making a movement as if she would kiss her feet.

The following morning, and just before my departure, the Pole, who had come to say good-bye to me, called Osman to his side.

"The Effendi is paying two medjidis a day for his horses," remarked Vankovitch, "and six piastres for a chicken! Oh! Osman! thou descendant of a line of thieves! What is the meaning of this?"

The Turk changed colour for a moment; but then, collecting himself, replied,—

"The Effendi's horses are not like other horses, they eat more, and work more. We and he, too, we all like large chickens. The Effendi is rich, and he pays; he is big, and he eats a great deal. He is not giving more money for barley now than he gave when he was in Constantinople. The people at the Khans tell me the price; I give them what they ask.

It would not do for me to be mean with my lord's gold. In future I shall know better. I will find out the proper value of everything, and will only pay what is just."

I interrupted him.

"Osman," I said, "you are a thief! However, as we leave Yuzgat to-day, there is no time for me to get another servant. Only beware! for if I find you deceiving me any more, not all the hairs in the Prophet's beard shall save you from being discharged."

"The Effendi knows what is best," said Osman coolly. "He has brain, and I—I am the dust in his sight. Another time we will not give so much for our barley, we will tighten our purse-strings to the chicken-sellers. We have all been deceived, we will be so no longer."

We rode through an undulating country, in the direction of Sivas. The track was firm and good; there was an abundant supply of water throughout the district; numerous flocks and herds were grazing by the side of the path.

After marching for six hours and a half, we halted at a Turkoman village, called Kulhurdook, which contained forty-five mud hovels. With much difficulty I obtained accommodation in a filthily dirty barn. Here our horses were also sheltered; side by side with them stood several cows and oxen. A small piece of carpet covered the ground in one corner of the building. The proprietor, bringing me a pillow which once had been white, but was now black with dirt, placed it under my head, Radford and Osman lying down by the side of the horses.

There were several mostaphas, or men belonging to the last army reserve, in this village. They eagerly inquired if there would be war, but did not express any wish to fight their country's battles. This struck me as the more remarkable, for elsewhere I had observed great martial ardour amongst the rural classes. I afterwards learnt that several men who had been enlisted from this village had been killed in Servia, hence the unwillingness of the mostaphas to go to what they considered certain death.

I tried to sleep: this was impossible; some little insects, which the manager of the Crystal Palace advertises as "industrious," proved their industry by making fierce onslaughts on my body. Repeated groans from Osman made me aware that even his skin was not proof against the attack; whilst my English servant, who had given up all idea of sleeping,

was walking about with a pipe in his mouth, and probably
doing anything but bless his master who had brought him to
such an out-of-the-way region.

"Can you not sleep, Radford?" I inquired.

"Sleep, sir! No! They are running up my legs like coach
'osses. Hosman's skin is like an ironclad, but they give him
no peace; they worry awful, that they do. I have been
trying to smoke them off me, but 'bacca is nothing to these
fleas. We shall be eaten alive if we stay here much longer—
I know we shall!"

Having come to much the same conclusion, I ordered him
to saddle the horses, and, to the astonishment of the proprietor
of the hovel, we left our quarters three hours before daybreak.

Presently the country became more mountainous. It
reminded me a good deal of the Saxon Switzerland, the
scenery being very picturesque as our path wound round some
wooded slopes.

We were in a country abounding with pine forests. The
telegraph-wire to Sivas was stretched not far from our track.
Many saw-mills, turned by the mountain streams, showed
where the telegraph-posts had been made; they had then been
dragged by oxen to their destination.

Our road ran through a pleasant valley, and by the side of
a mountain stream known as the Gogderi Soo. In a few
hours we arrived at a river, called the Tchekar Ermak. It is
crossed by a weak stone bridge, the stream being about thirty
yards wide by four deep. We halted for the night at the
village of Tchirklik, a two days' march, or thirteen hours from
Kulhurdook.

I was accommodated in a house which actually possessed
two rooms. They were not constructed in the side of a hill,
as the other dwellings in the neighbourhood, but of wood—one
room being reserved for the proprietor's cattle, sheep, and
camels, the other for himself and harem.

I was permitted to sleep in the stable. Osman, with
Radford and our horses, were lodged in a hovel at the other
end of the village.

In the middle of the night I awoke with a feeling of suffo-
cation, my throat was dry and parched, my eyes began to
smart; a crackling noise overhead could be heard. It gradually dawned upon me that the house was on fire. I now
discovered that the flames from the fireplace had ignited some
boards in the chimney: they, in their turn, had set fire to the

roof. If the proprietor, who was sleeping in the next room, were not immediately aroused, his house would in all probability be destroyed. The building was surrounded by a courtyard with high mud walls. The space outside the dwelling was infested by dogs. They at once came smelling around me.

Shutting the door, to prevent the flames from bursting out inside, I went to the harem. The entrance was barred from within. The proprietor and his wives were fast asleep, they paid no attention to the noise which I made at the door.

It is of no use standing upon any ceremony with a man when his house is being burnt down : drawing my revolver, I fired two shots in the air ; thinking that the sound of the reports would arouse the sleeping inmates. The effect was instantaneous : the whole family awoke, the man, greatly alarmed, thinking that an attack was being made on the village by a tribe of Kurds ; slowly drawing the bolt, he looked through a crack in the door.

"Come !" I said, " your house is on fire ! Be quick, or it will be burned down, and your camels and oxen be suffocated ! "

The proprietor bounded out of the room. He was followed by the harem ; the ladies, in the confusion, did not think of covering their faces, and were very scantily attired. They ran to a well in the yard and brought some pitchers of water. The proprietor by this time had climbed to the roof of his house. It was a windy night. The gusts were a source of considerable inconvenience, to the water-bearers ; their hands being occupied with the pitchers, they could not arrange their garments. The latter fluttered above the ladies' heads, to the great discomfort of the proprietor, who, much enraged at his house being on fire, was equally annoyed at his wives' legs being exposed to the view of an unbeliever.

To relieve his mind, I clambered on to the roof. From this position the ladies' limbs could no longer be seen. After pouring several buckets of water on the charred rafters, we managed to extinguish the flames.

CHAPTER XXI

It was a bright moonlight night. Not thinking it likely that
we should obtain any more sleep, I determined to start at
once, and take advantage of the weather. Desiring Radford
and Osman, who had been aroused by the reports of my
revolver, to saddle the horses, we set off in the direction of
Sileh Zela, a town which contains 3000 houses, and a barracks
which will hold at a pinch 1500 soldiers.

Sileh Zela stands in the centre of a natural basin, the hills
which form its sides being at a distance of six or seven miles
from the town. A small rising ground near the principal
street is occupied by the ruins of an old citadel. A stream
runs through the heart of the city. The soil in the neighbourhood is very rich ; corn abounds throughout the district.
The inhabitants do not seem to have suffered from the famine
which a few years ago so depopulated the Angora district.

Half a battalion of infantry, about 400 strong, was drilling
in a plain immediately in front of the town. The inhabitants
had turned out, men and women, to witness the instruction of
the troops. The white dresses of the ladies, contrasting with
the blue uniforms, red caps, and the many-coloured dresses of
the inhabitants, formed a bright and vivid picture. It was a
glorious day. The sun poured down its rays with a force
more suggestive of July than January. The drill was just
over as we neared the town. We rode into Sileh at the head
of the regiment, the band, which consisted of about twenty
musicians, performing a wild and discordant march. Halting
at the house of the Caimacan, I dismounted and proceeded
to pay him a visit. He was in the audience-chamber, sur-

rounded by clerks, who were on their knees, and submitting different documents for his approval.

The great man himself was squatted on a divan; the members of the town council were by his side. The Cadi, whose head was enveloped in a gigantic yellow turban, was engaged in smoking a long chibouk. A crowd of men were in the anteroom, some with petitions in their hands, others apparently prisoners, judging by the guards who stood beside them.

It was evidently a busy day. The Caimacan, not taking any notice of my arrival, continued attaching his seal to the different papers.

At last he stopped, and, turning to me, salaamed and apologized for his apparent rudeness. It appeared that the half battalion which I had seen drilling was to march the following morning for Constantinople, *viâ* Samsoun. The Caimacan was engaged in making arrangements for its departure. Carriers would have to be sent forward to the different villages between Sileh Zela and Samsoun, to apprise the local authorities of the approaching arrival of the troops. The chief difficulty which the Caimacan experienced was the want of money, he presently observed, " *Asker tchok, lakin para yoke,*" "We have plenty of soldiers, but no paras" (money).

The colonel of the battalion now entered the room, and after having been introduced to me, observed that he had heard in the event of hostilities England would be neutral.

"What! desert her old friend of the Crimea?" said the Caimacan, turning to me. And the Cadi, grinning in a ghastly manner at the rest of the company, remarked that England had many paras, and that perhaps she would send some of them to the Sultan.

This created a revulsion of feeling in my favour—the assembly having been a little annoyed at the colonel's statement about the neutrality of Great Britain.

"Well," I said, "you will probably have an ally in Austria."

"An ally in Austria!" said the colonel; "no, certainly not. There are more Slavs than Magyars in the Emperor Francis Joseph's dominions. However, Andrassy, a Hungarian, is at the head of affairs, and by all accounts he rules the emperor. Perhaps Andrassy may prevent Austria from allying herself with Russia against us."

"We shall have to fight our own battles this time," continued the colonel; "and, please God, we will win."

An old Imaum, who was seated in a corner, now put in a word, and said that if there were a war, he too would go at the head of the Imaums. I had observed this same propensity for fighting amidst other Mohammedan priests. In fact in Asia as in Europe the most bellicose members of society are often those gentlemen whose profession is that of peace.*

"We shall have Yakoob Khan of Kashgar with us," observed the Caimacan.

"No we shall not," replied the Colonel; "the Russians have stirred up a quarrel between Yakoob and the Chinese, so as to prevent him giving us any assistance."

"Will any other Mohammedan states help you?" I inquired.

"Yes, all of them will fight for Islam."

"Russia is large," continued the officer, "but she will have to divide her forces. She will have to be on her guard against the Khivans, Bokharians, and Turkomans in Asia, she must also protect herself against a rising of the Poles in Europe."

The Caimacan, now rising from the divan, walked with me to a small house in the neighbourhood which was reserved for the use of travellers.

There were very few Armenians in Sileh, the population being made up almost entirely of the followers of the Prophet. The ancient city is nearly a mile from the present site, and tradition tells us that it was built upon the so-called mound of Semiramis. I found the castle in a very dilapidated state, the wall round it bore signs of having been constructed from the ruins of some very ancient edifice; here and there were heavy blocks of marble and other broken debris which had been let into the sides of the enclosure.

According to the inhabitants, there is a secret passage leading from the citadel to a small square several hundred yards below the hill; this is very likely the case, for although now a third-rate town, Sileh was once a city of considerable military importance.

Whilst I was looking at the antiquities, Osman had been engaged in buying some tea and sugar, the supply which I

---

* Whilst writing these lines I have come across some verses written by a Bishop who calls himself a Christian, and an answer to them by an American writer. The Bishop seems to have forgotten that his mission is one of peace. His verses will be found in Appendix XI.

had brought from Constantinople being almost entirely exhausted, the tea and sugar having gone more rapidly than the other provisions. On my remarking this to Radford, I was informed that Osman had a sweet tooth, and had declared that tea was good for his stomach.

I called the Turk to my side.

"Osman," I said, "you have nearly finished my tea and sugar. What is the meaning of it?"

"Effendi, I like tea, I like sugar; but what I like most of all is to hear my lord's liberality praised. Whenever I am drinking tea, and the village people see me putting much sugar in my glass, they honour me. In this manner they honour my lord."

"I should like to be honoured in some other way for the future," I observed; "and Radford tells me that you are always praying instead of saddling the baggage-horses."

"Quite true, sir," remarked Radford, who gathered from my gestures what the conversation was about. "Quite true; he has worn off the nap of my new great coat a-praying on it. He is always on his knees whenever there is some work to do."

"Now for the future, Osman," I continued, "should I give orders to commence loading the animals at daybreak, you must get up two hours before sunrise: there will be then ample time for your devotions. In the meantime, when you pray, you are to kneel on your own jacket, and not on Radford's."

"Is my brother angry?" said the Turk, pointing to his fellow-servant.

"Yes."

"Well, I will not offend him any more."

And shaking hands with the Englishman, Osman manifested his friendship by borrowing a little tobacco.

On leaving Sileh Zela we rode by numerous gardens, planted with all kinds of fruit-trees, and enclosed by high walls built for the most part of dried mud. The road then continued through a series of vast circular basins, each from six to seven miles in diameter, and similar to the one which surrounded the town. The walls of these basins were formed of many coloured sand-hills. The plains below were sowed with every kind of grain.

We passed Tartars on their way to Sileh Zela, the women walking along the road, and the lazy husbands on horseback, riding in front of their wives.

Turkoman and Circassian villages abound throughout this district. The inhabitants were eager to hear about the war. When the Russians drove the Circassians from the Caucasus, the Sultan gave the exiles land in Anatolia.   The wild mountaineers thirst for the opportunity of revenging themselves upon the Muscovites.

We left the corn-growing country behind us, and emerged upon a plain thickly planted with tobacco. On one side of the track, the mountains were covered with vines, on the other were many-coloured sand-hills.

Presently a wonderful phenomenon presented itself to us. A thick, black cloud, which all the morning had hung above a mountain-top, burst over our heads, and then being gradually wafted onward, it poured down its waters on the sand-hills. The sun, which was shining brightly, formed a magnificent rainbow—the glorious orb joined earth to sky, its matchless colouring lit up the whole of the firmament.

The waters dashed down the sides of the hills. The torrent bore with it a million particles of coloured sand. In a moment the rivulets at our feet ran white, red, and then crimson. The thunder roared in the distance. A flash of lightning streaked the horizon with gold.

The sun was setting ere we reached our halting-place, and as we rode up the main street of the village of Bazar, our horses had to wade through about three feet of water—the result of the recent storm. I obtained quarters for the night in a small, but clean wooden house belonging to a Turkish gentleman. He was formerly an officer in the army, and had been employed at Kars during the siege.

"Pacha Williams proved himself to be a great man," observed my host.   "He was always busy, and not like other Pachas, who spend their lives in the harem. He went out at all hours of the night to inspect the fortifications.   There was another Englishman with him—a young man of fair complexion, but with a heart like a lion."

"Teesdale?" I observed.

"Yes, that was his name. The hearts of our poor Osmanlis were cheered when they saw this young Englishman sharing all their privations, never grumbling, and always cheerful. If the war breaks out again, God grant that you may send us many more such officers? Is Pacha Williams still alive?"

"Yes."

" Is he a very great man in your country ? "

" Yes."

" You English are a wonderful nation," continued my host. " You reward the Pachas who are brave and skilful. In our country if a captain has a relation in the harem of the grand vizier, the officer is sure to rise to high command ; but with you a man must have merit to succeed."

CHAPTER XXII

Tokat—The Caimacan of the town—The battalion is to march to Samsoun —A naturalized Englishman—The road from Tokat to Sivas—The population of Tokat—The rich inhabitants bribe the gendarmes—The want of funds—The officials' salaries in arrear—Armenian schools in Tokat—The Greeks ; not much reliance to be placed upon them—Khiva —Tashkent—Samarcand—Mussulmans in India—The Black Sea and the Russian fleet—Old soldiers in Tokat—The Armenians and Greeks to be supplied with fire-arms—Good governors—Osman Bey—A Circassian on Russian atrocities—A statement by the Russian authorities—Seven hundred families near Labinsky—Men, women, and children at the breast butchered—English sympathizers with Russia—The Russians sow the seeds of dissension amongst the Circassians—Yonn Bek—Many gold imperials offered to him.

It is only a few hours' march from Bazar to Tokat, the track running parallel to the river of the same name. There are many villages by the side of the stream. The valley widens, and then narrows again as we proceed towards the town. Tokat at last lies before us. It is a long, straggling city, and on the left bank of the river.

We were met by a Zaptieh. He conducted me to a house set apart for travellers. Shortly afterwards I received a visit from the Caimacan (governor). This official was an active, bustling little man, and much more energetic than any of the governors I had previously met.

An order had arrived for him to send 1000 men immediately to Samsoun. The battalion would march the following morning at daybreak. He proposed that I should go and see the start.

An engineer now called, a Pole by birth, but a naturalized Englishman. He was engaged in making a road from Tokat to Sivas ; he had been in Tokat five years, and the work was not half completed. Indeed, judging by the system adopted for the construction of public work in Anatolia, it will be a wonder if the road is ever finished.

According to the engineer, Tokat has a population of 25,000 inhabitants. Of these there are 8000 men who should each work four days a year at the construction of the road.

"It is a pitiable sight," continued the Pole. "The Zaptiehs are ordered to bring the people. A rich inhabitant bribes the gendarmes: they leave him and seize some impecunious individual. The latter is brought to me, and I tell the fellow to commence digging. The man digs so long as I am in sight, but the moment my back is turned, down goes the shovel, and he lights a cigarette. The result is that I have been here five years, and only five miles of road are finished."

The engineer complained of the want of funds in the public chest. His pay was only 10*l.* per month, and it was never paid punctually. Meantime, the authorities had discharged several engineers in their employ, on the ground that every piastre in the treasury was required for the maintenance of the troops.

There were several Armenian schools in Tokat, and the Turks and Christians got on very well together. However, the Caimacan was of opinion that not much reliance could be placed upon the Greeks, i.e., in the event of a war between Turkey and Russia.

"They are very cunning," remarked the governor. "They will not declare themselves at once, but will wait a little, and hang back to see which side is the strongest. They still dream of the old Greek Empire, and think that some day Constantinople will be a Greek capital. This is not very likely to happen," he continued. "If Russia were to conquer us, and to take Constantinople, she would not be willing to hand it over to the Greeks. What Russia takes she keeps. Look at the Caucasus. Look at the Crimea. Look at Khiva, Tashkent, and Samarcand. Some day she will try and conquer India, and what shall you do then?"

"Probably take our Indian troops, and, joining with the Afghans, and inhabitants of Kashgar, drive Russia out of Central Asia," I remarked.

"That is easier said than done," said the governor. "But, talking of the natives of India, is it true, as I have read in our newspapers, that many Mussulmans in India, have petitioned your Queen to help the Sultan?"

"Yes," I replied, "I believe so."

"Then why does she not oblige them? Your interests are

bound up with our interests. We do not wish to lose Constantinople. It would be our death-blow. It would be your death-blow if the Black Sea belonged solely to Russia, for her ships could remain there in perfect safety, and, running out at any moment, might attack your commerce in the Mediterranean."

"There are a great many old soldiers in Tokat," observed the engineer, "men who fought in the Crimea. They have asked me if there is any chance of England joining Turkey, and are longing to serve, with English pay and English rations."

"The men who leave to-morrow go without any pay," said the Caimacan, "but they march cheerfully. We shall have to fight it out to the end," he continued; "if Russia does not destroy Turkey, Turkey must destroy Russia! I will sell my watch and everything I have in the world to raise funds for the war. We must all do the same."

Whilst we were conversing an order arrived for the Caimacan to supply all the Armenians and Greeks in Tokat with firearms, and have them instructed in drill.

"I must go," he observed, and, rising from the divan, he left me alone with the engineer.

"He is a most energetic man," said the Pole, pointing to the retreating figure of the Caimacan. "If Turkey had more governors like him, she would not be reduced to her present straits. The great mistake in this country is the continual change of Caimacans. When we have a good governor, we never keep him for more than six months; the present man has been here about that time, he does not rob the people, and is thoroughly honest: we shall probably soon lose him."

Several of the principal persons in the town now came to call upon me; amongst others, a certain Osman Bey, a Circassian, and a chief of a large band which had emigrated from the Caucasus a few years previous. He was dressed in the Circassian style, with a sheep-skin coat, tightly buckled round his waist, embroidered leather trousers and high boots; a black Astrakhan cap surmounted his bronzed features. He was a fine tall fellow, and immensely popular with the inhabitants of Tokat.

After conversing for a little while about my journey, and the state of the roads between Tokat and Erzeroum, he proposed that I should accompany him to his house, drink tea there, and be introduced to his relatives. The engineer came with us.   After walking through some lanes, where the mud reached considerably above my ankles, we arrived before a square-built, whitewashed house.   A solid wooden door, absolutely possessing a knocker—an article of luxury not known in Tokat, save to the richer inhabitants, gave admission to a small courtyard.   This, in its turn, led to the apartments reserved for Osman Bey and the members of his family.

He had sent a servant on before, to say that he was on his way.   About fifteen Circassian gentlemen were seated around the room.

"We Circassians have heard a great deal of your nation," said Osman Bey, as he motioned to me to take a seat.   "We once thought that England was going to help us to drive the Russians out of our country.   However, you did not come; they outnumbered us, and they had artillery opposed to our flint guns.   What could we do?   We resisted as long as possible, and then, sooner than be slaves, came here."

"If there is a war, shall you all go to the front?" I inquired.

"Yes, every able-bodied man amongst us.   We do not pay any taxes to the Sultan; he gave us our land, and we owe him a debt of gratitude.   Not only that," continued the speaker, and at the same time drawing a long keen knife from his sash, and flipping his nail against the blade, "but we shall have an opportunity of cutting a few Muscovite throats!"

"I hope you will not kill the women and children!" I observed.   "Nobody cares about the men; but in Europe we have a horror of people who massacre women and children."

"We shall do as the Russians do, and as they have always done," observed my host grimly.   "They have killed our old men, have cut to pieces pregnant women, and have tossed the children on the bayonets, whilst the soldiers have satisfied their lust upon our wives, and burnt them to death afterwards!* Well, if they do the same thing now, we shall follow the example set us, and shall continue doing so, until England or some other power interferes to save our countrymen from the devilish tyranny of these Muscovite butchers.   Let me give

* This statement, coming from a Circassian, may be deemed by some people in England, like the Right Hon. Robert Lowe, M.P., who believe that Russia is the protector of the unprotected, and the refuge of those who have no other refuge, as hardly worthy of credence.   Unfortunately for humanity it is confirmed, so far as the massacre of pregnant women and of children is concerned, by the official report of a British Consul.   See Appendix VII.

you one instance of their cruelty. A few years ago the Russian authorities informed the Circassians that whoever wished might leave the Imperial dominions and go elsewhere. This was probably done to discover what natives were well disposed or otherwise to the Russian rule. There was no real intention on the part of the Government to allow any of its subjects to pass the frontier. Seven hundred families belonging to some villages near the town of Labinsky, thought that it was a *bonâ fide* permission. Leaving their district, they started for the Turkish frontier. A short time afterwards they were surrounded by Russian troops, cavalry and artillery, and ordered to return. The fugitives said that they had permission to leave Russia. The officer in command insisted that they should at once retrace their steps. The command was not immediately obeyed, the troops fired at the villagers, and then charged them with the bayonet; only thirteen Mohammedans survived to tell the tale. All the rest, men, women, and children at the breast, were cut to pieces."

"Are these assertions really true?" I said to another Circassian.

"We know it, to our cost," he replied. "This is only one instance which Osman Bey has just given you, and which you have written down in your note-book; but there are many more equally horrible. The Russians have made a hell of our beautiful country. They are worse than the fiend himself."

"Do your country-people like the Russians?" said Osman Bey.

"Some do," I replied; "but they do not believe in these horrible cruelties which you have been just relating to me."

"Well, then, tell them to travel through our country—that is, if the Russians will let them—to go to our villages and talk to the country people; but not in the presence of Russians, as the poor sufferers would be afraid to speak, knowing well the fate which would await them when their questioners had departed. Let any of the people of England, who now sympathize with Russia, do this, and then let them form an opinion about the merits of the case."

"When you return to your own country will you publish what I have said to you?" said Osman Bey.

"Yes," I said, "every line. Listen to what I have written, so that there may be no error."

And I translated to him my notes, the engineer aiding me in the task.

" Are all your countrymen of one mind in their hatred of the Russians?" I inquired.

"Unfortunately, no," said Osman Bey. "The authorities have been clever enough to sow the seeds of dissension amongst our ranks. For example, they will often give the post of ' stanishna' (a local authority) in the different villages to a Circassian of a low degree. This gives him authority over our nobles. Ill-feeling is thus created between the two classes ; it is utilized by the Russians."

"One of our number is doing his best to avenge himself on the Muscovites," said another of the party, a good-looking young fellow, apparently about twenty years old, and Osman Bey's nephew. "His name is Yonn Bek ; he has taken up his abode in the Farsa Shaguash mountain near Ekaterinograd, and kills the Russians whenever he can meet them. He has been pursued ; but he has depôts in the mountain where he keeps provisions, and the Russians have never been able to trace him to his lair. The authorities have offered Yonn Bek a great many gold imperials if he would leave the country, as the man has done so much mischief there ; but Yonn declines, and says that if the Russians have not been able to capture him in eight years, and he has been able to do them so much damage, what would not happen to the foe when the war breaks out and he is joined by other men like himself?"

CHAPTER XXIII

The servant of the house—The Onbashee—Five piastres—Osman detected— The guilty man—Vankovitch's remarks—The sentence—May I put Osman in prison?—The barracks—Two old Khans—The women weeping—Immense enthusiasm—Numbers of volunteers—Parading for the march—Men crying—We shall eat the Russians—The Sergeant— The Major of the battalion—The Dervish—A Circassian—The Imaum of the regiment—The Muleteer—Baggage animals required for the regiment—A bitter cry—The women's wail—The old Major—The soldier's hymn—The standard of the battalion—Go in safety—God be with you.

THE following morning the servant of the house in which I was lodging entered the room and observed that a Zaptieh corporal, or Onbashee, who had escorted us into the town on the day of my arrival, wished to see me.

"Tell him to come in," I said. In a few minutes the

Onbashee opened the door; approaching me, he took from his waistcoat five piastres, and placed them in the palm of his hand.

"What is this for?" I inquired.

"Osman!" answered the Onbashee, with a sigh.

"Osman! What has he been doing?"

"Osman gave them to me, Effendi; but you said that he was to give me half a medjidi—he has kept the difference for himself!"

It now flashed across my mind that the previous evening I had desired Osman to give the corporal half a medjidi as a baksheesh, and that I had told him to do so in the presence of the servant of the house. The latter had informed the Onbashee. Osman, who wished to appropriate to himself the difference between five piastres and the larger coin, was thus detected.

I sent for the culprit. He was aware that his knavery had been discovered. Instead of coming to me with his usual assertion that he was the most industrious man in the world, he stood in the corner of the room, an object of derision to the Onbashee, who was regretting the loss of his half medjidi, and to the servant of the house, who had been the means of disclosing Osman's dishonesty.

Addressing the guilty man, I asked him why he had not given the Zaptieh the half medjidi, and added that the previous evening, when he had told me of the expenses of the day, he had charged me with that sum.

Osman had hardly anything to say for himself. Presently he stammered out something about his only having five piastres in his pocket.

"That is a lie, Effendi!" here interrupted the Onbashee. "He had many coins in his hand when he gave me the five piastres."

I at once made up my mind to get rid of Osman. Vancovitch's remarks about the Turk's dishonesty also recurred to my memory. Osman was undoubtedly a rogue; I determined to procure another servant.

"Osman," I said, "you have robbed a Mohammedan, a follower of Islam, and one of your own religion. If you had confined yourself to robbing me, I could have understood it, for you might have reasoned to yourself as follows: 'The Effendi is a giaour, and there is gold in his purse.' But to rob a brother Mohammedan, and a poor man; to rob him of the pittance which I had given him.—this I can only under-stand by the assumption that you are a greater scoundrel than I thought you were! You are no longer my servant. You darken the threshold no longer!"

"I am innocent, Effendi!" cried Osman.

"Well, prove your innocence, and I will say no more about the matter."

"Effendi, the Onbashee is a liar!"

"Very likely, but then the servant must be a liar as well, and he saw you give the five piastres to the corporal. Now what interest has the servant in telling a lie about the matter?"

This was too much for the delinquent; lowering his eyes, he walked out of the room, through a long row of servants, who had come from the neighbouring houses to hear me administer justice.

The sentence appeared to give great satisfaction to the Onbashee.

"May I put Osman in prison?" he eagerly inquired.

"I have no authority on such matters," I replied.

"No, Effendi; but the Caimacan likes you, and if you asked him to do so, he would put Osman in prison. Just a day or so, Effendi! Please do!"

"Why do you want to put him in gaol?" I asked.

"Because, if he is once shut up, we will not let him out till he has returned me the difference between your present and the five piastres."

"No," I said: "here is the difference," at the same time giving him a small sum of money "But now go and inquire in the town for a man who wants a situation, as I want a servant immediately."

Just then a sergeant entered the room. He brought word from the Caimacan that he was waiting for me, and that the battalion would leave Tokat in about half an hour.

I at once rode to the barracks. They consisted of two old Khans, which surrounded a courtyard, the Khans being used as barracks when there were troops in Tokat, and at other times of the year as lodgings for wayfarers. The streets lead-ing to the Khans were lined with women, muffled up in long white sheets, and weeping piteously. The battalion was drawn up in two ranks inside the courtyard. The men were standing at ease, and engaged in talking to their numerous friends and relatives. Immense enthusiasm prevailed amidst the bystanders. Numbers of volunteers were offering their services.

"Look at these men, sir," observed Radford, who was riding behind me; "they do not look as if they liked going as soldiers : bless my heart alive, if they ain't a-crying !"

I glanced in the direction he was pointing, and saw thirty or forty men with most woe-begone faces, and some of them in tears.

"Why are you crying ?" I said to one of their party. "Are you afraid of being killed ?"

"No, Effendi, we want to go with our brothers in the battalion and to fight by their side ; but the major will not take us, he says that his battalion is complete. Do ask him to let us accompany him ! Our hearts are full of sorrow at being left behind."

A captain in the regiment, a short, podgy-looking man, with very fat cheeks, now came to them, and tried to console the volunteers by saying that their turn would come soon, and that they should go with the next battalion.

It was a curious spectacle : the soldiers dressed in a neat dark blue serge uniform, and with their feet in sandals, surrounded by little knots of relatives clad in every kind of attire that can well be imagined ; fathers embracing sons, brothers rubbing cheeks with brothers, and the sergeant and corporals vainly endeavouring to get their men into some sort of order ; the fat captain in the background engaged in trying to console the rejected volunteers ; and the younger portion of the crowd looking inquisitively at the new Martini-Peabody rifles which had only arrived from Samsoun the previous evening. Some of the soldiery were showing how quick their rifles could be loaded and fired. The rapidity of the system created great astonishment amidst the crowd.

"The giaours come from the country where these guns are made," said a bystander, pointing to Radford and myself.

"These giaours have more brain than we have," said another.

"If they help us, we shall eat the Russians !" exclaimed a third. We became the object of still more curiosity when a sergeant, coming to me, said that the Caimacan was in the major's room, drinking coffee, and hoped that I would join him there.

"He is going to drink coffee with the Governor—he is a great man !" said one of the bystanders. Some of the volunteers, rushing up, entreated me to intercede with the Caimacan, and perhaps he could induce the major of the battalion to take them with him to the war.

The major, and several other officers were squatted on a carpet in a small and rather dirty room overlooking the court-yard. The Caimacan was seated on a chair, a dervish sat by his side. The latter individual was a portly-looking man, wrapped up in a roll of brown cloth, and with a gigantic sugar-loaf hat on his head. The hat was made of grey cloth, and would have made the fortune of the leader of a nigger band. Several more officers now came into the room, amongst others the fat captain. They each in turn bent before the dervish, who placed his hands above their heads, and pronounced some sort of a blessing.

A Circassian entered the building. He presently informed us that five thousand of his nation, who resided in the neigh-bourhood of Tokat, had expressed a wish to go to the seat of war, and to bring with them their own horses and arms.

By this time the sergeants had succeeded in arranging their men in the ranks, and the major going downstairs, followed by the Imaum or chaplain of the regiment, the latter addressed the battalion. The Imaum was attired in a lieutenant's uni-form, but with a green turban round the fez, as a distinctive mark of his profession.

The Chaplain's discourse was not a long one. It was listened to with great attention by the populace. When he had finished the ranks were again broken by a crowd of eager, excited Mussulmans, who rushed up to embrace their friends.

As I was descending the steps, my attention was called to a man who was seated on the stair. He was sobbing like a child; at the same time striking his chest with the palms of his hands.

"What is the matter?" I inquired.

On his looking up, I recognized the muleteer whom I had hired to bring my baggage from Sileh Zela to Tokat. The man on seeing me sprang to his feet, then throwing himself on the ground, he began to embrace my legs, at the same time kissing my boots.

It appeared that several baggage animals were required for the battalion which was about to march. The Zaptiehs of Tokat had pressed the muleteer into their service, and had taken his mules.

" Do speak for me, Effendi ! " he said. " They will take me to Kars. I shall be a ruined man. And my wife expects me home—she is in a delicate state of health ; I shall shortly be a father."

" It is useless," said the Caimacan, who overheard his prayers. " We must have baggage animals, he continued ; " you will not be taken to Kars, only to Samsoun ; you will be paid for the hire of your animals. Dry your eyes, and do not block up the steps."

" It is a great pity, and I am very sorry for these poor fellows," observed the Caimacan, turning to me ; " but what can we do ? It is war time, or very soon will be so : some of us must suffer."

" Listen to those poor women there," he continued, as we rode through the gate, preceded by the brass band of the regiment playing a melancholy march. A deep wail could be heard even above the noise of the instruments. The wives, mothers, and other female relatives of the soldiers, had not been permitted to enter the barracks ; but from an early hour they had taken up a position along the streets. The bitter cry, which was joined in by hundreds of voices, announced to the people in the very outskirts of the town that the battalion was on the march.

Presently the band ceased playing ; and the old major, his long white beard streaming in the wind, began singing the words : "God is great. There is but one God, the God, and there is but one Prophet, the Prophet, and he is the Prophet of God."

The soldiers took up the strain, ten thousand bystanders joined in the verse—it even silenced the women's wail—and resounded along the banks of the river. Here taken up by some people on the ruined citadel, the words were re-echoed back to us ; there wafted by the breeze to an adjacent hamlet, the peasantry swelled the chorus. The standard of the battalion, with the crescent embroidered on a green border, was raised high in the air, and several of the crowd, rushing up to the major, implored him to take them in his ranks.

It was a striking scene—these weeping women in their shroud-like dresses ; the many-coloured garments of the men ; the excited soldiery—the still more excited major ; and the immense religious enthusiasm.

Snow-capped mountains barred the way before us, and the

river, its banks set fast with ice and hoar-frost, glittered in the distance, and reflected the rays of a midday sun.

Large stacks of wood had been piled up near the stream. The timber had been cut in the forests above the town, and been floated down the river to Tokat. It is chiefly used for smelting copper, the Government having some smelting works in the neighbourhood. According to my informant, they were established thirty years ago by a German; after his decease they had been bought by the Turkish authorities.

The Caimacan thought that he had accompanied the battalion far enough. Drawing a little on one side, we let the soldiers pass us. The standard-bearer waved his flag, the old major saluted by lowering the point of his sword as he rode past, and with the words, "Go in safety, God be with you. We shall meet in Erzeroum," we parted.

CHAPTER XXIV

Osman Bey—A Circassian feud—Will there be a rising in the Caucasus ?—
If England were to help us—A wonderful servant—Mohammed—His
Captain—An Armenian doctor—Business is flat—The Christian popu-
lation to be armed—Visitors asking favours—Your reward will be in
heaven—A subscription—Promotion through favouritism—A sad story
—A cruel father—A servant arrested for debt—Failure of justice.

Soon afterwards I met Osman Bey, my acquaintance of the previous day. He was on the point of leaving for a Circassian hamlet in the neighbourhood. It appeared that a feud had arisen between the people of this village and another one in its vicinity; the Bey was going there to calm, if possible, the angry feelings of the inhabitants.

He remarked that in the event of war breaking out between Turkey and Russia he should go to the Caucasus.

"Will there be a great rising in that country?" I inquired.

"It is very doubtful," was the answer; "our people have risen several times;* no foreign power has assisted us, and the result is that we have been decimated by our enemy. My countrymen are afraid of doing anything, unless they feel certain that they will be aided in their attempt. If England were to help us," he continued, "and could only capture one

---

* For statement made by Circassians on this subject, see Appendix X.

Russian port on the Black Sea, the Circassians would have confidence, and there would be a rising throughout the length and breadth of our land."

On returning to my house I found the Zaptieh who had been defrauded by my late servant. He was awaiting me with a candidate for Osman's place.

"Effendi, I have brought you a wonderful fellow," said the gendarme; "if you send him with a message, he will fly; he will guard your purse more carefully than his own."

It appeared that the wonderful man's name was Mohammed; he was a redif soldier. His battalion would march in the course of a week or so to Erzeroum. To avoid going with the troops he proposed that he should engage himself as my servant until we reached that town, and then he could join his battalion.

"But will your commanding officer give you leave to accompany me?" I inquired.

"If the Effendi asks him," interrupted the Zaptieh.

Mohammed was apparently not above twenty-five years of age. He had a pleasant, frank expression, and I determined to engage him, that is, if I could obtain the sanction of his captain.

I now went to see this officer. He at once agreed to the proposal; that is, if I would pledge myself to give up Mohammed at Erzeroum.

"How can I pledge myself?" I remarked, "he may run away on the road."

"That is true," said the officer; "but he is a straightforward fellow—he will not do so. If I had the power, I would let you take him as a servant for all the time that you remain in the country; but I have no authority to do this, I am merely a captain."

The matter was settled. Returning to my house, I informed the man of his officer's consent.

Mohammed was to have the same wages as Osman, and as he had a horse of his own, which he wished to take to Erzeroum, I was to pay for the forage of the animal, and could make use of him for the baggage. This would be very useful; hitherto I had been obliged to hire a horse, owing to my loss of Obadiah. Up to this time I had been travelling on the postal track. It was possible to find horses. After leaving Sivas, the next town I should reach, there would be no more postal-stations; I should then have to trust to my

being able to hire animals from the peasantry, or be obliged
to purchase another horse.

"I have a wife," said Mohammed; "will my lord give me
a little money!"

"How much do you want?"

"Two liras."

"I wonder if he will bolt with the money, like the Tartar
I engaged last winter in Orenburg." This idea at once
occurred to my mind. On second thoughts, I remembered
that he was well known to the Zaptieh, and to many of the
other inhabitants of Tokat; so I acceded to his request.

An Armenian doctor called to see me. He had been
educated in the States, and spoke English with a most
unmistakable Yankee drawl.

"How is business here?" I inquired.

"Very flat," said the medical gentleman; "the people do
not put much faith in doctors, that is, until they are really ill,
and then we have a busy time of it. They pill themselves," he
continued, "and go in for herbs and old women's remedies;
they get them cheap, and grudge the money which they must
pay to a regular practitioner."

"You do not look very well," said the doctor.

"Thank you, there is not much the matter," I replied.
The fact was that I had a splitting headache, owing to the
charcoal pan or mungo which warmed the apartment. The
gas from the charcoal being lighter than the air, fills the
upper part of the room. The Turks and Armenians generally
squat on the floor. They do not feel the effects of the fumes
so much as a person who is seated on the divan.

Another Armenian now paid me a visit. He was the
telegraph inspector in Tokat, and he informed us that orders
had just been sent from Constantinople to buy up all the
available horses in this neigbourhood.

"Things look warlike," he continued, "and the doctor,"
pointing to his compatriot, "will have plenty of practice
before long. The whole Christian population is to be
armed. It is clear that the Government has not much
faith in the Conference, and is doing its best to prepare
for war."

The Armenians in Tokat complained of the slack way in
which justice was administered throughout that district.
According to the doctor, if a man committed a crime, and
could get away for a year or two and then return to his home,

he would not be pursued by the authorities ; that is, unless the aggrieved parties made a formal complaint.

"Yes," said another visitor, "three months ago fifty-four malefactors escaped from the prison. Forty of them shortly afterwards surrendered ; the rest made their way to the mountains. Their ringleader, who is a murderer, has been recently seen in Tokat : no one has cared to arrest him."

Four young Turks entered the room ; the eldest could not have been more than three-and-twenty.

"What do you want ?" I inquired.

"We do not wish to go to the war," replied one of them, who took upon himself to be spokesman for the party.

"Why not ?"

"Because we are married men and have children."

"I cannot help you."

"Yes, Effendi, you can ; you might speak to the Caimacan, and he could free us from military service."

"His duty is to send you to the front," observed the doctor.

"Yes, but he evidently likes the Frank, for we saw them riding together, and if the Effendi would only ask him, he could not be so inhospitable as to decline."

I was a little annoyed at this remark, and observed,—

"I certainly shall not ask for anything of the kind. Other people who have wives and children are obliged to go, then why not you ?"

"But they did not love their wives so much as we love ours," persisted the man.

The Caimacan now called. Upon his arrival the four visitors, after grovelling almost in the dust before him, took their departure.

"What did they want !" said the Governor.

I told him.

"It is very unpatriotic of them," he observed. "The cunning little dogs, to ask you to intercede on their behalf ! But they shall all go with the next battalion !"

I was evidently destined to have a succession of visitors on that afternoon, for no sooner had the Caimacan gone than another official arrived. He at once commenced a conversation by saying that he had been employed in collecting the redif soldiery from the different villages in the neighbourhood, and had also started a subscription amongst the wealthier inhabitants to provide the men with warm shirts.

" You have acted very kindly, and doubtless with the best motives," I remarked. " Your reward will be in heaven."

" Yes," said the man, who did not seem quite to relish the idea of his reward being so indefinitely postponed ; " but the Effendi is going to Sivas ? "

" Yes."

" He will see the Pacha there."

" Very likely."

" Then will he tell the Pacha of my great merits, and ask him to give me some higher employment ? "

" If it pleases Allah, you will receive some higher post," I piously observed. " Our destinies are in his hand."

" Yes," said the man, " so they are. But for all that, I wish that you would speak to the Pacha for me."

From the two examples I have here cited, it will readily be seen that a system of promotion through favouritism is very deeply rooted amidst the Turks. I had been seen riding with the Caimacan. It was thought that I might see the Pacha at Sivas—this was quite sufficient to induce some of the inhabitants of Tokat to believe that any request I might make to the Pacha or Caimacan would necessarily be granted.

" It was fortunate," here remarked the engineer, " that you told Osman to give the baksheesh to a Corporal, and that a Turkish servant heard you give the order. If the fellow had been a Christian, the servant would never have taken the trouble to mention it to him. But the fact of the Corporal being a co-religionist was too much for the servant. It has enabled you to detect the fraud."

" This is one of the worst features of the country," he continued. " The Turks will not do anything to aid a Christian at the expense of a Mohammedan, even if the Mohammedan is most clearly in the wrong. And it is much the same with the Christians in respect to their co-religionists. The result is that the Armenians and Turks do not pull well together. The law, too, is faulty, and requires amendment."

" Let me give you an example," continued Mr. Gasparini, " and one which has come immediately under my notice, for it affected my own servant. It sounds like a romance, but alas ! is too true ! My servant's name is Karatel Mermenk Ovooloo. He is an Armenian ; his mother died when he was a child ; his father remarried, but behaved very badly to his second wife, continually illtreating her, and making his son bring another woman to the house. The lad was very fond of his stepmother, who was at that time seriously ill; at last he refused to bring his father's paramour to their home. The father beat him severely and apprenticed the lad to his own trade, that of a coppersmith. The mother soon afterwards died, with an anathema on her lips at her husband's paramour. The latter, strange to say, died herself three weeks afterwards. In the meantime, the father gave the boy three piastres a week for his clothes. The lad could not clothe himself for that sum, he left his home and went into service. The parent succeeded in having the boy turned away from several situations, but at last I took him. Now, only the other day, the father went to the Cadi, and swore that his son was in a coppersmith's business with himself, and in consequence must pay half the tax on his trade. There is no truth whatever in the statement, but the father's word has been taken, and my servant arrested, and kept in prison for three days. The sum is only twenty-six piastres, I would gladly pay it myself, but I have no money; the government will not give me my salary; so here we are at a dead-lock."

CHAPTER XXV

Mohammed's horse—The Effendi's barley—The road from Tokat to Sivas—
    A very pretty girl—Tchiflik—Complaints made against the Circassians
    —Highly cultivated soil—The Tchamlay Bel mountain—A Turk killed
    —A wonderful gun—Yenihan—The Yeldez Ermak—The Kizil Ermak
    —Sivas—A ruined citadel—The importance of Sivas from a military
    point of view—My entry into Sivas—The guard—An Italian engineer
    —Three American missionaries—A house pillaged.

THE following morning, Mohammed arrived at an early hour, bringing with him his horse, a wretched brute to look at; he had not a particle of flesh on his bones, and was half blind with one eye.

"This is my horse, Effendi," said Mohammed proudly; "is he not a magnificent animal? My having this horse will save the Effendi the expense of hiring or buying another one."

"I hope that I shall get a baksheesh at Erzeroum," he added.

"Of course," I said; "that is, if the brute reaches Erzeroum. But it strikes me that you have not been giving him anything to eat lately!"

"No, Effendi, I was afraid that if he looked too well he would have been taken for the use of the troops; but no one will even glance at him as he is. He has a wonderful appetite, and will make up for lost time; no one will recognize him, after he has eaten the Effendi's barley, for a day or two; he will soon be fat and strong."

The road from Tokat to Sivas is a good one for the first few hours. My friend the engineer's work had been very fairly done; our horses were able to get over the ground at from five to six miles an hour. The track led through a succession of hills and valleys. In some places the engineer had been obliged to cut the road for several hundred yards in the solid rock.

Presently we passed a small Circassian village. Several good-looking women, coming to the roadside, offered chickens and geese for sale. One of the Circassians was a very pretty girl, and would have carried off the palm amidst many European belles. Her face was not veiled. There was a great deal of expression in her large, dark eyes. They flashed excitedly as she sought to induce me to buy her wares.

"I am tired of chicken," I said; "I should like a little meat."

"There is no meat here," replied the girl. "We ourselves live upon bread and eggs: buy some eggs."

And running back to a house, she brought out about fifty eggs; the price being eightpence of our money.

Now we came to Tchiflik, an Armenian village. Here there were thirty houses; and as six hours had sped by since we left Tokat, I determined to halt for the night, the more particularly as Mohammed's horse showed unmistakable signs of fatigue.

The Armenian in whose house I stopped, complained of his Circassian neighbours. According to him, they had hazy ideas as to the difference between *meum* and *tuum*. Several cows belonging to the villagers had recently disappeared. It was strongly suspected that some Circassians were implicated in the robbery.

The country in the neighbourhood was very highly cultivated. The farmers' granaries were full of corn. Hundreds of cows and cattle could be seen grazing along the side of the road.

We arrived at the Tchamlay Bel mountain. As we were ascending a narrow pass which overhung a steep precipice, the guide, a Zaptieh, observed that only five days previous a Turk had been killed on this very spot. It appeared that there was a band of brigands in the neighbourhood. Five of them had attacked a party of four Turkish merchants, who were returning from Sivas with, as it was believed, a considerable amount of gold on their persons. Three of the Turks ran away, leaving their companion, who showed fight, but was shot down ; the brigands had taken away from him thirty-five liras, besides two horses. An hour later, when the news was brought to a village, several of the inhabitants turned out on horseback to pursue the robbers : it was too late, they had made their escape and carried off the booty.

"Do not be alarmed," said the guide as he concluded his story. "I am with you ; the brigands will be afraid. Look here !" he carefully unstrapped a long, single-barrelled flint gun from his saddle-bow. The barrel was tied on to the stock by a piece of string.

"It is a wonderful gun," said the guide. "It belonged to my grandfather, I once shot a deer with it."

"Was the deer far off ?" I inquired.

"Very far," was the reply. "So far," pointing to a rock about 1000 yards from us. It was clear that however well the guide might shoot with his gun, he was equally good with the long-bow. I began to be a little doubtful about the story he had just told us of the brigands.

We rested for a while at Yenihan, a large village with 200 houses ; the population is composed half of Armenians and half of Turks. The Caimacan had gone to the mountains in search of some redif soldiery. He had experienced considerable difficulty in inducing these men to leave their homes, and join the army in the field.

There was nothing particular to see at Yenihan. Sivas was only nine hours distant : I determined to make a long march on the following day, and give our horses a rest in that city. The track was good. Ox-carts—the chief means of transporting baggage in this part of Anatolia—have no difficulty in travelling along the road to the Yeldez Ermak, a rapid stream which is about seventy yards wide. It is crossed by a good stone bridge on arches. The river, though fordable in the winter, would be impassable in the early spring if it were not for the bridge. It is a tributary of the Kizil Ermak, and meets that stream about twelve miles S.E. of Sivas. The district is hilly, but is highly cultivated. In about four hours we reached the Kizil Ermak, a broad, deep **river**. It is crossed by a stone bridge. A road on the opposite bank leads to Divriki.

We did not cross the bridge, but continued on to Sivas, which lay before us, with a background of rising slopes. A citadel, in a ruined state, frowned down upon us from the centre of the city.

Sivas, the capital of Armenia Minor, is situated at the head of the valley of the Halys of the ancients. It is the most important military position in this part of Turkey. It commands the sole route which descends with the waters upon the plateau of Asia Minor. Sivas is the key to the Peninsula on the Asiatic side ; the Turks ought to fortify this place, particularly when they are threatened in Asia Minor by the Russians. Should the latter succeed in forcing the first line of defence, consisting of Kars, Ardahan, and Bayazid, and afterwards take possession of Erzeroum, there will be no other fortified town between themselves and Scutari.

The governor had sent an officer with some Zaptiehs as an escort for our party. As we were entering the principal street a servant approached us with a fine Arab horse, and said that the Pacha hoped that I would honour him by riding his favourite animal to the quarters prepared for my accommodation. It appeared that the Bey in Angora had telegraphed to the governor of Sivas about me, hence the preparations which had been made.

I dismounted from my own quadruped, and mounted the Pacha's horse. I now found that the stirrup-leathers, even when let out to the last hole, were much too short, I was sitting with my knees nearly up to my chin.

The whole population of Sivas had turned out to welcome me to their city. I should have liked to have made my entry in as dignified a manner as possible. Dignity soon became out of the question. The Arab horse, unaccustomed to sixteen stone on his back, began to kick. To avoid ignominiously coming off, I was compelled to take my feet out of the stirrups, and ride without these appendages to the saddle.

Luckily the rooms prepared for us were not far distant. On arriving in a small square, the officers and Zaptiehs halted before a small, but clean-looking house, which faced the Pacha's residence. On the other sides of the square were the prison and the barracks. The guard turned out from the last-named building, and presented arms as we dismounted.

The officer of the escort, taking my hand, led me up a staircase to the apartment set aside for my accommodation.

Soon after our arrival, I was waited upon by an Italian engineer, who was employed at Sivas by the government. He was the only European in the city, which contains 7000 houses; however, there were three American missionaries who had been settled in Sivas for several years past with the object of making proselytes.

The Italian was accompanied by an Armenian who spoke French. The latter gentleman was very indignant with the Pacha, who had shut up the shops belonging to the Christians during the previous week. It appeared that some of the redif soldiers had pillaged a house in the market-place. Several hundred more redifs were expected to arrive at Sivas; there were hardly any regular troops to keep order. The governor had taken the precaution of closing all the shops belonging to Armenians during the stay of the redifs in the town. This was a precautionary measure. It had given great umbrage to the Christians. My visitor loudly denounced the proceeding.

"Are people ever tortured here?" I inquired.

"No," said the engineer; "the law is, or rather the judges are, much too merciful. There has been only one execution during the last three years. The culprit was a soldier; his first wife had been seduced by a neighbour. He put her away and took another, but at the same time said to his neighbour, 'If you seduce this woman I will kill you!' The threat had no effect. The soldier's second wife was treated as the former one had been : he revenged himself by killing the adulterer; for this offence he was hanged."

"Are people ever impaled here?" I inquired, still having the two English priests who wrote some letters to the *Times* about what they said they had seen when travelling on the Danube, in my mind's eye.

The Armenian smiled.

"No, not so bad as that. I believe a robber was impaled eighteen years ago; at all events, there is some tradition to that effect."

Shortly afterwards my visitors left the room.

CHAPTER XXVI

The prison in Sivas—Christian prisoners—The gaoler—Kurds and Circassians—A few Armenians—False statement made to me by Christians—The old murderer—The firman for his execution—Kept in suspense—Our Governor dislikes shedding blood—Issek Pacha—He may die—His residence—The law in Turkey about murder—Mercenary dealings—Lax justice.

The following day I walked across the square to the prison. I had not said anything to the authorities in Sivas about my intended visit to this establishment. I wished to see it under its everyday aspect, and at the same time to find out if there were so many Christians prisoners as the Armenians in Yuzgat would have had me believe.

I found the gaoler seated in the doorway, he was smoking a long pipe.

" Can I see the prison ? " I asked.

" Certainly, Effendi."

Going before me, he led the way to a lofty but narrow room. Here there were twenty-seven prisoners, clothed in rags and tatters ; each man had his wrist fastened to his instep by a light iron chain. No gaoler slept in this room with the prisoners. They would not have had any difficulty in freeing themselves from their manacles had they tried to do so.

" What do you give them to eat? " I inquired.

" A loaf of bread (about 2 lbs. weight) every day, and some water," was the reply. " However, many of them have friends in the town, and they are supplied with provisions from outside."

" What are the prisoners mostly here for ? " I asked.

" For robbery and murder. We have a great many Kurds and Circassians for horse and cattle stealing. Then there are a few Armenians, the latter chiefly for crime connected with money matters."

" How many prisoners are there altogether ? " I remarked.

" One hundred and two."

" And how many Christians ? "

" Six ; all the rest belong to Islam."

As the population of Sivas is fairly divided between the two sects, it was very flattering for the Armenians that there should be so few of their number amongst the prisoners. But, after what I had been told at Yuzgat, my belief in the truthfulness of their community was very much shaken.

In another part of the gaol there were several prisoners without chains. They were walking about in an enclosed courtyard. One of them, an old man who was very much bowed down by years, appealed to us. Taking my hand he touched it with his forehead, and then besought me to speak to the Pacha for him.

" What is he here for ? " I inquired.

" For murder," was the reply ; " and a very cold-blooded murder too."

" He is a Circassian," continued the gaoler, " and the firman for his execution arrived at Sivas two years ago."

" Yes," said the old man, in a whining voice, " two years ago ! and I have been kept in suspense ever since. It is an awful thing, Effendi—I never know from one hour to another that it may not be my last ! "

" Why was he not executed ? " I inquired of the official.

" Our Governor dislikes shedding blood," said the gaoler, " and he has put the firman away in a drawer."

" Yes," interrupted the aged murderer ; " Issek Pacha is a kind man, he will not put me to death ; but he is very old— he may die ! The Governor who will succeed him might find the firman, and order me to be hanged ! "

" Well, what do you want me to do ? " I asked.

" Only, Effendi, to beseech the Pacha to tear up the firman ! " cried the old man in imploring tones. " Let me end my years in the prison, for here every one is kind to me ; and let me not be strangled at the end of a rope on the scaffold ! "

" Well, I will speak to Issek Pacha," I said ; and with difficulty escaping from the murderer, who threw himself on all fours and frantically embraced my legs, I walked to the governor's residence.

He was seated on a sofa at one end of a large hall, and surrounded by attendants with documents awaiting his signature. He at once rose, and motioned to me to sit down by his side. After the customary salutations, I mentioned to him that I had just visited the prison and had seen the old murderer.

" Ah ! you have seen him," said the Pacha gravely, at the same time slowly stroking his stomach. " He is in a great state of mind, I believe, lest I should die before he does, and my successor order the sentence to be put into execution. But he has nothing to fear ; I have the firman safe in my drawer, and am trying to arrange the matter with the relatives of the murdered man."

It appears that there is a curious law in Turkey, to the effect that if a man has committed a murder, and the order for his execution has come from Constantinople, the Pacha whose duty it is to have the sentence carried out need not do so, provided that the relations of the murdered person request that the assassin's life may be spared.

This frequently gives rise to mercenary dealings between the assassin and the relatives, for the latter hold his life in their hands. If the murderer is rich, he will often have to give up all his property ; and then if the relations pardon him, the law enacts that he must spend fifteen years in gaol. The manner of carrying out this part of the sentence is extremely lax. Should the friends of the prisoner be able to scrape together enough money to satisfy the officials connected with the prison, the murderer will be allowed to escape and remain at large in his native town.

Later in the day two Armenian gentlemen called upon me. Presently one of them remarked that Issek Pacha was immensely rich, and that many tales were in circulation about him.

" Yes," said his companion, " there is a story to the effect that one day the Grand Vizier was walking by the side of the Bosphorus with the late Sultan Abdul Aziz. A beautiful yacht, the property of Issek Pacha, happened to be anchored close to the royal palace. ' What a magnificent vessel ! ' said the Sultan. ' To whom does it belong ? ' The Grand Vizier," continued the Armenian, " did not much like the Governor of Sivas, and replied, ' It was the property of Issek Pacha, but he has sent it here to be placed at your majesty's disposal.' ' Write and say that I accept it with pleasure,' said the Sultan. The first notification which Issek Pacha had of this transaction was the receipt of an official letter from Constantinople enclosing the Sultan's thanks for the present.

" A subscription had been recently started in the vilayet or province of Sivas, with the object of collecting funds to enable the Government to continue the war. Ten thousand liras were collected. The Pacha sent the money to the Grand Vizier without exactly stating the sources from which it was derived. The minister at once ordered the receipt of this sum, as coming from Issek Pacha, to be acknowledged in the public journals ; he also desired a secretary to write an official letter to the governor to thank him for his large donation, and say in the postscript that when the rest of the people in the province of Sivas had sent in their subscriptions, he was to forward them immediately to Constantinople. Our Pacha did not like this letter," continued my informant. " However, what could he do? he is an enormously rich man, and, though it went very much against the grain, he sent a fresh 10,000 liras to the Porte."

It was clear that the Armenians did not love their Pacha. From what I subsequently heard, their dislike to him originates in the fact that he is not amenable to bribes. That he is not a miser can be easily shown. Misers are not in the habit of expending large sums of money in the construction of public buildings. Issek Pacha at the time of my stay in Sivas was having a large mosque built in the town of Erzingan, at his own expense. It was said that this building would cost him 40,000 Turkish liras.

Three American missionaries called ; they had been settled for several years in Anatolia, and had succeeded in making some converts amidst the Armenians, but they had not in any one instance induced a Mohammedan to change his faith.

I inquired if it were true, as stated at Yuzgat, that Armenian boys and girls had been carried away from their parents, and shut up in Issek Pacha's seraglio.

"No! no," said one of my visitors. "At all events, we have never heard of anything at all authentic as to such proceedings." When I mentioned the subject of impalement, and asked if they had ever known of any Christians who had been impaled by the Pacha's orders, the three missionaries seemed very much surprised at the question, one of them observed that the Turks were by no means a cruel race ; but that their system of administering justice was a bad one.

I now learnt that the proprietor of the house in which I was living was a shoemaker. The Pacha had hired from him the apartments which I occupied, and which were generally given to travellers. Mohammed, when he gave me this piece of information, suggested that it would be a good opportunity for me to buy him a pair of boots.

" Such beautiful boots as there are downstairs," he continued, " the Effendi could get both his feet into one of them. They will keep out the cold. If I do not have something over my slippers I shall be frost-bitten before we reach Kars !"

The proprietor brought the boot for my inspection. He had a very Jewish type of countenance, and at once commenced driving a bargain with Mohammed.

"But you told me downstairs that the boots were 125 piastres, and now you ask 165 !" observed the Turkish servant indignantly.

"They are my boots, and not yours !" said the Armenian, "and I shall charge what I like for them !"

It appeared that the difference of opinion between Mohammed and the shoemaker had arisen owing to the Armenian thinking that he would be paid in *caime*, or bank notes, and not in silver. Caime in Sivas had fallen to 165 piastres the lira. It was formerly 125 ; so by the depreciation of the paper currency the shoemaker would lose 40 piastres on every pair of boots he sold, if purchased from him at the present rate of exchange. Many of the Turks were alarmed at the constant fall in the value of their paper currency. They objected very strongly to being paid any large sums in Turkish bank-notes. According to the son of Crispin, only ten years previous the Government had issued an immense quantity of caime, and had said that in the following month of March this paper would be accepted in payment of the taxes.

"March arrived," continued the shoemaker, "we took our caime to the tax-collectors. They would not receive it. A vast number of the notes then issued are still in the possession of merchants in this town, and are valueless."

When I was in Yuzgat Mr. Vankovitch had asked me to intercede with Issek Pacha for an Italian lady, the widow of a Pole who had died a few months previously in Sivas. The Pole had been the chief engineer in the district, and at the time of his death was owed about £120 by the Turkish authorities. His widow had applied to the Pacha for this sum, but was refused payment on the ground that she had a son, and that her late husband's father was still living.

"You must write to your husband's Ambassador," said the Pacha, "and ask him to inform us how the law of succession is applied in his country, we will then pay you everything to which you are entitled."

In the meantime an inhabitant took pity upon the Italian lady, and had received her into his harem. Here she was now living, and anxiously awaiting a reply from Constantinople to her letter. Months passed away, no answer came. The poor woman had exhausted the small resources which she possessed at the time of her husband's death.

CHAPTER XXVII

I WAS thinking of calling upon the Italian lady when
Mohammed, running into my room, informed me that the
governor was actually coming in person to call upon me, and
that it was a great honour; for some time before this the
Khedive's treasurer had passed through Sivas, and Issek Pacha
had not deigned to visit him, but had conversed with the
Egyptian from the street.

"See what a great man you are, Effendi!" said the
delighted Mohammed. "The equal of a Pacha too! fortunate
is my fate that I have been assigned to you as a servant!"

The governor drove up to the door in a vehicle which very
much resembled a brewer's dray. It was the only carriage of
any sort or kind in Sivas. This fact alone added considerably
to the Pacha's importance in that town. He was a corpulent
man, and required a great deal of pushing at the hands of his
two attendants to make him pass through the doorway of the
carriage; two steps enabled the person inside the vehicle to
descend to the ground,

Issek Pacha, turning with great caution, walked backwards,
his two servants holding his feet and guiding them to the
steps below. After resting a few seconds, to recover from
this exertion, the governor slowly mounted the staircase which
led to my apartment.

He now told me that twenty-five years ago the Turks and
Christians got on very well together, but ever since the
Crimean war the Russian government has been actively
engaged in tampering with the Armenian subjects of the
Porte, and has been doing its best to sow the seeds of dis-

affection amongst the younger Armenians, by promising to make them counts and dukes in the event of their rising in arms against the Porte.

"If it were not for Russian intrigues," continued the Pacha, "we Turks should be very good friends with the Christians. But Ignatieff is very clever, he will not let us alone, and does his best to create discord in our ranks."

I mentioned the case of the Italian lady, and asked him if he could not do something for her.

"It is a very difficult question," replied the Pacha; "her husband, the engineer, was a refugee Pole, and had lost his nationality as a Russian subject. Moreover, his father lives in Russia, and may claim that the son's property should be administered according to Muscovite laws. Then there is an infant child; and, besides this, the lady herself is an Italian, and is expecting another baby. We have written to Constantinople for instructions, when they arrive we shall know what proportion of the husband's property is due to the widow."

"What should you advise to be done in the matter?" he inquired.

"My opinion is that you ought to give the lady sufficient money to pay her expenses so far as Constantinople; for there she can speak to her own ambassador, and arrange the business more easily than it can be done here."

"Not a bad idea," said the Pacha. "I will advance two months of her husband's salary."

"*Gell!* come!" he cried to a crowd of servants who were waiting outside, and whilst one attendant handed him a cigarette, and a second some coffee, the Pacha desired a third to tell his treasurer that he wished to speak to him immediately. This official now arrived.

"I want two months' wages from the sum owing to the late engineer to be brought here at once," said the governor.

"But no order about the distribution of the property has come from Constantinople," replied the treasurer hesitatingly; "if we pay any money to the widow, we shall be held responsible for it ourselves."

"No," I said, "I will be responsible for the amount. If the authorities at Constantinople say that you have done wrong, I will repay you the money."

"Certainly not," said the Pacha; "the responsibility is mine. My orders are to be instantly obeyed," he added.

"Is the money to be paid in caime or silver?" asked the treasurer.

"Silver," was the reply. "When the poor woman's husband died, caime was worth as much as medjidis, but now there is a great difference, she must not be the loser. Run!" he cried.

"On my head be it!" replied the treasurer. In a few minutes he returned with a small sack of silver.

"Will you take it to the lady yourself?" said the governor, handing me the bag. "And when do you leave Sivas?" he added.

"Probably in three days' time."

"Well," continued the governor, "you will pass by Erzingan, where I have some property, and I hope you will stay in my house. Nay, no thanks. It will be doing me an honour, and I have written for rooms to be prepared. I shall send some Zaptiehs with you," he added.

"I do not want any."

"Nay, but you must have some. You will have terrible hard work in crossing the mountains between this and Divriki. There are already two or three feet of snow on the track. In some places you will require men to dig a way before your party. You do not know what the cold is in this country," he continued. "I was once nearly frozen to death myself, going from Kars to Erzeroum, just about the time of the Crimean war. I had 500 soldiers with me; a snow-storm came on, we lost our way. My men strayed in different directions. I had furs, and was able to resist the cold, but when we counted up my party the next morning, more than half the men were frost-bitten, and several had died during the night. There is another reason why you require several guides," added the governor. "The path over the mountains is covered with snow, and there are deep chasms and fissures alongside the track, some of them are more than a hundred feet deep. The guides carry poles, and will sound the path before your horses, otherwise you will not have much chance of reaching Kars."

"The Conference is over," said the Pacha, as he rose from the divan. "The news has been telegraphed to us from Constantinople."

"What has been the result of it?" I inquired.

"Nothing? What else could you expect? Particularly when Russia, the cause and origin of all our difficulties, was permitted to have a representative at the Conference—and such a representative—for General Ignatieff is a cunning old fox ?"

Then shaking hands with me—which I afterwards learned from Mohammed was a very great honour—the Pacha waddled downstairs, and drove to his official residence.

Later in the day I rode to the missionaries' home, a pleasant little house situated in the outskirts of the town. On their arrival in Sivas they had taken an abode from some Armenians, but the latter demanded such an exorbitant rent for the house in question that the missionaries determined to build one for themselves.

My friends' names were Perry, Hubbard, and Riggs. They received me with that hospitality which an Englishman always receives from Americans, no matter whether they meet him in the States or elsewhere.

Two of these gentlemen had brought their wives with them from America. Several ruddy-faced and pretty children who were playing in the room showed that the climate of Sivas was in no way an unhealthy one.

The ladies liked the place ; but when they first came here they had to put up with a great deal of annoyance, owing to the Turkish little boys. The latter, unaccustomed to see women walking about in European costume, and with their faces uncovered, had sometimes followed them in the street and thrown mud at their dresses. Whenever this occurred, and any elder Turks were present, they had chastised their young compatriots and put an immediate end to the disturbance.

"I dare say," observed one of the missionaries, " that it was a strange sight for the people in Sivas to see our ladies walking about the town. However, if a Turkish woman were put down in the streets of New York, I reckon that she would have a crowd at her heels before long."

This remark reminded me of an episode which had recently occurred in America, and which had found its way into the newspapers. It appeared that a Chinese lad was selling sweets and lollipops in New Orleans, when a burly native, coming up to him, kicked over the tray and the boy's wares. The lad, without a word of remonstrance, picked up his lollipops. The man a second time upset them into the mud. The child looked at his tormentor, and, collecting his sweetmeats, said to him, "Your are a Christian and I am a heathen ; I should be sorry to change places with you !"

"There are bad people all over the world," remarked one of the missionaries ; "the poor ignorant Turks are not nearly so cruel as some people would have us believe."

"No, they are not cruel," observed another gentleman, "but they are pig-headed—that is their great fault. They will not advance with the times in which they live ; if they adopt European inventions, they copy them blindly, and without adapting them to circumstances. Soon after the telegraph was invented, the Turks determined to have special lines, and to use the Turkish alphabet ; the man who was employed to arrange the system copied it blindly from our own. Now 'E' and 'I,' the fifth and ninth letters in our alphabet, are those which occur very frequently in an ordinary message ; in Europe the telegraph dial is so arranged as to facilitate the transmission of the letters most often employed. The Turk, when he came to 'I,' and found it was the ninth letter in our alphabet, placed the ninth in his own on the same footing, whereas that letter is, comparatively speaking, but seldom used."

"A few years ago," observed one of the missionaries, "there was an Englishman here connected with the Anglo-Indian Telegraph. We were then as well supplied with information as the people in London or New York. It was the time of the French war, and all the news was sent daily from England to Hindostan. Our friend used to tap the wire, and send us a little budget of information every morning ; but now he has gone, and all that we hear is several weeks or months old."

"There was actually a great deal of difficulty in introducing the potato plant," remarked another gentleman ; "this will give you an idea of the nature of the people with whom we have to deal. Some foreigners brought over the seeds and planted them. They came up very well ; the soil is admirably suited for their growth. But the natives would not eat the potatoes. It was not until the military authorities, who were short of provisions, supplied them to the soldiers in lieu of other edibles that the soldiers would partake of this vegetable. They soon acquired a taste for it, and potato culture is gradually spreading throughout the district."

"I tell you what it is," said another missionary, "the Turks about here are just the inside-outsidest and the outside-insidest, the bottom-side-upwardest and the top-side-down-wardest, the back-side-forwardest and the forward-side-back-wardest people I have ever seen. Why, they call a compass,

which points to the north, ' Quebleh,' south, just for the sake
of contradiction, and they have to change their watches every
twenty-four hours, because they count their time from after
sunset, instead of reckoning up the day like Christians."

The peculiarity of this gentleman's expressions rather struck
me at the time. It was clear that he had not formed a
favourable opinion of the Sultan's Mohammedan subjects ; but
when I changed the conversation to the Armenians, I found
that the company looked upon them as being quite as ignorant
as the Turks, and much more deceitful.

The good missionaries found the conversion of these superstitious and ignorant Christians of the East a very difficult
and uphill task. Indeed I subsequently heard from some
Armenian Roman Catholics, who might have been prejudiced
in making the statement, that most of the converts to Protestantism were from amongst the Armenian shop-keepers
who supplied the mission with goods.

" Supposing the Russians were to conquer Anatolia, what
would be the position of the Protestant mission ?" I inquired
of my hosts.

" We should be immediately turned out of the country to
make way for the Russian priests," was the answer. " The
Tzar's Government does not tolerate any religion save its
own."

This remark struck me, coming, as it did, not from an
English Protestant, but from an American, and from an
inhabitant of that country which, in spite of its Republican
institutions, has always been thought to have a great sympathy
with Russia.

So the Government of this last-mentioned Empire would
not brook any foreign mission in its territory, and the
Emperor would not be likely to allow American missionaries
to impart to the Russian idolators a knowledge of the
Protestant faith.

Protestantism implies freedom of thought. The right of
investigation would be very displeasing to a despotic set of
rulers. The superstitions and debased form of worship
attached to the Greek religion have no chance of being
replaced by our pure Protestant faith, until such time as the
autocratic system of government which prevails throughout
Russia is terminated by a revolution.

CHAPTER XXVIII

THE following day I rode to an Armenian monastery, which is known by the name of the Monastery of Nishan or of the Cross. It stands on a rising slope, about two miles from Sivas. Its Gothic towers, more than 500 years old, look down upon the town and neighbouring villages, and can be seen for many miles around.

A large garden, over thirty acres in extent, enclosed by a high wall made of dry clay, supplies the monks with fruit and vegetables. It bounds the monastery upon one side ; on the other there are several farms, which furnish cattle, sheep, and such other live stock as may be required.

A long low passage with damp walls led the way, with many a winding turn, to the apartment which had been reserved for my use.

. Here I found the bishop and several other priests belonging to the community. The ceiling of the room was of hand-somely-carved oak, and divans, as in the Turkish houses, supplied the place of chairs. Some Armenian merchants now arrived, and shortly afterwards dinner was announced.

It was a fast day. The bishop himself could not partake of the dishes. However, he gave permission to the other guests to break the fast, and a turkey stuffed with apples—the *pièce de resistance*—was nothing to the hungry visitors ; the dinner being in the Turkish style, made up of a series of surprises to our stomachs.

According to one of the Armenians, the Turkish finance was in an utterly hopeless condition.

" Our Government," he remarked, "first said that it would only issue paper money to the amount of 3,000,000 liras, and we have caime to the value of 11,000,000 liras in circulation !"

"Yes," said another merchant, "the lira is now at 160 piastres, but if there is a war it will rise to 500."

"The Government will be the loser in the long run," he continued, "every one is speculating for the fall, and we are buying up all the gold we can."

I now learnt that the Armenian merchants in Sivas employed the telegraph very freely in their monetary speculations. The inhabitants in general only knew of the rise or fall in the value of their paper money by the post, which arrived once every fortnight. The value of caime in proportion to gold was reckoned according to the date of the post's delivery. But, as the Turkish bank-notes were becoming more and more depreciated every day, the Armenian merchants who employed the telegraph were able to make large sums by buying up all the gold in the district, and pocketing the difference between the actual exchange and that which passed current at Sivas.

The walls of the monastery were not thick enough to keep the breath of scandal from reaching the abode of the recluses. I was told of a former governor of Sivas, who had been extremely popular throughout the district, and who in forty days had actually established order in the town and neighbourhood. It appeared that this Pacha was a very good-looking man. One day, when he was at Constantinople, a sister of the late Sultan Abdul Aziz chanced to see him. She wished to marry the Adonis; "but unfortunately," added my Armenian informant, "he was in love with his own wife, a pretty woman. He declined the Sultan's offer to take his sister, who was not good-looking, as chief lady in the harem. Soon afterwards the Pacha died at Smyrna under very suspicious circumstances. It is generally supposed that he was poisoned."

"His Eminence is freed from all such dangers," whispered another of the guests, as he called my attention by a nudge with his elbow.

"How so?" I asked.

"Why, he cannot marry. Our bishops are not allowed this indulgence. Should a priest take unto himself a wife, he can never become a bishop."

"How does your system answer?" I inquired.

"Answer! very badly. They are not allowed to have wives of their own; but they look after the welfare of the ladies in their congregation. Are your Protestant bishops allowed to marry?"

" Yes."

" Well, it would be a good thing for the married people in Armenia, if our bishops had the same permission."

I now went to see the chapels belonging to the monastery.

An altar in one of them was profusely decorated with gold and other ornaments. It was erected to the memory of the four martyrs of Sivas who were torn to pieces by the Pagans about 1500 years ago. It is said that our Saviour shortly afterwards appeared to the inhabitants of the town in the form of a bird, and alighted upon a large stone near the place where the four Christians had been murdered. The stone was subsequently taken to the monastery, and this altar had been erected upon it. In another chapel, there was a picture of one of the kings of Armenia in the act of being consecrated by an archbishop of Sivas. The holy father who called my attention to this picture pointed to the suppliant form of the king, who was kneeling before a priest, and to a monk who was writing the date of the coronation on a scroll of parchment, and looking down upon the sovereign.

"Things are very different to what they were then," remarked the priest. " In those days even kings had to obey the holy Church. They do not think anything of us now," he added, with a sigh ; "instead of giving presents to the Church, they take away from it the few privileges and the little wealth it has left."

" Have you any privileges belonging to your order ? " I asked.

" Only one ; we have not to pay any duty upon salt, and I suppose that even this slight exemption from taxation will be taken away from us ere long."

A throne belonging to a former king of Armenia was next produced. It was made of ebony, and in form much resembled a shut-up garden-chair, but one of gigantic dimensions. The sovereign for whom this throne had been made, died several hundred years ago at Sivas. The worthy fathers differed a few hundred years as to the date of the monarch's decease, and so it is impossible for me to give it. His bones were taken to Van, and interred there ; however, his sons reigned for many years afterwards, and held their court at Sivas.

"Our nation has had a great many reverses," said the bishop ; "but who knows what is in store for us ? "

" We do not want any Russian rulers ! " said an old Armenian merchant. " When I was a child," he continued, "the Russians made war upon the Persians. A general, second in command of the Russian forces, was an Armenian. The head of our Church helped the Russians, and 25,000 Armenians were levied to aid them in the war against the Shah. The Persian army was annihilated; twenty-five cities were destroyed; the invading forces advanced towards Teheran. The Shah then made a treaty with Russia."

"What has that got to do with your dislike of the Russians?" I inquired.

"Listen!" said the old man. "After the war was over, the Russian chief was alarmed lest the Armenian general, who was a very skilful officer, might make himself King of Armenia. He accused him of treason, had his eyes taken out, and sent him a prisoner to Russia." *

"The Russians would not have been pleased if we had been made independent at that time," said a priest. "They have always looked upon us as a certain inheritance, all they want to do is to take our territory without having to fight for it."

"We revenged ourselves upon Hassan, Khan of Persia, who had defiled one of our churches near Ararat," remarked the old merchant. "He was taken prisoner and transported to the church which he had desecrated. He was afterwards tied face to face with a dog, and given the same food as that animal. The Persian soon died of shame or starvation."

There is but little export trade from Sivas. Tobacco is the staple produce of the country. All the articles imported are very dear, owing to the expense of transport from Samsoun, the roads between Sivas and that port being very bad.

Sugar, I was informed, costs eighteenpence a pound. If an enterprising inhabitant were to start a manufactory of this article of consumption, he would speedily make an immense fortune. Beetroot and a peculiar sort of sweet carrot abound throughout the district. The first-mentioned vegetable can be bought for eight shillings a ton. It might be grown for very much less. Any amount of water-power could be brought from the neighbouring mountains to bear upon machinery. Coal is also to be found in the neighbourhood. This part of Anatolia is supplied with sugar from Constantinople. If it were manufactured on the spot, the profit would

---

* I wrote this anecdote down at the time. It is given precisely as the Armenian narrated the story. I have not been able to find a corroboration of the statement in any historical document. Very little is known of what took place during this war.

be very great, for the cost of carriage would be saved ; in all probability it would utterly supplant the Constantinople sugar, and soon find a market throughout the whole of Asia Minor.

CHAPTER XXIX.

On leaving the monastery, we rode to the principal mosque of the town.   I was struck by seeing a large ostrich egg suspended from the ceiling by a silver chain.   On my asking the Turk who showed me over the building, why this egg was hung there, he replied,—

"Effendi, the ostrich always looks at the eggs which she lays ; if one of them is bad, she breaks it.   This egg is suspended here as a warning to men that, if they are bad, God will break them in the same way as the ostrich does her eggs."

Mohammed met me as I was returning to my house.   He was very much excited.

"What is the matter ?" I inquired.

"Effendi, a regiment is about to march to Erzeroum.   It will be a grand sight.   The Pacha will accompany it out of the town.   The dancing dervishes will go before the band. Other dervishes will be there with sharp knives ; they will cut themselves, but the blood will not flow !   It will be a miracle ! And all this we can see from the Effendi's window ! "

" Happy are you, O Mohammed, to be able to see such wonderful sights without paying for them," I remarked ; then, giving him my horse, I went upstairs to my room.

An immense crowd had gathered in the square ; the part facing the barracks was thronged by hundreds of idlers who were eagerly pressing against the gates.   Presently they were thrown wide open.   The governor, in his dray-like carriage, issued from the portals.   He was accompanied by the colonel of the regiment, who was mounted on a superb grey, and rode by the side of the Pacha's vehicle.

Next came six dancing dervishes clad in sackcloth, and with long cowls over their green turbans. They in their turn were followed by about twenty men—some carrying what appeared to be bill-hooks—others, maces with leaden balls attached to them by chains, and bright steel skewers.

"This is delightful!" said Mohammed, who, by way of seeing better, had climbed on to the top of the divan, torn away the piece of paper which supplied the place of a pane of glass, and, having thrust his head and shoulders through the aperture, was staring with his mouth wide open at the procession.

"Please God they will soon begin to cut themselves!"

However, he was doomed to disappointment; the dervishes had already cut themselves in the barrack-yard, and were not inclined to repeat the performance.

On they went in serried ranks, followed by the troopers, all of whom were excellently mounted on horses averaging about fifteen hands, and which looked in capital condition. The men were armed with American revolvers and repeating-rifles, whilst a short curved scimitar hung by each man's side.

"How long will it be before they reach Erzeroum?" I inquired of Mohammed.

"About a month," was the answer; "but they are going by a short route by Kara Hissar, and we by Divriki, Arabkir, and Egin, which will be a long way round. We shall arrive first at our destination, as the regiment will not march more than sixteen miles a day."

The Pacha ordered his coachman to draw up the carriage on one side of the road; the dervishes raised a mournful yell. The regiment, passing onward, was lost to view behind an avenue of poplars.

The following morning I started at daybreak in the direction of Dudusa, a village about five hours from Sivas. For some distance we marched alongside the left bank of the Kizil Ermak. The track was very heavy. The baggage-horses had great difficulty in making a way through the mud. Presently we came upon some firm soil. The scenery changed from a flat expanse of plough-land to a winding chain of rugged heights. Chain succeeded chain. Snowy crests were piled up in rear of each other like the billows of the deep. Our path led round these mountain peaks. From time to time we caught a glimpse of the Kizil Ermak, which, white as silver, flowed through the vale at our feet. Nature's walls on all sides of us were of every colour ; at every moment, red, blue, and grey sandstone met our gaze.

We round a neighbouring crag ; a vast rock of the purest marble lies before our party. Huge blocks strew the borders of the path ; they sparkle beneath the sky, and rival in their Parian whiteness the snowy heights overhead. On the summit of an adjacent hill is the monastery of Dudusa, and at its foot the village of the same name, made up of straggling houses, built at long intervals apart—some of mud and marble ; others—where the inhabitants had been too idle to transport the blocks from the adjacent rock—of dried clay : and a few of the abodes of the better-to-do farmers actually boasting glass windows ! In other houses the panes were replaced by paper or pieces of some transparent alabaster, which is found in large quantities in the neighbourhood.

Dudusa is an Armenian village. I now learnt that Issek Pacha was very popular amongst the villagers. I must say that I was a little surprised at this, after the way the Armenians in Sivas had abused their governor. Two months previous, some Turks, from a neighbouring hamlet, had made a raid on the flocks belonging to the inhabitants of Dudusa, and had carried off fifty sheep. Information of the robbery was given to the Pacha, he at once sent out a party of soldiers. The robbers had been arrested. They were expiating their offence in prison.

I had heard at Sivas that a redif battalion which had lately marched to Erzeroum had outraged some women near Dudusa. I took the opportunity to inquire if the story were true. Like many other statements which had been made to me by the so-called Christians in Anatolia, it turned out to be a fiction. The redif soldiers had passed that way. The only thing which could be said against them was that they had not paid for the bread with which they had been supplied, as the military authorities had not given them any money. There were no officers with the troops, but the men had given the name of their regiment. On application to head-quarters, the amount due would be transmitted to the villagers.

I did not stay long at Dudusa, but, after lunching at the priest's house, continued the march towards Kotnu, another village about twenty-seven miles, or about nine hours from the capital of the province.

It was dusk long ere we reached our halting-place. In passing over a narrow wooden bridge, one of my horses put his foot down a hole between the planks, and nearly broke his leg. Misfortunes never come singly. A moment later, the poor brute strayed a few yards from the track. He was at once bogged in the treacherous soil. Everything had to be unstrapped from the saddle, a rope was attached to his surcingle, and then, by means of the other horses, he was dragged from the slimy trammels. It was hard work loading him again.

The thermometer had fallen to considerably below zero. The wind howled and blew the snowy flakes in our faces. The horses would not stand still. Our matches were wet through. We could not light them. Under such circumstances we had to arrange the baggage.

The Zaptiehs who had been sent to act as guides would not help ; they sat still, cursing their destiny which had made them accompany a mad giaour like myself, who had chosen to travel from Scutari to Kars all the way by land, instead of going the greater part of the distance by sea, like a sensible true believer. I have but little doubt that the same train of thought was passing through Mohammed's and Radford's mind. However, the latter never flinched, and Mohammed had evidently won his friendship, for, on my asking my English servant how he liked his new companion, he replied, "Sir, he is worth three of Osman at any time, save prayingtimes, and then there is not a pin to choose between them. They must be awful sinners, these Mohammedans, if they require five prayers a day to settle the account with their consciences. Mohammed ain't that artful as Osman was. He don't choose the moment when there is work to be done, to set to work at his victuals, or to flop down on his knees to say his prayers. Mohammed has his pray all to himself afterwards, and then it don't so much signify ! "

"What ! Has not Mohammed so good an appetite as Osman ? "

"No, sir, Mohammed has more of a Christian's appetite ; he is satisfied with what I put before him, he don't go prigging out of the tin like that there other Turk, Why, I watched Osman one day eating a chicken which I had kept back for your supper ! A few days before, I had missed one out of the pot, and had taxed him with it ; he then said, ' *keupek*,' dog, as if a dog would go and lift up the lid of the tin ! I used to call Osman ' keupek ' afterwards, and he did not seem to like it. The other Turks, when they want to give it a fellow, tell

him that he is the grandson of a dog ; but I called Osman the
original animal—dirty hound that he was too—quite spoiled
my coat, that he did ! "

And my servant, lighting a short wooden pipe, the wonder
of the Turks, smoked furiously—the rapidity of his puffs
probably denoting an extreme dislike to his late fellow-servant.

CHAPER XXX

Snow—The path covered by it—The scenery—Upset in a snow-drift—
Nearly down a chasm—Probing the ground—A consultation—Teaching
my followers manners—May he die of the plague—A baggage-horse
knocked up—Yarbasan—A dirty village—The farmer committing himself to Providence—Visiting his friends—The Zaptiehs—Their remarks
—The giaour threatened to beat us—The Inglis giaour is different to
the Armenian giaour.

Snow fell heavily during the night. The next morning our
path was covered to a depth of quite two feet. In the valley
it was as much as our horses could do to force a passage
onward ; but, as we ascended a mountain path, the snow,
though deep, was in a frozen state, and afforded a firm
foothold.

The scenery was very picturesque as we gradually climbed
the steep. The bushes and pine-trees which studded the
mountain's sides were wreathed in flossy snow ; crags of all
shapes and colours glinted out above the pale white carpet.
A thick veil of azure clouds hung on the peaks of the distant
hills ; then, gradually dispersed by the rising sun, it broke up
into a hundred different forms, and, ascending higher in the
sky, opened out other mountains to our vision. Layer upon
layer of seemingly ever-ascending ranges barred the way in
front. They sparkled beneath the rays of the golden orb.
They flashed and glittered like the billows of the mighty deep.
My eyeballs acted and felt as if they would burst beneath the
glare. The village at our feet disappeared in the distance ;
shrubs and such-like traces of vegetation were now no longer
to be seen. We had arrived in the midst of what seemed to
be a vast white ocean. The intensity of the light created a
kind of mirage along the surface. The various crests and
ranges seemed to rise and fall. They became more wave-like
than before. Not a living thing was in sight save ourselves.

Ever and anon a boom, as of thunder, announced the fall of
an avalanche.

The cry of " Look out !" from a Zaptieh in rear of our party
awoke me from the contemplation of Nature's marvellous
scene. A second later, and I found myself on the broad of
my back in a snow-drift ; the animal which I had been riding
was pawing the air with his fore-legs, like a spaniel the first
time he is thrown into the water ; before any one could reach
my horse's head, over he fell—the soft substance fortunately
saving my body from the effects of the collision. It appeared
that I had strayed half a yard or so from the track, hence this
disaster. The Zaptieh in front of our party dismounted,
taking a wand, six feet in length, from his saddle-bow, he
began to advance with great caution, and to probe the ground
before him at every step he took.

"There are deep holes," said Mohammed, wading through
the snow to my assistance. " If we fall down one of them we
shall remain there, and in the summer the eagles will pick our
bones. It will be better for all of us to walk and lead the
horses," he continued. " Even then we shall have great difficulty in effecting a passage. The chief Zaptieh has been saying
that it would be better if we were to return to Kotnu and try
to cross the mountains to-morrow."

The snow had recommenced falling ; it was difficult to see
what lay before us. However, we had accomplished more than
half of the day's march. In all probability the path would
soon become more difficult. I determined at all hazards to
push on, and the more particularly as I had no time to waste,
owing to my limited leave of absence. Forward we waded
through the gradually-rising drifts. Each man followed his
neighbour in Indian file ; presently the leading Zaptieh who
was engaged in sounding the path before him, buried the six-
feet wand in the snow ; he thrust his elbow down after the
stick ; there was still no bottom. We were off the track. A
false step might at any moment send us down the chasm.
A consultation took place between the Zaptiehs, the head man
urging forcibly upon our party the necessity of returning.
But when we faced the other way, the wind cut against our
eyes with great violence. The particles of snow were so
blinding that it was clearly much more dangerous to return
than to proceed.

" It is our fate ! " remarked the chief Zaptieh to the comrade
by his side.

"Destruction seize the giaour who may be the cause of all our deaths!" said another.

"Let him die of the plague!" added a third.

This rather strong language was uttered in a loud tone, and as if the speakers did not care whether their observations met my ear or not.

"I tell you what it is!" I cried rather sternly to my unruly followers, and at the same time drawing my revolver; "I cannot reach you with my whip; but if you make any more insulting remarks, I shall send a bullet in your direction to teach you manners!"

"For the sake of heaven be quiet!" cried Mohammed to the Zaptiehs—for he, being directly in the line of fire, did not wish to expose himself as a shield to the delinquents.

"There will be no baksheesh unless you are as docile as horses," continued my Turkish servant.

This last remark, combined with my threat—which, it is needless to say, I had no intention to put into execution—brought the guides to their senses. Presently the stick of the leading Zaptieh struck against the track, and, after wading through the snow for some three hours more, we descended the side of the mountain. The snow disappeared as we reached the vale below, and deep mud, reaching above our knees, covered the track before us. It was terrible hard work for the baggage-horses. One of them, stumbling, fell prostrate in the mire. No amount of pressure would induce him to get up; so, taking off his pack-saddle and dividing the baggage as best we could—placing some on the saddle-horses and carrying the rest ourselves—we struggled on to a glimmering light which marked our quarters for the night.

The village of Yarbasan was reached. Sending back some of the villagers for the abandoned animal, I prepared to make myself as comfortable as the circumstances would allow.

In the meantime Radford and Mohammed were busily engaged in unloading the other baggage-horse. The pack-saddle was too broad to pass through the narrow gateway; all the luggage had to be unstrapped in the street—such a street as it was too! Imagine a farm-yard of the dirtiest description, and without any straw to absorb the filthy refuse; but even this does not convey to my own mind the hideous state of the road through Yarbasan. The inhabitants possessed many cattle, which were each evening driven into the village, so as to be out of the way of wolves. It had never occurred to the mind of the oldest villager to remove the deposits of their cows and oxen. If a farmer wished to pay a visit to a neighbour across the way, he simply tucked up his dressing-gown under his arm-pits, took off his slippers, broad trousers, and stockings, then, committing himself to Providence, he would wade through the dirt to his friend's house.

"Why do you not clean the street?" I inquired of my host, an old Turk, who, having just come in from the country, was rubbing his legs with some straw before the fire.

"The mud will dry up in the summer months," replied the man; "why trouble our heads about it now?"

The inside of the dwelling was not so clean as an average pig-sty. Horses, oxen, cows, and sheep were stowed away in the same room as ourselves. The Zaptiehs had squatted down in one corner with the host, Radford and Mohammed lay stretched out in the middle of the floor.

In a few minutes a woman arrived from some other house in the neighbourhood. She was clad in a long strip of cloth, which enveloped the upper part of her body; her legs and feet were covered with mud. Putting down a large wooden tray, on which were several thin cakes of half-cooked paste, and a basinful of oily soup, she retired. The proprietor of the house, after offering the dishes to me, returned to the Zaptiehs. In the meantime, closing my eyes, I tried to doze off to sleep. Presently the gendarmes thought that I was in the land of Somnus, and my attention was aroused by the familiar term of "giaour."

"Only think of our being ordered to accompany an infidel to Divriki in the winter!" observed the chief of the party.

"Yes, and for him to threaten to whip us!" said the other.

"He would have done it too," said Mohammed, joining in the conversation. "My Effendi is not like the Christians about here. He is an Inglis!"

"So the Inglis giaours are different to the Armenian giaours?" observed the Zaptieh.

"Very different: the Armenians talk, but the Inglis strike. Hush! hush! we shall awake him!"—and the conversation gradually died away in a whisper.

CHAPTER XXXI

THE baggage-horse was very little the worse for his long march
of ten hours on the previous day. Yarbasan was not a lively
place to stop at ; I determined to push on to Divriki.

We passed a range of hills—red-coloured stones lying in
profusion along the track—and, descending a deep incline,
arrived on the banks of the river Dumrudja (Kumer Su), a
rapid stream, here about fifty yards wide. A quantity of
wood was floating on the waters. This had been cut in the
pine-forests higher up the channel, and afterwards been tossed
into the river to find its way to Divriki. There was no bridge
over the stream, the water being more than four feet deep. A
consultation took place amongst the Zaptiehs.

"What are they talking about ?" I inquired of Mohammed.

"Effendi, they say that if any one of our horses were to
stumble, it would be a bad thing for the rider. There is a
waterfall a few hundred yards down the stream."

The large pieces of timber which were whirling round and
round in the middle of the river were also a source of anxiety,
for should any of these huge beams strike a horse, the animal
would have been swept off his legs for a certainty. After a
minute or two spent in consideration, the Zaptiehs determined
to cross the river, every horseman riding abreast of his companion. The stream would then press against the outside
horse ; he, however, would be supported by the one alongside
him ; each animal, in turn, being assisted by the other quad-
rupeds of the party.

It was as much as our horses could do to reach the opposite

bank. After several thanksgivings to the all-merciful Allah,
we once more began to climb into the clouds. A dense mist
prevailed. Presently almost everything was hidden from our
view. The snow became deeper and more blinding; at last
the pack-horses came to a standstill. Unloading the baggage-
animals, we distributed the luggage amidst the saddle-horses,
and, wading onward, continued our march through the snow.
This in some places was nearly breast high.

On the summit of the mountain stood a little house built of
rocks, which were loosely piled the one upon the other; and,
resting here for a minute or so to recover our breath, I was
informed that it had been erected by a charitable Turk in
Divriki, as a shelter for benighted travellers.

"Blessings on his head!" said the Zaptieh who gave me
the information. "This shelter has saved several lives
already. If we had arrived here two hours later, it might
have been the means of saving our own. The wind is rising,"
he continued, "and the sooner we reach Divriki the better."

Presently the little town appears in sight; a thin skirt of
poplar-trees encircles it as in a frame. An old ruined citadel,
perched up on a seemingly inaccessible rock, faces us from the
opposite side of Divriki. A tower on a still higher peak, but
communicating by a hidden path with the citadel, serves as a
place of refuge for the garrison, should the first-mentioned
stronghold ever be taken by assault. A rapid stream—the
Tchalt Tchai—runs below the citadel. The town is said to
contain about 3400 houses, of which 3000 belong to Turks,
and the remainder to Armenians.

Behind the houses and in the distance were fresh layers of
snow-covered mountains: the valley in which the town lies
had not felt the onslaught of winter; it was still covered with
deep mud.

One of the Zaptiehs galloped forward with a letter to the
governor from the Pacha at Sivas. Presently the official rode
out to meet me. He was accompanied by an escort of
gendarmes under the command of a captain. The latter, who
was mounted upon a spirited little Arab, caracoled his steed
to and fro—now bending over the saddle and trying to touch
the ground with his hand—then going through all the motions
of throwing the Djerrid—evidently wishing to astonish the
weak nerves of the newly-arrived giaours.

"Lor! what a cropper!"

This remark from my English servant disturbed me in a

conversation with the governor. On looking round, I saw the captain rolling in the mud. His saddle had turned—hence the fall.

"Serve him right, sir!" remarked Radford, catching my eye. "He was a spurring his horse that cruel; now pulling him up short on his withers, and then loosing him off like an express train. He was trying to show us how he could touch the ground. I believe, sir, the fellow thinks that we know nothing about riding, and that is why he wanted to do a Astley's performance out here in Hasia!"

The Caimacan led the way to a large house, belonging to a Turkish gentleman, a personal friend of the Pacha of Sivas. My host received me very courteously. He was under the impression that I had come to Divriki on some business connected with mines, and seemed surprised when he was informed that nothing but a wish to see the country had induced me to ride through Anatolia.

"There are mines in the neighbourhood," said the Turk, "and, according to tradition, some very rich ones. They were worked several hundred years ago—that is, when people lived who had brains—but now, alas! every man's head is like a blown-out calf's skin. The people do not know how to get at the treasures which lie hid beneath the ground, and, even if they did, would be too idle to do so."

I observed that, judging from the ruins about Divriki, all the houses must formerly have been built of hewn stone.

"Yes," said my host sorrowfully, "our ancestors were wise men. They lived in stone houses, we are satisfied with buildings made of dried mud. What do you build your houses of in England?" he inquired.

"Of bricks made of clay burnt in a fire."

"Yes," said the Turk, "you English have advanced. You know more than your grandfathers. Why have we not done the same?"

"Probably because you keep your women shut up in a harem, and do not educate them," I replied. "Turkish mothers are very ignorant, and, consequently, cannot instruct their children. The result is that your sons are only half educated. Besides this, you choose your wives—at least I am told so—for their looks, and without any regard to their attainments."

"The Inglis is quite right," said an old Turk, a friend of my host. "If I want to breed a good foal, I am as particular about the mare as the sire. He means that we leave the mares out of the question, and then complain that our stock is not so good as that of other nations."

" But hundreds of years ago our women knew quite as much as the Frank women," observed my host.

" Yes," replied his companion, " and then we could hold our own against the Franks. But the Frank women have been educated since those times ; the Effendi thinks that we ought to educate our wives in the same way."

" It would be difficult to do so," said the Turk coldly. " Their women uncover their faces ; I have heard that some of them declare that they are the equals of their husbands. What ridiculous creatures they must be," he continued, " not at once to accept that inferior position which Allah in His wisdom has awarded to them ! "

The following day I walked to the citadel, accompanied by my host. The building had been erected 600 years ago, as a defence against the Persians, who at that time frequently made encroachments into this part of Turkey. The solid masonry, which in many places had been allowed to go to ruin, showed that the walls had been originally built with great care. Two thousand men could have been quartered in the citadel, which now, uninhabited save by dogs and lizards, is rapidly succumbing to the elements. Convenient embrasures had been left on that side of the rampart which was easiest to assault ; through them the defenders could pour down the celebrated Greek fire so much used in the middle ages.

The river, which ran below the citadel, separated us from the tower which was used as a final place of retreat should the citadel be stormed. On my asking how the garrison could cross the water, there being no bridge in the vicinity, I was informed that a subterranean passage led beneath the stream to the other bank, and, then entering the side of the rock, a winding staircase gave access to the tower. The defenders were thus able to retreat from the citadel without their movements being seen by the enemy.

It was a glorious afternoon. The view of Divriki, of its numerous minarets and domes, lying as it were in miniature below us, was very lovely. Lofty mountains, in winter garb, surrounded the suburbs on every side ; and the silvery river, threading its way through the more distant quarters of the town, bubbled and splashed against the rocks and boulders.

The murmur of the waters was blended with the hum of the population. The cries of the herdsmen mingled ever and anon with the report of a fire-arm in the distance.

"Is there much game in the neighbourhood?" I inquired of my companion, who, leaning against one of the battlements in the tower, was straining his eyes in the direction of the shot.

"No. A few wild goats are sometimes to be seen on the rocks. The sportsman, whoever he is, has probably managed to come upon some of them unawares. I have a beautiful gun," he continued; "I will show it you afterwards."

"Is it for partridges or for big game?" I asked.

"For big game. It is rifled," he replied, "but I often load it with shot, and shoot at partridges, that is when they are all huddled together on the ground. Do you shoot much in your country with ball?"

"Yes; there is a great meeting once a year near London. All the best marksmen attend, and the Queen gives a prize to the best shot."

"Does she give many paras?"

"A great many—several hundred liras."

"Now could one of your best shots hit that cow?" pointing to an animal about 400 yards distant.

"Yes."

"What a marvel!" said the Turk. "Even the Kurds could not do that, and they shoot very well. They manufacture their own powder," he continued, "and very good powder it is too. The powder sold by the permission of our Government is very bad and dear; besides that, a man is only permitted to purchase a very small quantity at a time. There is plenty of sulphur, saltpetre, and charcoal in the mountains, and the Kurds supply themselves."

I afterwards learnt that all the powder which is furnished to the troops in Asia Minor is sent from Constantinople. There is no gunpowder manufactory in this part of Asia Minor. It is a great pity that the Turks have not long ago started an arsenal in the neighbourhood of Erzingan, which could have supplied the troops on the Turco-Russian frontier with cartridges and small-arms. As it is, every cartridge served out to a soldier before Kars costs the Government fifty per cent. in addition to its original cost, owing to the difficulties of transport.

"The Pacha at Sivas wrote to me to make your stay at

Divriki as pleasant as I could," presently remarked my companion.

"How did you like him?" observed an Armenian who now joined us.

"Very much."

"He is civil to all Europeans," continued the Armenian. "Probably he took a fancy to you because his astrologer had worked out your horoscope, and had reported favourably upon it."

"You do not mean to say that the Pacha believes in such things?" I observed.

"Yes; he never makes a journey without first of all consulting his astrologer."

There was no very active trade in Divriki. The Armenians supplied the people of the town with the few goods which they might require, at exorbitant prices.

In addition to this, most of the Christians were usurers. Any Mohammedan who chanced to require a loan had to pay his Armenian fellow-citizen a very high rate of interest. However, in this respect, Divriki is not an exception to the towns in Anatolia, and in almost every district which I visited I found that the leading Christians in the community had made their money by usurious dealings. In some instances, old Turkish families had been entirely ruined; their descendants were lying in gaol at the suit of Armenian money-lenders.

CHAPTER XXXII.

Usury laws in Turkey—An Armenian in prison for debt—The Caimacan—
The Turkish creditor—Hanistan Ereek's father—A Government cannot
be imprisoned for debt—The redif soldiers—Their unwillingness to
serve—The Armenians not to be trusted—Yanoot—A picture of desolation—A Jordan road—Turkish soldiers do not grumble—Arabkir—A
silk-merchant—My host—His library—Pretty covers—A Russian servant—He was taken prisoner during the Crimean war.

I WAS now to learn that the usury laws in Turkey are also used against the Christians. On returning to my house, a servant informed me that an Armenian was downstairs, and wished to see me.

He had been in Paris, and could speak a little French. This he so interlarded with Turkish that it was rather difficult to follow him. The man's name was Hanistan Ereek. At length I discovered that, twelve years ago, his father had borrowed 300 piastres from a Turk. Soon afterwards the father died, and the son, leaving Divriki without paying the debt, had gone to Europe. On his return the creditor had him arrested for the sum of 6000 piastres. This Hanistan Ereek refused to pay; he had been imprisoned for three months in consequence.

The Caimacan was in the room at the time the man made his complaint.

" It seems a hard case," I remarked.

" It is our law," was the reply; " if he had been a Turk, the same thing would have happened."

" No, it would not have happened! 300 piastres could never have amounted to 6000 piastres?" cried the Armenian indignantly.

It appeared that the case was one of hard swearing. The Turkish creditor had produced a piece of paper, on which was written that he had lent a larger amount than 300 piastres to Hanistan Ereek's father—the document in question bearing the latter's signature. This the son swore was a forgery. However, the Turk had been believed, and the Armenian had been sent to prison.

" What would have been done if this case had happened in your country?" asked the Caimacan; " would you not have put the man in prison for debt?"

" No; a son is not liable for his father's debts."

" Well, each country has its own laws, which doubtless are good for the respective inhabitants," observed the governor; " but if my father had died owing a sum of money, I should have thought that it was my duty to pay it."

" A very proper resolution," I remarked; " but supposing that a Government has contracted a debt, do you not think that its successors are bound to pay the interest of the loan?"

The Caimacan stroked his beard and looked at the Cadi, who presently answered,—

" We could not put a Government in prison."

" No," I observed, " but your nation owes my nation more than a hundred millions of liras, and not only you do not pay us any interest, but you have even proposed to repudiate the debt altogether!"

" How can we pay?" said the Cadi; " we have no gold, only caime, and your people will not take that. When the Russians leave us alone, then we shall be able to pay."

" And in the meantime I suppose I am to go back to prison ? " said the Armenian.

" We shall see," said the Caimacan gravely ; " the law must be carried out."

I have, perhaps, given the above case more prominence than it deserves, but I have done so because in this instance the governor of Divriki and a Christian were confronted in my presence, and the Armenian made his complaint without the slightest hesitation or fear. Now if the Christians had been so ill-treated as some of their co-religionists would have had me believe, Hanistan Ereek would not have been likely to have dared to come forward and find fault with the Cadi of his town, who had adjudicated upon the matter.

According to the governor, the people in his district had not shown much readiness to go to the war. In some of the villages, the redif soldiery were very reluctant to leave their homes, and could only be made to do so by the Zaptiehs of the province, who were most of them engaged at present in this duty.

" Why do you not give the Armenians arms ? " I inquired.

"They would turn them against us, and join the Russians," was the governor's reply. " In some districts which are very near Russia, and where the Armenians have the opportunity of seeing the Russians as they are, and not as they pretend to be, the Christians prefer being under the Turkish rule ; but the Armenians in our central provinces are constantly being tampered with by Russian agents. If we were to give the Christians arms, Allah only knows what would take place ! "

I left Divriki at daybreak the following morning, and continued the march towards Arabkir.

We ascended once more into the clouds, and, after a four hours' ride, halted to bait our horses at the village of Yanoot —if, indeed, it deserves the name of village—for it consists of a few huts, and about twenty-five inhabitants make up the entire population.

Now a curious phenomenon presented itself before us. We were passing a chain of hills which traversed our track from north to south. The northern side of every height was covered with deep snow, on the southern declivities some igneous rocks were exposed to view and glared in the sun. Here the rays were so fierce that not only there was no snow, but the weather became oppressively warm. A few hundred yards further, and winter attacked us again in all its rigour. Our horses were tried to their utmost in forcing a way before them.

The road became very rugged. An immense quantity of loose sharp pebbles were lying on the track. Our horses could not see them and were constantly falling on their knees. Not a village or solitary house was met with during our march. It was a picture of desolation. A few magpies, which from time to time flew mournfully across the path, were the only living things besides ourselves.

"Well, sir, this is a Jordan of a road," remarked my servant Radford, referring to some popular song, as the horse he rode fell down for the fifth time that morning. "That cemetery in Constantinople, where we tried the 'osses, was a bad place for riding, but it was nothing to this. Mohammed, he don't seem to take any account of it whatever. I never see such fellows as these Turks; they don't seem to be able to muster a grumble amongst them, no matter what they may have to undergo! Why, sir, some of them soldiers as we saw at Sivas had not received a day's pay for twenty-five months, and they seemed quite content and happy like; whilst, as for rations, it is true that the men fill themselves to bursting when they have the chance, but when they have to go without their grub they don't grumble! I wonder, sir, what our soldiers at Aldershot would say if they had not received a ha'p'orth of pay for two years, and had to march sometimes from morning to night, with nothing inside them save a whiff or so of tobacco?"

Radford was right in his remark about the track being a Jordan road—that is, if a Jordan road is the quintessence of everything that is stony and disagreeable. We had to lead our horses. Hour after hour sped by; we still seemed to be no nearer to any signs of Arabkir. Now we were up to our waists in snow and quagmire, and then we were lying between our horses' heels, the result of a slip from some half-hidden boulder.

At last we arrived at a spot close to the town. Here the rocks were of a crimson hue, their sides were covered with pebbles of ebon blackness. We mounted our horses, and, riding along a precipice-bounded path which leads into the long straggling city, presently halted at the house of an Armenian gentleman, who was kind enough to offer us a lodging for the night.

My host was a silk-merchant. He had started in business a very few years previous. This district being suitable for breeding silk-worms, he had speedily amassed a fortune. He was now one of the wealthiest men in the province, and not only supplied the Arabkir district with textures of his manufacture, but sent them by caravans to the limits of Asia Minor. He was very much respected by the Mohammedans in the town, and was on the best of terms with the Caimacan. The latter, when he heard of my arrival, called, and, after salaaming my host, told him that he should stay to dinner.

The apartment set aside for my use was hung round with engravings of all the sovereigns in Europe. A book-shelf in one corner was filled with French books, none of which my host could read.

"Do you know French?" I inquired.

"No!"

"Then what is the good of those volumes to you?"

"I am sorry for my ignorance," replied the man, "but I mean to have my child sent to Constantinople; there he shall learn French, and afterwards he will be able to read to me what is inside these books. Pretty covers, are they not?" he continued, pointing to the binding. "I bought them when I was residing at Erzeroum, and the merchant told me that they were full of wisdom. I have a European servant," he added.

"A Frenchman?"

"No, a Russian."

"A Russian!"

"Yes. You may well be surprised," he said, "for there is not much love lost between the Russians and ourselves. This man was taken prisoner during the Crimean war. When it was over he preferred remaining with us to returning to his own country."

CHAPTER XXXIII

My host—A Russian servant—The Crimean war—How the Russian soldiers were beaten—My father the Tzar—I would sooner be hanged!—The civilized way of eating a dinner—Knives and forks of Circassian manufacture—The Caimacan's opinion of knives and forks—My host's wife —His mother—Your Queen likes riding—An Armenian lady inquiring about balls—The barracks—The appearance of Arabkir—The prison— The inmates—The troops—A nation of soldiers—If Allah wills it— Capital required.

My host now called out in a loud voice, "Atech!" (fire!) "I want to show you my Russian servant," he remarked.

The door opened. A man of about fifty years of age, with an unmistakable Calmuck cast of countenance, brought a piece of live charcoal, between a pair of iron tongs, and placed it in the bowl of my host's chibouk; then, retiring to the end of the room, and crossing his arms, he awaited a fresh order.

"So you are a Russian?" I said, addressing the man in his native tongue.

"Yes, your excellency."

"And why did you not return to your own country after the Crimean war was over?"

The man looked down upon the floor; presently he remarked,—

"I was beaten."

"Who beat you?"

"I was beaten all day and all night. My colonel beat me. The sergeant boxed my ears, and the corporals kicked me!"

"But did you get flogged more than the rest of your comrades?"

"No, your excellency; at that time we were all beaten. I am told that now the officers do not flog their men so much."

"You are a deserter," I remarked.

"No, your excellency, I did not desert. I liked my father the Tzar too much to run away when he required my services. I was taken prisoner; when the war was over, I would not return to Russia. That is all I have done."

"Well, and if the Russians come here, as it is quite possible they may, what shall you do then? For you would, in that case, have a very fair chance of being hanged."

"It would be a dreadful thing, your excellency, but I must take the risk. I would sooner be hanged than go back."

"But things have improved in Russia since your time."

"A little," replied the man. "Little by little we advance in Russia. It is a nice country for the rich, but it is a dreadful country for the poor!"

"Is Turkey better?"

"Yes, your excellency, no one is beaten here; when a man is hungry, no Turk will ever refuse him a mouthful of food— that is, if he has one for himself. I hope my brothers will not come here," continued the man, pointing presumably in the direction of the Caucasus. "Allah has given our father

the Tzar much land; why does he want more?" and, after
putting some more red-hot charcoal in the bowls of our pipes,
the Moujik left the room.

My host's frequent journeys to Erzeroum, where he had
occasionally met Europeans, had given him a taste for the
civilized way of eating a dinner. He pointed with some pride
to his knives and forks. They had been brought to Erzeroum
from the Caucasus, and were a mixture of silver, lead, and
gold—the three metals being blended together by the Circassian
artificers, and then formed into the articles in question.

The Caimacan was also supplied with a knife and fork;
however, this gentleman did not seem to understand the use
of his plate, and ate out of the dish.

"Which do you like the best—to eat with a knife and fork,
or with your fingers?" I inquired.

"With my fingers," replied the Caimacan. "It is so much
cleaner," he continued. "I first wash my hands, and then
put them into the dish; but I do not clean my own fork—
that is the duty of the servant, who, perhaps, is an idle fellow.
Besides this, who knows how many dirty mouths this fork
has been stuck into before I put it in mine?"

Later in the evening, and when the governor had retired,
my host said that his wife and mother would come and sit
with us for a little while.

"I am not like the other Armenians in Anatolia," continued the speaker; "I have determined to shut up my female
relations no longer."

"Do they not cover their faces?" I inquired.

"Yes, in the street they do, but not inside the house."

The ladies now entered. They were dressed in loose yellow
silk dressing-gowns. Making a profound reverence to my
host and self, they seated themselves on a divan in the farther
corner of the room, tucking their legs underneath them, and
assuming the same position as my companion.

"It is a great honour for them to see an Englishman," he
observed.

"Yes," said the old lady, "and what a distance you have
come! Our roads are bad, and travelling is very disagreeable
for ladies," she continued. "To have to go always on horseback, or in a box slung on a mule, is not comfortable. Do
English ladies ride?"

"Yes."

"And why should they ride?" observed my host's wife,

"Have they not carriages and railways in your country, so that when a man travels he can take a woman with him without any difficulty?"

"Yes, but they ride for pleasure! Our Queen is very fond of riding, and often does so when she is in Scotland."

"Your Queen likes riding! That is a miracle!" said the old lady.

"I do not like it at all—it makes me so sore," said her companion; "but you Franks are wonderful people, and your women seem to do what they like!"

"Would not you like to do the same?" I inquired.

"A woman's place is to stay at home, and look after the children," said my host's mother gravely.

" Do not the husbands in England often become jealous of their wives?" inquired my host,—"and the wives of their husbands?" interrupted the old lady.

"Yes, sometimes."

"Well, there is a great deal to be said on both sides of the question," observed the Armenian. "It will be a long time before we follow you in all your customs."

"You have places in your country where the men and women meet and dance together in the same way as our gipsies dance—at least so I have been told," remarked my host's wife.

"Not exactly like your gipsies," I replied; "but we have what are called balls, where men and women meet and dance together."

"The husband with his own wife?"

"No, not always. In fact, more often with the daughter or wife of a friend."

"I should like to see a ball very much," observed my host.

"We had better go," said his mother, "it is getting late;" rising from the sofa, she made another very obsequious reverence, and left the room with her daughter-in-law.

The following day I rode to see the barracks. Arabkir is built in such a straggling fashion, that, although it only contains about 3000 houses, it extends for a distance of six miles. The houses are built on each side of a deep ravine. The streets, which are very precipitous, lead, in some instances, over the flat roofs of the dwellings. The latter were many of them built of stone, and an air of cleanliness prevailed throughout the town.

Large gardens, planted with all sorts of fruit-trees,

surrounded the houses. Long avenues of mulberry-trees were to be met with in every direction.

I stopped for a few minutes at the prison, and, dismounting, walked into the building. There were only seven prisoners—six Turks and one Armenian—the latter for attempting to pass false money, the Mohammedans for robberies and debt.

The population in Arabkir is equally divided between the Turks and Armenians. It was very creditable to the latter that there should be only one Armenian in the gaol. By all accounts, there was very little crime in this district, and the prison of Arabkir would be often for weeks together without a single criminal within its walls.

We arrived at the barracks, a square building, with long dormitories for the troops, and which were fairly clean. It contained at the time of my visit 500 redif (reserve) soldiers. They were shortly to start for Erzeroum. There were quarters for three times that number of troops, and another battalion was expected very shortly.

The men had not received their uniform. It was to be given to them at Erzeroum ; they were clad for the most part in rags and tatters, and had been armed with the needle rifle. I was informed that the Martini-Peabody weapon would be shortly served out to them. A squad of men was being instructed in the manual exercise in one of the passages. I spoke to the officer, and inquired if the battalion had ever been out for target practice.

" No," replied the man, apparently surprised at the question, " we want all our ball-cartridges for the enemy."

" But if your men do not practise at a target in the time of peace, they will not be able to hit their enemies in the time of war."

" We are a nation of soldiers," said the officer. " Every Turk carries a fire-arm. You have doubtless observed this on your journey," he continued.

" Yes ; but the weapons are for the most part old flint guns, which, if fired, would be quite as dangerous to the owners as to the foe, and are of no use whatever as a means of enabling your soldiers to aim correctly."

" If Allah wills it, our bullets will strike the Russians," observed the Turk.

" If Allah wills it, there will be no war, and all this instruction which you are giving the men in the manual exercise will have been wasted. What is the good of teaching your soldiers anything?" I continued; "if Allah wills it so, they can defeat the enemy with chibouks and nargilehs (pipes) just as easily as with Martini rifles!"

"This is the effect of the doctrine of fatalism," observed my Armenian host, who had accompanied me to the barracks; "it is the cause of half the apathy which characterizes the Turks. Why, they only commenced making roads after Sultan Abdul Aziz's visit to Europe."

"But you Armenians are equally to blame in that respect," I observed. "Only look at your own town. There are no roads, the streets are not paved, and they are full of ruts. The inhabitants are half of them Armenians; then why do not you Christians set the Turks an example, and begin by making a road to Divriki?"

"We are quite as apathetic as the Mohammedans," replied the Armenian. "The same observation which you have just made has been repeated to us fifty times over; but there is no one who has energy enough in his disposition to commence taking the initiative."

"Why do not you set about the business yourself?"

"I have my own affairs to look after. We are not public-spirited, or like Englishmen," continued my companion; "each one of us thinks of his purse first, and afterwards of how to benefit his fellow-townsmen. What a good thing it would be for the country if you English were to come here!" he continued. "All we want is a little of your energy; with it and capital, Anatolia would soon become one of the richest countries in the world."

CHAPTER XXXIV

The Mohammedan school—The Governor—The Schoolmaster—His impertinence—An Armenian song—The Russians at Tiflis—Are the Russians so very degraded?—The Hodja, or Schoolmaster—He is put in prison—The fanatics amongst the Turks—A school required for Hodjas—Qualified teachers wanted—Do the Turks insult your religion?—Malattia—A cross tied to the tail of a dog—We want newspapers—Even they contradict each other—The streets are slippery—The precipices—Shephe—The Kurds—Few Zaptiehs in the province—Hara Bazar—The village of Ashoot—Arab horses—Deserters—The Usebashe—God is evidently on our side.

FROM the barracks we rode to the Mohammedan school Here there were about thirty boys, all squatting on the floor, and engaged in spelling verses of the Koran. A few badly-drawn maps of the different quarters of the world were hung round the whitewashed walls. The governor accompanied me to the school-room. On his entrance the boys at once stood up and salaamed. The Hodja school-master made a gesture, as if he too would rise ; but then, seeing me, his countenance changed. He sank back into a sitting position.

"This is done to show his contempt of you as a giaour," whispered an Armenian. "This is how he insults us Christians."

The Caimacan turned a little red when he saw the school-master thus seated in his presence. However, he did not make any remark, but accompanied me to the Armenian school.

There were about a hundred boys in the establishment. The moment I arrived they commenced an Armenian song, headed by one of the masters—an elderly gentleman, who sang through his nose. A performer on an ancient harpsi-chord, which from its signs of age might have belonged to Queen Anne, accompanied the vocalists. The words, I was informed, were about the glories of Armenia, what a fine nation the Armenians were, and how some day Armenia will lift up her head once more. My host interpreted to me these verses.

"Do you think that Armenia will ever be independent ?" I inquired.

He shook his head.

"Russia will very likely be here in a year or two, and then we shall be much more oppressed than we are at present. Why, the Russian Government will not allow this song to be sung in our schools at Tiflis. Everything is done to make my fellow-countrymen in the Caucasus forget their own language and nationality, and to thoroughly Russify them. If the Russians were to come here, our religion would soon disappear," he continued.

"But some of your priests rather like the Russians ?"

"Some people would sell their souls to obtain a cross or an order," said another Armenian. "But every patriot amongst us who has read of what our country once was will scorn the idea of being degraded into a Muscovite."

"Are the Russians so very degraded ?" I remarked.

"They possess all the vices of the Turks, and none of their good qualities. They drink like swine ; many of their officials embezzle the public money; and as to lying, they can even outdo the Greeks in this respect."

"You have not a high opinion of the Tzar's people?" I observed.

"No, Effendi; better a hundred times remain as we are than be forced to submit to his rule."

"Is that really so? I thought that you were always complaining about the want of liberty in Turkey," I remarked.

"Yes, Effendi, all we wish for is to be placed on the same footing as the Turks themselves. This is the Sultan's desire; a firman has been issued to that effect, but it is a dead letter. The Cadis ought to carry out the law; they will not do so. They ought to be forced to carry out the Padishah's orders."

On returning to my quarters, the Caimacan, who accompanied me, remarked,—

"Effendi, did you notice the Hodja's (schoolmaster) conduct?"

"I did."

"I was sorry to remark that he did not stand up when you entered the room."

"It was a very bad example for the boys; they could plainly see that their preceptor did not hold the chief magistrate of the town in much respect," I observed.

The Caimacan hesitated for a moment, and then remarked,—

"Oh! it was not on my own account that I spoke, but for the sake of the Effendi, who is an Englishman. It was an insult to him."

"Not in the least," I remarked. "How could it have been, when you were present? Why, you would have taken notice of it immediately."

"I did," said the Caimacan drily, "and the schoolmaster is in prison!"

"Is in prison? What for?"

"For contempt of his superiors."

"How long shall you keep him there?"

"That depends upon you, but he has been shut up about two hours already."

"I should think that it would be sufficient," I remarked.

"Shall I send and have him released?" said the Caimacan.

"Yes, if you think that he has sufficiently atoned for the way in which he insulted you; but make him come here and apologize for his conduct."

My Armenian host now came to me.

"Do not ask for that," he remarked. "All the fanatics amongst the Turks would be furious with me if they heard that the schoolmaster had been forcibly brought to my house to apologize to you, a giaour. The fellow has had a good lesson," he continued, "and will be more particular the next time he sees a European."

"Are there many fanatics in this neighbourhood?" I inquired.

"Not more so than in other parts of Turkey; it is everywhere very much the same. What ought to be done," continued the speaker, "would be to establish large schools, and insist upon the parents sending their children to be taught. If Mohammedan and Christian boys and girls were to meet in the same schoolroom, and learn their lessons together, they would be more likely to mutually respect each other in after-life. To carry this idea into execution, it would first be necessary to procure a staff of efficient schoolmasters. There ought to be a college for Hodjas in Constantinople, where Mohammedan and Christian young men could be educated, and pass an examination as to their efficiency. We should then have qualified men as teachers, instead of the ignorant fanatics who now usurp the office. There is another reform which we require," continued my host, "and this is that the Mudirs, Caimacans and Pachas in the different provinces should not be exclusively Turks. The various posts ought to be open to every sect. We are all, Christians as well as Mohammedans, the Sultan's subjects; then why make a difference? If the Turkish lower orders saw that Armenians were sometimes selected to be Pachas and Caimacans, they would be more likely to respect the Christian community."

"Do the Turks often insult your religion?" I inquired.

"No, not often, but they call us giaours (infidels)."

"Yes," said another Armenian, a professor at the Armenian school, and who could speak a little French; "in Malattia there are twelve thousand inhabitants, made up of three thousand Christians and nine thousand Turks. Only three months ago some Mohammedans in that town made a cross and tied it to the tail of a dog. The hound ran through the streets of the town; the little boys threw stones at him, and the holy symbol was dragged in the mud."

"This is very horrible," I remarked. "Did you see it yourself?"

" No, but I have heard of it."

" Who told you ? "

" A man in Arabkir."

" Had he seen it ? "

" No, he had not been in Malattia, but he had been told the story. Every one has heard of it."

" We are in the East," I observed to my host, " and it appears to me that you Christians are very much given to exaggeration."

" Yes, Effendi ; we want newspapers. If we only had newspapers we should then know the truth. How fortunate you must be in England to have so many newspapers ! "

" Even they contradict each other sometimes," I remarked.

" Perhaps. But you are a great nation ; I should like to be an Englishman."

" So should I," said the schoolmaster.

The mercury in the thermometer fell very much during the night. It was a frosty morning. The steep streets of Arabkir were extremely slippery. It was difficult enough for a man on foot to avoid falling ; as we led our horses down the treacherous inclines, the poor brutes skated about in all directions.

We crossed a rapid stream, fifty yards wide, on a fairly strong bridge—this river runs into the Euphrates, forty miles south of Arabkir—and next had to lead our animals through a difficult and mountainous district.

The track was very narrow. It generally sloped towards a precipice. In some instances there was a clear drop of at least 400 feet within six inches of our horses. The surface upon which they had to walk was like glass. A slip would have been certain death ; it was marvellous how they avoided stumbling. In about three hours' time we reached Shephe, an Armenian village. I halted here for a few minutes to bait our animals.

The proprietor of the house where we dismounted spoke highly of the Caimacan at Arabkir. However, he freely cursed the Kurds, who in the summer-time committed many depredations in the neighbourhood. In the months of June and July, no man's life was in safety. There were so few Zaptiehs in the province that the robbers could carry on their trade with impunity.

Presently we passed a stream called the Erman Su. It is spanned by a good stone bridge. On reaching the other side,

I found myself in a broad, well-cultivated plain. The ruins of a large city lay heaped up by the river's banks. This was the site of Hara Bazar, an Armenian town which flourished long before either Arabkir or Egin were built. The ruins lay some little distance from the path; I did not visit them. My guide informed me that the débris consists of enormous stones. These are the wonder of the villagers, who generally build their houses of mud. They cannot conceive what manner of men were their ancestors who had taken the trouble to bring such massive slabs from the distant mountains. The village of Ashoot stands in the middle of the plain, and is composed of fifty-one houses, all belonging to Mohammedans. The inhabitants, for Turks, were extremely wealthy; some nice-looking Arab horses stood in my host's drawing-room. He was the chief person in the village, and presently informed me that twenty soldiers, who were on their way to Erzeroum, had deserted, a few days before, from a hamlet about six miles distant. He had been on their track, and would certainly have shot the culprits if he had been able to catch them. There had been no officer with these soldiers. The men had been left to find their way to Erzeroum without even being accompanied by a sergeant.

"Three days ago," continued my informant, "a battalion, 800 strong, came to this village. The officer in command demanded from the inhabitants nine mules for the transport of his sick men. The amount to be paid by him for the hire of the animals to Egin was fixed at 200 piastres (about 1*l.* of our money). The officer omitted to settle the account. The villagers have applied to the police authorities at Egin for the sum, and are very angry because it has not been paid."

A Usebashe (captain) now called. He had just arrived from Erzeroum, and declared that there was a report in that town to the effect that Yakoob, Khan of Kashgar, had attacked the Russians near Tashkent—had utterly defeated them, and taken 20,000 prisoners and twenty guns.

"Allah grant that it may prove true!" said my host. "Twenty thousand sons of dogs in captivity! This is something! I hope Yakoob has cut all their throats."

"God is evidently on our side!" said the village Imaum.

"The Russians say He is on theirs," I remarked.

"Yes," replied the Imaum. "Infidels even can take the name of the Highest One in vain. But this time they will be punished, and the Prophet is already arranging a plan for their destruction."

CHAPTER XXXV

Radford—His health — The farmer's house—The high elevation—My brother will look down the precipices—The Frat—The scenery—A caravan—How to pass it—The weather—Turks in Egin—A coracle—Beautiful fish—Sick soldiers—Twenty-four hours without food—Egin—The Caimacan—The Cadi—His story—Daniel—Samson—His riches, his 10,000 wives, all of them fat and lovely—His treasure-chests—The lovely daughters of the mountaineers—The officers died ; the Pachas died ; and last of all, Samson died—The fate of the Russians.

I WAS beginning to be a little alarmed about the health of my servant Radford. So far he had not been ill, and had resisted the fatigue of wading through deep snow, of bad sleeping accommodation and indifferent fare. He had complained of a pain in his heart, during our march that morning, and had not been able to walk up-hill save at a very slow rate. On arriving at the farmer's house, he had lain down in a corner, and, according to Mohammed, was very ill. I went to him, and, feeling his pulse, found that it intermitted. He was feverish, and complained of a pain in the head.

" Would he be able to march the following day ? "

" He thought he should."

I was exceedingly doubtful about it ; and, leaving word with Mohammed to call me, should his fellow-servant be taken worse in the night, I lay down by the side of our horses and tried to go to sleep.

I myself, for several days past, had experienced considerable difficulty in wading through the snow, but was inclined to believe that this was owing to our elevation above the level of the sea, and that the diminished pressure of air upon my body, combined with the hard work, was the real cause of this weakness. However, the fact remained that the poor fellow was knocked up. It would be impossible to remain for more than a day or two in our present quarters. I determined to push on as fast as his health would permit to Erzingan ; for once there we should be within a nine days' march of Trebizonde, and it would be possible, if he were still poorly, for me to send him home to his relations.

To my great delight he was a little better in the morning,

though still very weak. He would have been unable to walk ;
he had strength enough left to sit on a horse. I gave orders
that he was on no account to go on foot, and resolved to let
him ride my horse from time to time, should his own animal
be unable to carry him through the drifts.

" My brother will be on horseback all the day. He will
look well down the precipices," said Mohammed with a
chuckle.

He had observed that the Englishman did not relish riding
a few inches from a chasm, and Mohammed was rather amused
to learn that his fellow-servant would now no longer have the
chance of walking by the precipices. He himself, though not
particularly brave in other respects, never seemed to value his
neck when on horseback. No matter how steep the slopes
might be, Mohammed seldom or ever took the trouble to dismount from his animal, which, under the influence of two good
feeds of barley every day, had improved considerably since the
march from Tokat.

" Why should I dismount ? " Mohammed would say. " If
I am to slip and be killed, it will happen, and I cannot
prevent it."

The fellow had been accustomed to a mountainous country
all his life, and had previously been employed as a Zaptieh.
This may account for his coolness on horseback. But, at a
later period of the journey, and when it was necessary for us
to descend some rapids in a boat, Mohammed showed unmistakable signs of fear, and was not at all to be consoled by
Radford's remark that, if he (Mohammed) were to be drowned,
it would be his fate, and so would not signify.

We reached the crest of a lofty height. A wide stream
appeared below our feet.

" What is the name of that river ? " I inquired. The welcome announcement, " The Frat," made me aware that at last
I had arrived on the banks of the Euphrates—here a broad
stream about 120 yards wide and nine or ten feet deep.
Numerous boulders half choked up the river's channel. The
waves splashed high in the air as they bounded over these
obstacles ; the sound of the troubled waters could be distinctly
heard even at our elevation.

We continued the march alongside the bank of the world-
renowned river. The path was cut out of the solid rock. In
some places the track was not above four feet wide. No
balustrade or wall had been made to keep a horse or rider from

slipping down the chasm. Presently the road wound still higher amidst the mountains. The river beneath us seemed no broader than a silver thread.

On we went. The sound of bells made us aware that there was a caravan approaching. Our guide rode first. A few moments later, about 100 mules, all laden with merchandise, could be seen coming towards our party. We should have to pass them; how to do so seemed a difficult problem to solve. The track was not wider than an average dinner-table.

The guide soon settled the matter. Taking a whip, he struck the leading mule; the latter, to avoid punishment, ran with his load up a steep slope along the side of the path. The rest of the animals followed. There seemed to be scarcely foothold for a goat, but the mules found one. They were removed from the path on which we stood; my people could advance in safety.

Numbers of vines clad the lower part of the mountain slopes. Here and there a few châlets made of white stone could be seen. These, I was informed, belong to the wealthier Turks of Egin, who come to reside here during the grape season.

Below us some fishermen were seated in a boat apparently made of basket-work. It looked like a Welsh coracle, but was of much larger dimensions. They were engaged in fishing with a sort of drag-net; one of them was busily employed in mending a smaller one of the same kind.

"Beautiful fish are caught here," said the guide. "Some are 100 okes in weight (about 260 lbs.). The people salt, and eat them in the winter."

We met some sick soldiers lying across the path. They had fallen out of the ranks and were basking themselves in the sun, utterly regardless of the fact that their battalion was, ere this, a two hours' march ahead of them.

"What is the matter with you?" I inquired of one man.

"Footsore," was his reply, at the same time pointing to his frost-bitten feet.

"And with you?" to another.

"I, Effendi, I am weak and hungry.

"What! have you had no breakfast?"

"No."

I then discovered that these soldiers had been twenty-four hours without food! There was no grumbling at this break-down in the commissariat department. The men were solacing themselves with a cigarette, the property of one of the party, and which he was sharing with his comrades.

Our route leads us by some high rocks. They are broken into strange and fantastic forms; they rear themselves up on each bank of the Euphrates, and frown down on the waters below. Here domes and pinnacles stand out in bold relief; there, the figure of a man, shaped as if from the hands of a sculptor, is balanced on a projecting stone, and totters on the brink of the abyss.

Mulberry and apple-trees grow in wild profusion along the banks. We leave them behind. The track steadily ascends. We are more than 1200 feet from the waters. I gaze down on the mighty river; it winds its serpent-like coils at our feet. They twist and foam and lose themselves behind the crags. Higher we go.

Vegetation disappears, we are in the realms of snow; continuing for some miles over the waste, the path descends into a valley. Egin lies before us.

It is a long, straggling town, with a population of 10,000 souls, and much resembles Arabkir. We rode over the roofs of many houses ere we reached our destination—the house of an Armenian merchant, who had ridden out himself to place it at our disposal. The following day I called upon the Caimacan— a little man, who spoke Italian very fairly. He had been only seven months at his present post. The Cadi was seated at his side. After the governor had announced that the Conference was a failure—a piece of news which I had heard before—the Cadi observed that he should like to tell me a story.

" He relates a story very well," said the Caimacan.

" We all like his stories," said the rest of the company.

" By all means," I said; and the Cadi, thus encouraged, began,—

" Many thousand years ago there was a prophet—he was a great man, he was a marvel—his name was Daniel ! "

This last word was duly repeated by the assembled guests; and the Caimacan gave a little cough.

" I have heard this story before," he observed; " but it is a good one. Go on."

" Well," continued the Cadi, " Daniel had a dream. In his dream he saw a young man, Samson was his name. Samson was beautifully dressed; his clothes alone would have cost all the gold and caime that have ever been circulated at Constantinople. The rings on his fingers were encrusted with precious stones—beautiful stones—each one more bright and lovely than the eye of the most beautiful woman whom mortal man has ever seen.

"But, Samson himself was pale, his features were wasted away; he was very thin, and, on carefully looking at him, Daniel discovered that he was dead. There was a large scroll of paper lying at his feet. No other man could have deciphered the letters on it; but the Prophet read them at once, and he galloped his eye over the scroll with the same rapidity as a hunter in pursuit of a hare——"

"He read very quickly!" interrupted the Caimacan.

"Daniel was a Hodja" (learned man), observed the Cadi indignantly; "of course he did!"

"Samson had conquered almost the whole world," continued the speaker; "but there was one very poor and mountainous country which did not acknowledge him as its lord.

"Samson had 10,000 wives, all of them fat and lovely. The keys of his treasure-chests were in themselves a load for 10,000 camels. He was all vigorous and able to enjoy every blessing which Allah had bestowed upon him——"

"Was he not satisfied with 10,000 wives?" remarked one of the audience.

"No," said the Cadi. "Some men are never satisfied; Samson was one of them. He wanted more. His heart was not full, he wished to conquer the poor country, and take a few wives from the lovely daughters of the mountaineers. He came with an enormous army. The people fled. The troops ate up everything. There were no more provisions. There was nothing left even for the king. Samson offered 10,000 sacks of gold for a handful of millet-seed. It could not be purchased. The soldiers died; the sergeants died; the officers died; the Pachas died; and, last of all, Samson died.

"Let this be the fate of the Russians if they come here," added the Cadi. "The Tzar has much land—he is rich—he has many more soldiers than we have, he has everything to make life happy. Yet he is not content; he wishes to take from his poor neighbour the pittance which he possesses. Let Allah judge between him and us," continued the speaker. "And God alone knows who will be victorious!"

"We shall beat them!" said the Caimacan.

Soon afterwards my visit came to an end.

CHAPTER XXXVI

The Armenian church—The devotees—The ladies—The priest—His toilet
—Little boys—A song for the Queen of England—These Armenians
are very dirty—A hymn sung in English—The inhabitants of Egin—
Turkish doctors—A *post mortem* examination—Price of meat—Russian
agents—The massacres in Bulgaria—The Hasta Dagh mountain—The
descent of the glacier—I never thought as how a horse could skate,
sir, before!

I NOW went to the Armenian church. It was carpeted with
thick Persian rugs like a mosque. Several pictures in gaudy
frames were hung against the wall. The building was
crowded with devotees; the galleries being filled with women;
their faces were invisible, owing to the lattice-work. However, some bright eyes peering inquisitively through the holes
in the screen were quite sufficient to turn a man's thoughts in
their direction.

The priest put on his robes—several little boys assisting
him in his toilette; a heavy, yellow silk garment, with a cross
emblazoned in gold upon the back, was drawn on over his
every-day apparel. Some more little boys bustled about with
long candles, and seemed to do their best to get into each
other's way, then the service began.

Two songs were sung by the choir—first one for the Queen
of England, as a sort of compliment to the nationality of the
foreign visitor; and then another for the Sultan. The old
priest next addressed the congregation, and said that they
must do everything in their power to help the Sultan in this
war against Russia, who was a mortal enemy to the Armenian
religion.

The Caimacan was standing by me in the church, and
seemed pleased at the discourse.

"It is good! very good!" he said. "I wonder if the
priest means it."

The worthy Turk's meditations were suddenly interrupted.
Some insect had bitten him.

"These Armenians are very dirty, they do not wash," he
added. "Let us go."

Everybody bowed as he walked down the nave, and we
then proceeded to the Protestant church.

This was nothing but a large room in the clergyman's house.
On our entry, some boys sang a hymn in English. They
pronounced the words tolerably well, though they were

ignorant of their meaning, the clergyman who spoke our language having taught his pupils merely to read the Roman characters. There were no pictures or images of any kind in the room. A simple baptismal font was its sole ornament. After the hymn had concluded, the clergyman, without putting on any extra vestments, addressed his congregation in a few straightforward and practical sentences, saying that as it was the duty of the Jews to pay tribute to Cæsar, it was equally proper for all true Christians to respect the Turkish authorities; that the Turks were on the eve of a great struggle with a power which oppressed all religions but its own, and consequently it was the duty of all Armenian Protestants to aid the Government in the forthcoming struggle, and shed the last drop of their blood for the Padishah.

The inhabitants of the town are not a trading community, most of them live by agriculture. There was a considerable amount of grumbling to be heard about the bankrupt state of the country; I learnt that many of the farmers had invested their savings in Turkish bonds, and had lost their capital. A Greek doctor who gave me this information had been established for many years in Egin.

" What do you think of the Turkish doctors?" I inquired.

" They are very ignorant," he replied; "but what can you expect in a country where it is not permitted to study anatomy, &c., in a practical way?"

" What, do they not allow dissection?" I asked.

" No. And even if you were convinced that a patient had died of poison, it would be very difficult to obtain permission to make a *post mortem* examination of his body. The result is that poisoners go unpunished. The Turkish surgeons are so ignorant that they cannot even tie up an artery, much less perform an average operation."

The Caimacan now joined in our conversation, which was in Italian, and began to find fault with the old school of Turks, which is an enemy to education, and bigoted about religious matters.

" I make no difference between a Christian or a Mussulman," said the governor. " All religions are good, provided that the man who practises them is honest."

" What we require are schools for the elder Turks," he continued; "something to force them to advance with the age, and to make them forget that old maxim, 'What was good for my father, is it not good enough for me?' Until they forget this, there will not be much improvement in Turkey. A company once offered to make a railway from Diarbekir to Constantinople, and, if Sultan Abdul Aziz had not spent all the money he borrowed from you English people in palaces and his harem, the railway might have been made. Meat is here only one penny a pound; at our seaports you have to pay fourpence for the same quantity. We have mines, too, but no means of transporting the mineral if we worked them. I have been at Egin six months," he continued. "I may be dismissed at any moment. What inducement is there for a man to try and improve the condition of the people, when all his work may be upset by his successor? We Caimacans are underpaid," he added. "We have not enough to live upon. If we received a better salary, and our positions were more stable, there would be less bribery throughout the Turkish empire."

"Do you believe that there are many Russian agents in the neighbourhood?" I inquired.

"Undoubtedly; particularly at Erzeroum, and there they intrigue with the Armenian clergy. In the other towns the Armenians will not have much to say to them. The Russians are more unpopular near the frontier of the two empires than elsewhere. We are spoken of very harshly in Europe," continued the Caimacan. "The massacres in Bulgaria were very horrible, but they were the work of a few fanatics, and brought about by Russian instigation. It is hard upon us for people to judge of the entire Turkish nation by the misdeeds of a few Circassians."

My host insisted upon seeing me off, and the following morning we walked down to the narrow wooden bridge which spans the Euphrates—here about forty yards wide.

After crossing the river, our course lay across the Hasta Dagh (mountain). Presently we came to a glacier. The frozen surface extended for at least one hundred yards. The incline was steeper than the roof of an average English house.

How was this to be passed? Radford looked at Mohammed. The latter gave a grunt.

"What do you think of it, Mohammed?" I asked.

"Effendi, we shall go down very fast. If the Lord wills it, we shall not break our bones."

"If we do not take this route," said the guide, "we must

make a détour for at least two hours. I think the horses can manage it, Effendi."

" Very well," I said, " you can try."

The guide rode his horse to the glacier. The poor animal trembled when he reached the brink.

"*Haide*, get on?" cried Mohammed from behind, and, striking the quadruped on his flanks, the animal stretched his fore-legs over the declivity, almost touching the slippery surface with his girth.

Another crack with the whip, away went the guide and horse down the glacier. For the first fifty yards the man succeeded in keeping his steed's head straight. A slight inequality in the ice gave the animal's hoof a twist in another direction ; horse and rider went round in mazy circles ; they had nearly obtained the velocity of an express train, when they were suddenly brought up by a snow-drift. There was not much damage done, and now I prepared to make the descent. It was not an agreeable sensation. I was on the edge of the precipice. The yelling Mohammed was castigating my animal from behind. I felt very much like Mr. Winkle, as described in the "Pickwick Papers," the first time he was on skates. I would have gladly given Mohammed five shillings or a new coat to desist from the flagellating process. However, the die was cast. My followers were looking on. What the guide had done it was very clear that an English-man ought to do. I committed myself to Providence. Away we went. The steam roundabouts in the Champs Elysées in Paris revolve at a great pace ; a slide down the artificial ice-hills in St. Petersburg will sometimes try a man's nerves ; but the sensations experienced in these manners of locomotion are nothing to what I felt when sliding down that glacier. Was I on my horse or was I not? Now we were waltzing madly down the slippery surface, and then my boots were touching the ice itself, owing to my animal's position. One moment we ricochetted from a rough piece of the hard substance, and were flying in the air, as if jumping the Whissendine brook ; a second later we were buried, as the guide had been, in six feet of snow.

Next came the turn of my followers. Their descent was a fearful thing to witness, but, fortunately, not half so dangerous as it appeared. With the exception of some damage to the luggage and saddlery, there was little harm done.

" I never thought as how a horse could skate, sir, before ! "

remarked my English servant, as he slowly extricated himself
from the snow-drift. "It was more than sliding, that it was
—a cutting of figures of eight all down the roof of a house!
And then I was buried alive in snow, to finish up with!
Mohammed will have something to pray about, if he has to
go down any more of these hills, for nothing but Providence
can save a man's neck in these here parts."

CHAPTER XXXVII

Hasta Khan—The Kurds—Their summer depredations—Our Sultan ought
to be Padishah in his own dominions—The English Consul—A story
about the Kurds—The Delsin—Arresting the major—The major's
dinner with the chief—Acknowledge the Padishah—A sore back—The
mule which is offered in exchange—The pack-saddle—The Euphrates
—Coal in the neighbourhood—Kemach—The Caimacan—Djerrid—A
National Guard—A miniature Gibraltar—Turkoman horses—Numerous
wells—One of the faithful.

On we went, fortunately not down any more glaciers, and,
after being upset about twenty times in the snow-drifts, reached
Hasta Khan. This was a house built on the road-side for
travellers. It was kept by an old Turk. According to him,
the Kurds in the neighbourhood were engaged all the summer
in robbing their neighbours, and were hardly ever brought to
justice.

"They take our cattle," said the man, "and they bribe the
police. There is no sort of order here. What we want is
our Sultan to be Padishah in his own dominions."

I subsequently heard from the English Consul at Erzeroum
a story which rather corroborated the Turk's account of the
Kurds.

It appeared that in the Delsin, not far from Erzingan, a
major commanding a battalion of infantry received orders to
apprehend a Kurdish chief. Somehow or other the Kurd
heard of this. One day, taking with him about five thousand
followers, he managed to surround the place where the troops
were encamped. Riding up to the commander's tent, he
accosted the officer—who was much surprised at the unexpected presence of the culprit—with the words,—

"Peace be with you! I have come to dine here this
evening."

It was a very disagreeable position for the major, but what

could he do ? His battalion had been taken unawares ; it was surrounded by the Kurd's followers, and all of them were armed men. He put on the best face he could about the matter, and gave his guest an excellent dinner. The following morning the Kurd said to him,—

"I dined very well last night, and slept comfortably. I have accepted your hospitality, and now you must accept mine. I am going to take you to dine with me. Nay, I am!" he continued, to the officer, who appeared a little indignant at the proposal, "and every man under your command as well. They shall all dine and sleep in my encampment this evening."

"It was a disagreeable position for the major," observed the Consul at Erzeroum, when he related the story to me. "He was ordered to arrest the Kurd, and now the Kurd was about to arrest him ! However, resistance was useless. His battalion was surrounded by Kurds, who, at a sign from their chief, would have massacred every Turk on the spot. The only thing for the officer to do was to accept the invitation. The Kurd, when the soldiers arrived at his mountain home, commanded his servants to make preparation for a feast. Several hundred sheep were killed, to be cooked for the occasion, and the stream on the hill-side ran red with the blood of the slaughtered animals."

After dinner the major tried very hard to persuade the Kurd to recognize the Sultan as his lord.

"You need only nominally acknowledge our Padishah," remarked the officer ; "you have 30,000 sheep : give 1500 piastres (10*l*.) a year to the Sultan. You have 10,000 retainers ; give him 10 to serve in his army. I can arrange the rest. You are a very rich man, but this need not be known at Constantinople."

"I have never given any one of my children to serve another master," replied the chieftain, proudly. "Your Padishah is Sultan at Stamboul, but I am Sultan here!"

The following morning, the Kurd allowed the battalion to return to their quarters, and presented the major with an Arab charger as a memento of his visit.

"All the circumstances were reported to the military authorities at Erzeroum," added the Consul when he related the story, "and the officer was afterwards promoted."

Shortly before leaving Hasta Khan, Mohammed came to me with a smile on his countenance. I at once thought that

something disagreeable had happened. The Turk seldom
indulged in a smile. Radford, too, in spite of his illness,
seemed rather more cheerful than usual. I began to be a
little alarmed.

"What is the matter?" I inquired.

"*At*—the horse!" said Mohammed.

"Yes, sir," said Radford, who had accompanied him, and
had acquired the habit of sometimes interlarding his English
with a few words of Turkish; "the At has a hawful sore
back, and all the 'air is off it."

"Which horse?"

"The old pack-horse, the roarer."

Mohammed shook his head mournfully.

"We had better sell him," he said. "One of the Zaptiehs
has a mule; he is not a big mule, but he is a nice animal,
sleek and comely, besides being strong. The man says that
if the Effendi will give him five liras and the horse which
makes a noise, that we may have his mule."

The animal in question was a brute which the gendarme
rode, and which was always trying to run away. I had
previously gathered from the fellow that his mule had
escaped three times whilst he was being saddled. However,
the gendarme had forgotten that he had told me of this, and
in all probability had offered Mohammed a share of the five
liras, should I be fool enough to accept the proposal.

"Let me see the pack-saddle!" I exclaimed.

On looking at it I found that by cutting out a considerable
portion of the lining, it would be possible to prevent any
weight pressing upon the horse's sore place.

"He can carry his pack," I remarked to Mohammed.

"If I cut the saddle he can," replied my servant; "but it
will cost twenty piastres to mend it again."

"Yes," I observed, "and it will cost five liras to exchange
the horse, besides which we should have a worse animal than
at present."

"The Effendi knows best," said the Zaptieh, with a grin.

"He knows," said Mohammed.

"Shall I have a little backsheesh?" remarked the gendarme,
rather alarmed lest his endeavour to deceive me might have
done away with his chance of a present.

"Inshallah!" I replied; and, this matter being arranged,
we continued our march across the mountains.

Presently we had to descend almost to the bed of the

Euphrates. Here there were traces of copper ore. A little farther on we came to a place where what seemed to be iron ore was lying strewn along the mountain side; I was informed by the guide that a few miles to the east there is a substance in the earth which the villagers use as fuel. According to my informant it is hard and black, and gives a bright flame; so in all probability coal is also to be met with in these regions.

As we approached Kemach, the Euphrates became narrower; in many places it was not more than thirty yards wide. The stream was very rapid. Any man, no matter how good a swimmer he might be, would have a poor chance for his life if he were to fall into the torrent. Here and there large rocks and loose stones, which have been washed down from the mountain sides, block up the channel; they check the waters for a second. The river bubbles and roars; it lashes furiously against the boulders, and, leaping over them, rushes headlong with a fall of at least four thousand feet to the ocean.

The Caimacan of Kemach and a few of his friends were engaged in playing at Djerrid near the outskirts of the town. It was a lovely scene. The sun was setting on the snow-capped mountains; the river ran at my feet; bright-coloured vegetation and many-tinted rocks looked down upon us from either hand; cascades and waterfalls dashed over the rugged crags; whilst the Caimacan and his party, who were immensely excited with their game, shouted "Allah! Allah!" as they rode at each other and hurled the wooden missile.

The governor stopped playing when he saw our party, and, riding up, asked the Zaptieh who I was. He then introduced himself and the company to me. They had been busily engaged in learning drill all the morning. An order had been received from Constantinople for the Caimacan to form a National Guard. Every able-bodied man in the district had at once enrolled himself as a volunteer. On entering Kemach I was struck by a high rock, which might have been a miniature Gibraltar, and which stands immediately behind the town. The rock was about 500 feet in height, and a ruined citadel on the summit towers above the Euphrates and the town.

The Caimacan and his friends were well mounted, their horses being of a very different stamp to those which I had seen during my march from Constantinople. They were most of them fifteen hands high, and one or two over sixteen. On inquiry, I found that they were Turkoman horses. I also learnt that most of the animals in the district had been bought by Government agents for the use of the army at Erzeroum.

A large proportion of the houses in Kemach are constructed of dried mud. Numerous wells, with high cross-bars and long iron chains for the buckets, were to be seen along our path. One of the faithful, on a tower above our heads, was calling the Mohammedans to prayer. His loud but melancholy strains were being listened to with great attention by Mohammed and my English servant. It appeared that Mohammed, through some strange inadvertence, had omitted praying at mid-day. Radford was a little alarmed lest the Turk might make up for his shortcoming by an extra-long prayer that evening, which would have kept him from attending to the horses.

CHAPTER XXXVIII

Kemach—Its population—Barley is very cheap—An English traveller— Conversation about the impending war—If we beat Russia, will England permit us to take back the Caucasus?—Yakoob Khan—The Poles to be freed—Germany to have the Baltic Provinces—What about the Crimea? —We ought to cripple Russia—The floggers of women—Crossing the Euphrates—Radford is poorly—Erzingan—The intendant of Issek Pacha—Pretty Armenian women—An intelligent Turk—Iron, silver, gold—Coal—Lead-mines worked by the Kurds—The peasantry and coal—The Government and the mines—A relation of the Pacha of Sivas—The old doctor—Firing a patient for gout.

THERE are 800 houses or about 4000 inhabitants in Kemach, and barley is very plentiful throughout the district, the price for the maintenance of my five horses not exceeding sevenpence per day.

This town had been visited by an English traveller about five years previous; whereas no Englishman, so far as I could learn, had been in Divriki or Arabkir in the memory of the oldest inhabitant.

The Caimacan, who informed me about my compatriot having been in Kemach, was very curious to learn my opinion about the impending war; and when I told him that I believed England would remain neutral, remarked,—

" Yes; but if we beat Russia, will England permit us to take back the Caucasus?"

" I really do not know, but I should hope so."

" Well," continued the governor, " if we beat Russia this

time, we ought to cripple her. We must take back the districts she has conquered in Central Asia, and give them to the original possessors, or else form one Mohammedan empire in Central Asia, under Yakoob Khan, who nominally acknowledges the Sultan. We ought to free the Poles in Poland, and give Germany the Baltic Provinces."

"You seem to know a little about political geography," I observed.

"Yes," said the Caimacan, "I take an interest in the subject, and I love my country. Until we can hem Russia in on every side, she will always be a thorn, not only in our side, but also in that of Europe."

"Well, what should you do about the Crimea?" I inquired.

"That we should keep ourselves. Russia would then have to be more or less an inland power, and Moscow would become her capital."

"Do you like the Russian system of government?" inquired the Caimacan.

"No."

"I am not surprised," said the official. "Foreigners say that there is no liberty in Turkey, but I should like to know which Government is the most liberal. Mohammedans tolerate every religion, whilst the Russians make converts by force, and flog women and children to induce them to change their faith.* The Russian faith is very different to the English religion, is it not?" he added.

"Yes, we do not worship idols, or venerate mummified bodies."

"What do you worship?"

"The one true God, and Jesus Christ His Son."

"We worship the one true God, and worship Him through Mohammed His Prophet. But Mohammedans dislike idols and all that sort of thing, quite as much as you do."

The following morning the Caimacan was up at daybreak to see me off. He accompanied us a little way on the road. The moon was throwing her pale beams on the old citadel as we rode beneath the turrets. In a few minutes we crossed the Euphrates on a narrow wooden bridge, and, continuing for a short distance over mountains, came again upon the valley of the river. Here there were green fields in abundance. The country in summer-time is said to be rich in corn and

* The Caimacan did not exaggerate, judging by Consul-Gen. Mansfield's official Report, see Appendix I., also Appendices II. and III.

barley.   Hundreds of cattle and sheep, grazing on some rich
pasture-lands, testified to the wealth of the inhabitants.

It was an eleven hours' march to Erzingan.   By the time
we neared that city our horses showed symptoms of being
thoroughly exhausted.   Indeed, there was no reason to be
surprised at this.   They had marched a thousand miles since
we left Constantinople.   The last two hundred miles had
been exceptionally fatiguing, not only on account of the snow
and constant mountain-climbing, but also owing to our high
elevation and the rarefied nature of the atmosphere.   Radford
was weak, and from being a fourteen-stone man had come down
to about eleven.   His clothes hung on his wasted limbs.
Some rest would be absolutely necessary to enable him to
reach Erzeroum.

The road became much better as we entered the suburbs of
Erzingan, and, to my surprise, I was met by a man in a four-
wheeled chaise.   He announced that he was the intendant of
Issek Pacha, the governor of Sivas.   The governor had
written to him to say that I had promised to reside in his
house during my stay at Erzingan.   A servant advanced and
took my horse; I dismounted, and getting into the vehicle,
drove to the Pacha's residence.

Some pretty Armenian women were standing on the roofs
of their houses.   They were not so particular about veiling
themselves as their compatriots in Sivas.   They stared at the
procession with wondering eyes.   The Pacha's carriage was
not often seen in the streets of Erzingan.   It was the only
vehicle of the kind within an area of 150 miles.   It was only
brought out on state occasions, religious ceremonies, or when
some very important visitor arrived.   This was quite enough
to set the ladies in Erzingan on the *qui-vive ;* the European
dresses of my servant and self whetted their curiosity still
more.

Erzingan is different to either Egin or Arabkir, both of
which towns are built upon the sides of a mountain.   Erzingan
stands in the middle of a large plain, the Kara Su—Black
Water—as the Euphrates is here called, running through·the
plain a few miles south of the city.

I now made the acquaintance of a very intelligent Turk.
He was an officer with the rank of major, but employed as
the superintendent of a large manufactory, which had been
established to supply the troops in Asia Minor with boots.
He had spent three years in France, where he had studied

everything connected with the trade in question. In addition to this he was a fair chemist and mineralogist.

He informed me that there were ebony forests in the neighbourhood of Erzeroum. A great deal of this wood used formerly to be bought by Armenian merchants and despatched to France. Of late years this branch of industry has been neglected. Iron, silver, and gold could be found here, but the people were much too idle to search for these metals. The lead-mines were worked to a small extent by the Kurds. These mountaineers required this substance for bullets and shot. The lead in the towns of Asia Minor was all brought from Constantinople. It was, consequently, very dear; this had led the Kurds to make use of the metal beneath their feet. According to my informant, there is coal of a good quality in the neighbourhood of Kemach. However, the peasantry do not like the idea that this mineral may some day replace wood as an article of fuel. Cutting down trees is easy work in comparison with mining. The villagers do their best to keep the people in the towns from burning coal; and they make their livelihood by bringing firewood from the mountains, and selling it at a large profit to the citizens.

The Government take twenty per cent. of the net produce of all mines which are worked in Anatolia, and only two-and-a-half per cent. from the price fetched by sheep, oxen, and horses in the market. The result is that the people think it more profitable and less laborious to breed cattle, than to dig in the earth for treasure.

I called upon a relation of the Pacha at Sivas. He was a stout, middle-aged man, and at that time ill in bed. I was shown into his room. During my conversation with him, an Italian doctor came to see the patient. The medical gentleman was the only European in Erzingan, he had been there half a century; his age, according to himself, being ninety-two years. The old man's appearance belied his assertion. He at once commenced talking with me in his native tongue.

" What is the matter with the invalid ? " I inquired.

" Drink, my good sir, drink ! " said the old gentleman. " He is forty, and I am over ninety, but, please God, as the Turks say, I shall outlive him. If the upper classes of Mohammedans were only sober, they would live for ever in this delightful climate. But what with their women, and what with their wine, they shorten their existence by at least thirty years. This man would have been dead ten years ago if he had lived in Constantinople."

" Why so?"

" Because of the climate. He would have drunk himself into a dropsy."

" What are you talking about?" said the sick man.

" I was saying, Bey Effendi," said the doctor, " how very popular you are in the neighbourhood, and how much every one loves you!"

The sick man smiled benignantly, and the old gentleman continued,—

" I should have been sorry if he had divined the topic of our conversation. He would never have employed me again, and might have called in the Turkish practitioner, an ignorant ass, who does not know so much about anatomy as a butcher in the market, and who treats cases of inflammation by firing his patient."

" What! would he fire the Bey's foot?" I inquired.

" God knows! but he is quite capable of doing so, if the Bey would let him."

The doctor now felt his patient's pulse, and administered a few words of consolation; then, promising to send some medicine, he left the room.

CHAPTER XXXIX

Erzingan—The Mutasarraf Pacha—Widdin—Russian official documents—
Names of high functionaries—General Ignatieff—Your Indian frontier
—The Kurds will be excited to massacre the Armenians—The probable
final result of the war—If Turkey were to join Russia—The boot
manufactory—The shoe-makers being drilled—The gaol—Coiners—A
jealous woman in prison—The unfortunate shopkeeper.

I NEXT visited the Mutasarraf Pacha, the civil governor of Erzingan. He was an active little man, of about sixty years of age, full of energy. He seemed to have more of the Gaul than the Osmanli in his disposition. Formerly he had been civil governor at Widdin. Whilst he occupied this post some of his Zaptiehs had arrested a Russian. The latter had documents on his person which clearly showed that he was an agent of a society in Moscow, formed with the object of creating a revolution in Bulgaria. Abdul Aziz was then Sultan, and the Mutasarraf Pacha forwarded the documents to Constantinople. Ignatieff's influence was at that time paramount with the Sultan. No notice was taken of the papers. Very shortly afterwards the Pacha was removed from Widdin to Erzingan.

"Were there any names upon the document?" I inquired.

"Yes, names implicating some very high Russian functionaries. I hope that we shall soon be engaged in hostilities with Russia," said the Pacha. "Ever since the battle of Sedan she has been secretly at war with Turkey, and trying to stab us under the guise of friendship.* Ignatieff encouraged Abdul Aziz in his extravagance. He knew that this would lead to bankruptcy, and to a rupture of the alliance with England; and you may depend upon it, that the Russian Ambassador was one of the first men to advise his majesty to repudiate the debt. They are very clever, these Russian diplomats," continued the Pacha; "and however poor Russia may be, she has always enough gold to sow the seeds of sedition and rebellion in her neighbour's territory. You will find this out for yourselves one day."

"How so?"

"When she touches your Indian frontier; by that time you will have enough to do to keep your native troops in order. Will England help us in this war?"

"I do not know; but it is not likely. You see the Turkish Government is very unpopular with us, because it does not pay the interest of its debt, and also because of the massacres which have taken place in Bulgaria."

"Say for the first reason," replied the Pacha, "and I agree with you, for you English, by all accounts, dearly love your gold. However, I should have thought that by this time your people had learned that we were not the originators of the massacres in Bulgaria."

"Who caused them, the Russians?"

The Pacha nodded his head affirmatively.

"If there be a war in Asia Minor, they will do their best to excite our Kurds to massacre the Armenians in the neighbourhood of Van, and will then throw all the blame upon our shoulders."

"Do you think that the Russians will be able to conquer you in Asia Minor?" I inquired.

---

* These remarks of the Mutasarraf Pacha resemble those made on the same subject by other Pachas in Asia Minor. All these Turkish gentlemen had the same opinion of the Russian Ambassador.

"No, we are the strongest in this part of the world. The Georgians, Tartars, and Circassians hate the Russians, and will rise against them; besides that there are no roads."

"But Russia has taken Kars before."

"Yes, but she will not do so this time, and I should not be surprised if we were to go to Tiflis instead."

This I subsequently found to be the prevailing opinion amidst all the civil and military Pachas in Asia Minor.

"What do you think will be the final result of the war?" I now inquired of the Pacha.

He shook his head sorrowfully.

"If we have no ally, it will go hard with us; but your countrymen will be mad if they do not help us."

"Why so?"

"Because, when we find that we have no chance against our foe, what is to prevent us from turning round and allying ourselves with him; that alternative might be preferable to annihilation. And when Russia has our fleet, the Dardanelles, Batoum, and another port or so in the Black Sea, she might leave us alone at Constantinople. Anyhow, if she has once crushed us, we shall no longer have the power of lifting our heads, and however much we may dislike the alternative of slavery or destruction, shall end by being menials of the Russians."

The following day I walked with the Turkish major to see his boot manufactory; a large building on the outskirts of the town. Four hundred and fifty men were employed in the business.

An order had arrived from Constantinople for all the workmen to be drilled. Two hours per day had been allotted for this purpose.

The shoemakers were drawn up in two ranks outside the building.

The officer who was instructing them commenced putting his men through the bayonet exercise. Many of the towns-people were amongst the spectators. They were greatly pleased at the eager way in which the men gave their thrusts into the air.

"If we only had some Russians to run through!" said a corpulent, middle-aged Turk.

"Ah! if we had," replied his friend. "Our bootmakers alone would be enough to make all the Cossacks turn pale and run!"

The manufactory was clean, and great order prevailed in the arrangements. Forty thousand pairs of boots had been made during the previous two months; my companion had received instructions from the authorities to forward 12,000 more to Erzeroum. The order had only just been issued, and was urgent. The result was that the leather which under ordinary circumstances would have been left in the tan for four months could only be soaked for five weeks. The major complained that he had not been supplied either with a machine to triturate the bark, or with a steam cutter's machine, which would have very much facilitated the work.

" I have written to the authorities at Constantinople about the matter," remarked the officer; " a reply has come to say that the articles in question are on their way. They will probably arrive when the war is over," added the officer despondently. " In the meantime some of our soldiers will have to march barefoot."

The thread used in the manufacture came from an English firm, Finlayson, Bousfield, and Co., of Glasgow; and the officer, as he showed me some of the packets, observed,— " that formerly he had been supplied with French thread. It was a little cheaper than the sort now employed; but after some trials he had discovered that the English article was three times as durable, and consequently far more economical in the long-run."

The boots manufactured in the establishment were made to lace high up over the ancle, and with very thick soles. They are much heavier than those furnished to English troops, and would be apt to tire the soldiers during a long day's march. In one room a number of Armenian and Turkish lads were working sewing-machines.

All the hands in the manufactory were paid by piecework. The boys could earn from one to five piastres per day, and some of the men forty. Owing to the pressure of business, the work-people were employed sixteen hours per day, fourteen hours in the manufactory, and two at drill.

I now went to the gaol. Here there were nineteen prisoners. They were made up of seventeen Mohammedans and two Christians; the latter had been arrested, one for coining money, the other for murdering his wife. Whilst walking through the building, I heard a great noise in one of the cells, and a woman's voice.

" What is she doing ?" I inquired of the gaoler.

" Effendi, it is a curious case," said the man; "she has a husband, but is very much in love with a young Armenian shopkeeper. The latter is a married man, and does not return the enamoured female's affection; however, she is continually leaving her husband's house and invading the Armenian's premises. The husband became annoyed and complained—he thinks that the Armenian encourages his wife. Anyhow," continued the official, " the affair created a scandal, the Cadi did not like it; he has ordered the woman to be shut up for a day or two, and the Armenian as well."

" What, together ?"

" No, Effendi, apart; it is rather hard upon the man," he added; " but who knows? perhaps he encouraged her."

" Why is she making that noise ?"

" Because she has learnt that the Armenian is in the prison, and she wishes to be confined in the same cell with him. He does not want it himself, and of course it would not do; for what would the husband say? A jealous female is a first cousin of the devil," continued the gaoler: "it is bad enough when she is jealous of her own husband, but when she is jealous of some other woman's, that is ten times worse."

CHAPTER XL

LATER in the day, the Mutasarraf called at my house, and at once commenced his favourite theme, politics.

" What do the people in your country say about Russia's conduct in Servia ?"

" Many of them do not like it," I replied.

" It was a cowardly act on the part of the Tzar, was it not ?" said the Pacha; " he pretended to be at peace with our Sultan, and allowed Russian officers and soldiers to take part in the fight against us. I tell you what it is," added the speaker, "Ignatieff wishes to cut off another arm from Turkey, by making Bulgaria independent, like Servia. If we are to die, better to perish at once than be torn to pieces limb by limb!"

"But I thought you told me this morning that in your opinion, sooner than that this should occur, your Government ought to join Russia?"

"Yes, I did," said the Pacha, "and if we were to join Russia and attack Europe, who will do nothing for us now, what would happen then?"

"Yes; what would happen then?" said the Hodja, or schoolmaster, a friend of the Pacha, and who had accompanied him during his visit.

"Europe would probably swallow up both Turkey and Russia!"

"You do not really think so," said the Pacha.

"We have a great many troops," said the Hodja.

"Yes; but not many officers."

"He is right," said the Pacha sadly; "our officers have not much brain, but we have one chance," he added.

"What is it?"

"If the Circassians were to rise, the Russians would have so much on their hands that they would be unable to advance."

"Is it likely that there will be a rising?"

"There is sure to be one," said the Pacha; "but it is doubtful whether it will be general, or confined to some districts;" and shaking hands with me he left the room with his companion.

The Pacha was an energetic man, and very popular with the inhabitants. He had been at Erzingan but a few months. He had found time to put the streets in tolerable order, and to make the town one of the cleanest in Anatolia. He was desirous of purchasing some machinery with the object of making cloth from the cotton which grows in this district. As it is, the raw cotton is sent to England, and is then manufactured into the articles required. The Pacha would have liked to save all this expense and have the work done on the spot. He had tried to form a company, with the object of realizing his idea; but there was no energy in Erzingan—the people were afraid of risking the little money they possessed; it was impossible to carry the project into execution.

I now went to the Mohammedan School.

"Will you ask the boys some questions?" said the Hodja.

I remembered the success which I had obtained with the sum put by me to the lads at Yuzgat; and at once gave it. The schoolmaster was at his wits' end for a solution. However, later in the day he came to my house and said—

"You set me a sum this morning—I cannot do it. I should like to ask you one."

"Go on," I remarked.

"Three men," said the Hodja, "who were accompanied by their three wives, arrived at a river. The husbands were all jealous of their wives. There was one boat in which to take the party. The bark would only hold two persons, and no woman could be trusted by her husband unless there were two men with her. How did they cross the river?"

"Can you do it?" said the schoolmaster.

"I will think it over," I replied.

"This sum has puzzled our Mutasarraf for six months," said the Hodja; "it is a beautiful sum!"

"Do you know the answer?" I inquired.

"Unfortunately, I have forgotten it," he replied.

I proceeded to visit the Mosque, which was being built at the expense of Issek Pacha, Governor of Sivas. It had been in the course of construction for three years, and was only half finished. The walls were made of stone and marble, which had been brought from some quarries, about eight miles from the town. It was said that when the mosque was finished, it would be the handsomest one in Anatolia.

I met the Italian doctor as I was returning to my quarters.

"So you have seen the mosque?" he said.

"Yes."

"Well," he continued, "the Turks in some ways resemble us Catholics. Issek Pacha probably thinks that by building a magnificent mosque, he will be less likely to be fried in a future state of existence; and we are told that if we leave money to the priests, to say masses for our souls, we shall not have to remain so long in purgatory."

"It all comes to the same thing," said the old gentleman. "It is no matter where a man is born, whether in the Mohammedan East or in the Christian West, his Imaum or Priest will always get money out of him in some manner or other."

"In this instance," I remarked, "the money has gone to build a mosque and not to Imaums."

"Yes," said the Italian, "but whenever a priest or dervish

asks a good Mohammedan for anything the latter will never refuse. The result is that the religious profession in Turkey is made up of as many idlers and beggars as can be seen in my own country."

Provisions, according to the doctor, were not very dear in Erzingan. A good sheep could be bought for six shillings; 80 eggs for a shilling; two pounds and a half of bread, or rather of the thin unleavened cake which takes the place of the staff of life in Anatolia, for a penny; whilst eight pounds of potatoes could be purchased for the same price. A nice-looking horse would not cost more than 10*l.* Fuel was dear in proportion to the other articles of consumption—charcoal costing a farthing the pound.

"Erzingan is not a bad place for poor people to live in," added the old doctor. "I have resided here nearly half a century. A man can get on very well if he has 50*l.* a year."

On leaving the town I found a fair carriage road, which led in the direction of Erzeroum. This state of things was not to last long, and after marching two or three miles we were riding once more along a track.

Marshes extended for some distance on either side of our route. A number of geese and ducks, some of the latter of a very peculiar breed and different to any I had hitherto seen, were feeding in the fields around us. I tried to approach them, so as to have a shot, as goose or duck would have been an agreeable change to the chicken fare which awaited us in every village. But the wild geese in Anatolia are quite as wary as their kindred on this side the Channel. It was impossible to stalk them.

I began to disbelieve in the stories which have been written about the amount of sport which can be obtained in Anatolia. With the exception of a few snipe, partridges, and hares, I had seen literally nothing in the shape of game since our departure from Constantinople. Deer were said to exist in some of the forests, but I had never even heard of any being exposed for sale in the different markets.

Should an Englishman ever think of undertaking a journey through Anatolia, and have the idea that he will be able to combine shooting with the pleasure of travel, he will find himself very much mistaken.

Now we overtook three hundred Kurds—redif soldiers on the march to Erzeroum. There were no officers with them. The men had to find their way as best they could to their destination. They were armed with needle rifles, but had no uniform, and were clad for the most part in rags and tatters. Many of them had no shoes or even slippers, but were walking with bare feet through the snow. A few men were riding on mules, and on a closer inspection I found that these poor fellows had been frost-bitten. Some of them had lost their toes on the march.

CHAPTER XLI

IT was bitterly cold as we gradually climbed the mountains which lie between Erzingan and Erzeroum, and after a nine hours' march we halted for the night at a little village called Delan. There were only twelve mud hovels. The three hundred Kurds stowed themselves away as best they could. I was fortunate enough to obtain a resting-place in a stable. My horses were packed together as closely as possible on one side of the building. There was just room for my followers and myself on the other.

The inhabitants of this little hamlet were Kurds, and the people did their best to make the newly-arrived soldiers comfortable. The latter were all fed at the expense of the villagers ; each inhabitant giving as much bread as he could spare towards the rations of his countrymen. So far as I could learn, none of the soldiers had any money with them, and it was a five days' march to Erzeroum. But they evidently had solved the problem of how to get on without money ; a week later I saw them arrive at their destination, and, with the exception of a few men laid up with frost-bite, they were not much the worse for their journey.

It was very slippery as we descended the slope which leads from Delan. We drove our horses before us ; the little animals tacking from side to side, like ships beating against the wind, and putting their feet down with the greatest caution, so as to make sure of the ground before them. We then had to lead the animals up the mountains, Radford having great difficulty in wading through the snow, owing to his state of debility. Fortunately we soon arrived at a place where it was possible to ride. Here another path branched off to the village of Kargan, but continuing by our old track we shortly came to a fine stone bridge, called the Kutta Kupri. It is about seventy-five yards wide, and spans the river Euphrates.

We passed through a series of natural basins, each of them two or three miles in diameter, and after an eight hours' tiring march put up for the night in the village of Mohallata. It contains about 100 houses, and a small barracks, with quarters for a squadron of Zaptiehs.

A battalion of redifs had also halted here. The men had marched from Erzingan without having had anything to eat since they left that town—the soldiers had gone more than thirty hours without food. There were no grumblers in the ranks.

One of the sergeants appeared rather an intelligent fellow; I spoke to him about the matter.

"We came to a village," he said; "there was nothing to eat, and so we went without our dinners."

"Did the men make any remarks?"

"No, Effendi, they knew that the people would have given them food if they had any to spare. When we beat the Russians, go to St. Petersburg and conquer all their country for our Padishah," said the sergeant, "we shall have many paras, there will be plenty to eat. But our Padishah is poor now," continued the man sorrowfully, "he cannot give us any pay, there is no money in Stamboul."

The captain of the Zaptiehs accompanied me in my walk through the barracks. This officer was anxious to obtain his promotion.

"I am forty years of age," he remarked, "and a captain's pay is very little. It is not enough for me to keep a wife. I want to be married, but before that event can take place I must be a major. Shall you see the Pacha at Erzeroum?" he added.

"Yes."

"Will you speak to him for me, and recommend me for promotion?"

"How can I? I do not belong to your army, and am only here as a traveller."

"But you are an Englishman!" exclaimed the Zaptieh excitedly. "That is quite sufficient. The Pacha would know that no Englishman would recommend any one without a reason. I should be promoted!"

"My good sir," I observed, "I have only seen you for a few minutes; how could I solicit your promotion on the ground of your merits?"

The captain was not to be rebuffed.

"I will write down my name," he said, "and then you will speak to the Pacha."

Taking a dirty piece of paper from his pocket, he scribbled something and handed it to me.

Forward again for twelve more hours, our horses slipping up, or varying the performance by falling into snow-drifts, and we came to a spot where the Erzingan track meets the Trebizond and Erzeroum road. Here most of the snow had been cleared away. There was but little to impede our progress. Large caravans of several hundreds of horses and mules were bringing cartridges from Trebizond; bands of Bashi Bazouks were with them and on the march to Kars.

We rode along the left bank of the Kara Su (Black Water), the name given to the Euphrates in this district, and presently were met by some Zaptiehs. Their leader, advancing a few steps, said that he had been ordered by the Pacha to meet me, and escort my party into the town.

Erzeroum lies at one end of a large plain. It is surrounded on the north, south, and east sides by hills. A few detached forts had been thrown up on these heights. The town itself is encircled by an intrenchment of loose earth—this defence was in no place more than three quarters of a mile from the city.

I rode to Ismail Pacha's residence. It is a large building in the middle of the town, and is also used as an office by the military Pacha.

Ismail, the civil governor, is a Kurd by birth. Some of his female relatives have made influential marriages: this, added to the talents which the Pacha possesses, has raised him to his present high position.

He did not think that war would take place between Turkey and Russia. A pacific speech made by Lord Derby had been telegraphed from London to Erzeroum. It was the opinion of many of the townspeople that the Tzar did not mean to break the peace.

"It will be much better for us if we fight now," said the Pacha, when he gave me the above-mentioned information. "If war is postponed, Russia will continue her intrigues* amidst our Christian population."

A few months previous the Tzar had sent a decoration to the Armenian Bishop of Erzeroum. The order had been forwarded through the Russian Consul. The latter, instead of asking Ismail to give the decoration to the Bishop, had ignored the Pacha altogether, and had not even invited him to the ceremony.

This had been converted into an Armenian demonstration. The relations between the Mohammedans and Christians were not so friendly as could be desired.

Erzeroum is the principal depôt for the caravan trade which is carried on by the merchants in Teheran and their *confrères* in Constantinople. *Timbaki*, the tobacco used in nargilehs, is exported from Persia to this part of Asia Minor. Of late, the Turkish authorities have increased the duty on timbaki from eight to seventy-six per cent. This has been done in consequence of many Turks liking the Persian plant better than that which is grown in their own country. The price of ordinary timbaki was formerly only twenty-five piastres an oke at Constantinople, whilst Turkish tobacco of the same quality costs as much as sixty-one.

Ismail Pacha was doubtful whether in the event of war he would be able to keep the Kurds quiet in the neighbourhood of Erzeroum. Russian agents had been busily engaged for some time past in attempting to suborn these mountaineers. Money had been lavished upon their chiefs. Anxiety was expressed as to which side they would take.

"The Russians are nearly as poor as we are," continued the Pacha, "but they have enough money left for the purpose of intrigue. If the war breaks out, it is not at all improbable that they will bring about a massacre of Christians in Asia Minor. Some of the Kurds would obey any order they might receive from St. Petersburg. It would go very hard with us in the court of European public opinion, if any fresh rebellions had to be suppressed by strong measures on our part."

* See Consul Taylor's Report on this subject, Appendix XII.

CHAPTER XLII

The Pacha's interpreter—The Russian Consul—The telegram—*Un ennemi acharné* of Russia—Mr. Zohrab—The Russian Government encourages photography—The paternal Government — Spies — Pregnant women massacred—How to frighten the mountaineers—Go and complain to the *Kralli* of the English. Ask her to send you an oculist—A blood-stained placard—A proof of Russian civilization—Two Circassian chiefs —Their statement—The value of the Caucasus—A Memoir drawn up by the Emperor Nicholas for the instruction of the present Emperor Alexander—Our inheritance is the East—The Circassians must be freed.

AN Armenian, the Pacha's interpreter, now entered the room. Presently he observed that the Russian Consul at Erzeroum had just received a telegram.

"He read it to me himself," said the Armenian. "He wants its contents to be made known to you. It is from the Russian Authorities in the Caucasus, and has come *viâ* Batoum. It runs as follows : "Two months ago, an English-man, a certain Captain Burnaby, left Constantinople with the object of travelling in Asia Minor. He is a desperate enemy (un ennemi acharné) of Russia. We have lost all traces of him since his departure from Stamboul. We believe that the real object of his journey is to pass the frontier, and enter Russia. Do your best, sir, to discover the whereabouts of this aforesaid Captain. Find means to inform him that in the event of his entering our territory, he will be immediately expelled.'"

The following day I went to the English Consulate. Mr. Zohrab is our Consul in Erzeroum. He is a good Turkish scholar, besides knowing most of the European languages.

I soon learnt that there was no exaggeration in the inter-preter's story. It was said that the Russians had procured my photograph, and hung it up in all the frontier stations, so as to enable their officers to recognize me should I attempt to enter Russian territory.

I must say that I was rather surprised to find that the Paternal Government still took so much interest in my move-ments. From the fact of the Russian agents having lost all trace of me since I left Constantinople, I presume that my movements were watched during our journey on the steamer, and also in the capital. This was doubtless done with a kind motive, and to prevent my being assaulted by any fanatical

Mussulmans. When I was in St. Petersburg, only twelve months previous, General Milutin, the Russian Minister of War, had shown a most fatherly interest in my safety; he was much alarmed lest I might be assassinated by the Khivans or Turkomans in Central Asia. It was very kind of him. I had evidently not sufficiently appreciated the philanthropy of that gallant officer, and of the Government which he serves.

I could hardly believe that the Russian Authorities were so interested in my welfare as to set spies to travel with me on board a steamer or to track my steps in Constantinople.

I much regret that my short stay in that city had not permitted me to call upon an old acquaintance, General Ignatieff, the Russian Ambassador to the Porte. I should then have been able to give his Excellency my solemn assurances that I had not the slightest intention to cross the Russo-Turkish frontier. However, possibly the term " solemn assurances " does not convey quite the same meaning to a Muscovite diplomate as to an English officer ; it might have been that his Excellency would not have placed any reliance on my promises.

The odd part of the matter was that I had not even dreamed of entering the Tzar's dominions. I was not ignorant of the state of Russia. Mr. Schuyler had proclaimed to the world that several of the Tzar's officials were corrupt. The scarcity of gold and the overwhelming paper currency proved the bankrupt state of the country. Every traveller could testify that many of the inhabitants of European Russia were drunkards. Major Wood in his book, the " Sea of Aral," had declared that some of the conquerors in Central Asia were worse. These facts were well known throughout Europe. I had travelled in Russia myself. Then how could the Russian Authorities be so childish as to think that I, of all people, wished to revisit the empire ? On second thoughts, I could only account for it by the supposition that they were afraid lest I should travel through the Caucasus, and discover their method of dealing with the Circassians.

A few years ago, a British Consul called attention, in an official Report, to this subject. From what the Circassians whom I had met during my journey had said, there was every reason to believe that the following manner of treating Circassian ladies is still sometimes resorted to by the Russian promoters of Christianity and civilization. Consul Dickson remarks, in a despatch dated Soukoum Kalé, March 17th,

1864, " A Russian detachment captured the village of Toobeh, inhabited by about 100 Abadzekh, and after these people had surrendered themselves prisoners, they were all massacred by the Russian troops. AMONG THE VICTIMS WERE TWO WOMEN IN AN ADVANCED STATE OF PREGNANCY AND FIVE CHILDREN."

Some people who call themselves Christians, and who sympathize, or for political motives pretend to sympathize with Russia, attempt to gloss over these facts by observing that the Circassians are a nation of freebooters, and that it is necessary to rule them with a rod of iron, and through their fears.   So in order to strike terror into thieves and other malefactors, it is justifiable to murder pregnant women, and fire upon little children !

Amongst other ways of compelling the Circassians to submit to their conquerors was one so fiendish, that if proof were not at hand to confirm the statement, I should hesitate to place it before the reader.

In order to frighten the mountaineers and civilize them *à la Russe*, the Tzar's soldiers cut off the heads and scooped out the eyes of several men, women, and children ; then nailing the eyeless heads on trees, they placed placards underneath them, saying, " Go now and complain to the Kralli of the English, and ask her to send you an oculist."

An Englishman, Mr. Stewart Rolland, of Dibden, Hants, has travelled in Circassia.   He can authenticate my statement.   One of these bloodstained placards is in his possession. He will show it to any one who wishes to see for himself a proof of Russian civilization.

It may be asked why these Muscovite gentlemen were so inveterate against Great Britain.   The Circassians formerly were of opinion that England would help them against their foe.   Some years ago* they actually sent two chiefs, to state their grievances to the people of this country.   These chiefs being asked why they counted upon England's good offices, said,—

"We have been told that the English nation is a great nation, and a nation that protects the distressed.   Our wives and our children, our little ones and our old men, said to us with groans and tears, ' You must go to that nation, and get us help.'   And we replied, ' We will go, and we will tell that

* See statements made by the Circassian Deputies, Appendices IX. and X.

nation that if they do not give us help, we shall become the slaves of Russia, or shall be destroyed by Russia. We grown men will not become slaves, but who knows what will happen to those who come after us; and once enslaved, they will be an army in the hands of Russia to attack the great English nation.'"

The Circassian chiefs visited England in 1862. Some Englishmen thought that it would be dangerous to interfere with a strong power like Russia, for the sake of a few mountaineers. The assistance asked for was denied. The Russian authorities did not value the Caucasus so lightly as our English officials.

This can be shown from the following extract * from a memoir drawn up by the Emperor Nicholas for the instruction of the present Emperor Alexander :—

"Our inheritance is the East, and we must not suffer our activity in that quarter to relax for a single moment. Our aim is, and remains, Constantinople, which is destined in our hands to become the centre of the world, and the eternal door to Asia. For a long time England has had the supremacy of the ocean ; but the same position which we have attained on land will be occupied by our maritime power. The possession of Constantinople, the Dardanelles, the whole littoral of the Black Sea, are indispensable to us. The sea is to become one great Russian port and cruising-ground for our fleets. The Emperor Alexander claimed Constantinople and the Dardanelles, when Napoleon proposed the partition of Turkey to him. At a later period, at the Congress of Vienna, he himself made a like proposal. The great Catherine foretold in prophetical spirit, that the execution of the grand scheme would be reserved for her second grandson. The Emperor Nicholas has taken the task upon himself. Everything of a higher order on which Mussulman life rests has disappeared. Old forms and habits are upset; all higher education and activity are wanting ; the complete dissolution is near at hand. Europe will try to oppose our taking possession of Turkey. Our conquest advances step by step, without any considerable sacrifice on our part. It extends already to the vicinity of Stamboul. Our apparent moderation restrains even our enemies from taking up arms. Things, too, are not quite ripe yet. The erection of forts and the arming of all

* This extract is quoted from a remarkable pamphlet, entitled "Circassia," published by Hardwicke in 1862.

important spots on the Black Sea is an indispensable pre-
liminary. We have to continue our struggle with the tribes
of the Caucasus. It is sometimes troublesome, but it exercises
our armies, and covers our preparations in the Black Sea.
Our moderation in the Treaty of Adrianople deprived England
itself of every pretext for interference ; yet we obtained everything that we wanted. By fostering Egypt, we continued
afterwards to weaken Turkey. Events of the utmost importance to the splendour of our arms are not far distant. We
keep the Divan in good disposition towards us, and at the
same time in dependence upon us. It is most important to
confirm the Sultan in his pseudo-reforms, and to push him on
in the same way ; but it will be expedient to throw obstacles
in the way of any real improvement for the military regenera-
tion. Of equal importance is it that the Porte should never
get clear of financial embarrassment."

The possession of the Caucasus is undoubtedly most
important to Russia. It enables her to make preparations
for a march westward towards Scutari, and another southward in the direction of the Persian Gulf, without considering
the possibility of her some day taking a fancy to the Bay of
Iskenderoon.

Should Russia ever take possession of Armenia,* Persia
would be at the mercy of the Tzar. The latter would
command the highlands of Asia Minor. He could descend
upon the valleys† of the Euphrates and Tigris.‡ Syria would
be exposed to his attack. We should have to be on our guard
lest he might wish to invade Egypt. It is quite true that
England could easily defend Syria against all the Tzar's forces
—but this would cost money. We should have to increase
our military expenditure by several millions a year. This
would not be agreeable to the British tax-payer.

People may argue that the Caucasus is far off from the
points which I have mentioned ; so it is ; the Russian frontier
town in Asia Minor, Gumri, is more than 1000 miles from
Scutari. It is not likely that in one, two, or even three
campaigns, the Tzar's troops would be able to reach that town.
The policy of the Russian officials is a safe one. They do not
attempt to swallow at one time more territory than they can
easily digest.

---

* See Appendix IV.
† See Routes which cross the Euphrates and Tigris, Appendix XIV.
‡ See Importance of Syria from a Military Point of View, Appendix XV.

This is what the possession of the Caucasus means to Russia. Should the fortune of war ever enable us once again to place our heel upon the throat of the Muscovite, we must not forget the Circassians. The people ought to be freed to act as a barrier between Russia and the Sultan's eastern dominions.

CHAPTER XLIII

The European society in Erzeroum—The Russian Consul an energetic man —How to depopulate a country—Russian passports—Consul Taylor— The intrigues of the Russian Consul—The Armenian upper classes— How corrupt they are—The soldiers in Erzeroum—Discontent— *Métallique*—The military hospital—Recruits from the South—The head surgeon—The wards—A valuable medicine—A bad habit— Wasting ammunition.

THERE was not much European society at Erzeroum. It was made up of the English, French, and Russian Consuls and their families; no other European, so far as I could learn, being in the town. The Russian official was an energetic man. A short time previous he had discovered that some Circassians had the intention to leave the Caucasus, and enter Turkey. He had telegraphed the news in cypher to the Russian authorities. Troops had been sent to the Circassian villages. The inhabitants had been caught in the act of packing up their goods and chattels. Very strong measures had been taken. It was not likely that any similar attempt would be made by the inhabitants. There were now hardly any of them left.

An empty house is better than a bad tenant; this seems to be the policy of the Tzar's generals in the Caucasus. It is undoubtedly cheaper to hang a prisoner than to imprison him. The Russian officers have great ideas of economy in this respect. The Russian Consuls at Erzeroum had been engaged for some time past in intriguing with the Armenians. Many Christians belonging to the higher monied classes were in favour of Russian rule—almost all of them being supplied with Russian passports. The traffic in such documents carried on in the Erzeroum district was very great. No large town in Armenia is free from pseudo-Russians. Consul Taylor, writing from Erzeroum to the Earl of Clarendon on March the 19th, 1869, remarks about the Russian Consul, who was then in that city, as follows: "The exaggerated pretensions,

overbearing conduct, and ostentatious display of the Russian
Consul in his relations with the local authorities, in which it
is needless to say other Consuls do not indulge, coupled with
the unaccountable servility of the Turkish officials here in
their intercourse with him, tend among an ignorant people to
give a false value to his particular importance or rather to
that of the country he serves—which by still further strengthening their belief (alluding to Armenians) that no other
power than Russia is so able or willing to help them—makes
them eager to apply to him in their differences, and to acquire
DOCUMENTS that to them appear claims to the interference
of a foreign power in their behalf. That the INTRIGUING,
meddling conduct of the RUSSIAN CONSUL is approved, I
may state that although in disfavour with the Embassy at
Constantinople, he is SUPPORTED by the AUTHORITIES
in the CAUCASUS, to whose diplomatic Chancery at Tiflis
he is directly subordinate. It is the POLICY of the RUS-
SIAN GOVERNMENT, and therefore of its AGENTS, to
encourage such ideas— as also to exaggerate real existing
evils, or trump up imaginary complaints, in order to keep up
that CHRONIC DISAFFECTION so suitable to the line
of conduct it has always pursued in the limits of Eastern
countries."

I now learnt that a very large sum of money had been
nominally spent in throwing up some earthworks round Erzeroum. They were said to have cost a million of liras; nobody
seemed to know how the money had been spent. I had not as
yet visited the fortifications. From what I could gather, the
defences were in a very bad state. It was stated that they
would be utterly untenable in the event of an attack.

One thing seemed to be the unanimous opinion of all classes
in Erzeroum—with the exception possibly of the Russian
Consul, whose acquaintance I did not have the pleasure of
making; this was, that should the Armenians ever get the
upper hand in Anatolia, their government would be much
more corrupt than the actual administration. It was corroborated by the Armenians themselves; the stories which they
told me of several of the wealthier and more influential of
their fellow-countrymen thoroughly bore out the idea.*

The soldiers in Erzeroum were very discontented about the
way in which they had received their pay, or rather, I should

* See Mr. Taylor's Report to the British Government on this matter,
Appendix XXII.

say, some of their back pay, as the amount owing to them was now more than twelve months in arrear. Where formerly they used to be paid in *métallique*—a debased coinage of silver mixed with copper, but which always keeps its value of about 140 piastres to the lira—they were now being paid in *caime* or bank-notes. Caime had depreciated enormously, a lira being worth at Constantinople 200 piastres. The Governor of Erzeroum had issued an order that a paper piastre was to be considered as equal to a metallic piastre. This did not prevent things from rising in value. The soldiers were not able to buy half so much with their caime as formerly with their *métallique*. They had petitioned the Governor on this subject, and were in hopes that he would let them be paid after the Constantinople rate of exchange.

The following day I went to the Military Hospital, a large building in the middle of the town. Many of the patients were suffering from typhoid fever, and others from frost-bite. The men who had marched from the southern provinces of the empire had felt the extreme cold in Erzeroum. Their clothes, well adapted for the climate of Bagdad, were no protection against the low temperature on the mountains. There were also several cases of ophthalmia and pneumonia.

The head surgeon in the hospital was a Greek, and one of his assistants a Hungarian. They both appeared to be intelligent men, and bewailed the lack of resources for the hospital.

"We have enough at present," said the Hungarian; "but it is the time of peace. When the war breaks out we shall require medicines and instruments; how the Government will be able to pay for them I do not know. Every para* will be required for the soldiers in the field. Notwithstanding the best intentions on the part of the authorities, the wounded will many of them be left to rot."

The wards were well ventilated. But, owing to the dearth of accommodation, patients laid up with typhus were lying next to men suffering from ophthalmia. It was impossible to separate the different cases. The doors, too, did not fit. On opening one of them, a current of cold air cut through the room, and attacked those patients who were suffering from inflammation of the lungs. Hollow coughs could be heard from all sides of the apartment.

The name of every inmate, and the nature of the case, was

* A small coin, but often used as a general term to express money.

written in French over his pallet, and the sufferers seemed to be much attached to their attendants.

"One of the most valuable medicines in this hospital," remarked the Greek, as I finished my inspection, "is wine. The Turks who come from the south suffer from poorness of blood. They have never drunk wine before, their law prevents them; when they receive alcohol as a medicine the effect is marvellous."

I now walked to one of the barracks, to see the cavalry regiment which had left Sivas whilst I was in that town. It had just arrived in Erzeroum. An officer accompanied me through the stables. They were large and lofty. The saddles, arms, and accoutrements were clean and bright, and the men appeared very particular about these matters; the colonel telling me, with a certain amount of pride, that notwithstanding the long march from Sivas, he had no cases of sore backs amongst the horses in his regiment.

Unfortunately there was only one other cavalry regiment in that part of Anatolia. The Turks, in the event of war, would have to depend upon their Circassian irregulars for outpost duty. Now if there is one branch of warfare which requires study more than another it is outpost duty. The safety of an army depends upon this being well done. Intelligent cavalry officers are the eyes and ears of the commander of an expedition. A general who is not supplied with a numerous and efficient cavalry is like a deaf and blind man; he knows nothing of what is going on around him.* My companion was well aware of this. He regretted that there were not more cavalry regiments on the frontier.

"We shall do our best," he said, "but there are only 400 troopers; when we are killed there will be no one to replace us."

He was not so sanguine about the result of the war as many of the officers with whom I had conversed.

"I fought against the Russians in the Crimea," was his remark on this subject. "They have very little money," he continued; "however, we have less. We shall have to buy arms from abroad. So long as we have gold, your manufacturers will supply us; when we have no liras left, there will be no more rifles and cartridges. We have plenty of men. We can recruit from the Mussulmans throughout Asia. We

* Fortunately for the Turks in the present war, the Russian cavalry has so far proved itself very inefficient.

can put into the field quite as many troops as the Russians. The latter are not to be despised as soldiers, they will die in their places. Our men will do the same. It will be a question of money, and the longest purse will win."

From the cavalry barracks I proceeded to a large Khan, originally constructed for travellers, but now given over to the troops. Here a battalion of redifs (reserves) was quartered. They had just received their uniform—a blue tunic and trousers, very much like the dress worn by the red French infantry, and were armed with Martini-Peabody rifles—a quantity of these fire-arms having been recently purchased from an American firm.

The rooms in which the troops were lodged had nothing to recommend them ; they were dirty and low, besides being overcrowded. The officers' rooms adjoined the men's dormitories, and were equally filthy.

A captain was drilling his company in one of the passages, and was making the soldiers go through the motions as if they were volley-firing. The moment the men had their rifles to the shoulder he gave the word "fire ; " there was no time allowed for taking aim.

The same fault I subsequently observed in a battalion which was ordered to form a square to resist cavalry. The band was placed in the middle of the square, the men, so soon as the music struck up, commenced firing independently—the object of each soldier being to discharge his rifle as rapidly as possible, the officers encouraging them in this bad habit.* If the same system is to be carried on in a war with Russia, the Sultan's army in Anatolia will soon be without ammunition.

CHAPTER XLIV

A conversation with the Pacha—The English Parliament opened—What will they say about Turkey ?—Can the people at your Embassy speak Turkish ?—The French are brave soldiers—The fortifications—The roads—The water supply—The posterns—Important military positions —A dinner with our Consul—He relates a story—A Kurdish robber— The colonel—His young wife—How the Kurd wished to revenge himself—Many of the Kurds are in Russian pay.

ERZEROUM was certainly the land of rumours, or, to use a slang expression, "shaves." Shortly after returning to my

* This actually happened in the first engagement in the neighbourhood of Deli Baba.

quarters, the Pacha called and said that he had received a telegram to the effect that England, Germany, and Turkey were to be allies in the coming struggle.

" Do you believe it ? " I inquired.

" Well," replied the Pacha, " the Germans, it is said, do not like the Russians, and Russia is believed to be an ally of France."

" If Germany does not fight France soon," observed another Turk, " France will be too strong for Germany."

" That is what I think," said the Pacha : " Germany sees the nation that she has beaten making every effort to become strong, so as to revenge herself for her defeat. Bismarck will not be likely to await that event."

A Turkish engineer officer now entered the room. He informed us that a telegram had arrived to say that the English Parliament had been opened.

" What will they say about Turkey ? " continued the officer.

" Probably some more about the Bulgarian atrocities," I replied ; " but I really do not know."

" You English people," observed the engineer, " think that you know a great deal about what is passing in foreign countries. You know nothing at all about Turkey. Can the people at your Embassy speak Turkish ? "

" One can."

" All our officials in England can speak English," said the engineer. " Our newspapers say that you receive your information from people who are sent to travel for different English journals, and that hardly any of these men can speak Turkish : is that the case ? " he continued.

" Our newspapers, as a rule, are very well informed."

" They wrote a great many falsehoods about us in Bulgaria," said the officer ; " our journals say that the writers were bribed by Russia."

" Englishmen do not sell their pens," I observed ; " this is a habit which is more likely to exist in your country than in my own."

" If England, Austria, and ourselves fight Russia," said the Pacha, " we shall annihilate Russia. Do you think France will be against us ?'

" Probably not."

" I should be sorry if France were our foe," said the Pacha ; " the French are brave soldiers, and were our friends in the Crimea."

" Allah only knows what will happen," said another of the company ; " we are in His hands ! "

I now mentioned to the Pacha that Mohammed had come with me as a servant from Tokat, and inquired if I might keep him during my stay in Asia Minor ?

" Is he a soldier ? " said the Pacha.

" Yes."

" Well, there will be no fighting at present ; he can remain with you till you reach Batoum ; a battalion from Tokat is in that town, he can join there."

Later in the day, I rode round the fortifications, accompanied by a Turkish officer. There were nineteen small forts —those on the Kars side being on an average 3000 yards from the town, but those in the direction of Ardahan only 1000.

On the south a mountain descends to within a very short distance of Erzeroum. There is a direct road from Van to Moush, and from that town to the mountain which commands the city. I learnt that no preparations had been made to defend this height, but, Inshallah, so soon as the winter was over, a redoubt would be thrown up in that direction.

Two water-channels lead from this mountain into Erzeroum ; if an enemy once had possession of the eminence, he would be able to turn them off from the town. There are a few wells in the city. The water-supply is insufficient for the requirements of the population.

Erzeroum is entered by three posterns, known by the name of the Stamboul, Ardahan, and Kars gates. The roads from them lead to Ardahan, Kars, Van, Erzingan, and Trebizond. On the Van road, and about five miles from Erzeroum, there is a position known as the Palandukain defile ; here it had been proposed to build a fort—that is, so soon as the weather became a little warmer. It was also the intention to construct another at Gereguzek, eighteen miles from Erzeroum, on the Ardahan road. The officer now remarked that the Deve Boinou Bogaz, five miles from Erzeroum, and on the Kars road, would be a good place for a fort, whilst redoubts, in his opinion, ought to be thrown up at Kupri-Kui—a place nine hours from Erzeroum, and where there is a branch road to Bayazid. He added that some more defences should be made at the Soghana defile, which is twenty-four hours from Erzeroum. If this were done, it would be very difficult for the Russians to advance by that route.

The important positions on the Bayazid road are at Deli

Baba—a narrow gorge through high mountains, and which pass, the Turk declared, was impregnable—at Taher Gedi, a five hours' march from Deli Baba, and at Kara Kilissa; after which the road is level to Bayazid.

The forts around Erzeroum were many of them armed with bronze cannon, which had been manufactured at Constantinople. The artillerymen had very little knowledge of these pieces. The officers in command of the different batteries were ignorant of the distances to the different points within range of their guns.

A million of liras had been spent in the construction of the defences of Erzeroum; after riding round them, it was difficult for me to imagine what had been done with the money.* As it is, this sum has been entirely wasted; Erzeroum, if assailed by a resolute foe, would not be able to offer any resistance— the easiest points of attack being by the Ardahan or the Van road.

Later in the day, I dined with our Consul, Mr. Zohrab. There was an Armenian present, the Pacha's interpreter, and also Mr. Zohrab's dragoman, a gentleman who I believe is of Arab parentage. The conversation after dinner turned upon the Kurds; the Consul, lighting his cigarette, remarked that there were several curious anecdotes with reference to these wild mountaineers.

On being pressed to relate one, Mr. Zohrab began,—

" Not long ago, and in the neighbourhood of Karpoot, a Kurdish robber attacked a Turkish merchant. The robber was wounded. He fled from the scene of his crime, and took refuge in the house of a Kurd known as Miri Mehmed, a rich and powerful sheik or chief. News of the outrage reached Erzeroum. The Pacha sent orders to the colonel of a regiment in the neighbourhood of the sheik's encampment to arrest the robber. The chief soon heard of this. He was able to dispose of several thousand armed men. He was not at all inclined to submit. In the meantime the officer, who did not know how to arrest the Kurd, wrote to the sheik and invited him to dinner.

" The colonel had lately taken to himself a young and beautiful bride," added the Consul, by way of a parenthesis. " Most of the officers in his regiment were married men. The day fixed for the dinner arrived. At the appointed hour the

* Since my stay at Erzeroum, the defences of that city have been strengthened.

sheik rode down to the encampment. He was unaccompanied by any retainers, dismounting at the door of the colonel's tent, he passed the threshold. The officer received his guest very courteously, gave him a magnificent entertainment, and, after the dinner was over, asked him to give up the Kurdish robber. To this, however, the Kurd would not agree. 'He has eaten bread and salt in my house,' was his reply. 'I shall not surrender him.' The officer exerted all his powers of persuasion, finally, discovering that the Kurd was obdurate, he arose, and, taking a document from his pocket, showed him that his orders were to arrest the sheik himself sooner than that the robber should be allowed to escape. 'So you mean to arrest me?' said the Kurd. 'You probably think that, because I am unattended, I have no one at my beck and call. Wait! If I have not returned to my encampment in three hours' time, my men will come here to look for me; and I tell you what will happen. I shall take the wife you love best, I will revenge myself by dishonouring her before your eyes. My men shall do the same to the wives of every officer in your regiment!' The colonel was dreadfully alarmed at this," continued the Consul. "He knew that the sheik was quite capable of carrying his threat into effect, he trembled at the vast superiority of numbers on the side of the Kurds. He went down upon his knees, and implored the chief for mercy. The other officers were equally alarmed. They entreated the Kurd to depart. The colonel, kneeling down on the ground, embraced the sheik's feet as a sign of humility and respect. The chief was inflexible," added the speaker. "He stood motionless as a block of stone. He made no remark. At last the colonel, goaded to a state of frenzy, sprang to his feet and cried out to the chieftain, 'You are worse than a Christian! you are not a Mohammedan! You have eaten bread and salt in my house, and yet you wish to do me this great wrong.' 'And what did you wish to do to me?' said the Kurd. 'You thought that I was without my followers and unprotected. You wished to take me a prisoner to Egin; and then what would have been my fate? Perhaps I should have been put in gaol or hanged, as has been the lot of some of my tribe. But,' added the sheik, 'you have thrown in my teeth the remark that I am worse than a Christian! I will show you if I am so. My followers will be here in a very short time. They shall not harm your women. To-morrow morning I will go with you to Karpoot; but only on one condition—that we ride there without any of our men. I will send for my wife whom I love, and you shall take your wife whom you love. They shall accompany us. We will go together to the governor of the town.' The next day they started," added Mr. Zohrab. "The governor was first of all for treating the Kurd very severely ; but when the news had been telegraphed to the authorities, and all the facts of the case were known, an order came to release the chief."

"From whom did you learn this story ?" I inquired.

"From a Hungarian doctor who was attached to the battalion in question, and who was an eye-witness of the greater part of the scheme."

"Some of these Kurds are very chivalrous fellows," remarked an Armenian. "However, they are great robbers, and a curse to the neighbourhood. They often bribe the Pachas," he continued, "and when troops are sent to force the mountaineers to submit, the general in command, instead of surrounding the mountain, or blocking up all the passes, will purposely leave one or two defiles open. The Kurds then escape, and the Pacha telegraphs back to Constantinople that perfect order reigns throughout the district under his command."

"What will the Kurds do in the event of a war with Russia ?" I inquired.

"They will go with the side which pays them the most money," was the reply. "They are many of them known to be in Russian pay, and presents are continually being sent by the authorities in the Caucasus to the chiefs in this part of Anatolia."

CHAPTER XLV

The weather—The number of troops in the town—Wood is very dear—
    Tezek—The shape of the town—Trade with Persia—Ismail Pacha's
    head servant—Have the Russians arrived ?—No, Effendi, but the
    Pacha has hanged himself ! that is all—The Pacha's wives—He was
    gay and handsome—The Consul's dragoman—An attack of dysentery
    —Starting for Van—Major-General Macintosh—His opinion about the
    Kurds—The Bazaar at Van—Fezzee Pacha—Kiepert's map—Erzeroum
    is very weak—Fezzee Pacha's opinion about the impending war—The
    curious Caves.

It was bitterly cold at Erzeroum. The thermometer had fallen below zero. The half-clad recruits could be seen running up and down in front of their barracks, endeavouring to keep themselves warm. There were at that time about 12,000 troops in the town. The number was continually changing, every week fresh battalions of redifs arrived from the interior, and then the older soldiers were marched off in the direction of Bayazid, Kars, or Ardahan.

Wood was dear in the market. The inhabitants had to trust to their tezek, the dried excrement of cows, bulls, and oxen. The town is in the form of a pentagon. Its appearance from afar off has been compared by a traveller to a ship of enormous size, raised by the waves and thrown into a neglected bay. The mainmast is an old tower which stands out conspicuously amidst the mud-built houses.

Formerly there used to be a great trade between this town and Persia. All the caravans going from the latter country to Trebizond pass through Erzeroum, and halt a few days to dispose of some merchandise. Of late years, a great deal of the Persian trade has found its way *viâ* Khoi and Erivan to Tiflis. The caravans between Persia and Erzeroum are not so numerous as they were some eighteen years ago. Two per cent. duty is charged upon all merchandise going from Erzeroum to Persia, and eight per cent. upon imported goods. Any article manufactured in Erzeroum, and sent out of the town without being marked with the Government stamp, as a sign that it has paid the duty, is liable to be confiscated.

The following morning I was awoke by Ismail Pacha's head servant. It was bitterly cold. He proceeded to make a little fire in the stove. From time to time he looked at me in an excited manner, then he would blow the fire. There was evidently something on his mind.

"What is it ?" I inquired. " Have the Russians arrived ? "

"No, Effendi, but the Pacha has hanged himself ! that is all ! "

" Not Ismail Pacha ? " I exclaimed, at once thinking of my hospitable old host.

" No, Effendi, not Ismail, but a military Pacha—a young man, only forty. Woe is me ! He has hanged himself ; our Pacha has gone to his house, with all the other Pachas. The body is quite cold ; if the Effendi were to go there, perhaps he might bring it to life again."

" I am not a Hakim," I said.

" Yes, Effendi, you are. Mohammed has told me that you have some medicine."

" Nonsense ! But what made the Pacha hang himself ? "

" Effendi, no one knows for certain. It may have been owing to his wives ; some people say that he had lost all his money by lending it to the Sultan. Allah only knows ! I should say his wives had something to do with it."

" Why so ?"

" Because he was gay and handsome. His wives were jealous. They were always scolding him—that is, whenever he went to his harem. If he had not been a military Pacha, he might have abandoned his seraglio, but he could not leave Erzeroum ; the wives knew it, they had him in their power. He was such a nice gentleman ! "

Later in the day I met the Consul's dragoman. He was of opinion that the Pacha had not committed suicide, but that some one in his house had saved him the trouble. This was the impression of many people in the town.

" Anyhow," continued my informant, " no one will be the wiser. The poor fellow is in the ground ; coroners' inquests, or any sort of judicial inquiry as to the causes of death, are unknown in this part of the world."

Radford was still looking ill. I wished to leave Erzeroum. It was necessary for me to make up my mind as to what was to be done with him. It is a six days' march from Erzeroum to Trebizond : once there he might have gone on board a vessel bound to Constantinople. But on my proposing this plan, the poor fellow so entreated to be allowed to continue the journey, that rather reluctantly I consented.

When long forced marches have to be made through deep snow, an invalid is a source of great inconvenience. In addition to this, I was anything but well myself ; a sudden chill had left me with an attack of dysentery. The food supplied us by the Pacha at Erzeroum consisted of very rich dishes. It was not the best thing for the digestive organs.

I was eager to commence the journey to Van ; however, if both man and master were to fall ill on the march, it would be next to impossible to reach that city. When I announced to Ismail Pacha my intention of starting for Van, he did his best to dissuade me from the undertaking.

" It is a fourteen days' march," he observed. " You will be in a country infested by Kurds, many of whom are in Russia's pay.* The Russian Consul in Erzeroum is aware that you

* Major-General Macintosh, writing in 1854 on the subject, remarks that "in their desire to win over the Kurds, the Russian authorities proceeded so far, that on the pretext that they were a migratory people, they

are here, he also knows that his Government looks upon you as an enemy—this I have heard from the interpreter. Should the Kurds kill you, your countrymen would very likely throw the blame on us. Take my advice," said Ismail Pacha ; "do not go to Van. There is nothing to be seen in that town. Go straight to Kars, you will then meet with no Kurds on the road."

But I had made up my mind to see Van, and the more particularly because I had been informed by many of my Armenian acquaintances that the bazaar there had been recently set on fire by some Turkish troops, and that the Christians had been robbed of all their effects by the Mussulman soldiers. The bazaar was represented to me as having been of gigantic dimensions. The Armenian merchants in Van were said to have been reduced from a state of affluence to one of abject poverty.

I was anxious to ascertain for myself how far this story was true ; and as it is perfectly impossible to trust to any evidence in the East, save to that of your own eyes, I had determined to visit the seat of the conflagration.

Another Pacha called upon me, Fezzee Pacha (General Kohlmann), the chief of the staff in Erzeroum. He was a Hungarian gentleman, and had formerly been engaged as one of the leaders in a revolution in his own country. At that time he had been ordered to blow up the bridge over the river at Buda-Pesth, but had not done so. Shortly afterwards he entered the army of the Sultan. He showed me one of Kiepert's maps of Asia Minor, dated 1856, but with numerous corrections, which had been made subsequently by European officers in the Turkish service. The Pacha had enlarged this map by photography, he had then distributed facsimiles of it

claimed a right for them to cross the frontier for the purpose of grazing their cattle ; and that even in Turkey they should still be looked upon as Russian subjects, and have no imports to pay on that side." He continues, "I have no doubt it is the interest of Russia that the Kurds should to a certain degree be weakened and scattered, though it has been her crafty policy, while urging or encouraging Turkey in this course (referring to attacks upon Kurds), to pretend to be their champion and friend. She has pursued a similar course among the Turkomans to the eastward of the Caspian ; and when in a contiguous part of Asia I heard of dresses of honour having been given to the chiefs, at the same time that the Shah of Persia was encouraged to attack them from the south. The more these various tribes of barbarians weaken themselves by their incessant conflicts, the more they are paving the way for the dominion of such a power as Russia."

to the officers under his command. He was a fine-looking old man, nearer seventy than sixty, but upright as a lad of sixteen, and with a pleasant, frank smile which did one's heart good to witness.

The Turks, as a rule, are not in the habit of smiling; indeed, Radford often used to expatiate on the extreme melancholy which prevailed throughout all the Mohammedan classes ; his favourite remark being "that they looked as if they had found a sixpence and lost half-a-crown." General Kohlmann was an exception to this rule. He had adopted the Mohammedan religion, but this had not taken away from him a keen sense of the ridiculous. I have seldom found myself in pleasanter company than that of the chief of the staff in Erzeroum. He had been in Kars during the last siege, and was personally acquainted with Sir Fenwick Williams, Colonel Teesdale, and several other Englishmen ; besides having a great deal to say about the gallantry and skill which had been shown by the British officers during the investment of the fortress.

"Shall you remain much longer in the Turkish army?" I inquired.

"I am waiting here in hopes that there will be a war with our enemies the Russians," said the old general, "and, if we can only beat them, shall then return to Constantinople, and take my pension."

In the Pacha's opinion, Erzeroum was very weak and could not stand a siege. He did not apprehend any danger from an attack along the Van road, as there is a very strong position near Meleskert, and one which the Russians would not be able to take without enormous loss. He did not believe that the Tzar's troops were so strong * in the Caucasus as was generally supposed. If the general could have had his way, he would at once have commenced the war by an attack in that direction.

Later in the day, I heard from an Armenian that there were some curious caves in the neighbourhood of Erzeroum, and which no one had ever explored. They were said to extend for miles, and to pass under the different detached forts. My informant declared that a priest who had been in them for a short distance had said that they contained gigantic halls, and seemingly never-ending passages.

I now asked the Pacha if I might undertake the exploration

* Subsequent events have proved how right General Kohlmann was in his opinion.

of the cavern. It would bo interesting from a military point
of view to know where the passage ended. Should there be a
war, an attempt might be made by Russian agents to blow up
the batteries with gunpowder.

Ismail Pacha readily gave his consent, and at the same time
ordered an officer of engineers to take some men with lanterns
and pick-axes to aid me in the task. The English Consul,
Mr. Zohrab, and his two sons, expressed a wish to join the
party. It was arranged that we should meet the following
morning at the consulate, and go from there to the caves.

CHAPTER XLVI

WHEN I arrived at Mr. Zohrab's residence, I found that
gentleman and his boys, two English-looking lads with ruddy
cheeks, prepared for a journey to the centre of the earth, if
the subterranean passage would only lead us there; and riding
by a Turkish cemetery, which is just on the outskirts of Erzeroum, we proceeded onward towards our destination—a hill a
short distance from the walls of the city.

A few melancholy-looking dogs were walking about the
dead men's home. A grave-digger was busily engaged in
making a hole in the frost-bound ground with a pick. Further
on a small band of people, howling and making a great noise,
showed that another follower of Islam had just been committed to his last abode. Some of the monuments were
surrounded by wooden railings. Others had the names of the
departed written on them in Arabic characters. Every stone
was upright, none of them being placed horizontally on the
ground, as is the custom with the Christians in the East.

Some soldiers were standing near a small aperture in a
neighbouring hill. One of them advanced as we rode up the
slope, and said a few words to the officer.

"We have arrived," said the latter, and, dismounting, we followed his example.

The hole was not a large one. To enter the cave it was necessary for each man to lie flat on the ground, and gradually squeeze his body through the aperture. The first to attempt the passage was a thin Turk; he looked as if he had never been properly fed, and was as emaciated in appearance as some of the dogs about the cemetery. Holding a candle in one hand and a box of matches in the other, he disappeared head-foremost down the cavity. I prepared to follow, not without some misgivings, as I was not at all sure whether there was room for me to pass.

"You will stick?" said the Consul. And I did stick.

However, by the aid of a friendly shove from those behind, and a hand from the little Turk in front, I succeeded in entering the cavern. The others in turn followed. The passage became higher, we could walk upright. There were still no signs of any barrier, all of a sudden we arrived at a branch tunnel. Leaving some soldiers to explore this passage, we continued onward and presently came to a small cavern to the left of our path, the latter being now blocked up by some loose stones.

The soldiers began clearing away the débris. The rest of our party sat down in the cave and began to discuss the grotto. The officer was of opinion that it had been made several hundred years ago, as a refuge for the women and children of Erzeroum, in the event of that city being attacked by an enemy.

"Erzeroum is supposed to have been the site of the Garden of Eden. Perhaps this is the spot to which the serpent retired after the fall," remarked another of the explorers.

The officer shook his head; he did not believe in serpents. He stuck to his original idea.

The soldiers by this time had succeeded in clearing away the débris. An aperture was exposed to view. It was about the same width as the one through which we had previously passed, and, on reaching the opposite side, several tunnels were found, branching in different directions.

Taking a ball of string, we attached it to a stone by the entrance. Gradually unwinding the cord, we advanced along one of the passages—now crawling flat on our stomachs, and then stumbling over heaps of rubbish—the Consul, who was rather blown by his exertions, remaining in the first room, and solacing himself during our absence with a cigarette.

Presently a candle went out. We had to send for another. Two or three small caverns were now passed. Finally we arrived at the bare rock. There was no exit. We had explored the caves on one side.

Retracing our steps, we tried the other tunnels, but, after a very short time, found that they too ended in the bare rock. There was nothing more to be done, and, returning to the open air, I soon afterwards reached my quarters. My faith in Armenian stories was still more shaken by the events of the morning. I had been told that I should see gigantic caverns: they had turned out to be small places, most of them not more than twelve feet square.

The officer who accompanied me was intelligent for a Turk, but he could not understand our getting up so early and riding through deep snow, merely to explore an old cave. Curiosity about antiquities does not enter into a Turk's composition. He lives for the present. What has happened is finished and done with.

That evening I dined with a general of engineers. Some officers on his staff and Fezzee Pacha were amongst the guests. After dinner the son of my host—a child of ten years of age —came into the room, accompanied by an attendant. The boy was dressed in a cadet's uniform, and had a very pleasant cast of countenance.

" He is a pretty boy," I remarked to his father.

" Mashallah ! " interrupted the old Hungarian. " Say Mashallah," he added, " or else the father will be afraid of the evil eye ! You have no idea how superstitious the Turks are," continued the speaker, in French ; " if you had not said Mashallah, and subsequently anything had happened to the child, they would then have declared that it was owing to you."

The engineer general was much surprised to learn that almost every Englishman could read and write, and would not believe me till the Hungarian had corroborated my statement.

" It is wonderful ! " exclaimed our host. " Only think ! A whole nation of Hodjas—schoolmasters ! No wonder that the English people are so clever. It would never do for us Turks," he added.

" Why not ? "

" Because it would make our poor people dissatisfied to find that they knew as much as their masters, but were only receiving a servant's wages. Does it not make your lower orders dissatisfied ? " he inquired.

" No, because their masters know something beyond reading and writing."

" You English are a marvellous nation," said the Pacha ; " but, I should not be surprised if one day you had a revolution. Why, some of our Pachas cannot write, and yet they get on very well. All your labourers being able to read and write—this is a miracle ! "

I said farewell to my host, and to our hospitable Consul, who had done his best to dissuade me from the journey. The following morning we started for Van.

It was a windy day. The postman who was carrying the Van letter-bag did not much fancy the march.

" It will be all right for a few hours," he remarked ; " but if it is like this to-morrow, we shall not be able to pass the mountains."

I now learnt that, owing to the wind and snow, the track was sometimes blocked for days together, the path too was slippery, and there were precipices on either side.

Presently we met a caravan of camels from Persia—the huge beasts were covered with icicles, owing to the extreme cold. The men who accompanied the caravan were clad in sheep-skins, and wore high black hats. The track was very narrow, not being more than twelve inches broad ; on either side of it there were five feet of snow. The camels had to make way for the postman, who preceded us. With a crack from his whip, he sent the foremost of them off the track, and breast-deep in the drift. The other camels, more than a hundred in number, followed in their leader's wake. There was one mule left in the path ; on approaching, we found that he bore two ladies. They were the wives of the Persian merchant, and were seated in large baskets—a pannier being slung on either side of the animal.

The postman proved to be more chivalrous than I expected. Spurring his horse, he made his animal leave the track. Man and steed were half buried in the snow. We followed him. The mule was now able to pass with the ladies, who seemed much alarmed lest their quadruped should stumble. The women appeared to be very uncomfortable in their conveyance. One of them was much heavier than the other, the Persian had balanced her weight by putting a huge stone in the pannier containing his thinner wife. Some parts of the road along which they had come led by the side of a precipice. It must have been very disagreeable for the ladies to have sat still in their baskets, and have looked down the abyss, with nothing save the sure-footedness of their animal to insure them against eternity.

This caravan had come from Khoi and Bayazid—the owner reported that the roads were in a dreadful state. He had been twenty days performing the journey. We halted that evening at an Armenian village called Herteff, containing about ninety houses, and a short distance from Kupri Kui. I was not sorry to reach a resting-place. My illness had weakened me. I had discovered this when we were obliged to wade on foot through the snow, and was now quite as great a cripple as Radford had been when on the road to Erzeroum.

The owner of the house where we stopped was not a cleanly object. His domicile was as dirty as his person. His wife and children were manufacturing some tezek for fuel in one of the two rooms the house contained; this room was given over for the use of my party and self. It was bitterly cold outside. To keep the habitation tolerably warm, the owner had blocked up a hole in the roof, used as ventilator, chimney, and window. The smell of the tezek, and the ammonia arising from the horses and cattle, was excessively disagreeable. There was no other accommodation to be obtained. Mohammed presently informed me that two merchants had been waiting three days in the village. They wished to go to Van, and had made several attempts to cross the mountain, but in vain.

The wife of the Armenian host, and her children, were not at all coy about showing their faces—at least so much of them as the dirt did not hide from our view. They squatted round my English servant, who was making tea, and watched his proceedings with great interest. Now the woman, sticking her filthy fingers into the basin, took out a lump of sugar; then, putting it in turn into each of her children's mouths, she had a suck herself. "Give it me!" suddenly exclaimed her husband. The lady did not show any signs of readiness to surrender the prize. The man sprang to his feet; thrusting a finger and thumb into the mouth of his helpmate, at the same time clasping her tightly round the throat with the other hand, so as to avoid being bitten, he extracted the delicacy. Holding the sweet morsel high in the air, he dis-

played the treasure to the assembled guests; then, greatly to
the woman's indignation, he placed it within his own jaws.

CHAPTER XLVII

IN the next room, which was only separated from us by a
railing about three feet high, there were buffaloes, cows, calves,
and pigeons, besides the relatives of the Armenian, the postman, and a Kurd. The latter individual had a wonderful
turban in the shape of a bonnet on his head. It was made of
blue satin, and adorned with gold thread. He was evidently
very proud of this attire, and told the Armenian that he
had purchased it at Erzeroum, and that, when he had
finished wearing the turban, he should give it to his favourite
wife.

Presently an Armenian woman brought in a wooden tray,
on which were several of the cakes which are used as bread
by the inhabitants, and some oily soup.

The Kurd, postman, and Armenians, squatting round the
dishes, devoured the contents with rapidity.

Mohammed was lying in a corner of my room; from time
to time a groan escaped his lips. I discovered that he was
suffering from rheumatism. Radford had put a mustard
plaster on him by way of alleviating the pain. Mohammed
had been told that he was to keep it on all night. The
mustard was rapidly creating a blister.

"Atech—fire!" said the Turk, pointing to his back.

"Yes," said Radford. "Hottish—I should say it was. It
will be better presently."

"Turkish is very like English, sir," observed my man to
me. "You see that he says it is 'hottish.'"

"Nonsense!" I replied. "He says 'atech—fire.'"

"'Atech,' or 'hottish,' it don't make much difference, sir;
the plaster is raising a beautiful blister. I should not be
surprised if Mohammed left off complaining about his haches

and pains after this. I don't think that as how any other Turks will ask me to doctor them again !"

Radford was wrong. The sound of Mohammed's groans attracted the Kurd's attention: accompanied by the Armenian, he came to the side of the sufferer. They minutely inspected the plaster.

"It is a wonder !" said the Kurd. "The plaster is cold, but Mohammed says he is on fire. Where has the Frank put the flames? I should like a plaster too." Turning to Radford, he held out his hand for one.

"Plasters are for sick people, not for men in a good state of health," I observed.

"But I am not well," said the Kurd.

"What is the matter with you?"

"I have a pain here;" taking off his slipper, he showed the remains of an old frost-bite. "The cold did this," he added : "the fire there," pointing to the wet paper, "will put it right again."

I had considerable difficulty in explaining to the man that the plaster in question would be a useless remedy.

The following morning the wind blew harder than before. The mountain which barred our progress was entirely hid from view in what seemed to be a whirlwind of snowy particles. The cold, too, was intense. The thermometer was still several degrees below zero.

"It is no good starting," said the postman, coming to me ; "to-day the sun does not shower its rays upon our destiny. Fortune is against us. We must wait here till the wind goes down."

The two merchants had made another attempt to ascend the mountain a little before daybreak. They had found it impossible to cross the passes. The track was hid from their view by the snow. They were half blinded by the flakes which the wind carried with it in its course.

There was nothing to be done but to wait patiently. In conversation with a Turkish lieutenant, I discovered that it would be possible to reach Bayazid, and from Bayazid there was a road to Van. It would be a much longer route than the one which led direct from Erzeroum to Van.

The officer interrupted me in my reflections, and proposed that we should go to Bayazid.

"Who knows," he continued, "how long we may have to wait here? The mountain is sometimes impassable for two or three weeks at a time; and, besides this, the smell in this room is enough to poison any one. These Christians do stink," he added, pointing to my Armenian host and hostess, who, begrimed with dirt, were squatting in a corner—the woman engaged in making some cakes with flour and water, and the man in looking for what it is not necessary to mention amidst his clothes.

The Russian moujik is not a sweet animal; a Souakim Arab, with hair piled up two feet above his head, and covered with liquid fat, is an equally unpleasant companion; but either of these gentlemen would have smelt like Rowland's Macassar oil in comparison with my Armenian host, who, apparently, had no ideas beyond that of manufacturing fuel from cows' dung. His conversation was entirely engrossed with this subject. It was also an important topic with the rest of his family, who were all longing for the frost to go, so as to commence making the article in question on a large scale.

Wood is very dear in these parts. The inhabitants would die if they had not a supply of fuel. It is not surprising that they take a considerable interest in their tezek. But to hear this subject discussed from morning to night, and in a room with an atmosphere like a sewer—besides being ill at the time—was a little annoying to my senses. I made up my mind that, if the weather did not improve in the course of the next twenty-four hours, I would continue my journey towards Bayazid.

The lieutenant would accompany me in that direction. He was a very cheery little fellow, and not at all disposed to hide his own lights beneath a bushel. He had been a lieutenant about six years, and took an opportunity to mention to me this fact. He knew that I had stayed with Ismail Pacha in Erzeroum, and was in hopes that I would write to the governor, and casually mention his, the lieutenant's name as a gallant and exceedingly efficient officer.

There was no improvement in the weather. The following morning I left Herteff for Bayazid—the postman remaining behind with the letters.

We crossed the Araxes on the ice. The river was said to be only two feet deep. Kupri Kui was about one mile from our track. Here there is a bridge over the stream, which is about thirty yards wide, besides being deep. Our track was firm and level. There were no mountains to cross. Every now and then we passed by villages; they all contained soldiers, and, so far as I could learn, there were about 8000 troops echeloned between Erzeroum and Bayazid.

After a seven hours' march, we halted at Yusueri, an Armenian village. From here it was a three hours' ride to Deli Baba, a celebrated gorge or mountain pass, and the most important place, from a military point of view, on the road to the Russian frontier.

The women in the house where I was lodged were busily engaged in making some large earthenware jars. Taking some clay from the soil, they knead it for several hours with their fingers, and then form it into the shape they require. In every house there is a hole left in the floor, which is used as an oven. The women place the jars in this receptacle, and, filling the space between them with tezek, set fire to it. They afterwards colour the pottery by some process of which I am ignorant. The result is an extremely well made and serviceable article, in which they keep their corn, flour, and household goods.

Now we came to the famous pass of Deli Baba. It is about a quarter of a mile long. High and precipitous rocks are on either hand, and the gorge is not more than forty yards wide at the exit from the defile towards Bayazid. It is a spot where a thousand resolute men, well supplied with ammunition, might keep at defiance a force of a hundred times their number. However, in spite of the extreme importance of the position, nothing had been done to strengthen any part of it.

"We are going to throw up earthworks, and place some batteries here when the winter is over," was the reply of the lieutenant, when I interrogated him on this subject.

"When the winter is over:" "Not to-day, to-morrow:" this is the stereotyped answer which a Turk has always at the tip of his tongue. Until the Sultan's subjects can shake off the apathy which prevails throughout the empire, it will be difficult for them to hold their own against other nations.

CHAPTER XLVIII

Our track led over some low hills. The ground was covered with deep snow. We had to dismount, and struggle as best we could through the treacherous soil. The sun shone bright above our heads ; the reflection from the white surface at our feet was blinding in the extreme. We staggered about, and followed in each other's track, like a number of drunken men, and after eight hours' incessant toil reached Daha, a Kurdish village.

We were here informed that the road to Bayazid had been blocked for eight days ; and that the village was full of caravans which had made daily attempts to force a passage forward. All the inhabitants were going to turn out at day-break on the following day. They intended, if possible, to clear a track from Daha to the next village.

The daughter of my host took a great deal of interest in her father's guests. She was a tall, fine-looking girl, with a high cone-shaped head-dress made of black silk. A quantity of gold spangles were fastened to this covering. A red jacket and loose white trousers enveloped her limbs and body, her feet were thrust in some white slippers. If only she had been properly washed, she would have been a very attractive-looking young lady. But soap and water were evidently strangers to the Kurd's dwelling, if I might judge by the surprise the girl evinced when Radford commenced washing his pans after he had cooked my dinner.

"So you wash the dishes and pans in your country ? " she remarked.

"Yes."

"But it gives a great deal of trouble," observed the girl ; "and it does not make the dinner taste any better."

The voice of her father on the outside of the dwelling made the young lady aware that she would probably receive a scolding if she were found talking to a European. Sticking her fingers into a tin box, and seizing a handful of biscuits, she ran into the stable.

"She is very dirty," observed Mohammed, who had overheard the conversation ; " but, for all that, if she were well washed, she would fetch a good price as a wife for some Bey in Constantinople. It is a pity that you are not a follower of Islam, Effendi," continued my servant ; " she is tall, she would make a good wife for you."

I now learnt that certain Turkish merchants were in the habit of visiting the Kurd district in the summer months. If they meet with a pretty girl, they buy her from her parents, and then, taking the young lady to Constantinople, make her go through a course of Turkish baths, and feed her well. Under this régime the girl's complexion improves. She will command a considerable price as an addition to the seraglio of some magnate or other. If she succeeds in gaining the favour of her lord, she does not forget the relatives at home, but sends them money and presents, besides interesting herself for the advancement of her brothers and other relations. The result of this is, that a Kurd has no objection to part with his pretty daughter. If she is well sold at Constantinople, this is looked upon, by the young lady's family, as rather a feather in their cap than otherwise.

"Rich men generally get pretty wives," said Mohammed, as he concluded giving me this information. "Is it the same in your country, Effendi?"

"Occasionally," I replied, "but not always. The girls are sometimes allowed to choose for themselves. There are instances when they prefer a poor man to a rich one."

"What do their fathers say to this?" said Mohammed. "Do they not beat their daughters if they do not like the rich man?"

"No."

"I cannot understand that," said Mohammed. "If I had a daughter, and she might marry a rich man, but she preferred a poor man, I should whip the girl till she altered her mind!"

The owner of the house entered the room. He was accompanied by three of his sons, all fine looking lads. They were dressed in green serge, and in a costume which somewhat resembled that worn by the foresters in the opera of Freischütz. Several daggers and pistols were stuck in their sashes, enormous orange-coloured turbans adorned their heads. They squatted down beside the Imaum of the village—a thin man dressed in a white sheet.

The father rose from the divan, and, standing before me, pointed to his tooth.

"What is the matter with it?" I inquired in Turkish—a language which is generally understood by every Kurd, though few of them speak it well.

"It aches; I have heard, Effendi, of your great skill as a hakim (doctor)," continued the man. "Mohammed has told me how you set his shoulder on fire with a piece of wet paper. This is very wonderful, perhaps you could cure my tooth."

Now it is one thing to be able to prescribe a mustard plaster, it is another to be called upon to act as a dentist. However, the Kurd's children were all expectant. They evidently believed that if I put a mustard plaster on their parent's tooth, that this would relieve him immediately.

Mohammed was also of this opinion. He went through a sort of pantomimic performance in the corner of the room, suggestive of the sufferings which he had undergone, and of the subsequent benefit which he had received.

A thought occurred to me. I remembered that, three years before, my servant Radford had extracted the tooth of a maid-servant in a country house in Norfolk. Why should he not extract the Kurd's tooth? And if he were able to do so, would not my reputation as a hakim be higher than ever amidst the inhabitants of Kurdistan?

"I am not a hakim for teeth," I remarked to the patient. "I am a hakim for the stomach, which is the nobler and more important portion of a man's body."

The Imaum and the Kurd's children made a sign of assent to this; the Kurd himself did not seem to see it.

"You are in my house," he said. "You have accepted my hospitality—cure my tooth!"

"Well," I continued, "I have a servant with me; he is a hakim for teeth. If you like he shall look in your mouth."

"By all means!" said the Kurd.

In a few minutes a servant of my host arrived, leading Radford by the sleeve of his coat.

"Do you want me, sir?" inquired Radford, touching his cap. "This dirty chap," pointing to the man who had brought him to the room, "came into the place where I was a cooking, laid hold of me with his dirty fingers, and without saying a word led me here!"

"Yes," I said; "this gentleman," pointing to the old Kurd, "has something the matter with one of his teeth. Look at it."

My servant, without moving a muscle of his countenance, seized the patient by the nose with the fingers of one hand; then, thrusting a finger of the other into the sufferer's mouth, looked well down the gaping orifice.

"It had better come out; but it is very tight in his 'ead," remarked my man. "If I only had a pair of champagne nippers, I would have it out in a trice."

"Could not you pull it out with a piece of string?"

"No, sir; could not get a purchase on it;" and with that remark my servant released the Kurd's head.

"What does he say?" said the sufferer, rather alarmed at our conversation in a language unknown to him, and the more particularly at the grave demeanour of my servant.

"He says that the tooth had better be extracted."

"Will it hurt much?" inquired the Kurd excitedly.

"Yes, a good deal."

This observation of mine appeared to afford great satisfaction to the Imaum and the Kurd's children.

"Have it out?" they all cried.

But their parent did not see the matter from his sons' point of view. He remarked in an indignant tone of voice,—

"Silence!"

Then, turning to me, he inquired if I could not give him some medicine for his stomach.

"But your tooth hurts you, not your stomach," I observed.

"Yes," replied the man, "but, for all that, I should like some medicine."

Taking some pills from my medicine-chest, I gave them to him. The old man, putting three pills in his mouth, commenced chewing them with great gusto.

"My tooth is better already," he remarked, and in a few minutes prepared to leave the room, accompanied by his sons and the Imaum. The latter was very much disappointed that my host's tooth had not been operated upon.

"If it had been my tooth, I should have had it out," he observed to me *sotto voce;* "but he is afraid."

The Kurd overheard the remark.

"You would have done nothing of the kind," he replied. "You would have swallowed the medicine like me!"—and a whelping cry from a dog outside the door announced to us that the old gentleman had vented his bile on the ribs of the animal in question.

CHAPTER XLIX

Clearing the way—Leaving Daha—My father was well cleaned last night— The wonderful medicine—Charging the snow-drifts—Turkoman steeds —The Persians—The lieutenant—Zedhane—Molla Suleiman—Toprak Kale—A sanguinary drama—The Caimacan—The rivals—An Armenian peasant — The marriage ceremony— The Circassian Governor — The Kurd's mother—Revenge—His father's bones—The Circassian's wives —The Governor in bed—The fight—The feud between the Kurds and Circassians—Camels in the water.

ON the morrow we were up before daybreak, and not only ourselves, but almost all the male inhabitants of the village. They had turned out, some on horseback and others with spades and shovels, to try and force a passage through the snow. In addition to these men there were two caravans, comprising between them over 200 camels, and accompanied by fifty Persians. It was very cold. The lieutenant was doubtful whether we should succeed in clearing a way before us. According to the Kurd, there were still six feet of snow in many places along the track.

Just as we were leaving Daha, the eldest son of my host approached and apologized for the absence of his father. There was evidently something on the lad's mind, he hesitated as he said "Good-bye."

"Is there anything I can do for you?" I observed.

"Yes, Effendi, there is," said the boy, delighted at the ice being thus broken for him. "But I am afraid to ask for it."

I now began to be a little alarmed, thinking that possibly the lad had set his heart on possessing my little express rifle or revolver, both of which he had much admired on the previous evening.

"What is it?"

"Effendi," replied the boy, "I know that it is contrary to our ideas of hospitality for a host to ask for a present from a guest; but in this case my father——"

"What does he want?" I remarked a little hastily, as it was anything but agreeable sitting still in the cold.

"He was so well cleaned last evening," continued the lad;

" he has never been so well cleaned before ! He would like you to give him some more of that wonderful medicine."

All the luggage was on the pack-horses. But the boy so entreated me to comply with his request that I could not refuse. Unpacking my bag, I gave him a box of pills. The lad's face became radiant with delight. Taking off the lid, he took out a couple and ate them on the spot. Then, touching his head with my hand, he hurried off in another direction.

" He is a rogue," said Mohammed, chuckling. " He does not want the medicine for his father. It is for himself. He wants to set up as a hakim in the village. When once it is known that you have given him some medicine, he will be a person of great importance in the neighbourhood."

Presently we came to a place where the camels, which were in the van of our party, had come to a halt. One of the animals had almost disappeared in a snow-drift, nothing save his long neck could be seen. The men coaxed and whipped their unruly beasts, all was to no purpose, they would not move a step.

I thought that we should have to dig out the road with shovels. However, the Kurd who directed the operations did not resort to this measure. Ordering one of the Persians to make his camels retire about 200 yards, the Kurd called twenty of the best mounted of the villagers to his side, then striking his horse and shouting wildly, he galloped along the track and charged the drift. In a second or two nothing could be seen but the head of the rider, his steed was entirely hidden from our view. After a few struggles the man backed the animal out of the snow, having made a hole in it some twenty feet long by four wide. The next horseman rode at the place, like his leader. Each Kurd followed in succession. They finally forced a passage.

It was a wild sight to witness—these Kurds in their quaint head-dresses, and on strong, fine-looking steeds of Turkoman breed, many of them quite sixteen hands high, charging the snow-drifts, yelling and invoking Allah—the Persians, phlegmatic and still, seemingly not caring a straw about the matter —the lieutenant encouraging the Kurds by cries and gesticulations, but having too great a regard for his own safety to gallop at the ridges—and the leading horseman now far in front, his horse apparently swimming through the snow as he slowly burst the barrier,

It was hard work even following in the steps of the Kurds. If a horse or camel deviated a hair's breadth from the line marked out, he would be often buried in a drift, and a long time be wasted in extricating him.

The track led over a succession of rising ground until we reached Zedhane, an Armenian village with about thirty houses.

We were close to the village of Molla Suleiman, and were not far from Toprak Kale—a town in which a sanguinary drama had been enacted but a very few months previous. I will relate the story as it has been told me by an eye-witness of part of the scene.

Four years ago a Kurd was Caimacan at Toprak Kale. His grandfather had been a sort of king of Bayazid; the family being well off and having relatives married to some magnates in Stamboul, had considerable influence in the district. However, many complaints had been made about the conduct of this Caimacan. He was removed from his post. It was given to a Circassian. This gave rise to a feud between the ex- and the new governors—the Kurd often vowing vengeance against his newly-appointed successor. Shortly before my informant's visit to Toprak Kale, the Kurd's father had died. His family was in mourning.

An Armenian peasant, who resided in Toprak Kale, was about to be married. It is the custom amongst the Christians in this part of Asia Minor, when the wedding ceremony is concluded, to beat drums, hire a band of what they call musicians, and fire guns in the air, as a sign of general rejoicing.

The peasant, knowing that the Kurd's father had recently died, went to the ex-Caimacan, and asked his permission for the wedding to take place, as it would be impossible to have it without the music, gun-firing, &c.

The Kurd consented, provided that he received a present, this the Armenian gladly promised to give. The marriage ceremony began, but when the Armenians in Toprak Kale commenced beating drums, &c., &c., the noise reached the Kurd's mother's ears. She hastened to her son, asked him how he could allow people to insult his father's memory, and insisted that he should instantly put a stop to the proceedings.

The son allowed himself to be persuaded, and sent some servants, who broke in the heads of the drums. The peasant was very indignant. He at once proceeded to the Circassian, the actual Caimacan, and related everything that had happened.

" Did the Kurd accept a present from you ?" inquired the governor.

" Yes."

" Very well," continued the Caimacan, " go back to your house. My servants shall accompany you. Make more noise than before. Get more drums ; beat them harder than ever, and do not spare your powder. I will show the people in Toprak Kale who is Caimacan—the Kurd or myself."

This was done. When it came to the ears of the Kurd's mother, she told him that he must be revenged on the foe, or his father's bones would not be able to rest in peace in the tomb. The Kurd consented. That evening he went to the Caimacan's house, accompanied by two of his brothers, and inquired of a servant where his master was.

" In the harem," replied the attendant, much surprised at so late a visit on the part of the ex-Caimacan.

" Go and tell him I am here," said the Kurd ; then, without waiting for an answer, he pushed aside the man, and tried to force a way into the apartment reserved for the Circassian's wives. The governor was in bed at the time. He heard the noise : snatching his sword from the sheath, he rushed to the entrance. The Kurd fired at him with a pistol, the ball going through the Circassian's shoulder ; but the latter was able to cut down his foe. The Kurd's relatives now rushed upon the governor. He called loudly for assistance ; his brother, who slept in another room, hurried to the rescue, the result of the encounter being that three of the opponents were killed, whilst the Circassian governor was left desperately wounded on the field of battle.

In the meantime hundreds of Kurds, who had heard of the disturbance, came down from the adjacent mountain. They vowed that they would kill every Circassian in the neighbourhood. The Circassians trooped into Toprak Kale, and swore that they would exterminate the Kurds.

Fortunately the gentleman who related this story to me was able to despatch a mounted Armenian to the governor at Bayazid asking him to send some troops to the scene of the disturbance. The soldiers arrived in time to prevent a battle royal between the two factions. This probably would have ended in the annihilation of every Kurd and Circassian in the district, neither side being inclined to grant any quarter to its foe.

We rode through Molla Suleiman. All the houses in this village were filled with soldiery. On emerging into the open country I found that the path in front of us was blocked by a caravan coming from Persia. A pond was on the right-hand side of the path. The leading camel-driver led his animals along the frozen water, so as to avoid a collision with our party. He miscalculated the thickness of the ice ; a loud splash made us aware that it had given way beneath the camels. Five of the huge beasts were sprawling in the water, here about five feet deep ; their packs, containing timbaki, Persian tobacco, became dripping wet. The animals, frightened at the breaking of the ice, lay down on all fours. They refused to get up, in spite of the cries and the whips of their drivers.

CHAPTER L

WE met with some Armenian lads riding calves, and driving others before them, the driven animals carrying pack-saddles, which were laden with sacks of corn. The Christians in this district make use of their cattle as beasts of burden. It is not at all an uncommon sight to see Armenians, man and wife, riding to market on cows and oxen. Buffaloes are much in request with the inhabitants on account of the great strength of these animals. Some of the richer Christians possess from twenty to thirty buffaloes, two of which are considered a fair price for a girl—it being the custom of the poorer Armenians in certain districts to receive money from their sons-in-law, and seldom, if ever, to give any dowry to their daughters. On my remarking this one day, when in conversation with a Christian, the latter replied,—

"Our daughters are our maid-servants; when they marry we lose their services. It is quite right that the husband should compensate us for our loss. Europeans educate their girls very well, but the latter are utterly useless as cooks or sweepers. When they marry, the fathers lose nothing, but, on the contrary, gain, as they have no longer to pay for their daughters' maintenance or clothes. It is quite proper that you should give a husband something when he saddles himself with a useless incumbrance, and you have no right to find fault with us for our system."

Presently we met a dervish. His long black hair was streaming below his waist; he brandished a knotted stick. The fellow looked very hard at us, as if he were of the opinion that we ought to leave the track, and let our horses sink into the snow drift, so as to enable him to pass. The lieutenant did not see it in this light. This officer was a little man, but had a tremendous voice, which sounded as if it came from the very bottom of his stomach. He roared at the dervish; the latter, who was greatly alarmed, sprang on one side into the snow. Nothing but his head and face were visible—his dark eyes glared fiercely at the giaours as we rode past.

Kara Kilissa came in sight. It is a large village; every house was crammed with soldiers. It was impossible to obtain any accommodation. We rode on towards Kaize Kuy, another Armenian hamlet. The track descended for a few yards, and then ascended precipitously. I thought that we were in a gully. However, the Zaptieh and his horse, floundering in some water, made me aware that we were crossing a frozen stream, and that the ice had given way. It was very cold; the man was wet from head to foot; in a minute or two he looked like one gigantic icicle. Pushing on as rapidly as possible, we reached our quarters for the night.

The streams which traverse the tracks in many parts of Anatolia are a source of constant annoyance to travellers during the winter. The water becomes frozen; snow falls; it covers the glassy surface, and in time fills the space between the banks. There is nothing to warn the wayfarer that he is leaving the track, till he suddenly finds himself upon the ice : a horseman is fortunate if it is strong enough to bear him.

Now we saw some Persian women sitting cross-legged on their horses, like the men. Some of these ladies were mothers ; they carried their children slung in handkerchiefs round their necks. In a short time I came to their village, one amongst several others which are scattered about in this part of Turkey. The houses were clean inside, and in this respect a great improvement upon those inhabited by the Kurds. The floors were covered with very thick rugs, made by the wives of the proprietors. I was informed that the people in the district send their manufactures to Erzeroum.

The inhabitants formerly lived in the neighbourhood of Erivan. When the Russians invaded Persia, conquered the Shah, and annexed a part of Persian soil, many of the vanquished determined not to remain under the Muscovite yoke. Leaving their houses, they crossed the frontier and settled in Turkey. The Sultan gave them land. They expressed themselves as being much happier under their present rulers than their relatives who are Russian subjects. The latter would be delighted to pass the border-line and join their countrymen in Anatolia ; this the Muscovite authorities do not allow. " Once a Russian, always a Russian," is the answer given to the Persians on this question.

Our track led us along the right bank of the Murad, here about seventy yards wide. We came to a bridge which spans the river, the road on the opposite side leading in the direction of Van. We did not cross the structure.

Soon Diyadin was reached. Here there were two squadrons of cavalry, besides infantry. The commandant, in spite of the rumours of peace which had been telegraphed from Constantinople, was daily expecting an outbreak of hostilities. The Russians, according to him, had concentrated a large force of Cossacks in the neighbourhood of Erivan. It was believed that the war would commence by an attack upon Bayazid.

We rode for an hour over a low mountain ridge, and then entered a vast plain girt round by sloping heights. On our right front lay Persia. On my bridle-hand I could see the territory of the Tzar. The mighty Ararat is in front of us, and stretches upwards into the realms of space, its lofty crest hidden in some vaporous clouds.

It was extremely cold. A bright sun poured its rays down

upon our heads. The golden orb gave out no warmth, but it half blinded us with its splendour.

The people in this district suffer very much from ophthalmia : a traveller rarely finds himself in a house where one of the inmates is not labouring under this complaint.

The plain narrows. A broad lake of water is on our left. To our right front, and amidst the rocks, lies the little town of Bayazid. The ruins of an old castle are in the fields below. The track begins to ascend. It winds higher and higher amidst the crags. A few houses are passed, and the barracks, which contain two battalions of infantry. We come to the Pacha's residence. Dismounting, I proceeded to pay that official a visit.

He had been for some time in Egypt, and spoke Arabic very fairly, having great pleasure in showing off his proficiency in this language to the officers of his household.

I learnt that, six weeks previous to my arrival, the Russian authorities in Daghestan had ordered a levy of troops to be made amidst the inhabitants. The latter declared that they were Mohammedans, and said they did not wish to fight against their Lord, the Commander of the Faithful. They added that the Tzar formerly had promised that those men who wished might leave Russia with their wives and children, and settle on Turkish soil ; they asked for this permission for themselves.

"However," continued the Pacha, " the Russian authorities would not allow them to leave the country. Cossacks were sent to the district in question, and 400 people—amongst them women and children—were shot down and beaten to death!"

Bayazid is only a twelve hours' march from Erivan, the frontier town of Russia. There is a level road between these two stations. The Russians had a large artillery force at Erivan, and there were only two mountain guns in Bayazid. The Turkish officers were convinced that if an attack were made upon Bayazid, they would be unable to offer any effectual opposition. In their opinion it would be better for them to retire upon Karakilissa and Deli Baba, and make a stand at these points.

Major-General Macintosh, when writing about Kurdistan during the time of the Crimean War, remarks that he does not think there is a place of greater importance than Bayazid, in a military point of view, in the whole of Western Asia.

There is a continuous descent along the banks of the Euphrates to the Persian Gulf ; but as this great valley conducts through the range of Mount Taurus into Syria, its value to Russia, on this account alone, must be obvious. It is much nearer to her present frontier, and much more accessible than Erzeroum, which lies on the western branch of the Euphrates ; and should the contingencies of the present war render it possible for Russia to push on a force into the northern part of Syria, the good-will of the Kurds * at the moment of undertaking such an operation, would afford her an immense advantage. There is another exceedingly strong pass at Bayazid, on the Persian side, where a very small regular force might completely seal the entrance into Persia, from the side of Erzeroum, except through the roads of central Kurdistan. It may also be looked upon as a key to Kurdistan, and to Diarbekir, Mosul, and the whole course of the Tigris as far as Bagdad. I have no hesitation in saying that Russia, with the assistance of the Kurdish tribes, could speedily establish a route, and march an army down this valley into Syria.† The distance from Erivan to Aleppo is not above 500 miles, if so much, and the route by Aleppo, Diarbekir, and Van, to Aderbzou, from the Mediterranean, is quite practicable for an army.

I rode to see the barracks. Eighty years ago they formed part of a palace belonging to a Kurdish chieftain, a certain Mahmoud Pacha. He had expressed a wish to have the most beautiful residence in the world, and, after conversing with numerous architects upon this subject, had accepted the service of an Armenian. The latter had designed a very handsome building, with large glass windows, and everything that could be desired in the way of comfort. The Pacha was satisfied with the palace, but not with the idea that the Armenian architect might possibly construct a similar building for some other kindred chieftain. To prevent this Mahmoud ordered his executioner to cut off the Armenian's hands. This was done. The poor victim shortly afterwards died a beggar. In the meantime the Pacha was gathered to his fathers, leaving one son. This man, after committing all sorts of excesses, was bitten by a snake, and died at Alexandretta. His child

---

* Fortunately during the present war the Kurds have remained true to the Sultan, or Major-General Macintosh's predictions might have been realized.

† For importance of Syria from a Military Point of View, see Appendix XV.

was brought up at Bayazid, and afterwards became Caimacan at Toprak Kale. He had lost his life in the affray with the Circassians, which has already been mentioned in this work.

On entering the barracks, sometimes called the citadel, the irony of fate was clearly shown. The large window-frames which had been brought to Bayazid for Mahmoud eighty years ago, and at an immense expense, had all disappeared; their places were filled up with sheets of Turkish newspapers. The marble pillars and carving in alabaster over the portico were chipped and hacked about, the harem of the former owner was a dormitory for the troops. Four hundred soldiers slept in the rooms allotted by Mahmoud to his seraglio.

A Hungarian doctor in the Turkish service accompanied me over the building. Descending a flight of steps, he led the way to a large vault. Here lay the bodies of Mahmoud and of his favourite wife, in two tombs of the purest marble.

"He was a great rogue when he lived," said a Turkish officer who had joined our party, pointing to an inscription which merely said, "Mahmoud Pacha, son of Issek Pacha, lies here;" "but he is still now, and can do no one any harm. Peace be with his bones!"

CHAPTER LI

A spy—The news from Erivan—The border line—How he passed the frontier—The Mollahs—A war of extermination preached by them— A Turkish newspaper—Turks in Asia—Christians in Europe—The Conference—A Conference in St. Petersburg—The European Powers dislike Russia—General Ignatieff a judge instead of a prisoner—The hour for the evening prayer—A Turkish officer on prayer—His opinion about European Bishops—They eat mutton every day—A Turkish Captain.

WE leave the barracks. A beautiful view extends before us. We look down upon the red, green, and white plateau which divides us from the Tzar's dominions. In some places the sun has slightly melted the snow, the sand is exposed to view; in others, and nearer the lake which lies in the midst of the plateau, patches of vegetation can be seen. The clouds which overhung Ararat have been dispelled by the sun: the huge mountain, enveloped in its white pall, stands out in bold relief.

I now called upon the Pacha. Whilst I was conversing

with him, a servant entered and whispered something in his ear.

"Let the fellow come in," he observed; then, turning to me, he remarked that a Turk had just arrived from the Russian frontier, and brought the latest news of the military preparations in Erivan.

For some time past the Russians had prohibited any inhabitant of Turkey from crossing the border-line. It was difficult to obtain any authentic information as to the quantity of troops the Tzar's generals had massed in the neighbourhood. The new arrival succeeded in passing the boundary-line by saying to the Russian officers that he had been forcibly enlisted as a soldier, and was a deserter from his regiment. He had obtained permission to return to Turkey by declaring that he wished to bring his wife—who lived in a village near Bayazid—to Erivan: the Russian general had ordered him to obtain as much information as he could about the strength and disposition of the Turkish forces. He was a thick-set, sturdy-looking little fellow, with a bull neck and keen grey eyes; his attire consisting of a blue turban, a yellow shirt, and a pair of crimson trousers. According to him, the Mollahs were preaching a war of extermination against the Russians in Persia. However, the natives of that country were very lukewarm in their friendship to the Turks. It was not impossible that they would join Russia, or at all events allow the Tzar's troops to march through their territory in the event of an offensive movement against Van.

The Pacha took up a Turkish newspaper which he had just received from Constantinople.

"Listen!" he said. "The man who writes for this paper knows what he is about."

The article was to the effect that Russia wished to drive the Turks out of Europe because they were Mohammedans, and because in European Turkey the Christians were in the majority. "Very good," said the writer, "let us abandon Europe; but in Asia the Christians are in the minority. According to the same reasoning, the Russians and English ought to leave all their Asiatic possessions, and give them up to the original proprietors of the soil. Our Sultan has no objection to let every Christian in his dominions leave Turkey and go to Russia; but the Tzar, on the contrary, he will not let the Mohammedans in his empire cross the frontier: if they try to do so, he sends his soldiers; they cut the throats of our co-religionists. A Conference, composed for the most part of Christians, has been held at Constantinople to inquire into the way the Sultan treats his Christian subjects. Why should not a Conference be assembled at St. Petersburg, composed for the most part of Mohammedans, to inquire into the way the Tartars, Turkomans, and other inhabitants of Central Asia are treated by the Tzar?"

"Yes," said the Pacha, as he finished reading to me these extracts. "The European Powers dislike Russia, and, although they hate her, and know that she is the origin of all our difficulties, they are too timid to allow the fact. What a mockery it must have seemed to the representatives of England, France, and Germany, to find themselves sitting in judgment upon Turkey, and General Ignatieff, instead of being equally on his trial, seated at their side, and a judge instead of a prisoner! Does it not make you smile to think of it?" added the Pacha; "how the general must have laughed in his sleeve!"

Another officer entered the room. He had been educated in the military school at Constantinople. From frequent intercourse with Europeans, mostly Frenchmen, he had begun to look down upon the religious observances of his countrymen.

It was about the hour for the evening prayer. The Pacha, Cadi, and several other Turks commenced performing their devotions, regardless of the presence of a stranger. The new arrival, the Hungarian doctor, and myself, remained seated, the former remarking that it was very hard work praying, at the same time glancing rather contemptuously at his superior officers.

"Did you not pray when you were at Constantinople?" I inquired.

"Effendi, I did everything à la Franga (in European fashion). Europeans, from what I could learn, do not pray much."

"Not pray!" I observed; "what do you mean?"

"No, Effendi; the men, I have been told, go to the churches to look at the women; the women, some to pray, but others to look at the men and show off their fine clothes the one to the other. Is not that the case in your country?" he added.

"No. Of course there are exceptions; but the English people as a rule are religiously inclined."

"Effendi," continued the officer, "I have often heard

Frenchmen say that a Christian ought to be a poor man—that is, if he carried out the doctrines of his Prophet. But, my friends used to laugh and declare that their bishops and priests were rich men, and that some of the Protestant Mollahs were so wealthy that they could afford to keep carriages, eat mutton every day, and have servants to wait upon them."

"The fact of our bishops and priests eating mutton or keeping carriages does not make the Protestant religion the less true," I now observed.

"I do not know that," replied the Turk. "If I were to be taught a religion by a man who did not believe in it himself, or who did not carry out its doctrines, I should think that I was wasting my time."

The rest at Bayazid had done all our party good. The horses, which were still very emaciated on account of the long and frequent marches, had picked up a little flesh. I determined to leave Bayazid and accompany a Turkish captain who was going through Persia to Van with despatches for the governor of that town. The officer must have been sixty. He was quite grey ; but, he sat his horse like a centaur, and was more enthusiastic for the war than any Turk with whom I had previously conversed.

"You may get killed," I remarked.

"Please God I shall not," was his reply ; " others may die, and then there will be some promotion."

CHAPTER LII

WE turned our backs upon Mount Ararat, and, ascending a low range of hills covered with loose rocks and boulders, arrived at a Yezeed (devil-worshippers) village.

The houses were built in the sides of a hill. Cone-shaped huts made of tezek, and filled with that fuel, showed that the inhabitants had no objection to heat in this world, however hot they might expect to be in the next.

An old man, considerably above the middle stature, approached our party. Addressing the Usebashe, he invited us to dismount. It was about luncheon-time. I determined to avail myself of the opportunity afforded me to learn a little about the ways and habits of these strange people.

"Here we are, sir, with the worshippers of Old Scratch!" observed Radford, as he was preparing the mid-day meal, which consisted of a freshly-killed hen, boiled with some rice. "Mohammed has just been telling me something about them. All I know is that Old Nick has not much to complain of so far as his flock is concerned. They have been at our sugar already, and would have carried off Mohammed's tobacco if he had not been on the look out. I suppose they think it right to steal, so as to keep on good terms with their master."

The Yezeeds' religion, if such it may be called, is based upon the following dogma: that there are two spirits—a spirit of good and a spirit of evil. Allah, the spirit of good, can do no harm to any one, and is a friend to the human race. The spirit of evil can do a great deal of harm, and he is the cause of all our woes. From this starting-point the Yezeeds have been brought to believe that it is a waste of time to worship the spirit of good, who will not hurt them, and that the proper course to pursue is to try and propitiate the spirit of evil, who can be very disagreeable if he chooses. To do so they never venture to make use of the name of the devil, as this they believe would be an act of disrespect to their infernal master.

They are visited twice a year by different high priests, when certain rites are performed. These rites are kept a great secret. The Turks who gave me some information about the Yezeeds were unable to give me any details about the nature of the ceremonies. I was informed that the Yezeeds are divided into two sects; that the one looks upon the devil as the Grand Vizier of Allah, and the other regards him as the private secretary of the good spirit. It was said that the two sects hated each other to such an extent that, if a man belonging to the one which looks upon the devil as being the Grand Vizier of Allah were to enter a village belonging to members of the rival faith, the new arrival would have a great chance of losing his life.

The Yezeeds' priests are many of them unmarried. However, should a priest or sheik arrive in a village, the first thing which is done by the inhabitants is to offer their wives and daughters for his inspection. The sheik will select one. It will then be considered that he has conferred a very high honour on the young lady's relatives. There are different laws as to the subsequent treatment of these women. In one of the sects they are not allowed to marry, but are set apart ; and, in the case of a married woman, she is not permitted again to live with her husband. In the other sect they are permitted to marry, or if the lady has a spouse, she must return to him. It is then the duty of every Yezeed to make her rich presents, and the inhabitants of the village must maintain her husband and herself during the rest of their lives. Under these circumstances a woman who has been honoured by the attentions of a priest is looked upon by a youthful Yezeed in much the same light as a rich heiress by many impecunious younger sons in a European ball-room ; her hand is eagerly sought for in marriage. If she already possesses a husband, the latter considers himself as one of the most fortunate of men. The result of this is, that when a priest arrives in a village, great excitement arises amidst the population—every man hoping that his wife or daughter will be honoured by being selected. The ladies take immense interest in the proceedings. The visits of the reverend gentlemen are eagerly looked forward to by all classes of Yezeed society.

This information was given me by some Turks with whom I had conversed during my journey. I now asked my host if these statements were true. He at once repudiated them, and declared that they were inventions of the followers of Islam.

" Do you look upon the devil as the Grand Vizier of Allah ? " I now inquired.

If a bombshell had exploded in the room where I was sitting, there could not have been greater consternation than that which was evinced by the members of my host's family. Springing to their feet, they fled from the building—an old woman very nearly upsetting Radford's cooking-pot in her haste to escape into the open air. The captain looked at me, and then indulged in a sort of suppressed laugh.

" What has frightened them ? " I inquired.

" Effendi," he replied, " you mentioned the word 'Shaitan' (devil). It is very lucky for you," continued the old man,

" that there are five of us, and we are all well armed ; for, if not, the Yezeeds would have attacked our party for a certainty. Any disaster which may happen in this village during the next twelve months will be put down to you. If a man's cow or camel dies, the fellow will say that it is all your fault ; the sooner we continue our march the better."

It was getting late. The inhabitants had withdrawn to some distance from their houses ; they were gazing at our party with lowering brows. I would gladly have repaired the mischief that I had done ; but an apology might have only made matters worse. I was the more sorry, as I had hoped to have had the opportunity of questioning the Yezeeds as to some of their customs. What I had heard about them from the Turks was so different to what is related of this singular people by Mr. Layard in his admirable work, " Nineveh and its Remains," that I had become rather sceptical as to the veracity of my informants. The old captain, however, consoled me by saying that, on my journey from Van to Kars, I should have to pass by many other Yezeed villages, and would there be able to pursue my inquiries upon this subject.

Very shortly after leaving our halting-place, the guide stopped, and said something to the officer.

" What is he saying ? " I inquired.

" The summit of this hill is the border-line," was the reply. In another minute we had entered the territory of the Shah.

The track was good and firm ; although there was plenty of snow on the hills, there was but little on the plain below. After a few hours' march, we halted for the night in a village called Kelise Kandy.

The Usebashe was well known to the chief proprietor in the district, and, coming out to meet us, he invited our party to enter his house.

Kelise Kandy is a large village, and much cleaner than any of those which I had seen on the Turkish side of the frontier. The houses were well built, and many of them whitewashed. Several haystacks were in a yard belonging to our host ; hundreds of sheep and cattle stood in a large enclosure near his dwelling.

The proprietor was dressed at first sight a little like a European. He had a black coat ; a red sash was tied round his waist ; a pair of white trousers covered his legs. But a very high, cone-shaped, astrachan hat was on his head, and this article of attire, much resembling an extinguisher, did away with his otherwise slightly European appearance.

A number of servants, all armed with daggers stuck in their waist-belts, and with hats, if possible, still more like an extinguisher than that which their master wore, stood round the room. It was a good-sized apartment, thirty feet long by twenty broad. The floor was covered with a thick Persian carpet, of beautiful design, but not dear; indeed, I subsequently learnt that it had only cost fifteen pounds of our money.

Light was let into the room by some double windows—probably made in this fashion so as to keep out the cold. Our host, after motioning to me to squat down on one side of him, and to the Usebashe to squat down on the other, produced a cigar-case and offered me a cigarette.

He had been often in Erzeroum, and also in Russia, where he had imbibed a taste for smoking tobacco in this form. His acquaintance with the Muscovites had not prepossessed him in their favour.

"They want to conquer the Shah," he presently remarked. "They will make use of us as a stepping-stone to Van and Bagdad, after which they will annex their catspaw. We ought to have another Nadir Shah,' he continued. "If we had one, the Russians would not dare to laugh at us as they do."

"I thought that there were very good relations between the Courts of Teheran and St. Petersburg," I now remarked.

"The Shah is obliged to be on good terms with the Tzar," replied the Persian. "The Tzar is too strong for him."

"If there be a war between Russia and Turkey, which side will Persia take?"

The proprietor shook his head.

"We ought to go with Islam," he remarked; "but, better still, remain neutral. I am told that there are many Russian officers in Teheran. They are doing their best to influence the Shah in their master's favour. Nadir Shah once conquered you English in Hindostan," he added.

"No, he conquered part of India before we went there. However, now Hindostan belongs to us."

"I thought he had," continued the man. "I was told so in Russia; I was also informed that the Tzar of America had defeated you, and was an ally of the Emperor of Russia. Is that the case?"

"There is no Tzar in America," I replied; "we have had no war with the United States for many years."

"But you paid them a certain sum of money to prevent them going to war with you?" observed my host; "and not only that, but you pay Shere Ali, of Afghanistan, a large sum every year with the same object. Will Shere Ali fight against Russia if there is a war between the Tzar and Turkey?"

"I do not know."

"Some Muscovites say that Shere Ali is on their side," remarked the Persian. "But he is a clever fellow, and is not likely to join the weakest party."

CHAPTER LIII

Dinner—The Persian's wife is poorly—The wonderful wet paper—The *samovar*—The harem—Be not alarmed—She is in a delicate state of health—Jaundice—She feels better already—No medicine for your complaint—A mustard plaster would be useless—Sons of the devil—My lord's baksheesh—Commotion amongst the servants.

LATER in the day dinner was brought in—a chicken surrounded by a huge pile of rice. A Turk as rich as our Persian host would have provided his guest with fifteen or twenty courses, but the Persians are satisfied with one. I was not aware of the custom, and only tasted the chicken. Presently it was taken away; instead of a fresh dish making its appearance, some water was brought, in an ewer, for us to wash our hands.

"You Englishmen are very temperate," said the host, rising.

I did not tell him what was passing through my mind. I was ravenously hungry, and would gladly have had that chicken brought back again; but it was already in the hands of the servants outside. They were devouring the contents.

"You are a great hakim," now observed the proprietor.

"Who told you that?" I remarked, surprised that the reputation acquired in the Kurd's house had thus preceded me.

"The Uscbashe knows it. Mohammed, too, has told my servant. Praise be to Allah who has sent you here!"

"I am not a hakim!" I hastily replied. "I am an officer."

"Do not say that," said the Persian, who spoke Turkish fluently. "Do not deny the talents that Allah has given you. Your arrival has cast a gleam of sunshine on our threshold, and you will not go away without gladdening the hearts of my family."

"What do you want me to do?" I inquired.

"My wife is poorly: I ask you to cure her."

"But really I know very little about medicine. I have only a few simple remedies with me."

"Simple remedies indeed!" said the Persian. "A man who can set a person's shoulder on fire with a piece of wet paper!"

"What is the matter with your wife?"

"I do not know, but you will tell me."

"Well, I must see her," I replied.

"Impossible!" said the Persian. "She is in the harem. I cannot take you there!"

"But how can I tell you what is the matter with her if I do not see her?"

"Give me a piece of that wonderful wet paper; perhaps it will cure her."

"Effendi," said the Usebashe, turning to the Persian, "you cannot tell a horse's age without looking into his mouth. The Frank cannot tell your wife's ailments without looking at her tongue."

A consultation took place between my host and some other Persian visitors. It was at length agreed that, as a hakim, I might be admitted into the harem.

In the meantime a servant brought in a *samovar* (tea-urn), which the proprietor had purchased at Erivan; and whilst the Usebashe and myself were drinking tea, with lemon-juice instead of cream—as is the custom in Persia as well as in Russia—my host left the room and proceeded to the harem, to announce to his wife that I would see her.

Presently he returned, and, taking my hand, helped me to rise from the ground. Then, going first, he led the way across a yard, surrounded by a high wall and planted with fruit-trees, to a detached building, which I had previously thought was a mosque.

"This is the harem," said the proprietor. We entered an outer room; he drew a thick curtain which hung against one of the walls. An opening now appeared: stooping low, I entered the inner apartment. It was furnished, or rather unfurnished, like the one set apart for the Usebashe and myself. A pan of live charcoal stood in one corner. In the other, reclining on a quantity of silk cushions, was the wife of my host. She was enveloped from head to foot in a sheet made of some gauze-like material. There were so many folds that it was impossible to distinguish her features or even divine the contour of her form. Her feet, which were very small and stockingless, were exposed to view. She had taken them out of two tiny white slippers which lay by the side of the charcoal pan, and was nervously tapping the ground with her heel.

"She is alarmed," said my host. "Be not alarmed," he added, turning to his wife. "It is the hakim who has come to make you well."

These remarks did not tranquillize the lady. Her heel tapped the ground more quickly than before, the whole of her body shook like an aspen-leaf.

"She has never seen any man save myself in the harem," said her husband; "and you—you are a European."

"What is the nature of her illness?"

"She is in a delicate state of health."

"Can I look at her tongue?"

There was a whispered conversation with the lady. By this time she was a little more calm. Removing the folds of her veil, she allowed the tip of a very red little tongue to escape from her lips.

"Well, what do you think of it?" said my host, who was taking the greatest interest in these proceedings.

"It is a nice tongue; but now I must see her eyes."

"Why her eyes?"

"Because she may have what is called jaundice, and I must see if her eye is yellow."

"Perhaps she had better expose the whole face," said the Persian.

"Perhaps she had," I remarked.

And the poor little lady, whose nerves were now less excited, slowly unwound the folds of muslin from around her head. She was certainly pretty, and had very regular features, whilst a pair of large black eyes, which looked through me as I gazed on them, were twinkling with an air of humour more than of fear.

She understood Turkish well, as she came from the border, and, looking at me, said something in a low voice.

"She feels better already," said my host. "The sight of you has done her good; when you have given her some medicine, she will doubtless be quite well."

"What is the matter with you?" I said, turning to the patient.

She blushed. Her husband then remarked that she fancied strange dishes at her meals, and in fact was delicate.

It gradually dawned upon me what the nature of her malady was, and the more particularly as I was informed by my host that they had been married but a very few months.

"I have no medicine for your complaint," I remarked.

"No medicine!" said the Persian indignantly. "Mohammed has shown me the bottles and the little boxes. Besides that, you have the wet paper!"

"A mustard plaster would be useless."

"But she must have something!" said the husband.

Now, my medicine-chest was very limited in its contents. It merely contained cholera medicine, pills, and a few ounces of quinine, besides the prepared mustard plasters.

A pill, in the lady's condition, would not have been safe: I could not have answered for the consequences. Cholera mixture might have been equally disastrous in its effects. Quinine, I thought, could not do any harm; it is exceedingly nasty, an infinitesimally small dose leaves a very disagreeable taste in the mouth.

"You shall have some medicine," I observed. "Please God it will do you good."

"Inshallah! Inshallah!" replied my host devoutly; and accompanying me to the room prepared for the Usebashe and myself, I gave him three grains of quinine, to be taken in three doses, one grain in each dose.

"Will it do her much good?" inquired the Persian.

"That depends upon Allah," I remarked.

"Of course it does," said my host, and taking the medicine, he returned to his seraglio.

As we were leaving the house, I observed a great commotion amidst my host's servants. Mohammed was some time before he joined our party.

"What was the matter?" I asked.

"Effendi, they are sons of the devil, these Persians!" vociferated my man indignantly. "I waited behind to give them my lord's baksheesh, but they were greedy creatures, and one —a strong man—snatched all the paras out of my hand, and thrust the money in his waist-belt. The others cursed and called him many dogs, but the fellow did not care. They then wanted me to give them more money; I had none to bestow. They are like jackals, these Persians. They would cut a man's throat as soon as eat a pillaff!"

CHAPTER LIV

Villages — Arab Dize — Shadili — Shalendili — Karenee—Kurds—Radford
wishes to bleed the inhabitants—Persian men with their beards dyed
red—Every part of a woman is false—These Persians are a nation of
women—The old fire-worshippers' superstition—Gardens—Irrigation—
Soldiers—The flint fire-locks—They are unclean ones, these Persians—
The little dogs do some things well—A Persian will kiss you on one
cheek, and will stab you behind your back.

WE rode along a flat country. A few hills could be seen on
our bridle-hand. The track was in capital order for the march.
After passing several small hamlets—amongst others, Arab
Dize, Shadili, and Shalendili—we pulled up at a large village
called Karenee. It was inhabited by Kurds, all of them being
Persian subjects. Here there were 350 houses. Judging by
the number of people who came to ask for medicine, so soon as
I dismounted from my horse, the whole population was unwell.
It appeared that the Persian in whose house I had stopped on
the previous evening had sent word to the chief proprietor in
this Kurdish village, to say that a celebrated hakim was on
his way. No amount of expostulation saved us from the in-
trusion of the inhabitants. Every one wished me to look at
his tongue and to feel his pulse. Radford, who was in another
room, was interrupted in his cooking by a crowd of the
humbler Kurds, who believed that, when the master was so
great a hakim, his servant must necessarily have some medical
skill.

Presently my servant entered.

"What has happened?" I remarked.

"I cannot get on with my cooking, sir," was the reply.
"They will come and shove out their dirty tongues just over
my cooking-pot. Some of the people who have got nasty
diseases and sore legs insist upon showing them to me. Quite
turns me hup, that it does. I had two boxes of hantibilious—
I have given them all away. If I had only a pair of
champagne nippers, sir, I would draw the rascals' teeth;
perhaps that would take away their taste for my doctoring.
Do you think it would do any harm if I were to bleed one or
two of them, sir?"

"Could you stop the bleeding after the operation?" I
inquired.

"That, sir, is just what was passing in my mind. If I

thought as how I could, I would have taken a little blood from each of them in turn. It would have cooled them down a little, and they would not have been so anxious for my company in future."

On reaching a village about three hours' distance from our sleeping quarters, we heard that the short road over the mountains to Van was blocked by the snow, and that it would be absolutely necessary to go by Khoi, and by a circuitous route which I had hoped to avoid.

I did not believe the statement, and ordered the guide to take the mountain track. The man reluctantly consented. Higher and higher we ascended the steep which divided us from the capital of Armenia. The snow at each moment became more deep. At last the guide halted, and distinctly refused to advance.

"I shall lose my life," he said. "You can do what you like with your own, but I have children for whom to provide."

The Usebashe interfered.

"The fellow is telling the truth about the road," he said. "I too, like yourself, thought that he was deceiving us. We had better go to Khoi."

There was nothing to be done but turn round and continue towards that town. It was about fifty miles distant from us. We halted for the night at a Kurdish village called Melhamee. Here the inhabitants received us very discourteously. If it had not been for the Usebashe, who reminded them of the laws of hospitality which are prescribed by their religion, I much doubt whether we should have obtained a resting-place. They had learnt that I was an Englishman, and were under the impression that they would be pleasing the Russians if they threw difficulties in our way.

"We know who you are," said a Kurd, "and the people in Erivan know who you are too. The Russians are our friends," he continued.

"Take care that your friends do not eat you some day," said the Usebashe.

"They will eat you first, and we shall help them!" said the Kurd.

This aroused the captain's indignation. I thought that there would have been a disturbance. But, after a little more verbal warfare, the belligerents parted.

"All the people in this village are in Russian pay," said the Usebashe, "and that is why they are so hostile to you as well as to ourselves. These men," he continued, " are foolish enough to believe in the Russians, and think that because the Tzar's agents give them money and presents, this same sort of treatment will be continued. Poor fools ! they will find their mistake some day."

We rode by men driving before them oxen laden with wood for fuel. There were many villages on either side of the track. The Persian inhabitants, attired in loose blue garments, and with their beards dyed red, gazed curiously upon us as we passed.

Some of the greater dandies amidst these gentlemen had their finger-nails also stained ; and unless a man has his beard dyed a bright colour, he has very little chance of meeting with the approval of the fair sex. A stout red-haired Welshman would have what is termed *un grand succès* amidst the ladies in these regions.

" These Persians are ridiculous creatures," said the Usebashe. " Only think of the men dyeing their beards red ! One would have thought that black would have been a more appropriate colour."

" Some of our English women dye their hair a light colour," I remarked.

" With women I can understand it," said the Usebashe. " Every part of a woman is false, from her tongue to her smile, dyeing her hair red enables her to carry on the deception ; but for men to dye their hair red—they might as well form part of a harem at once ! However, these Persians are a nation of women."

And the Usebashe pointed contemptuously at a little knot of men who were seated outside a small dwelling, and watching eagerly for the moment when the sun would disappear behind the hills.

I have often wondered whether something connected with the old fire-worshippers' superstition has a lurking-place in the minds of the Persians or Kurds. Day after day, and at the same hour, I have seen the entire inhabitants of a village turn out and gaze intently upon the great orb of light slowly sinking into space on the distant horizon. I have questioned them about this subject. They indignantly repudiate the idea of any act of worship to the sun ; they say that they do so because it is their habit, and because their fathers, grandfathers, and ancestors did the same thing before them.

We rode by many gardens surrounded by high walls ; some

of these enclosures were five or six acres in extent. Cherry, apple, peach, and mulberry trees abound throughout the district. A plentiful water-supply, which is brought from the mountains by means of artificial dykes, irrigates the various orchards. Little trenches intersect each other at many places along the fields, and when the proprietor wishes, he can at once place his land under water. This must be an inestimable boon to the inhabitants during the hot months, as otherwise their entire crop would be destroyed by the heat.

Soldiers dressed in a dirty sort of French uniform, but with black sheepskin hats of the extinguisher shape, sat outside the guard-houses in the different villages. They looked askantly at the Usebashe as he passed—for the Usebashe was in uniform. A wonderful sort of blue cape covered the upper part of his person, and red knickerbockers, stuffed in high boots, his extremities. A curved scimitar hung from his waist-belt. The red fez on his head, and on our guide's, showed their allegiance to the Sultan.

The two men clad in European costumes were also a source of wonder to the soldiers. Some of them gripped the flint fire-locks with which they were armed, and made a movement as if they would like to have had a shot at our little party.

"Yes, you dogs! I have no doubt but that you would like to do so," said the old Usebashe, shaking his fist at them, after we had got to a safe distance. "However, your guns are only serviceable up to fifty yards; it takes you five minutes to load them! They are unclean ones, these Persians; do you not think so, Effendi?" continued the old Usebashe.

"I have seen so little of them I cannot judge. But their roads and houses are much better and cleaner than those which you have in Turkey."

"That is true," said the captain sorrowfully. "The little dogs can do some things well, but they are sly and deceitful. A Persian will kiss you on one cheek, and will stab you behind your back. He will call himself your friend, and will slander you to your neighbours. He will offer you the best horse in his stable: the offer comes from his lips, and not from his heart. When you know them better, you will find this out for yourself."

CHAPTER LV

VILLAGE after village were left behind us, still there were no
signs of Khoi. We had been told that it was only an eight
hours' march from Melhamee, two more sped by ere the walls
of the city were in sight. Soon afterwards we rode through a
narrow gate which gives access to the town, and presently
pulled up at a house belonging to the Turkish Consul, who is
the only diplomatic agent to be found in this city. He had
been educated in Constantinople, and spoke a little French.
For the last two years he had been established in Khoi, and
he greatly bewailed his thus being cut off from all European
society.

I now learnt that Russian intrigues had been the means
of very nearly creating a war between Persia and Turkey.
There is a Turkish border-hamlet, called Kashka Beulah,
about nine miles from Khoi. Some Persian soldiers had
recently attacked this village, and had robbed the inhabitants
of everything they possessed.

Whilst the Persians were engaged in their work of pillage,
some Turkish soldiers, under a Usebashe, arrived from an
adjacent guard-house. But the Persians were more numerous.
They captured the captain and seven of his men, and
brought them prisoners to Khoi. A Turkish lieutenant in
the guard-house heard of the fate of his Usebashe, and
arrested two Persian merchants who happened to be in the
neighbourhood. He sent them as prisoners to Van. The
Consul, on hearing of this, telegraphed to his Ambassador at
Teheran for instructions how to act. The latter official sent
back an answer that the Persian merchants were to be
immediately released. The Consul then wrote to the governor
at Van, informing him of the order he had received. The
governor, however, declared that he could not comply with it

without authority from Constantinople. After several weeks' delay, during which time the Turkish captain and his men had been kept in chains in the prison at Khoi, and had been treated like the commonest of malefactors, orders came from Teheran and Constantinople for the mutual exchange of prisoners.

A day was fixed. At the appointed time the Turkish Consul, with the prisoners and three hundred Persian soldiers, started for the frontier. Here he was met by the Persian Consul from Van. The latter was accompanied by the Persian captives and by an escort of Turks. The troops then retired to a short distance. The Consuls remained alone with their prisoners. The exchange was effected.

"What was the origin of the disturbance?" I inquired of the Consul.

"That is exactly what I wished to discover," replied that official. "I went to the governor of Khoi, who, by the way, is the Shah's uncle, and asked him why his regular troops had first of all attacked our village. The reply was, 'My orders came from some one of higher rank than I am.' Later on, it turned out that Russian agents at Teheran were the origin of the affair."

"I am very dull here," now remarked the Consul. "My wife died six months ago. I have not been able to find any one to replace her."

"Why do you not take a Kurdish girl?" observed the Usebashe. "They make the best of wives," he continued; "if their husbands have money they do not ask for any; if the husbands have no money the wives never bother their heads about the matter. In addition to this, they do not care about fine clothes. A long piece of calico and a pair of slippers content each one of them as well as all the silks and satins in the bazaar at Erzeroum."

"My late wife was a Kurd," replied the Consul sorrowfully. "She cost me very little."

A servant entered the room and lit the speaker's pipe.

"This man is my father-in-law," he added. "My mother-in-law cooks for me downstairs. When I married their daughter I wanted some servants; my wife proposed that we should engage her father and mother. I did so, and have found them hard-working people. When my poor wife died, I allowed them to remain with me. When I marry again, my new lady will probably wish her own relations to come here: I shall be obliged to get rid of my present servants."

"It is a very economical way of providing for a wife's relatives," I observed.

"Yes," said the Consul, laughing. "You could not make use of your mother-in-law as a cook in either Constantinople or London. Besides that, the women in your country cost their husbands a fortune in dress."

"Yes," I replied, "some of the women's dresses cost from 50 to 60 liras a piece, and, after having been worn once or twice, they are thrown away or given to the servants."

"Allah?" said the Usebashe, "50 or 60 liras! Only think of it!"

"The Inglis speaks the truth," said the Consul. "I have heard of this before, when I was at Constantinople. My last wife cost 10 liras," he continued; "I could buy five or six wives for the same price as a great English lady gives for her dress!"

"Why do you not marry a Persian woman?" I now remarked. "By all account they are very pretty, and you would have an opportunity of learning the language"—the Consul having previously bewailed to me his ignorance of that tongue.

"Marry a Persian, indeed!" interrupted the Usebashe. "The Persians will not give their daughters in marriage to us Turks. They are very selfish," he added. "We make no objections to our daughters marrying Persians. But the latter are most particular about this subject."

"You are both Mohammedan nations," I remarked.

"Yes, we are," said the Consul; "and the Armenians and yourselves are both Christian nations, but your forms of Christianity are very different. There is as much difference between a Persian and a Turk as between an Armenian and yourself."

"The Persians are very cruel," observed the Usebashe. "If a man commits a crime, and is detected, the authorities are not satisfied by taking the culprit's life, but often torture him first—sometimes by taking out his eyes, and at others by mutilation."

"The inhabitants do very odd things," said the Consul. "For instance, a short time ago there was an official in this town who was extremely unpopular. He died, and you would have thought that the matter was over; but no, six months after the man's decease, some of the townspeople went to the cemetery, exhumed the body, and hacked it to pieces. This was done by way of revenging themselves upon the official. There was a robbery in the bazaar," continued the speaker, " A man was taken up on suspicion of being implicated in the theft; he swore that he was innocent, but accused another man. The latter had nothing whatever to do with the robbery, but was unpopular in the town. Some people belonging to the bazaar went to the governor, and said to him, 'The man last arrested is the thief; you must order the executioner to cut his throat.' The governor was weak enough to consent, the innocent person was put to death. Soon afterwards the governor repented of what he had done. However, he was in need of money at the time, he determined to turn his repentance to some account. He ordered fifty of the richest people amongst those who had pressed him to execute the innocent man, to be imprisoned, and he kept them in gaol until such time as they had paid him a large sum of money."

I now walked round the fortifications of the town. They consist of a wall about thirty-five feet high, built of clay, with a brick foundation, and a dry ditch, which can be filled with water if necessary. There were sixteen old cannon on the ramparts. The Kurds and the inhabitants think that the place is impregnable. A battery of nine-pounders would be quite sufficient to destroy the fortifications, which are much out of repair. Any properly equipped force ought to take the city, which contains 7000 houses, in about half an hour.

The soldiers in the different guard-houses ran outside the buildings. They presented arms to the Consul as he walked with me through the streets. Presently we came to a place where two sentries had been posted. The men had put their flint muskets on the ground, and were engaged in gambling with each other—small balls of dried clay, something like marbles, taking the place of dice.

CHAPTER LVI

I ARRIVED at the bazaar. It is a very large building, arched
over in many places, and here and there is constructed of
bricks. It was a hot afternoon. The bazaar was delightfully
cool; many of the inhabitants had gone there merely with the
object of lying in the shade. At almost every step we took,
we came upon the forms of some recumbent Persians. It was
rather dark. The idlers' ribs must have suffered. A muttered
curse would be the only sign of the men's disgust; they would
turn over and be asleep again in another minute.

The bazaar was better arranged than any of the market-
places which I had visited in Anatolia. The shops belonging
to men who sold one kind of article were all side by side, and
not mixed up with the stalls belonging to traders in other
merchandise. Some carpets were very beautifully designed,
and could have been purchased for one-fourth of the price they
command in the London market. The cutlery mostly came
from Erivan in Russia. An immense quantity of gaudily-
coloured Russian calicoes were exposed for sale.

We came to a samovar (tea-urn) shop. The owner, a sleepy-
looking Persian, was very wide awake, so far as his interests
were concerned. He was engaged in a wordy warfare with a
Kurd who wanted to buy an urn for his house. The conversation became so loud, and the gesticulations of the Kurd
were so energetic, that I thought he was about to attack the
merchant. However, a minute later the affair was settled,
and the purchaser was drinking a glass of tea with the
salesman.

Most of the houses in Khoi are built of a sort of brown
clay. If it were not for the numerous mosques which are
painted blue and green, the town would be very sombre in its
appearance. Many of the doors to the buildings were supplied

with massive iron knockers—a rarity in Asiatic Turkey—and the many windows on the ground-floors, which were guarded by iron bars, rather reminded me of Cordova.

Streams of muddy water ran through the streets. Hundreds of women were busily engaged in washing the domestic apparel.

We passed by an open window, and, on looking in, I found that the building was used as a school. A master was seated on the window-sill, fifty or more children were clustered round his feet. He was teaching them pieces of the Koran, which the little ones were endeavouring to learn by heart. A class of lads, averaging, I should say, from fifteen to twenty years of age, were squatting in a corner occupied in learning how to write—a very rare accomplishment in Persia, and principally confined to the merchant classes. Some of the lads had escaped for a moment from the vigilance of their master, and were buying oranges from a pedlar. The fruit had been brought from Tabriz, as there are no orange-trees in the neighbourhood of Khoi. Suddenly the Hodja discovered their absence; he ran outside the school. He did not confine his blows to the lads, but allowed the pedlar to share them with his pupils.

We arrived at some pillaff shops; here legs and wings of chickens, surrounded by piles of rice, were placed before the merchants. One of them, taking a piece of meat in his fingers from a plate, handed it to me. He wanted my opinion of his wares.

"Good!" I said.

"Have you pillaff in your country?" he inquired.

"Yes."

"But not like my pillaff?"

"No, not so good."

This greatly delighted the trader: running out of his shop, he insisted that I should return with him and taste his sweetmeats. These last were some of them very well made, and had been manufactured with a considerable amount of skill—a trade going on in bon-bons between Khoi and other towns in the interior. The Persian ladies are very fond of sweetmeats, a large quantity of these delicacies being consumed in the different harems.

I wanted to buy some article of native manufacture in silver. It was impossible; the jewellers kept nothing by them ready made. They could have executed an order, but this would have been a tedious affair. After having visited the mosque in the town—a building which was rather more lofty than the Turkish mosques, but in other respects very similar—I began to think that it was time for me to continue my journey to Van.

It was very warm here, but the route from Van to Kars would be covered with snow, and I had only two months left of my leave of absence to complete the journey to England. The Consul pressed me to stay another day in his house. However, we had commenced making our preparations, and I was the more eager to leave the town as I had been given to understand that my arrival had caused great uneasiness to the Russian officials in Erivan. From their being so close to Khoi, they have begun to look upon this town as their own territory.

The paternal Government was alarmed lest I should be murdered by the Persians; and after the extreme solicitude the Russian authorities had shown for my safety when I was travelling to Khiva, I should have been deeply grieved to have given them any more annoyance on my account.

The following morning we left Khoi at daybreak. The city stands on a plain and is surrounded by a chain of hills, but they are at a considerable distance from the walls.

The latter gradually disappeared, and, after a march of two hours and a half along a good road, we arrived at Kotoor Boghaz, a famous pass which divides the territory of the Sultan from that of the Shah. There is no Persian military station in the neighbourhood. The Turks have built a sort of block-house at the entrance of the gorge. Here I found a small force, consisting of one captain, two lieutenants, forty infantry, and twenty-eight cavalry soldiers. Ahmed was the name of the captain. I now discovered that he was the identical officer who, six months previous, had been made prisoner by the Persians and taken to Khoi. He informed me that one Turkish soldier, Osman by name, had been killed in the fray, and that he himself had been kept in chains for forty days in the gaol at Khoi, during which time he had nothing given him to eat save bread and water. In addition to this he had to sleep on the bare floor. According to my informant, the Persian captives who had been sent to Van had been well treated. They had been given beds in which to sleep, and had been supplied with pillaff.

"What do you think was the cause of the Persians attacking the Turkish village?" I inquired.

"The Russians were the origin of the disturbance," replied the officer. "Whilst I was being taken a prisoner to Khoi, I heard the Persian soldiers say, 'The Russians are our fathers,' and they laughed at me as they said so."

"The sooner we fight Russia the better," continued the speaker. "She will not be half so troublesome to us in open fight as she is at present."

We proceeded onward through the Kotoor Pass. A little stream, called the Kotoor Su, dashed along at our feet, and gradually became wider as it received a succession of small tributaries from the adjacent mountains.

The defile presents a series of magnificent positions for defence. It is in many places not more than 200 yards broad. Precipitous heights look down upon the stream from either hand.

There are several mineral springs in this neighbourhood, some being of a sulphurous nature. These are largely used by the Kurds, who, if unwell, come here during the summer months and drink the waters.

Presently the guide turned off the path; ascending some rising ground, he dismounted by the side of a spring. Taking a tin cup from my holster, I desired him to fill it, after which I tasted the water. It was warm, and reminded me of the Sprudel spring at Carlsbad, but is much stronger. Two glasses full of this Kotoor water are equivalent in their effects to at least four of the Sprudel.

Snow lay on the ground beneath us. At first in patches, then becoming more frequent, it covered the winding path. A hail storm came on. A cutting wind whistled through the gorge. The sudden difference between the heat at Khoi, and the cold in the Kotoor Pass, struck a chill to our very bones. We had been marching for six hours; there were still five more ere we could reach a resting-place.

Dismounting from our horses, we ran by their side and tried to restore the circulation in our bodies. The rapid changes of climate in this part of Asia Minor are very dangerous to travellers. The natives have a saying, "A chill in the evening is death in the morn." If any one experiences a chill, and does not succeed in becoming warm again immediately, he is certain to feel some ill-effects. We passed by another hot-spring; it issues from the bank of the Kotoor river. The guido, borrowing my tin, dismounted, and began to wash his mouth.

" Why are you doing that ? " I inquired.

" For toothache," was the reply.

We now learnt that the Kurds have an implicit belief in the efficacy of this water for such complaints.

CHAPTER LVII

Kotoor—The Quarantine station—The medical officer in charge—The Governor of Kotoor—A Russian disguised as a Persian—Mineral wealth—The Russians would like this territory—A stepping-stone to Bagdad and Mosul—A loyal Kurd—Aleshkert—The people there take the strongest side—Moullah Hassan—Kurdish merchants—The postman—His mule—The mule in the water—My new yellow trousers—The saddle-bags in the river—Nestorian villages—How to buy a wife—Exchange and barter—A horse and two sheep—Van—The Pacha—The barracks—The garrison—Bitlis.

I was not sorry to reach Kotoor. The track had been very bad for the last half of our journey. An eleven hours' march made under such circumstances is tiring for man as well as beast.

There is a quarantine station in the town. The medical officer in charge has to examine all people travelling from Persia to Turkey by this route. This is done to prevent persons suffering from cholera or plague spreading these maladies throughout the Sultan's dominions.

The governor of Kotoor was a Persian by birth. His father had been in the Shah's service, but had changed his allegiance and enabled the Sultan to take possession of some land round Kotoor, which originally belonged to Persia. He now informed me that the Persians were forming a military camp at Salmas, and said that probably this was being done with the connivance of Russia.

The medical officer, an Italian, entered the room ; he was about eighty years of age, and had been in Kotoor since 1847. His emoluments consist of ten piastres per head, which he receives from every one who passes along the Kotoor road from Persia to Turkey.

" A Russian came here the other day," observed the doctor. " He was disguised as a Persian, and thought that I did not recognize his nationality."

" What was the object of his journey ? "

" Probably to stir up the Kurds, and invite the Armenians to rise against the Mussulmans," replied the doctor. " There is a great deal of mineral wealth in this neighbourhood," he continued; " coal and iron abound within two miles of this place."

" The Russians would like to take this territory for two reasons," remarked the governor; " first, because having Kotoor and Van, they would be able to make depôts and preparations for a march further south upon Bagdad and Mosul; and, secondly, on account of the mines in the district."

A Kurdish chieftain who lived near Bitlis had recently written to the Sultan, offering him the services of 20,000 men in the event of a war between Turkey and Russia. His offer was accepted, and the loyal Kurd's heart had been gladdened by the present of a magnificent silk turban and a sword.

The mountaineers near Kotoor could all be relied upon by the Turks. But there was reason to mistrust the sincerity and good faith of the Kurds in the neighbourhood of Moush and Aleshkert. They were said to have recently received large sums of money, besides arms, from Russia.

" If the Russians were to be worsted, the Kurds would be the first to turn these arms against their quondam friends," added the governor; " for the people about Aleshkert are proverbial for one thing,—namely, that they always take the winning side."

The following morning I said good-bye to the hospitable old doctor, in whose house I had slept. He had kindly given me a bed in one corner of his room—he himself, and the rest of his family, having slept in the other.

We rode towards Van. It is about sixty miles distant from Kotoor. Our track for the first hour ran within the mountain gorge—a continuation of the Kotoor Pass, but which here is several miles wide. After riding by several Kurdish villages, we began to ascend a succession of rising slopes. Plateau after plateau, each higher than its neighbour, were extended in front of us; the snow at each moment became deeper. It was evident that we could not reach Van on that evening. I determined to break the journey at the village of Moullah Hassan, which would be about a ten hours' march from Kotoor. Several Kurdish merchants had joined our party; they were travelling from Khoi, and drove before them oxen and calves laden with timbaki (Persian tobacco).

One of the Kurds possessed a mule. This animal, besides his master's personal effects, carried the post-bag from Khoi to Van. The Kurd led his mule for some time, but at length, tiring of this, he turned the animal loose, and drove him before our party, in company with the oxen and calves belonging to the other traders. We had nearly reached Moullah Hassan ; the mule had outstripped the rest of the caravan, I was riding behind him. The road suddenly dipped. There was a declivity in front of us. I lost sight of the animal. He had disappeared.

It was becoming dark. I pulled up my horse for a moment —it was lucky that I did so, for in another moment we should have been in a river—the dip being neither more nor less than the bed of the stream, which was covered over with a thin film of ice and two or three feet of snow. In another second the mule's head appeared above the surface. His frantic struggles showed that he was endeavouring to gain a foothold.

The proprietor of the animal came up.

" My new yellow trousers ! " was his first remark. A fearful oath then resounded from his lips.

He had bought some clothes at Khoi. They were in his saddle-bags and on the mule—the letter-bag being evidently considered by the muleteer as something quite secondary to his personal attire. He tried to reach the animal, but the ice breaking, let him into the water. In the meantime the exertions of the mule had loosened his surcingle, presently it gave way ; saddle, and letters, in addition to the wardrobe of the Kurd, slipped off the animal's back. They sank to the bottom of the river.

Our guide turning to the right, proposed that we should ride up the stream, and try and find a place where the ice would bear. This was done. About half an hour after-wards we found ourselves beneath the roof of a Kurdish farmer — the chief proprietor in the village of Moullah Hassan.

There were several Nestorian villages in the neighbour-hood ; however, the inhabitants of these hamlets possess the reputation of being dirtier than the Kurds, so the traveller who is wise will invariably elect to pass the night with the mountaineers.

The Kurd whose mule had fallen into the water entered the room. In one hand he bore something which was dripping wet. He salaamed, and then began to wring out the article he was carrying; the trousers were exposed to view. Once of a yellow colour, they were now a dull brown. The Kurd, stretching them out on the floor, gazed in a melancholy manner upon the soiled vestments.

"A horse and two sheep," he remarked with a sob; "Effendi, have pity upon me!"

"What does he want?" I inquired of Mohammed.

It appeared that the Kurd wished to buy a wife from a neighbouring farmer who had some marriageable daughters. Their father, nothing loth, and who was in want of a pair of broad yellow trousers, had consented, provided the candidate for his girl's hand would provide him with a beautiful pair, a turban, and some tea. Broad yellow drawers, or pants, as Yankees would call them, are not often to be met with in Kurdistan. They are brought from Erivan in Russia, and are greatly prized by the mountaineers. The Kurd had been to Khoi on purpose, had sold there a horse and two sheep; with the proceeds of the sale he had purchased the attire in question. He was now dreadfully alarmed lest the father of the girl should decline giving his daughter in exchange for the soiled apparel.

"But what can I do in the matter?" was my next question.

"Give me a baksheesh," said the Kurd, "and I will return to Khoi and buy some more garments."

The man had forgotten about the mail-bag, which lay buried beneath the frozen surface of the river.

Desiring him to go and fish up the letters, I promised that, later in the day, I would take his case into consideration.

The snow disappeared as we approached the town of Van. We rode by a small lake, about twelve miles from our halting-place. Continuing on over a succession of table-lands, the path sloped down towards the great lake or sea, to which the capital of Armenia gives a name.

Van stands in a plain and is surrounded by orchards filled with fruit-trees. The ground in the neighbourhood is highly cultivated, corn and other cereals flourishing throughout the district.

I had sent forward a letter of introduction to the governor of Van from Ismail Pacha of Erzeroum. The man to whom I had entrusted the epistle had not taken the trouble to deliver it. The governor was quite ignorant of my arrival.

I stopped at his house, and going up to the reception-chamber, found him busily engaged in conversation with an

official who had recently arrived from Constantinople, to inquire into the excesses said to have been committed by some soldiers upon the Armenians in Van.

The Pacha received me very courteously, in spite of my not having a letter for him ; he remarked, with a smile, that there were no hotels in Van as in Constantinople, and said that he would provide me with a room in a barrack which had been lately erected in the town.

The officer commanding the garrison now entered the room, and accompanied me to my quarters. The barrack was two stories high, and in the form of a square, with a courtyard for drill in the centre of the building. The officers' and men's rooms were on the first story, and below them the stables for the horses. The apartment given me was large and clean. The walls were whitewashed, the floor was covered with a Persian carpet. A large looking-glass—the first I had seen since I quitted our Consul's house in Erzeroum—was suspended from the walls.

There were only half a battalion of infantry and a battery of Krupp guns at that time in Van. The remainder of the garrison, consisting of one battalion and a half, had marched the previous week to the neighbourhood of Bitlis, where some Kurds had burnt down a Turkish guard-house.

CHAPTER LVIII

THE following morning I walked with the commandant to see the artillery at practice. The drill was fairly done. The guns were horsed with fine-looking animals from 15·3 to 16 hands high, mostly greys, and brought from European Turkey. The officer who commanded took great pride in his battery. A few hours after the drill was over, he accompanied me through the stables. The steel was bright, and the harness in thorough good order. When I remarked this to the commander he replied,—

"Effendi, I was educated in the Military School at Constantinople. If the rest of our officers had been there, we should have a better army. But, please God, for all that we shall give the Russians more to do than they expect."

I now went to see the citadel. It stands on a rock in the middle of the town, and is about 500 feet above the level of the lake.

Van is surrounded on three sides by a chain of hills, which are at a distance of from three to seven miles from the town. On the fourth side it is bounded by the lake which bears its name. There is a swamp towards the west, and close to the houses. This makes the place very unhealthy in the summer months—typhus and other fevers are prevalent in the district. The military surgeon, a Hungarian, who accompanied me in my ride to the citadel, observed that several complaints had been made to the authorities at Constantinople as to the sanitary state of Van, and a letter had been sent to the Medical Department recommending that the swamp should be drained. A Pacha had died of typhus only six months before ; this had thoroughly aroused the new governor. It had acted upon him like the death of a director, in a railway accident, acts upon the other directors of the line. However, nothing had been done up to the present time towards carrying the governor's and doctor's suggestions into effect.

I now learnt that the lake contains natron. The townspeople have a very simple manner of obtaining this substance. In the summer months they pour water from the lake into large shallow basins ; the heat of the sun evaporates the water, and carbonate of soda is deposited at the bottom of the vessels. It is afterwards sent to Erzeroum and Stamboul. The inhabitants of Van use this substance for washing purposes as a substitute for soap.

The road wound round the height on which the citadel stands. After about a fifteen minutes' climb our horses reached the summit. Here there were several very old guns, some dating back more than 250 years. Large piles of stone balls lay behind many of the pieces ; the commander, pointing at them, remarked that now-a-days they would not be of any use, although in the last century they had struck terror into the midst of a Persian host. The modern citadel, if it may be termed by that name, is merely a block-house, with accommo-

dation for about 100 soldiers. There are many galleries cut
in the solid rock, some of which were used in old days as
quarters for the troops, and others as dungeons for prisoners.
Some heavy chains were lying on the floors, or fastened to
rings in the rock. Presently we came to an enormous cavern
filled with stone cannon-balls. The commandant informed
me that these had been brought there just before Nadir
Shah's attack upon Van.

"Nadir Shah besieged this town for seven years," continued the officer; "look at the marks of some of his
handiwork." With these words he showed us a few holes in
the wall which had apparently been made by artillery fire.

Many ancient Greek and Assyrian coins had been found in
the neighbourhood of the citadel, and, according to the doctor,
the place abounds with inscriptions in characters which
cannot be read by any of the inhabitants.

There is a well of naphtha about fifty yards from the block-
house. The commandant, going with me to the spot, made a
soldier draw out some of the contents. The well was very
deep, and the inhabitants of Van had used the naphtha from
time immemorial. The doctor was doubtful as to whether it
was a natural well, or merely a large cistern which had been
filled many years ago with this liquid, possibly for the use of
the garrison.

"Are the guns in the citadel ever discharged?" I inquired.

"No," said the commandant, "they are all useless with the
exception of one small piece which we keep for firing salutes
during the Bairam. This rock is much too near the town to
be used as a fort," he continued. "A hospital ought to be
built here, or it would be a good site for a depôt of stores;
but as a defensive position it is useless against modern
artillery."

We came to a place in the rock where it descends abruptly
for several hundred feet. "An Englishman was let down
from here by a cord some years ago," observed the doctor.
"About 200 feet below this spot there is an inscription
cut on the stone. The inscription is about Semiramis.
Formerly we all wished to know what was the meaning of the
writing; but, no one in Van was bold enough to descend the
rock, or, even if some Armenian or Turk had dared to make
the attempt, he would have been unable to decipher the
characters. Well," continued the speaker, "an Englishman
came here and was lowered by cords over the precipice. If

he had fallen even from the spot where the inscription is cut, he must have been dashed to pieces, as it is a long way above the rocks. However, your countryman succeeded in taking an impression of the characters, and I believe a translation of them is in the British Museum. You can see the inscription from the town itself," he added. " The letters are very large, they occupy a place about twelve feet long by eight wide."

We returned towards the barrack. On the way I took the opportunity of looking at the characters on the rock. They are cut on four square blocks, each block being placed by the side of its fellow. Imagine four gigantic sheets of the *Times*, placed one alongside the other, and covered with huge quaintly-formed letters ; you will then be able to form an idea of the appearance of the inscription. As you look at the writing from the ground, it appears that in the third square from the right the letters are a little defaced, but in the others the characters stand out as clear as on the day when they were first chiselled. Several Armenian children were playing at soldiers in the street, their fathers and brothers were being instructed in drill in the barrack-yard. Some little military enthusiasm existed in the town even amongst the Christians, and the governor had promulgated the Sultan's edict that every one of his subjects was to be taught the use of arms.

I paid the commandant a visit. His apartments adjoined mine ; whilst I was with him several men arrived—some wishing to be soldiers, others desirous of being released from the conscription. A fine-looking Kurd was amongst the last-mentioned applicants. He was dressed in the usual picturesque costume of his race, but, in addition, wore a sort of white muslin shawl, which enveloped him from head to foot.

" You will make a capital soldier," said the commandant. " You had better serve."

" Bey Effendi," replied the man, " I am ruptured."

" Really," said the doctor, who was present in the room ; " on which side ? "

" The right," replied the man, pointing to his groin.

" Then you will do very well for the infantry," observed the Hungarian. " A man must be ruptured on both sides to be freed from service in that branch of the army."

The Kurd went away rather crestfallen. I then learnt that it is a common practice amongst those mountaineers who do not wish to serve, to purposely rupture themselves. This they do by pressing with their finger and thumb on the lower part of the stomach until a swelling arises. The operation hurts. After a man has ruptured himself on one side he does not feel inclined to repeat the process on the other. The doctor, who gave me the information, observed that the Kurds have a way of curing ruptures which is not generally known to the medical faculty. They burn the skin around the ruptured spot with a hot iron, the muscles will then contract, and this often effects a cure.

Three American missionaries called : they were living at a village about an hour's ride from Van. They had been there for some years, but had not succeeded in making many converts.

They described the country as being in a very unsettled state, and said that they had lately heard from some other missionaries near Bitlis that a Kurdish sheik in that neighbourhood had recommended them not to go to the mountains, as they were in the habit of doing during the summer months, for he could not guarantee their safety.

The missionaries at Van were eager to know what part England was likely to take in the event of a war. Although Americans, they are looked upon by the inhabitants as Englishmen, and the English flag is much more respected in Asia Minor than that of the United States.

The commissioner who had been sent from Constantinople, to inquire about the recent disturbances at Van, and the burning of the Armenian bazaar, entered the room. He informed me that immediately after the conflagration had occurred, fabulous reports as to the amount of the property destroyed had been published in the Armenian papers. It was first stated that 1,000,000 liras would not cover the loss experienced by the merchants in Van. Subsequently it was said that 200,000 liras in specie had been stolen by the Turkish soldiery, and that goods to the value of 300,000 liras had been destroyed by the flames.

When the commissioner arrived at Van, his first act was to make a list of all the merchants who had shops in the bazaar. Then, sending for each man separately, he asked him what was the nature of his merchandise, and at how much he valued his losses. When the commissioner added up the sums claimed by all the merchants in Van, he found that the total amount did not exceed 96,000 liras. In addition to this the Armenians acknowledged having saved goods to the value of 10,000 liras.

In the official's opinion 23,000 liras would cover the entire loss ; and from what I afterwards saw of the ruins of the bazaar, and judging from the small area over which they extended, I am inclined to believe that he had fairly estimated the damage.

The Armenian newspapers, probably instigated by Russian agents, had declared that the Turkish troops stationed in Van had first set fire to the bazaar, and then pillaged it in the confusion. The commissioner, after the most searching inquiries, was unable to discover that the troops were in any way implicated in the affair. Several Armenians kept petroleum and lucifer matches in their warehouses : his idea was that the fire originated either by spontaneous combustion, or through some one accidentally dropping a lighted match.

The soldiers had been called out to help to extinguish the fire. Thinking that the men might have stolen something during the conflagration, the commissioner asked the commander to issue an order for all the garrison to march to Erzeroum on the following morning. This was done. Shortly afterwards the different battalions left the town. The commissioner, accompanied by some Armenian merchants, met the troops on the road. The soldiers' baggage was then searched, and each man in succession. Nothing was found which could in any way connect the troops with the robbery.

CHAPTER LIX

I now walked to an extempore market which the Armenians are making use of until the old one is reconstructed. With the exception of quantities of rough silk brought from Persia, raw cotton, and carbonate of soda, which had been taken from the lake, there was literally nothing to see.

It was said that there were 20,000 inhabitants in the town ; I am inclined to believe that the number has been ex-

aggerated. The market-place which had been destroyed by
fire stood on a very small area of ground. The impression
conveyed to my mind was that the whole town did not contain
above 16,000 inhabitants. The Pacha receives a yearly salary
of 2200 liras, and is paid in gold. The other officials are not
so fortunate ; the pay of the commander of the garrison only
amounted to 20*l*. a month, and was always several months in
arrear ; in addition to this he was paid in Turkish bank-notes.
The Hungarian had a contract with the Government ; his pay
amounted to 17*l*. per month, and had to be given him in gold ;
in consequence of this, he was quite as well off as the
commander.

From the market-place I went to the Armenian church,
which stands in the middle of the town. It consists of several
rooms, one of them being very much like a wooden barn, the
others are built of stone with arched roofs. There was
nothing to be seen in the building save a few tawdry pictures
of saints ; it was carpeted in the same way as the Turkish
mosques. The priest who accompanied us, raising a curtain,
showed me an inscription in cuneiform characters cut in the
stone.

" This part of the building is very old," he said ; " it was
formerly a heathen temple."

" How old ?" I inquired.

"One thousand eight hundred years," said the priest.

" Nonsense, brother," said another. " It is two thousand."

" Say three thousand, and you will be nearer the mark,"
added a third.

It was evident that none of these gentlemen had any data
to go upon for their calculations ; I left the church rather disappointed. I had hoped that some of the divines might be
able to give me information as to the antiquities of the city.
The Armenian clergy do not trouble their heads about such
matters ; their time is so taken up in the performance of
idolatrous rites, and in looking after the welfare of the fairer
portion of their flock, that they have not a moment to spare
for the study of the ancient history of Armenia.

The Armenian who wishes to be a priest must serve in six
different grades before he can be ordained. He must be an
exorcist, porter, reader, sub-deacon, candle-lighter, and deacon.
If he has any interest with his bishop, he can pass through all
these grades in one day.

As a priest, he is allowed to marry ; however like the

clergy belonging to the Greek Church, if his wife dies, the Armenian cannot take unto himself a second spouse. He then may become a monk, and live, free of expense, in one of the monasteries. Next in order, but above the monks, are the bishops and the two patriarchs—one residing in Constantinople, the other at Jerusalem—the patriarch at Constantinople being looked up to by the Armenians as a sort of civil head, besides being their spiritual guide. We now come to the Catolicos, who is first of all in the ecclesiastical hierarchy. He lives in Russia, near Mount Ararat, and is the chief personage of the Armenian Church.

All bishops and priests have to wear beards. The bishops are ordained by the Catolicos, and a council of bishops consecrates the latter. The Armenian Christians worship pictures; confess to their priests; offer prayers for the dead, and ask for the intercession of their saints. An oil is used for the baptism of children. It is called *meira*. The Armenians believe that this oil has boiled without any fire having been placed under it, and they think that this has been effected through the miraculous power of the Catolicos. Whoever and whatever touches this oil is made holy, and is looked upon as having been sanctified.

The Catolicos sells the *meira*, and makes a very large sum by the sale of the oil. The other revenues of the Church arise from baptismal and burial fees, prayers for the dead, taxes imposed upon the people by the ecclesiastics, voluntary contributions, and money left in the wills of devotees.

According to an American missionary at Erzeroum, the Rev. Moses Parmelee, who has published a work which treats of the Armenian clergy, "many of the higher ecclesiastics become very wealthy at the expense of the poor people, whom they cheat and oppress."

He also remarks that the Bible of the Armenians is in their ancient language, which is not understood by the masses of the people.

They were a free nation till the beginning of the eleventh century, but later on the Moguls and Turks devastated Armenia, and the inhabitants have never raised their heads since.

There is a curious tradition connected with the Armenian faith. It is to the effect that, at the beginning of our era, some envoys from Abgar, King of Armenia, happened to be in Jerusalem. Whilst they were in the city they saw Jesus

Christ, and afterwards informed their sovereign of the
miracles which our Saviour was performing throughout Syria.
The monarch was a leper, and, thinking that the same super-
natural being who had saved so many lives in Jerusalem
might be able to do something for him, the king wrote, say
the Armenians, the following letter to the Saviour :—

"Abgar, son of Arsham, Prince of this land, to Jesus the
Saviour and benefactor of man. Greeting. I have heard of
Thee, and of the cures wrought by Thy hands without
remedies and without plants. For it is said that Thou makest
the blind to see, the lame to walk. The lepers are healed,
and spirits are cast out. Thou healest the unfortunate
afflicted with long and inveterate diseases. Thou dost raise
the dead. As I have heard of all the wonders done by Thee,
I have concluded that Thou art either God come down from
heaven, or the Son of God, to do such things. I therefore
have written beseeching Thee to deign to come to me and cure
my disease. I have also heard that the Jews use Thee ill,
and lay snares to destroy Thee. I have here a little city
pleasantly situated and sufficient for us both."

Jesus replied : "After I have gone I will send one of My
disciples, who shall cure thy malady, and give life to thee and
thine."

Some Armenians say that Christ caused the imprint of His
face to be left on a handkerchief, and gave it to the envoys,
telling them that it would cure their master. This is cited
to justify the adoration of pictures, which is part of the
Armenian faith. According to another tradition, the handkerchief never reached the leprous king ; for the envoys who
were carrying it to their master were attacked by brigands,
and it was stolen on the way. This version tells us that
Thaddeus subsequently healed the leprous sovereign.

It was the 7th of March. I had already spent several days
in Van, and, contrary to my hopes, had not benefited by the
rest. I was still suffering from dysentery ; instead of the
complaint getting better, it had become worse. By all
account we should be able to find milk in most of the Kurd
and Yezeed villages between Van and Kars ; so I determined
to start for the latter place and try what a milk and rice diet
would do towards restoring my health and strength. We
rode for two hours by the side of the lake ; then, leaving the
blue water, ascended a low range of hills. The sun's rays
were very powerful ; a mirage was formed before us. Miles

upon miles of water were reflected in the sky.   Presently we crossed a little stream known as the Mahmod Tchai, and after a short march halted at Gull—a small village with thirty houses, half belonging to Armenians, half to Mohammedans.

The morn breaks.   We ride over some high table-land, and then return to the lake.   Our route lies along its shores.   Sand-hills slope down to the water's edge ; myriads of starlings flit about the beach ; pelicans and other wild fowl sail along the surface of the deep.   After a six hours' journey we rest at Paz—a small Kurd village with only ten houses.

The following day we marched along a good track to Tishikoomlekui, a devil-worshippers' village.   Then crossing the Bendimah river—here about thirty yards wide—on a stone bridge, we continued to Karahana, and so on to Ardisch, an Armenian village with 200 houses and a resident Caimacan.

A pretty Kurdish girl, whom I had seen at Paz, accompanied us to the latter place.   I now learnt that the females in some parts of Kurdistan have a strange custom.   This is to beset any stranger who is about to enter or quit their village.   The girls dance round the wayfarer, and take the opportunity to divest him of his apparel.   When he is in a nude state, they seize their victim and carry him with them before some old matron,* complaining to her that their prisoner has grossly insulted them.   The man is lucky if he escapes with his clothes minus the cash in the pockets.

CHAPTER LX

WE reached Akserai.   I was informed by my host, an Armenian, that the Christians in this district live in constant dread of their warlike neighbours, the Kurds—and the more particularly of the Kurds from Persia.   These mountaineers sometimes made raids upon the villages, and committed all sorts of excesses on the women.   Only three months previous a scene of this description had taken place at Akserai.   The

---

[1] Major Millingen goes more fully into particulars about this custom of the Kurdish women.   See Appendix XIII.

Kurds had come there in the night : five of the females in the village had been ravished by the assailants.

The Armenian who gave me this information declared that he liked the Pacha at Van, but said that the latter was powerless to prevent these attacks. There were 5000 Kurds in the mountains, and all were well-armed men. Artillery could not be transported in those regions. The troops at the disposal of the Government were too few to be of any real assistance.

There were many hot springs in Lake Van, and I was assured that, in places, a man could not put his hand in the water without being scalded.

Fish, according to my informant, are only caught in the spring months. The finny tribe then descend the rivers to the lake, and are taken in large numbers.

The villagers draw three nets across the mouths of the rivers. There are funnels in the first two nets, which are left open for the fish to pass ; the apertures in the second net being much smaller than those in the first. When the men discover, by the pressure against the outer net, that they have as many fish as the trammels will hold, they close the funnels, and draw the nets together. The captives, in their endeavours to escape, leap several feet into the air, and the scene is a highly animated one. No large fishes are met with, their average size being from one to two pounds. When a sufficient number have been taken, the women salt them down, and they are kept for winter consumption.

There is a great deal of plough-land in the neighbourhood of Akserai, and, on inquiry, I learnt that corn is grown here in large quantities.

We rode along the shores of the lake for two hours, and, after traversing a well-cultivated country, reached Zerekli. Here many of the inhabitants were seated on the roofs of their houses—the women working and the men basking in the sun. A few soldiers could be seen mending their uniform, and an old Armenian woman was occupied in stitching a shirt belonging to a truculent-looking sergeant. This gentleman sat beside her, sans chemise, and smoking a long chibouk ; volumes of smoke from his pipe were slowly wreathing themselves in the atmosphere.

My host was engaged in mending the roof of his house. A buffalo, or some heavy animal, had walked upon it. The part near the chimney had given way.

Thousands of starlings were perched on some trees in the rear of the dwellings. Many of these birds could be seen hopping about in close proximity to a crowd of Turkish and Armenian urchins. The latter were very different to English lads; for if the starlings had settled down in one of our own villages, it would not have been long ere some boy or other had thrown a stone at them.

It was pleasanter sitting on the roof of the house than being an inmate of its subterranean recesses. But the night turned bitterly cold. A thick mist arose from the lake. It warned the villagers to retire within their dwellings, if they did not wish to risk catching a fever.

We followed their example, and in a short time experienced one of the plagues with which Moses afflicted the Egyptians. There were some loose boards in a corner of the stable; I took them, and tried to remove my body from the onslaught of the vermin by making a sort of scaffolding to sleep upon, three feet from the floor. However, it was all to no purpose. If my tormentors could not reach me by climbing from the ground, they ascended the sides of the building and dropped down upon the scaffolding from the ceiling.

Sleep was out of the question. Starting before daybreak, we continued our journey alongside the lake. Thousands of geese and ducks were skimming along the surface of its waters. In the distance some broad-bottomed boats could be seen. They were laden with wood, and were transporting this article of fuel to the adjacent villages.

We crossed two small rivers, and then, continuing through deep snow, arrived, after a six-hours' march, at Patnos. A river of the same name runs through the village, which contains fifty houses, and the stream, continuing its course a few miles farther, runs into the Murad. Patnos was garrisoned by a company of soldiers. A Mudir looked after the welfare of the inhabitants. The troops were not strong enough to cope with the Kurds in the neighbourhood. The result was that the misdeeds of the mountaineers went unpunished.

A few hours later, and we crossed the Murad river, here about sixty yards wide, the water being up to our horses' shoulders, and after an eight hours' march, halted in a Yezeed village called Dotah.

The Caimacan in this place was not very hospitably inclined. Instead of offering me a room in his own house, as had been the custom with the governors at our previous halting-places, he ordered an old Yezeed farmer to provide us with accommodation for the night.

The ancient devil-worshipper was anything but pleased at having to find a shelter for my servants and self. He had only two rooms, and one of the travelling priests or sheiks of his community was with him as a visitor. The sheik would want a room to himself, and there would be only the stable left for the old man, his family, our horses, and selves.

CHAPTER LXI

My host—The sheik's appearance—My host's two daughters—They attend upon the sheik—Caressing the flames—I love the fire—An insult to the Shaitan—Do you believe in Allah?—Allah can do no harm—The Yezeed fetish—The tomb of Sheik Adi—Your cows shall not die—Mohammed wants a fetish—A cure for rheumatism—The Melek Taoos—Do you ever pray?—What is the use?—Everything is fixed—You cannot force Destiny to change her mind—Hidden things—The balls of clay—Mr. Layard—The seven archangels.

MY landlord was not a sweet creature to look upon. The sheik who was his guest had a still more forbidding countenance; the latter gentleman, with his deep-set eyes, high, narrow forehead, coming almost to a point where it reached his skull, and long cockatoo-like nose, having a very demoniacal appearance. My host had two daughters, who had been deputed to wait upon the sheikh. They followed him about like spaniels, and vied with each other in obeying his commands.

I was seated beside the fireplace when the distinguished individual entered the room. He evidently expected that I was about to arise to receive him in a way becoming to his dignity, and made a sign as if to ask me not to move. I paid no attention to this gesture, but motioned to him to sit by the fire. This he did, and, squatting opposite me, unbared a pair of long shining arms and began to pass them through the flames, as if he were caressing the fiery element.

"You like heat?" I remarked, by way of commencing a conversation.

The man slowly raised his eyes, which glittered in his head and flashed like the embers on the hearth.

"Heat is good, Effendi. Fire gives warmth — without warmth we should die. Fire gives life, and destroys it. I love the flames,"

Mohammed came close to the fire and stooped down. The sheik's eyes sparkled brighter than before : he said something. My servant laughed, but moved away from the hearth.

"What did he say ?" I inquired.

"He was afraid, Effendi, that I was about to spit in the fire. They think that this is a great insult to the ——" Here Mohammed stopped ; he did not like to utter the word "Shaitan" (devil). The sheikh, who appeared much frightened at the beginning of the sentence, and had left off passing his arms through the flames, commenced repeating that operation.

"Do you believe in Allah ?" I remarked.

"Allah is good," was the reply. "Allah can do no harm."

My host now came up, and, bowing before the sheik, said something. The latter, placing his hand into his sash, produced two clay balls, which he gave to the proprietor—the latter receiving them with an air of the greatest satisfaction.

These balls had been manufactured with clay taken from the tomb of Sheik Adi—a saint who is highly reverenced by the Yezeeds—the travelling sheiks make a certain sum of money by selling them to the devotees.

"Your visit has brought happiness to my daughters and myself," observed the proprietor.

The sheik did not reply immediately, but presently remarked,—

"Your cows shall not die ; no robbers shall enter your doors ; illness shall not attack your family."

Mohammed approached.

"I too should like a ball," he remarked. "It might keep off my rheumatism. The Effendi's plasters do good, but they hurt. The ball would not cause me any pain. Give me one ; " and my servant held out his hand to the sheik.

"Go away !" said the latter in rather strong tones. "Go to your own saints, and let them cure you."

Then, rising, the man left the room, closely followed by the two daughters of the proprietor.

These girls were neither of them good-looking, and dirty to an extent which no man who has not been in the East could imagine.

It is said that there are pretty women amidst the daughters of the worshippers of the devil ; my personal observations do not lead me to place any credence in this statement.

I inquired of the proprietor if the sheik had brought the Melek Taoos (King Peacock) with him. This is a bird manufactured of bronze, which is occasionally carried about by the leading men amidst the Yezeeds, and which all devil worshippers are bound to reverence.

"No," replied my host; "our guest is not a Cawal (a sort of priest). Who told you about the Melek Taoos?"

"The Turks, and, besides, I have read about it, and seen a picture of the bird in a book written by a Frank."

"What a marvel!" said the host; "very few of our sheiks can read, much less write."

"Do you ever pray?" I inquired.

"Pray? like the Mohammedans?"

"Yes."

"No; what is the use? You Christians do not pray like the Mohammedans," continued the old man.

"No; but we pray to the Founder of our faith."

"Everything is fixed," observed the Yezeed; "then what is the good of praying? You cannot force Destiny to change her mind."

"Then what is the good of the balls you have just received? for if your cows are destined to die, they will die."

My host did not show any wish to continue this conversation, and he presently remarked,—

"We are talking about hidden things; no good will come of it."

"But if you have got the balls of clay," said Mohammed, joining in the conversation, "they ought to keep you from any harm."

"Who knows?" said the proprietor; and, rising from the ground, he lay down in a farther corner of the room, next some sheep, and was soon lost to consciousness.

Mr. Layard, who lived some time amongst the Yezeeds, remarked about these strange people:—

"They recognize one Supreme Being; but, as far as I could learn, they do not offer up any direct prayer or sacrifice to Him. My questions on this subject were evaded, and every topic was shunned connected with the attributes and existence of the Deity.

"The name of the devil is never mentioned, and any allusion to it by others so vexes and irritates them that it is said that they have put to death persons who have wantonly outraged their feelings by its use.

"So far is their dread of offending the evil spirit carried that they carefully avoid every expression which may resemble

in sound the name of Satan, or the Arabic word for 'accursed.'
When they speak of the devil, they do so with reverence as
Melek-el, the mighty angel. The Yezeeds believe Satan to be
the chief of the angelic host now suffering punishment for his
rebellion against the Divine will, but still powerful, and to be
restored hereafter to his high estate in the celestial hierarchy.
He must be conciliated and reverenced, they say, for as he
now has the means of doing evil to mankind, so will he
hereafter have the power of rewarding them. Next to Satan,
but inferior to him in might and wisdom, are seven archangels
who exercise a great influence over the world ; they are
Gabriel, Michail, Raphail, Azrail, Dedrail, Azrapheel, and
Shemkeel. Christ, according to the Yezeeds, was also a great
angel who had taken the form of man. He did not die on
the cross, but ascended to heaven."

CHAPTER LXII

Alongside the river Murad—Waterfalls—The Melaskert River—Tchekhane
—An attack of fever—Quinine—The doctor at Toprak Kale—He
arrives—The consultation—Excitement amongst the villagers—The
stethoscope—The audience—How clever these Franks are !—The
Effendi is going to die—Rheumatic fever—Pressed fruit—A native
remedy—A long night.

WE were once more in winter, deep snow lay along our path.
There were several Yezeed villages by the track, which began
to rise abruptly by the side of the river Murad, and was here
and there cut out of the solid rock.

In many places waterfalls dashed over the path, and we
were literally riding beneath a canopy of water, which fell
several hundred feet over precipices into the river below. At
others the torrent dashed across the track itself. We had to
advance with the greatest caution to avoid being swept down
the abyss.

I now crossed the Melaskert river. Here our guide had
a narrow escape of being carried away by the torrent.
Presently we arrived at Tchekhane, an Armenian village,
about eight miles distant from the town of Toprak Kale.

I had been suffering great pain during the last two marches,
and, on dismounting from my horse, should have fallen to the
ground, if it had not been for Mohammed,

The latter helped me to enter the house of my host, an Armenian peasant. Staggering up to the hearth, I threw myself down beside the fire. My legs seemed to have lost all their strength; I had great pain in the head and back. My pulse was beating very rapidly. It intermitted.

Thinking that it was an attack of fever, I desired Radford to give me the medicine-chest, and after taking ten grains of quinine, tried to sleep. This, however, was impossible—the insects in the house would have prevented slumber, even if the fever had not done so.

The night passed away. In the morning I found myself so weak that I could barely raise my head from the pillow.

"There is a doctor at Toprak Kale," observed my Armenian host. "He is a Frank: why not send for him?"

I did so; but the medical man did not arrive. I lay all that day racked by pain, and half devoured by insects.

In the morning I overheard the following conversation between Mohammed and the proprietor.

"There are many fleas; my Effendi cannot sleep."

"It is true," replied the Armenian; "but there are by no means so many here as in a Kurd village a few miles distant. The Kurds have been obliged to abandon their houses in consequence of these insects. They have had to live in tents for several months past."

Another night passed without my obtaining any slumber In the morning I had a visit from the doctor, a Hungarian who was attached to a regiment at Toprak Kale.

The news of the arrival of the son of Æsculapius was soon spread through the village. My bed-chamber, the stable, in which there were three cows, was speedily thronged by as many excited inhabitants as could find standing-room.

The doctor was a young man; he had not been long in Asia Minor, and could only speak a few words of Turkish. But he wore a uniform, and was accompanied by a Zaptieh. This was sufficient at once to strike awe into the Armenian villagers.

"Are you in pain?" said the doctor, in German.

"Yes."

"Where?"

"Behind the shoulders and in the side."

"I will examine you."

Producing a stethoscope, he placed one end of it upon my chest and the other to his ear. This proceeding gave rise to great astonishment amidst the assembled visitors, who eagerly pressed forward to witness the operation.

" Donnerwetter ! " said the indignant physician in German. " Haide, go away ! " This last word in Turkish to the Armenians, who, frightened at the sonorous sounds of the " Donnerwetter," had already withdrawn for a few steps.

There were also some Turkish peasants in the room. They had made friends with Mohammed. He had placed them behind two cows in a corner, so that they might have a good view of the doctor.

" What is he doing to the Effendi ? " inquired one of them of Mohammed.

" He is looking into his body," observed another.

Mohammed himself now craned out his neck in my direction.

" Effendi ! is he looking into your stomach ? "

" No ; he is listening to the beats of my heart."

" How clever these Franks are ! " said one of the Turks. " They do not even take the trouble to look ; they are quite satisfied by listening."

" I wish the hakim would put the instrument on my chest ; it would do me good," he continued.

" Perhaps he would if we asked him," added the other.

" Silence ! " said Mohammed. " The doctor is saying something."

The face of the medical gentleman became a little grave after he had sounded me. This gave great satisfaction to the audience.

" See how solemn he looks ? " remarked one of the bystanders ; " the Effendi is going to die."

" What is the matter with me ? " I inquired.

" Rheumatic fever ; and your heart is out of order," said the doctor. " You must lie quiet for several days, and I will send you some medicine. My battalion probably marches to-morrow," he continued, " and so I fear I cannot come here again."

Pocketing his fee, the medical gentleman mounted his horse, and rode off with the Zaptieh.

I had eaten nothing for two days, and my mouth was parched. Mohammed, seeing this, brought me some pressed fruit—a sort of wild cranberry, which the natives dry, and then, if any one has a fever, they soak the fruit in water and give it him to drink. The pressed berries are very nasty to look at. They much resemble tezek. For a moment I thought that Mohammed was giving me a piece of that fuel by way of a febrifuge. On tasting the beverage I found that the flavour was very agreeable. It was acid, and, in Mohammed's opinion, was a most valuable remedy for fever.

The day wore on. In the evening the cows inside my bedroom were joined by three buffaloes.

The air in the room became fouler and more dense. It was snowing outside, and the proprietor had covered the hole, which took the place of a chimney, with a large stone. I lay awake for the greater part of the night, every now and then drinking copious draughts of the pressed fruit dissolved in water. Nature at last succumbed. I had not slept for several nights. The figures of the cows and buffaloes became smaller : they gradually disappeared. The light given out by a piece of cotton steeped in some melted fat, and placed in an iron tripod, became more flickering : the sounds of my followers' snoring seemed to fade away. I shut my eyes and fell asleep.

I was awakened late the following afternoon by something cold and clammy against my hand. On looking up I found it was one of the cows. My arm was stretched out by her trough. The animal was licking my fingers with her tongue.

" I was afraid that she would awake you, sir," remarked my servant Radford, coming to my side. " I wished to drive her away, but was afraid of disturbing you."

CHAPTER LXIII

Mohammed's febrifuge—The doctor's medicine—Zedhane—Daha—Hassan Bek—Bash—The garrison—We cross the Araxes—The bridge made by a Circassian—Karakroot—The Circassian horsemen—The inhabitants —Their eyes and teeth—Gedjerharman—The plain around Kars—The streets of the town—The sewerage of the population—The civil governor—The river—The war with the Persians—Mount Kara Dagh —The fortifications.

THE rest had done me good. Mohammed's febrifuge seemed to agree. Later on, the doctor's medicine arrived. I took a dose, and felt myself much worse in consequence. I determined to stick to the native remedy.

Day after day passed by. At last I was able to raise myself a little from the floor. My appetite gradually returned ;

and one fine morning I determined to make an attempt to reach Kars. My servants lifted me on my horse : once on his back, I made them strap me to the high pommel in front of the saddle—a Turkish one.

The fresh air did wonders, and though very weak, I managed to reach Zedhane, a village which we had stopped at on our way to Bayazid, and which lay on the route between Van and Kars.

We rode to Daha, passing by Kurdali, a small village, seven miles from Zedhane, and with some strong positions, from a military point of view, in the neighbourhood. The track was very different to what it had been a few weeks previous. There was little snow, and we were able to reach Daha in five hours. Our course was almost due north, and ran through a broad mountain pass to Hassan Bek, a Kurd hamlet, and from there to Bash, an Armenian village with a hundred Khans. Here a battalion was quartered. The men had fought at Alexinatz, and, according to their lieutenant-colonel, an officer whose acquaintance I had made at Erzeroum, they were eager to cross bayonets again with the Russians.

We left Bash, and after a two hours' march crossed the Araxes on a rickety wooden bridge. It had been made by an enterprising Circassian. There is a ford several miles down the stream, but the Circassian had thought that, if he were to make this bridge, a great many passengers would prefer taking the short cut, and would gladly pay a few piastres for the privilege of crossing the structure.

We came to the village of Karakroot, in which the Circassian lived. The sheik, a fine-looking man, informed us that here there were only twenty-five houses, but there were 1005 houses which belonged to people of his nation in the neighbourhood. In the event of war, the inhabitants of this district could muster 2000 horsemen. The houses belonging to these Circassians were far cleaner than any which I had seen in the Kurdish or Armenian villages. They were all built of wood, with wooden floors. A small enclosure, made of sharp pointed stakes, surrounded each of the dwellings. There were quantities of buffaloes, cows, and sheep in some adjacent fields, and the granaries were said to be well supplied with corn and barley.

The inhabitants were smart-looking fellows, and all of them dressed in their national attire—in tight-fitting sheepskin coats, with the wool worn inside, and buckled round their waists by a narrow leathern strap, studded with buttons; broad leather trousers, stuffed into high boots, covered their legs, and small Astrachan caps their heads.

For arms, the men carried long daggers in their waist-belts —many of the hilts being beautifully worked in silver.

There were several women and girls in the village. They did not conceal themselves, as is the custom of the Armenian or Turkish women. We had the opportunity of looking at their faces. I was under the impression that the Circassian girls were very fair. This is not the case, they more resemble the Spanish belles, and have a clear olive complexion, through which you can discern the blue veins. One girl was very good-looking. She could not have been more than sixteen, and sat the horse on which she was mounted with more grace and ease than any of her male companions.

The chief features in all these women are their eyes and teeth. The former are very large, and the latter small, well-shaped and white as pearls. Tooth powder is unknown in this district. How they preserve their teeth so perfectly is to a European an enigma.

You see men of from sixty to seventy years of age who have never lost a tooth, each one is as white as the purest ivory. The Circassians have another advantage, from a European point of view, over the Kurds. They do not sleep in their cow hovels. The stables are separated from the apartments reserved for the family.

We rode by several more Circassian villages, and after passing Gedjerharman, which is a nine hours' march from Bash, came to a district inhabited by Turks and Armenians. The latter complained of their warlike neighbours the Circassians, and declared that a Turk had been killed the previous evening, in a quarrel with one of the mountaineers. All this part of the track was in good order. Seven hours after leaving Gedjerharman we entered the plain around Kars. In rear of the town, which is built in the form of a sickle or half-moon, are some high mountains. A series of detached forts occupying commanding positions defends the approaches to the citadel. This last stands in the north-west angle of the town.

Seven battalions of infantry were drilling in the plain. They presented a more martial appearance than any of the troops which I had previously seen in Asia Minor.

The streets of Kars were in a filthy state. Every house

was crammed with soldiers. The whole sewerage of the population had been thrown in front of the buildings. Fortunately the weather was cold. A very disagreeable smell could be perceived, as our horses stirred up the refuse beneath their hoofs.

We halted at the house of the civil governor. He had been kind enough to place a room at my disposal. The following morning I rode out to visit the fortifications. The river Kars Tchai runs through the town, and is crossed by three stone bridges, each about forty yards wide. The Persians in a war with the Turks had tried to turn this river, so as to cut off the water from the garrison, but failed in the attempt. I first went to Mount Kara Dagh, which is about 1400 yards from the town, and commands the road to the Russian fortress at Alexandropol or Gumri. A small barracks had been erected for half a battalion of infantry; some earthworks had been thrown up around the position, which was defended by twelve Krupp guns. The site for the powder magazine had not been judiciously selected; but, as it is possible that the war may not be over ere this work is published, the reader will pardon me if I do not mention its exact situation.

On the plain below, 1600 yards from the Kara Dagh, and 2000 from the town, was a small redoubt called the Hafeez Pacha Tabia; here there were nine guns, the battery facing the south. Fifteen hundred yards south-west of this point and 3000 from the town, stood the Kanli Tabia, an important redoubt, in very good repair, and with sixteen guns in position. The only other defensive works in the plain consisted of a small redoubt called the Sowaree Tabia, in which were two guns. No connecting lines had been made to join the different redoubts; the ground between them was entirely unprotected. On my mentioning this to an engineer officer who accompanied me, he remarked that it was winter, and the ground was hard; when the weather became milder, the troops would commence digging trenches and forming breast-works.

On the north-west of the citadel, and in a commanding position, stood the Veli Pacha Tabia with fourteen guns; and to the right of this battery, and slightly in advance of it, some earthworks had been thrown up at the suggestion of Bloom Pacha, a German officer; here there were five guns. The river separates these works from the Kara Kalpak Tabia, a strong position adjoining the Kara Dagh, and defended by ten guns.

In the citadel known as the Itch Kale, and which is slightly in rear of Bloom Pacha Tabia, and on the opposite side of the river, there were twelve guns. To the left of Veli Pacha Tabia was a battery of thirteen guns, known as the Tchim Tabia. Closely adjoining this battery, but more to the west, I saw the Tamar Tabia with twenty-three guns; here there was a barrack for one battalion. Five hundred yards in rear of the Tamar Tabia stood the Diktipe Tabia with thirteen guns; and about the same distance behind Diktipe, covering the northern slopes, the Tachmach Tabia with eighteen guns. On the east of Bloom Pacha Tabia there was a work with four guns, known as Inglis Tabia; and slightly in advance of this battery Williams Pacha Tabia with twelve guns. This made up all the defences on the north side of Kars. Most of these redoubts had been very much neglected; however, the town was better fortified on the northern side than from the south. Every facility was afforded to me for viewing the works in question, and I was permitted to take the angles between the different positions, besides being shown the exact bearings of all the powder-magazines.

CHAPTER LXIV

The garrison of Kars—Dr. Lanzoni—A probable outbreak of typhus—The two Pachas—Whose fault is it?—If God wills it, there will be no Cholera—If God wills it, the Russians will not come here—The hospitals full of men suffering from typhus fever—The International Commission—The Grand Duke Michael—Gumri—The Armenians and their nationality—The speech of the Grand Duke—The Master of the Armenian school—You shall go to prison—The Emperor Nicholas—Religious liberty granted to Armenians in Russia—The document—The Patriarch's death—Suspicious circumstances—Cossacks firing upon Mohammedans—Three children wounded—Clergymen of the Church of England—Hankering after the idolatrous practices of the Greek faith—Wolves in sheep's clothing—Colonel Lake—A little boy shot by the Cossacks—Russia the father of the fatherless—The Right Hon. R. Lowe, M.P.—The author of *the Bulgarian Horrors*—English officers and soldiers massacred in the Crimea—The Court of Inquiry—The Duke of Newcastle's speech—Russian officers butchering the English wounded.

THERE were at the time of my visit to Kars about 20,000 troops quartered in and about the town; but large reinforcements could be sent from Erzeroum should occasion arise for their services. Later in the day Dr. Lanzoni, of the Quarantine, called upon me; he is an Italian, and in the

International Service. On my alluding to the state of the streets in Kars, he remarked that he had written twice to the authorities at Constantinople, but that no notice had been taken of his letters. "We shall have an outbreak of typhus or plague in the summer," continued the doctor. "The mortality will be very great, if we are besieged before the filth is cleared away."

The civil governor entered the room. He joined in the conversation.

"It is the fault of the military Pacha," he observed. "The soldiers have made this mess in the streets, and the military Pacha thinks that the civilians in the town ought to clear it up. I have told him that this work ought to be done by the troops, but he says that the soldiers are the Padishah's servants, and that their duty is to fight, and not to be scavengers."

"What have you done about the matter?" I inquired.

"We have written to Constantinople," replied the governor.

"How long does it take for a letter to go there?"

"About three weeks."

"Yes," said the doctor, "three weeks to go, and three weeks to return, in all six weeks, without considering the delay there will be in answering the communication. We may have the cholera here long before that time."

"If God wills it, there will be no cholera," said the Pacha.

I interrupted him. "You are strengthening your garrison?"

"Yes."

"You will repair the fortifications?"

"Yes."

"You are supplying the troops with Martini-Peabody rifles at a great expense to your Government?"

"Yes."

"Well," I continued, "why are you doing this?"

"On account of the Russians," said the Pacha, "but why do you ask me these questions?"

"Because if God wills it, the Russians will not come here, and if He has decreed that Kars is to fall, nothing that you can do will prevent that event taking place."

"Then you think that armies are useless?" said the Pacha.

"No, but you would seem to hold that opinion, for you do not take the trouble to have the streets cleared, and say, if God wills it so, that there will be no epidemic."

"Allah is all-powerful. He knows everything that has happened and that will happen," said the governor devoutly. "We are all dust in His sight. If we have the cholera in Kars, it will be the military Pacha's fault."

Shortly afterwards my visitor left the room.

"I am very glad you spoke to him as you did," said the doctor. "Our hospitals are full of men suffering from typhoid fever; more than 10 per cent. of the poor fellows do not recover. This is a case in which the European powers ought to interfere," continued the speaker. "I am a quarantine officer, and am paid by the International Commission. It is my duty to prevent the cholera or any other infectious disease being brought from the East, but these Turks are doing their best to breed a plague in the heart of their principal fortification. Kars is only thirty miles from Gumri," he added; "if this place were to fall, the whole of Asia Minor would follow."

"Do the Armenians in this town like the Russians?" I now inquired.

"Not at all," said the doctor. "Only seven months ago the Grand Duke Michael visited Gumri, the Russian frontier fortress. When he was there he inspected the Armenian schools, and made a speech to the girls in one of these institutions. After a few remarks about the progress they were making, the Grand Duke concluded his discourse by addressing their mothers in these words, 'Rappelez-vous bien que le lait avec lequel vous nourrissez vos enfants doit être le lait Russe.' The Armenians are immensely vain of their nationality. This speech of the Grand Duke incensed them very much against him. The Russian prince made himself still more unpopular a few days later," continued the doctor. "In the course of a visit to the master of one of the Armenian schools, he observed some pictures in the schoolroom. 'What pictures are these?' he inquired. 'They are likenesses of some of the former kings of Armenia,' replied the schoolmaster. 'You have no right to have any portraits here save those of the Tzar and of the members of the Imperial family,' said the Grand Duke, 'you shall go to prison.'"

An Armenian gentleman entered the room; he corroborated everything that the doctor had said, and presently remarked that many years ago the Emperor Nicholas had given the Patriarch Mateos a document in which the Tzar granted full religious liberty to all Armenians in Russia. "Our Patriarch kept this deed always on his person," continued the speaker.

One day he died very suddenly, and under rather suspicious circumstances. His successor searched everywhere for the document, but could not find it. At length he discovered a copy : he then wrote to the authorities in Tiflis, and asked for a fresh paper. His request was refused, and at the same time he was informed that no such religious liberty had ever been granted to the Armenians."

"Is it true that the Russian authorities do not permit the Mohammedans to leave the Tzar's dominions?" I now inquired.

"Yes," said the doctor ; "a very few months ago a case came under my own observation. Some Mohammedans wished to leave Russia and escape to Turkey ; as they were passing the border-line, a band of Cossacks fired upon them. They continued their flight, but three children had been wounded and were afterwards treated in the hospital at Kars."

As I copy the above lines from my note-book, I cannot help thinking of some few Clergymen of the Church of England who, secretly hankering after the superstitions attached to the Greek faith, put themselves forward as champions of Holy Russia. But we need not be surprised. Those people who are so deadened to a sense of right and wrong as to imagine that they are doing God service by instilling into the ears of our wives and children sentences from the foul pamphlet entitled "The Priest in Absolution," can readily bring themselves to believe that killing pregnant women,* and flogging Christian women and children,† to make them change their religion, is justifiable on the part of the Russian Government. Priests like these would gladly re-establish the Inquisition in our midst. They could defend the massacres of St. Bartholomew, if the victims had been Mohammedans ; and on the seventh day of the week they stand up in their pulpits and preach the doctrine of peace by advocating the extermination of the Turks.

The above-mentioned way of treating Mohammedan little children is no novelty on the part of the Tzar's soldiery. Colonel Lake, in his work, the "Defence of Kars," remarks that, "brought up as savages from their infancy, some of these Cossacks will not scruple to commit the most barbarous actions. As an instance of this, on one occasion, during the earlier period of the blockade, a party of them made a dash at a small village by the river side called Karaba Kilissa, and though the inhabitants offered not the slightest opposition to

* See Appendix IX.　　　　　† See Appendix I.

them, they beat a little boy, twelve years of age, very cruelly with their whips, and finally shot him—the ball passing through his thigh and breaking the bone. It was heart-rending to see the poor old mother weeping over her dying child. He was packed up in an *araba*, or country cart, and sent down to the hospital, where he was attended by Dr. Sandwith. Every possible care was taken of the little sufferer, but he died under the amputation of the shattered limb."

We were told a few months ago by the Right Hon. Robert Lowe, M.P., that Russia was the father of the fatherless; judging from the way she has treated these Mohammedan children, it would not put her to much expense to provide for a numerous family.

It was a goodly spectacle this Holy Russia putting herself forward last autumn as the Champion of the Bulgarians, after she had done her best to foment* the disturbances which led to the massacres in their country. It may be refreshing to some of the believers in Muscovite philanthropy if I recall to their recollection what took place very recently in Central Asia.

"Kill the Turkomans, kill them all?" was General Kauffmann's order during the Khivan campaign.

"I suppose you mean in the Circassian style," was the dry remark of an old colonel, well acquainted with the Russian manner of making war upon the Circassians.

"Yes; kill them all! Spare neither age nor sex? Let none escape!"

Circassian† pregnant women cut to pieces!—does this go for nothing in the eyes of those gentlemen who called out for vengeance on the Circassians in Bulgaria? Circassian children butchered by Russian soldiery!—is this nothing to two clergymen of the Church of England, who denounced in the strongest language an imaginary atrocity of the Turks?

Are these things nothing to the Right Hon. W. Gladstone, M.P., who, writing last autumn about a friendly power, remarked, "What seems now to be certain in this sense (besides the miserable daily misgovernment, which, however, dwindles by the side of the Bulgarian horrors) are the wholesale massacres—

'Murder most foul, as in the best it is;
But this most foul, strange, and unnatural!'‡

---

* See Appendix IV., Russian Agents and the Massacres in Bulgaria.
† See Appendix VII., The Schoolmasters in Massacre.
‡ Hamlet, i. 5.

the elaborate and refined cruelty—the only refinement of which Turkey boasts!—the utter disregard of sex and age—the abominable and bestial lust—and the entire and violent lawlessness which still stalks over the land."

Two wrongs do not make one right. This is an old saying and a true one. The atrocities committed by the Russians in the Caucasus are no excuse for those perpetrated by the Circassians in Bulgaria; but the Circassians are Mohammedans, the Muscovites profess the doctrines of Christ. Why was the author of the "Bulgarian Horrors" silent when his own officials reported the crimes of the Russian soldiery? We have been told that Russia is the torch-bearer of civilization, and our military attaché at St. Petersburg, Captain and Lt.-Col. Wellesley, has stated that he believes the Muscovite soldiers are incapable of the atrocities laid to their charge. Mr. Gladstone has quoted this officer as an authority.

It may be that our military attaché is ignorant of what took place during the Crimean war. He was a child in petticoats at the time. But Mr. Gladstone cannot assign extreme youth in his own case as an excuse for bad memory. He was a member of the Cabinet, and, as such, had access to all official despatches. Let me ask him if he can remember the circumstances under which many of our officers and soldiers met their death at the battle of Inkerman, and when they were lying helpless on the field? Does he know how Captain the Hon. Henry Neville, of the 3rd battalion of Grenadier Guards, was butchered? and how Captain Sir Robert Newman, Bart., shared the same fate? Does he know how poor Disbrowe of the Coldstreams was tortured? *Possibly* all these things have escaped from his memory, but the Cabinet to which he belonged did not forget them at the time.

A Court of Inquiry* was held in the Crimea. It investigated the accusations made against the Russian troops. The proceedings of this Court of Inquiry, accompanied by a despatch, were forwarded by Lord Raglan to the authorities at home. In these papers will be found the names of many British officers and privates who were proved to have been brutally massacred by the Russian soldiers—when imploring mercy, and helpless owing to their wounds. Such horror was created in the minds of some of the Cabinet, that one of its members, the War Minister, the late Duke of Newcastle,

* The first witness examined at this Court of Inquiry was Sir Charles Russell, Bart., M.P. for Westminster.

alluded to the matter on the 12th of December, 1854, in the House of Lords, as follows. I give his own words :—

" The enemy which our men met were not content with the legitimate use of their weapons, but had the BARBARITY, THE ATROCIOUS VILLAINY, I will call it, TO MURDER IN COLD BLOOD THE WOUNDED SOLDIERS AS THEY LAY HELPLESS ON THE FIELD ; AND not the ignorant serfs alone did that, but MEN HOLDING THE POSITION OF OFFICERS. Our men have had to fight the savage and uncivilised Kaffirs, but in no instance have THEY EXPERIENCED SUCH BARBARISM AS WITH THE RUSSIAN SOLDIERS ! ! ! ! "

A number of families in Great Britain were in mourning after Inkerman. Many old fathers and mothers thought that their sons had been killed in fair fight. They have been deceived. The proceedings of the Court of Inquiry were in the War Office this summer. I challenge the author of the " Bulgarian Horrors " to ask the Government to lay these papers, with Lord Raglan's and Marshal Canrobert's despatches relating to them, on the table of the House of Commons. It is to be hoped that he will do so. The British public would then be able to judge for itself what sort of men the Russians are, and how thoroughly Russia merits the terms—The Torch-bearer of Civilization and the Protector of the Unprotected—which have been applied to her by the Right Hon. W. E. Gladstone and the Right Hon. Robert Lowe.

CHAPTER LXV

The march to Ardahan—Molla Hassan—A Turkish major—The garrison of Ardahan—The position of the town—The fortifications—Procrastination in military matters—The military governor—A colonel of artillery—The Russians might take Van—The Ala Dagh mountains—Freemasonry—The ancient Assyrians—To Livana by road—By the river to Batoum—Selling the horses—What they fetch—A bad bargain.

I STARTED early the following morning *en route* for Ardahan, a Turkish fortress about forty-two miles from Kars. The road was good for the first three hours, but then became very bad. We rode over some mountains covered with deep snow, and halted for the night in a small village called Molla

Hassan, inhabited by Kurds. A Turkish major had recently inhabited the room assigned to us. He had intended remaining there for some time; but the insects proving too much for him, he had taken up his abode in a Turkish village near Kars.

"These Turks have thin skins," said an old Kurd, my host, as he told me the story; "only think of their being frightened by a few fleas. You Ingliz are much braver people."

"My Effendi is very particular about these matters," remarked Mohammed; "if he is bitten, there will be no baksheesh."

The Kurd's face lengthened.

"I have a cart," he presently observed; "it is clean, it has been standing in the cold. The fleas are frozen. I will drag the cart into the road and the Frank can sleep in it."

This was done, and I managed to secure a few hours' rest, a very rare occurrence in a Kurdish village. The track was very bad between Molla Hassan and Ardahan; after marching for six hours and a half, we reached the latter place, which was at that time garrisoned by 12,000 soldiers.

Ardahan is surrounded on the north, south, and east by mountains—towards the west there are some heights about five miles distant from the town. The site is a bad one for defensive purposes. The roads which lead from the Russian frontier stations, Akellaki and Akiska, present a series of commanding positions which dominate the Turkish lines. A little river winds through a valley on the west front of Ardahan, and finally traverses the town. The stream is crossed by two wooden bridges without parapets.

An attempt was being made to fortify Ardahan on its western side by throwing up some earthworks only eight hundred yards distant from the houses. No guns had been placed in these batteries.

There were thirteen pieces in a fort on a hill called Manusa, about 3000 yards to the north of Ardahan, and in another position south of the towns on the Kars road. Here there were four small earthworks, called Ahali, Sangher, Gaze, and Kaptamele, mounting in all twenty-four guns. Three hundred yards to the east there was one more earthwork, called Kaiabashe, containing eighteen guns. Fort Manusa, the strongest point in the defences of the town, is commanded by a height called Ramazan. The Turks had not thought of occupying this last position; although should an enemy once succeed in placing some guns on the Ramazan height, Ardahan must eventually be taken.

On my pointing this out to an engineer officer who accompanied me, he acknowledged the truth of the remark, at the same time observing that, Inshallah, when the winter was over, he would fortify the height in question.

Procrastination in military matters is the great defect on the part of the Turkish authorities. But it ill becomes an Englishman to blame them. Perhaps no country is more negligent about these subjects than our own.

"The Russians will not come, Inshallah," remarks the Mohammedan, and he sits down and lights his pipe.

" It is extremely unlikely that Germany will invade Great Britain, or that India will ever be attacked," says one Englishman. " It is highly improbable that Russia will take Constantinople or the highlands in Armenia," remarks another; " when that moment arrives it will be time enough to go to war. We can then talk about a conscription for our army. We have more money than any other nation, and should be stronger at the end of a campaign than at the beginning." People who make use of these arguments, forget that France was a very rich country ; but that with all her money and her hastily levied troops she was unable to withstand the disciplined armies of Moltke.

The military governor was despondent as to his power of defending Ardahan. If he could have had his own way, he would have selected another position nearer the Russian frontier. It was now too late to do this, and the more particularly as the Pacha believed that hostilities would break out immediately. He had no cavalry at his disposal to bring him information about what was going on near the border. However, 2000 Circassian horsemen were shortly expected, and wooden sheds were being built for them close to the Kaiabashe earthworks. A colonel of artillery called upon me : he had been educated at Woolwich. He had not been in England for more than twenty years, but he spoke English remarkably well. On my observing that I had heard that the Russians had lately withdrawn their troops from Erivan, he remarked that the Muscovite general had probably done so through fear lest the Turks should advance upon Tiflis from Batoum.

" What would be the result if the Russians were to take Batoum ? " I inquired.

"They might remain there. It would be very difficult for them to advance inland," was the reply. "There are no roads. The Russians might take Van," he continued; "but even if they were to do so, they would find it very difficult to advance upon Erzeroum *viâ* Mousch. It would be almost impossible for them to transport their artillery over the Ala Dagh mountains."

"Would the Kurds help the Russians?"

"The Kurds would probably join the stronger side. I have been a great deal in the mountains, and know the Kurds well. There are freemasons amongst them," added the Colonel. "Their freemasonry dates back from the time of the ancient Assyrians."

I now learnt that it would be better for me to sell my horses in Ardahan, than to take them to Batoum. The shortest route to the last-named town was to go to Livana by road, and then down the Tschoroch river, to the seaport in question. We could hire five horses so far as Livana; if we were to take our own animals there, we should not be able to dispose of them. Calling Mohammed, I desired him to go to the market and inform any people who might wish to buy horses, that there were four for sale.

"Five, Effendi," said Mohammed; "I shall sell mine too. When we reach Batoum the Effendi will go to Stamboul; but I must join my battalion. That is, unless the Effendi will take me with him."

"Impossible, Mohammed," I replied. "I shall only remain for twenty-four hours in Constantinople, and from there go to my own country. You would be taken up as a deserter after I had gone, and perhaps shot. What would your wife say?"

"I could get a fresh wife at Stamboul."

"Go and sell the horses!"

A tear fell down Mohammed's cheek. He sighed deeply and left the room.

Presently Radford came to me,—

"Bless my heart, sir, if that 'ere Mohammed ain't a crying; he keeps on saying Stamboul, and wants to go there. He says, '*et à la Franga*, meat cooked in the European style, is nice; and that he loves my cookery!' the fact is, sir, he don't want to go to his regiment."

A sound in the courtyard attracted my attention; I went to the window. Mohammed was outside with the five horses; several Turks and Circassians were looking at them. The animals had very little flesh on their bones ; but they were in much better condition for work than on the day we left Constantinople. Mohammed's horse was in a wretched state ; he was nearly blind, from the effects of the snow. In addition to this he walked lame.

"He is a brute," observed an old Turk ; " take him away, Mohammed ; kill him for his skin, make leather of it."

"His grandfather was a magnificent animal," replied Mohammed indignantly. "His sire was the admiration of the people in Tohat. He himself is thin, he will soon get fat again. Anyhow," continued my servant, "my lord's horses are for sale ; unless you first buy mine you shall not purchase his animals."

Some conversation ensued ; a farmer at last offered 10 liras for the five horses.

"The Effendi gave 16 liras for the grey at Stamboul," remarked my servant.

"Ardahan is not Stamboul," replied the Circassian ; "the horses have carried the Effendi a very long distance."

"This proves that they are good animals," said Mohammed.

"It shows that they were good horses," observed the Circassian drily.

No one would bid any higher, and as I was in a hurry to start, I agreed to accept 7½ liras for my own four horses, letting Mohammed have 2½ for his own Rosinante-like steed. Seven liras and a half, or 6*l.* 15*s.*, is not a great price for four serviceable animals. I could have obtained the same amount for four dead horses in London. However, my stud had carried us for more than two thousand miles, over a country without roads, and for the greater part of the distance through snow. I could not complain that the animals had been dearly purchased. It cost me a pang to part with the little grey. He was a sterling good horse, and in England would have been worth from 60*l.* to 70*l.* The sale was concluded. In a few minutes I was receiving from the Circassian a pile of Turkish bank-notes, which he extracted one by one from some hiding-place next his skin.

CHAPTER LXVI

WE rode by several Turkish and Kurd villages in the direction of Ardanusch. The track was firm and tolerably level.
After a four hours' march we crossed the Ardahan river on a
wooden bridge about seventy yards long by sixteen feet wide.
The structure was very much out of repair; the planks were
loose in many places, here and there large holes in the timber
let us see the river below. We halted at Shadavan, a Turkish
village containing about thirty houses, and close to the water's
edge. I had intended to have made a longer march, but the
hired steeds were wretched brutes. They had shown unmistakable signs of fatigue. The proprietor of the house in
which we stopped owned large flocks of sheep, the country
round Ardahan being chiefly grazing land. He informed me
that for every thousand sheep he possessed, the tax collector
took from him the sum of thirty liras annually. There was
no tax for sheep under a year old, nor for cows and oxen.

Two hours after leaving Shadavan, the path crossed a high
mountain. It was covered with its winter garb; this fortunately was frozen hard and afforded a firm foothold. The
scenery around us became each moment more wild; fir-trees,
shaded in their cold white robes, embroider the sides of the
steep; huge rocks, their northern faces covered with snow,
but black as ebony towards the south, frown down on the
glistening carpet. The track wound higher and higher. A
thick oppressive mist enveloped us like a shroud. We were
above the clouds. The air became each moment more rarefied.
We breathed with difficulty, owing to our elevation. It
seemed at last as if we had reached the roof of the earth. A
plateau lay before us.

Onward we march. Our horses struggle through the drifts.
Every minute we have to stop to let them take breath. At
last the road begins to descend; now abruptly for a few
hundred yards, we slide down some glaciers; then it dips over
a succession of crests, each one lower than its predecessor.

We reach the regions of vegetation, and, continuing for some time our descent, find that winter has been left behind us.

There were many villages in this district; fruit-trees abounded throughout the neighbourhood. No more snow could be seen. The weather was oppressively warm. The Tschoroch river dashed along at our feet on its way to Batoum. Mohammed, pointing at the rapid stream, said something to my English servant.

"What is he saying?" I inquired.

"He don't like the idea of going in a boat, sir," replied Radford. "He is afraid that he will be drowned."

"Do you know how to swim, Mohammed?" I inquired.

"No, Effendi. Cannot we continue our journey by road to Batoum?" he added. "The road is safe, but the water is dangerous."

"Mohammed, it may be written in your kismet that you are to be drowned."

"Perhaps, Effendi. But——"

"But what?"

"If I am to die I would sooner end my days in a bed."

"You ought to be very glad to have the chance of dying," I now remarked. "Only think of the many wives who are awaiting you in the next world."

Mohammed here shrugged his shoulders.

"Effendi, you are a Christian."

"Yes."

"Do Christians believe in a future state of happiness?"

"Yes."

"Do they think that their heaven will be more delightful than this earth?"

"Yes."

"If a Christian is ill, does he send for a hakim (physician)?"

"Yes."

Then added Mohammed triumphantly, "Why does he do so? He ought to be delighted at the chance of speedily going to Paradise, and yet, Effendi, according to you, the Christian does his best to postpone the pleasure."

The track now became very bad; it led several times across the river, which was spanned by rickety wooden bridges. The may-trees were in full blossom. The voices of a thousand songsters chirruping amidst the branches echoed over the waters.

We enter what appears to be a vast amphitheatre. The Coliseum at Rome on a gigantic scale lies before us. Its walls are represented by a circular range of hills, the boxes looking down upon the arena by numerous châlets, they jut forth from the slopes. An enormous rock faces us. It stands out on one side of the amphitheatre, and might have been an emperor's throne. The boxes grow larger as we ride across the arena. The resemblance fades away. A speck appears on the crest of a neighbouring height; bigger and bigger it becomes.

"Kale, or the old fortress of Ardanusch," says our guide, pointing to it. Soon afterwards we put up for the night in a house belonging to the Caimacan of the district. This official informed me that it was only an eighteen-hours' march to Akiska, the Russian frontier station. The road to the border was a good one; artillery could be brought along it. There were no troops in Ardanusch, and the governor was much alarmed lest the Russians should commence the war by an attack upon his town. Whilst we were conversing, a servant brought him a letter which had been sent on by special messengers from Ardahan.

The Caimacan opened the envelope, "War!" he cried. "An order has come for me to call out all the Mostaphas (the last reserve) in this district. The Government would have never put itself to this expense unless our Padishah had felt sure that war was inevitable."

Leaving me, the governor went out to give the necessary orders for the execution of the Sultan's mandate.

We continued onward to Livana; the track was sometimes so narrow that we had to ride or lead our horses in Indian file. Now we come to a place where ten men could defend the road against an army, and then to a spot where the path has given way altogether, and fallen into the stream below. Our guide reins his horse backward. It is impossible to turn. We essay another route, and presently again strike the river. A large cayek was anchored by the bank. A man coming up to me proposed that we should go in his boat to Batoum.

"How much money do you want for taking us there?" I inquired.

"Ten liras, Effendi."

"Go away, sheep's son!" ejaculated Mohammed indignantly; "we will ride to Livana, which is only four hours' march from here; and then, if it pleases the Effendi to entrust himself to a boatman, I will get a ship for two liras—rascal that you are to ask ten liras for the hire of your little cayek!"

CHAPTER LXVII

THE road took a very circuitous course as we approached Livana. We were several hundred feet above the Tschoroch river, and could gaze down almost perpendicularly into the abyss below. Suddenly the sound of a shout reached our ears. We glanced in the direction of the noise.

"It is the cayek," said Mohammed eagerly. "The men are taking it to Livana. They will next propose that we should hire it from there to Batoum. Holy Prophet!" he continued, "how the waters roar, how near the boat goes to the rocks! My body groans, Effendi, at the idea of going to Batoum by water."

"You will very likely soon have to fight the Russians," I replied; "what difference can it make if you are drowned to-morrow in the Tschoroch, or are shot a few weeks later?"

"To-morrow is close at hand, Effendi. It would be better to die a few weeks later; besides that, when the Russians are shooting at me, I shall be shooting at them. I shall be frightened, but they will be frightened too. It is very different to travel on the river. I cannot drown the river, the river can drown me,"—and Mohammed shuddered as the cayek, darting round a neighbouring crag, suddenly disappeared from our view.

We crossed a stone bridge, which spans the Tschoroch, and began to climb the steep hill on which Livana is built.

I stayed at the house of the Caimacan, a Georgian by birth. He was popular with the Armenians. Several of the Christian merchants who came to visit me spoke very highly in his praise. Formerly there had been many robberies in the neighbourhood, but Alinihat Bey, the Caimacan, had arrested all the robbers, every man's life and property were now secure. I now heard, amongst other rumours, one which I had previously heard in Persia, to the effect that the Padishah of the United States had informed the Queen of England that if she were to

join Turkey against Russia, that he, the Padishah of the
United States, would ally himself with the Tzar. According
to the Caimacan, this had restrained England up to the
present time from allying herself with the Sultan. "You will
see the Pacha at Batoum?" observed the speaker.

"Yes."

"Will you do me a favour?"

"Certainly."

"Effendi, I have a Kateb (clerk), a good man—that fellow
on the carpet. Look how beautifully he writes! He is nice-
looking, too, and we all like him. But the Pacha, he has a
Kateb. The fellow is hideous, besides that, he has a node in
the middle of his forehead. The governor wishes to change
Katebs with me. He says that he does not like a man with a
node on his forehead; I do not like this either; and to sit all
day long with a man who is so disfigured would make me
very ill."

"It would make us all ill," observed the Armenians, eager
to please the Caimacan.

"Yes," continued the latter; "Effendi, you would oblige
us very much if you will tell the Pacha that I like my Kateb,
and do not wish to part with him. A man with a node is a
disgusting sight," he added.

"Very disgusting," said the Armenians—the man who spoke
loudest being a Christian with a hump-back.

In the meantime Mohammed had made an arrangement with
the owner of a large cayek to take us the following morning
to Batoum, which would be about a nine hours' journey by
water from Livana. We rode down to the bank of the river.
Here, close by the bridge, was a large boat. It was half full
of firewood, which was going to Batoum. Two oarsmen sat
in the stern of the cayek, and two more in the bows. There
were no rowers in the middle of the boat; this part was filled
with wood, some other passengers, my party and self. Our
fellow-travellers and the boatmen were Georgians. A very
stout old gentleman who sat behind me was arrayed in a bright
blue jacket and a large white turban; in addition to this he
carried a gigantic scarlet umbrella. A few drops of rain
began to fall; the umbrella was opened. Its happy possessor
looked proudly round; he was an object of admiration and
envy to the rest of his countrymen.

The boatmen, who were clad in brown serge jackets and
trousers, had their breasts covered with cartridge-cases, in the

Circassian style. Each man carried a long silver-mounted dagger in his waist-belt, and a black *cufia*, a sort of head attire, was worn by them instead of a turban. The river, which was very high, ran through the arch of the bridge at a great pace. Mohammed's face became an ashen hue as the captain of the cayek, loosening the cord which bound his bark to the shore, pushed off into the boiling torrent. For the first second or two the oarsmen could not get any command over their boat. It turned round and round, missing, as it were, by a miracle the many rocks in the channel.

The rowers all this time were raising wild cries to Allah. Mohammed, who had crouched down in the bottom of the bark, was grasping Radford's hand in a paroxysm of terror. In another moment the crew succeeded in gaining the mastery over their craft. They steered her into the middle of the river. The current was running like a mill-stream. We flew rather than floated along the waters.

Numerous rocks interrupt the channel; some of them are forty and fifty feet above the surface; others can only be detected by the foam and surf which bubble over their dangerous peaks. The mountains on either side of us are of igneous stone; they are covered with green bushes. A white line winds amongst the heights; it marks the track to Batoum, an eighteen-hours' march by land, but only nine by water. We pass the ruins of an old castle. We dart round a promontory. The scene changes. Vineyards deck the river's banks. Oxen can be seen ploughing the slopes above us. Many women, in bright red garments, and with white head-dresses, follow the plough. They knock to pieces the clods of earth with iron hoes. Waterfalls pour down the heights. The river grows wider; it becomes more rapid every moment. The wind is rising. The chief boatman remarks that we cannot arrive at Batoum that evening.

To reach the town it was necessary to enter the Black Sea; but to effect this in stormy weather, and in an undecked boat, would be impossible. We anchored for the night at the village of Miradet, four hours from Livana by the river, but twelve by land. I obtained accommodation in the house of the Mudir of the district. There were some cells in this building; in one of them was a prisoner—a deserter, who had run away from the army. There was a hearth in his dungeon, and Radford was permitted to cook there, the deserter taking great interest in the culinary operations.

CHAPTER LXVIII

I NOW learnt that corn is dear in this district, costing two
piastres and a half the oke. It is chiefly brought here from
the neighbourhood of Ardahan, the difficulty of transport
adding enormously to the price. Indian corn is grown in the
vicinity of Livana, but it is not easy to procure barley. This
last, however, is not so much required, as there are hardly any
horses in the neighbourhood.

Just above Miradet lie the ruins of an old bridge. At this
time of the year, the only way to cross the river is in the
cayeks of the peasants. I was informed that in the summer
months a horseman could ford the Tschoroch in some places
near the village. According to the Mudir, there are iron-
mines in the neighbourhood, but the inhabitants did not work
them.

There was a battalion of infantry, Bashi Bazouks, in his
village. The men, Georgians, were magnificent fellows, much
taller than the Turkish soldiers, and with that light and
elastic step which distinguishes mountaineers. A report had
just reached Miradet that the Persians were attacking Bagdad
with thirty-thousand men. In the opinion of the Mudir, this
was the precursor of an immediate outbreak of hostilities
between the Sultan's forces on the one hand and Russia and
Persia on the other.

We entered our cayek early the following morning.
Mohammed was more alarmed, if possible, than on the previous
afternoon. A passenger had been drowned two weeks before,
when going to Batoum. Mohammed had learnt this; he now
bandaged his eyes with a pocket-handkerchief.

"What are you doing that for?" I inquired.

"So as not to see the waters," replied Mohammed; "they
roar, my stomach aches."

" Tchok eyi (very nice), is it not ? " suddenly remarked Radford, nudging his fellow-servant violently in the ribs. We were in the midst of some rapids. Two or three violent bumps announced our close proximity to the rocks. " He will not laugh at me any more, sir, for not liking to look down precipices. Have a hegg, Mohammed ; " taking one from his own pocket, Radford handed it to the sufferer.

We had arrived at the open sea. Mohammed removed his handkerchief from his eyes, the motion of the cayek was different to that which he had experienced on the river. He gazed upon the egg for an instant, and then thrust it away indignantly ; the sea and his fears were too much for him ; he leaned against the side of the boat. Radford was thoroughly revenged.

The harbour of Batoum is one of the finest in the Black Sea. Numerous batteries mounted with heavy guns defend it on the sea side. Three large ironclads were anchored within thirty yards of the shore, the water being very deep.

I landed at the quarantine station, and now learnt that every house in the town, or rather village, was crowded with troops. The doctor of the quarantine offered me a room in the station ; I gladly availed myself of his kindness.

There were only 8000 men in Batoum itself ; the remainder of the garrison, consisting of 12,000 infantry, with some artillery, were stationed at Tschoroch Su, a strong position about six hours from the town, and defending the road from Poti. Mohammed's Tokat battalion was quartered here. It was probably the point against which the Russians would make their first attack, he was aware of that fact.

" Would you like to accompany me to Constantinople ? " I asked.

" No, Effendi, not for all the money in the world will I go there. One hour on the sea is very awful ; five days would kill me. My brother," pointing to Radford, " is brave on the water ; I am brave on the land ; we are both brave ; " seizing his fellow-servant's hand, Mohammed shook it heartily.

A major on the staff called. According to him, the Cossack outposts were in the habit of firing upon the Turkish troops. It appeared that on the 26th of March, 1877, a few Turkish soldiers were walking in the Sultan's territory, but on the edge of the frontier-line. Some Russian soldiers fired and shot three of them ; then, fording a river, which divides the two countries, the Cossacks carried the dead bodies and arms to the Russian side of the border. They afterwards complained to their officer that the Turks had crossed over on Russian soil.

" War has not been declared," I remarked.

" No," said the major; " the Russians are doing their best to make us attack them; but we shall not do so. They shall have the whole odium of the war, and Allah will judge between us ! "

I accompanied the officer to an encampment close to the coast. The tents had been pitched between the mouth of the Tschoroch river and the town. Three thousand infantry soldiers were quartered in this place. The sanitary arrangements of the camp left very little to be desired. Everything was clean and orderly. An air of smartness prevailed amongst the soldiers, which was refreshing to witness after what I had seen in other parts of the empire. The men's tents were banked up with stones to a height of three feet from the ground. Well-dug trenches carried off the rainfall. Many of the officers lived in huts which were surrounded by little gardens. All these battalions were armed with the Martini-Peabody rifle. I asked some of the men how they liked their new weapon, being curious to know if they objected to the recoil. There was no fault found with the gun on this score. The troops were highly pleased with the arm. They wished for nothing better than to have the opportunity of trying it upon their quarrelsome neighbours.

We next visited the market in the town, or rather village, for Batoum with its few hundred straggling houses does not deserve the former title. There was hardly anything exposed for sale. A solitary sheep was hung up in one shop. Some stale fish were lying on the counter of another. There were several money-changers in the streets; business, however, was slack, and these gentlemen lived by lending money on exorbitant terms to the Turks—the usurers being many of them Armenian Christians.

A Turkish steamer was to leave Batoum that night for Constantinople. I made inquiries as to when she would be likely to arrive at her destination.

" In five days," said the agent at the booking-office—a most saturnine-looking old Turk, " that is if the Lord wills it; but the Lord may will that the vessel shall lay to in Trebizond, and return here with troops without going to Stamboul."

Under these circumstances I determined to go in the

Turkish boat as far as Trebizond, and continue my journey in some other steamer to Constantinople. Mohammed accompanied me on board the vessel. The moment for parting at last arrived. The poor fellow was much affected. Some big tears began to roll down his cheeks.

"Will you go with me to Constantinople?" I inquired.

"To the end of the world, Effendi!"

"But think how ill you will be."

"Never mind, Effendi, only let me come. It is true that my stomach sank within me yesterday, but my heart is very full to-day; for am I not losing my lord as well as my brother?"—seizing Radford's hand, Mohammed wrung it heartily.

The vessel had got up steam; the deck was being cleared. Mohammed rubbed his eyes with the back of his hand and clambered down the side of the ship into a little boat. Several of his countrymen tried to comfort him. He was not to be consoled. As we steamed out of the harbour, I could still see the poor fellow straining his eyes in our direction.

"That Mohammed was not such a bad chap after all, sir," presently remarked Radford. "Them Turks have stomachs, and like filling them they do; but they have something in their hearts as well."

There was a great deal of truth in the observation. Those people in England who have declared that it is impossible to reform the Turks would do well to learn the Turkish language, and travel in the Sultan's dominions. Human nature is everywhere much the same. There is more good in the world than bad, or otherwise, as a French philosopher once said, the bad would have destroyed the good, and the human race would no longer exist. Give the Turks a good government, and Turkey would soon take her place amidst civilized nations.

This, however, would not be pleasing to the Sultan's powerful neighbour. Reform is impossible in Turkey so long as Russian agents* foment rebellion amidst the Sultan's subjects.

One of my fellow-passengers was a Turkish doctor. He had the rank of Pacha and was under the Army Medical Department. He had left Constantinople with orders to visit Kars, and report to his Government about the sanitary state of this town. On arriving at Batoum, he found that the tracks were still covered with snow. The doctor, who was suffering from heart disease, had determined to return to Trebizond.

* See Appendix IV.

" In what state is the road between Erzeroum and Kars?"
he now asked.

" Probably it is covered with snow."

" Dear me," said the Pacha, " I shall wait a little at
Trebizond for a change of weather."

" You had better go to Kars as soon as possible," I remarked,
" or there will be an outbreak of fever there."

" If I travel quickly," observed the official, " I shall die of
heart disease. A little sooner or later will not make much
difference to the people in Kars. I shall be able to leave the
service in a year and a half," he continued ; " if I were to
hurry myself, death might carry me off before I could enjoy
my pension. Please God there will be no war. We shall
have so many cases to attend. I was at Alexinatz," he
added.

" Did you have a great deal to do?"

" Yes, so few of our surgeons know anything about
anatomy ; dissecting a Mohammedan is contrary to the tenets
of Islam. But there were plenty of dead Servians, and so our
people practised upon them."

The following morning we arrived at Trebizond. There
was a French steamer on the point of starting for Constantinople. I had just time to take my luggage on board of her.
In a few minutes we were again steaming ahead. Three days
later, and after a most delightful passage, we anchored in the
Bosphorus. My leave of absence had nearly expired. There
would be another French vessel belonging to Les Messageries
Maritimes leaving on the morrow for Marseilles. I took our
tickets on my way to the Hôtel de Luxembourg, and eight
days afterwards arrived in London.

CHAPTER LXIX

My journey was over. A few weeks after my return to London, war was declared by Russia against Turkey. In the opinion of Her Majesty's Government, this was a most iniquitous and unnecessary step on the part of the Tzar. Her Majesty's Government did not conceal its views about the matter. The Earl of Derby, in a despatch to Lord A. Loftus, dated May 1st, 1877, made use of the following expressions:—

"They (i.e. Her Majesty's Government) have not concealed their feeling that the presence of large Russian forces on the frontiers of Turkey, menacing its safety, rendering disarmament impossible, and exciting a feeling of apprehension and fanaticism among the Mussulman population, constituted a material obstacle to internal pacification and reform. They cannot believe that the entrance of these armies on Turkish soil will alleviate the difficulty, or improve the condition of the Christian population throughout the Sultan's dominions. But the course on which the Russian Government has entered involves graver and more serious considerations. It is in contravention of the stipulations of the Treaty of Paris of March 30, 1856, by which Russia and the other signatory Powers engaged, each on its own part, to respect the independence and the territorial integrity of the Ottoman Empire. In the Conferences of London of 1871, at the close of which the above stipulation, with others, was again confirmed, the Russian Plenipotentiary, in common with those of the other Powers, signed a declaration affirming it to be an essential principle of the law of nations, that no Power can liberate itself from the engagements of a Treaty, nor modify the stipulations thereof, unless with the consent of the contracting parties by means of an amicable arrangement. In taking action against Turkey on his own part, and having recourse to arms without further consultation with his allies, the

Emperor of Russia has separated himself from the European concert hitherto maintained, and has at the same time departed from the rule to which he himself had solemnly recorded his consent. It is impossible to foresee the consequences of such an act. Her Majesty's Government would willingly have refrained from making any observations in regard to it; but Prince Gortschakoff seems to assume, in a declaration addressed to all the Governments of Europe, that Russia is acting in the interest of Great Britain and that of the other Powers; they feel bound to state, in a manner equally formal and public, that the decision of the Russian Government is not one which can have their concurrence or approval."

It is very clear, from this despatch, what the opinion of Her Majesty's Government was about the matter. However, neither Prince Gortschakoff nor his august master are easily affected by verbal remonstrances.

They had shown how little they cared for treaties by their conduct after the battle of Sedan.

"France is beaten, and who cares for England?" thought Prince Gortschakoff: he tore up the Black Sea Convention.

His august master, animated of course with the most peaceful intentions, wishes to destroy the Turkish Empire. Verbal remonstrances are of no use if applied to a semi-barbarous nation. Some people can be appealed to through their sense of right and wrong, others only through their skins. The Russian nation has a peculiarly thick skin; for this reason the rod ought to be a heavy one. England, allied with Turkey, and before the latter power is crippled, could easily apply it. The Tzar might be compelled to fulfil his solemn assurance about Khiva: Russia could be driven out of Central Asia, and forced to relinquish her hold on the Caucasus.

A Conference might then be held at St. Petersburg to arrange about the conditions of peace, and to inquire into the treatment of the United Greek Christians. Lord Salisbury could inform Prince Gortschakoff that some of the British nation do not approve of the Russian authorities ordering soldiers to flog Christian women and children,* by way of making them change their religion; and that others object to the Tzar's troops killing Circassian women in the family-way.†

---

* See Appendix I., The Floggers of Women and Children.
† See Appendix VII., The Schoolmasters in Massacre.

We have been told that these last-mentioned individuals were Mohammedans, and that Prince Gortschakoff's master would have liked to Christianize and civilize them ; but at the same time, and in spite of the assertion of a member of the late Liberal Government, that Russia is the protector of the unprotected, our plenipotentiary might be instructed to tell the Tzar that his soldiers should have shown their amiable qualities in some other manner. The subject of the Teke Turkomans, and how they were massacred—men, women, and children—during the Khivan campaign, could also afford our representative an opportunity for remonstrating with the Imperial Chancellor.

The latter should finally be distinctly given to understand that Englishmen do not look upon the establishment of a Constitution and a Parliament by the Turkish Government as an insult and defiance to Russia, whatever the Russians may do.*

In the meantime, and while I pen these lines, the Tzar's armies have crossed the Danube. They are quartered on Turkish soil. The Treaty of Paris has been once more broken by the Russian Government. The solemn assurances made by the Emperor have been cast to the four winds. A climax has been put to the breaches of good faith ; displayed first of all about Samarcand ; secondly, Khiva ; thirdly, the Black Sea Convention and immediately after the battle of Sedan. England has not declared war with Russia. There are still some people amongst us who place credence in the Russian Emperor's statement that he has no intention to interfere with British interests. "Let the Russians go to Constantinople," is the remark, "they will not stop there. The Tzar will dictate terms of peace in the Sultan's capital. The Muscovite armies will return to their own country. If the worst comes to the worst, England with her fleet could drive out the invader." Men who argue like this do not care to remember that Russia has broken faith with England four times in the last ten years. Should the Sultan be forced to succumb to his foe, and the Emperor's troops be once established in Constantinople, it would be almost impossible for a non-military power like England to dislodge them from the position. Whatever we might be able to do by sea would be counterbalanced by our inability to follow up the advantage by land. It must not be forgotten that Turkey is

* See Appendix IV.

fighting not only for herself, but also for the security of our Indian Empire.*   A few millions sterling would enable the Turkish Government to supply its soldiers with the munitions of war.

An English contingent force of fifty thousand men could defend Constantinople against all the Russian armies.   It is to be hoped that the Ottoman troops will do more than hold their own.   But this is doubtful.   The Tzar has thrown down the gauntlet to England by taking action on his own part against the Sultan.   We should accept the challenge, and draw our swords for Turkey.

* See page 333.

APPENDIX A. (I.)

THE FLOGGERS OF WOMEN

Lieutenant-Colonel MANSFIELD *to Earl* GRANVILLE.

Official. (Received Feb. 16.)

Warsaw, *January* 29, 1874

MY LORD,

It is with regret that I have to report to your Lordship a renewal of disturbances in the districts inhabited by the United Greeks in the Governments of Siedlce and Lublin, resulting in bloodshed, loss of life, and the MOST BARBAROUS TREATMENT inflicted on the peasants.

*   *   *   *   *   *

Several months since various of the United Greek priests represented to M. Popiel, the Administrator of the Diocese of Chelm, that the measures of assimilation had been but partially carried out; and that those priests who had done so were exposed to the gravest difficulties, amounting almost to persecution at the hands of the peasants.

M. Popiel applied to Count Tolstoi, who forwarded from St. Petersburg, within the last few weeks, a Circular, enjoining the strictest uniformity in the abolition of organs and benches, the disuse of the rosary, the bell at the mass, chants in Polish, and many other details, too numerous to be worth relation.

Such of the priests as had not, or were not prepared to execute the recommendations of the Circular, have been ejected from their cures. The number, however, is insignificant, as almost all had previously acquiesced in the views of the Government, and the Nonconformists had been eliminated.

As may be supposed, the peasants care nothing about the Synod of Zamosc, or about the purity and usages of the Primitive Church, Oriental or otherwise; but they have a deep-rooted veneration for the usages in which they and their fathers have been brought up.

The operation of Count Tolstoi's Circular has been most disastrous; in some few villages the peasants have entirely abstained from frequenting the churches; but in many the priests have been ill-treated, one having been stoned to death.

The aid of the police and military has been called in; in one parish three peasants were killed and many wounded. Isolated Cossacks are waylaid and murdered by the peasants. In some of the conflicts the military have been roughly handled, stoned, wounded by scythes, bones broken, and contusions, more especially among the officers.

In the district of Minciewicz, the peasants surrounded the church, and defied the military to introduce the priest. The former, with their wives and children, were finally mastered and surrounded, and were given the option of signing a declaration accepting the priest; on their refusal FIFTY BLOWS WITH THE "NAGAIKA"* (COSSACK WHIP) were given to every adult man, TWENTY-FIVE to EVERY WOMAN, and TEN to EVERY CHILD, IRRESPECTIVE OF AGE OR SEX; ONE WOMAN, more vehement than the rest, receiving as much as ONE HUNDRED.

*   *   *   *   *   *

I have, &c.,

(Signed)   C. E. MANSFIELD.

---

* Is this the way the Rev. Mr. Malcolm Maccoll would like to see the union of the Eastern and W stern churches brought about?

APPENDIX A. (II.)

CHRISTIANITY AS UNDERSTOOD IN RUSSIA

Lieutenant-Colonel Mansfield *to the Earl of* Derby.

(Received, February 22.)

Warsaw, *January* 29, 1875.

(Extract.)

I have the honour to report to your Lordship that 52,000 United Greeks in the Government of Siedlce have been received into the Russian National Church.

I need not recall to your Lordship's notice, the PERSECUTION of the UNITED GREEKS, which I have had to report for several years past, and which, within the last twelve months, has taken a more exaggerated form.

THE PASSING OVER OF THESE 50,000 UNITED GREEKS has been effected by various means, in which PHYSICAL MALTREATMENT has formed a not inconsiderable element.

In some parishes, THE MOST OBSTINATE having been sent to the interior of the Empire OR SIBERIA, THE REMAINDER, finding their substance being eaten up by the Cossacks, gave in to the pressure of the subordinate officials, and SIGNED THE PETITION DESIRING TO BE RECEIVED INTO THE RUSSIAN CHURCH.

In other districts money has been distributed, when it was seen that the resistance was less obdurate.

In others CORPORAL MALTREATMENT was resorted to, until the peasants gave in; but stating as they did so, that they yielded only on compulsion.

The details of the different degrees of compulsion in the various villages would take too much space to relate; but I cite as a specimen what I have heard, from a gentleman of whose veracity I have no reason to doubt, of what took place in a village on his property.

The peasants were assembled and beaten by the Cossacks, until the military surgeon stated that more would endanger life; THEY WERE THEN DRIVEN THROUGH A HALF-FROZEN RIVER UP TO THEIR WAISTS INTO THE PARISH CHURCH, through files of soldiers, where their names were entered in the petitions as above, and passed out at an opposite door, the peasants all the time crying out, "YOU MAY CALL US ORTHODOX, BUT WE REMAIN IN THE FAITH OF OUR FATHERS."

*   *   *   *   *   *

APPENDIX A. (III.)

RUSSIAN CIVILIZATION

In an extract from the *Monde*, published in some correspondence laid before the Houses of Parliament, I find the following remarks :—

" Russia is anxious for a second Congress, and asks all Europe to agree to it, in order to settle certain rules of humanity to be observed during a war, and she aspires to appear in the eyes of the world as a civilized nation full of charity; how can we reconcile this with the fact that this Power should be so barbarous in time of peace as regards its peaceful subjects, whose only fault is that of remaining faithful to the religion of their fathers ?

" The cruelties that the Russian Government perpetrate against the unhappy Catholics who are called United Greeks, are worthy of the horrors of the time of Nero. The Province of Podlachia, the people of which are Ruthenians, is more especially persecuted. There blood has flown in streams for more than a year. Troops have been sent there who behave as if they were in an enemy's country, for they live entirely at the expense of the people, who are not rich. The soldiers are authorized to kill for food all the cattle without exception, even the draught oxen.

" The inhabitants who remain true to their faith are delivered over to a THOUSAND TORTURES. The commonest form is to STRIP THEM, then ONLY CLOTHED IN THEIR SHIRT, THEY ARE STRETCHED ON THE SNOW AND BEATEN UNTIL THEY ARE NEARLY DEAD, as much from the effects of the blows as from the loss of blood and the cold they suffer. They are then taken to the ambulances. If they recover those ingenious tortures can be renewed on them, which Russia distributes freely to those who refuse obstinately to embrace that orthodox religion which is brought before them in so benign and attractive a manner.

" This Polish province contains at least 300,000 United Greeks, all under this same régime, for all are to be converted by this apostolic proceeding. The number of unfortunates crippled by the beatings is so great that it has been found necessary to organize many new ambulances. They are thrown into them; but it must not be imagined that they are cared for there. God alone is their doctor, for no trouble is taken either to treat or feed them.

" Moreover, this same treatment is adopted for sick and wounded soldiers. With the object of cheering them they are given a kind of soup made of gruel of revolting half-mouldy buckwheat, in which the grains are drowned in a quantity of hot water. In time of war THE SORES OF THE WOUNDED ARE OFTEN DRESSED WITH STRAW, BECAUSE THE LINT AND THE CLOTH WHICH ARE SENT BY CHARITABLE PEOPLE TO THE HOSPITALS ARE SOLD BY THE OFFICERS TO PAPER MILLS.

" All this may give some idea of what is passing there, where the passion of cruelty follows an unrestrained course, proud to be able to advertise its unrighteous zeal in sight of those whose orders are being carried out.

" One is filled with grief and astonishment when one thinks of the people exposed to tortures by Russian barbarity and wickedness. It is a counterpart of the Chinese persecutions, which the Muscovites seem anxious even to surpass.

" The heroism of the unhappy Podlachians is forgotten by all the world, they are delivered up to rapine and torture, deprived of union and hope, and bear all this with calm gentleness and perseverance; they are ready to die, so long as it is not outside the bosom of the Church, and after having betrayed their faith.

" What an example to all, and what a disgrace for those who, without being exposed to such trials, have not been able to persevere! ' "

APPENDIX IV

RUSSIAN AGENTS AND THE MASSACRES IN BULGARIA

Extract from Mr. LAYARD's *(H.M. Ambassador at Constantinople) Despatch to the Earl of* DERBY *dated 30th May, 1877.*

" SINCE my arrival in Constantinople my main object has been to prepare the way for peace. I have thought that in doing so I should best carry out the wishes and intentions of her Majesty's Government. I had this end in view, as I informed your lordship at the time when I induced the Porte to appeal to the Powers for their mediation under the 8th Article of the Treaty of Paris. I had little hope that war could be averted by this step, but it appeared to me that it might afford an opening for the interference of those Powers in the interests of peace on some future occasion. The opening of the war has not been quite so favourable to Russia as she appears to have expected. The extraordinary rise in the Danube has checked her advance on the side of Europe, and has enabled Turkey to increase her means of resistance. Although the Porte might, no doubt, have done more in this respect, there is no doubt that the difficulties of the Russian campaign in Roumelia have been much increased by the delay, and although Russia may succeed in the end, it will probably be at a greater sacrifice than she may have at first contemplated. The simultaneous attack on the European and Asiatic territories of Turkey has not, therefore, led to all the results upon which Russia apparently counted. According to information derived from various sources it would appear that the rise in the waters of the Danube, and the consequent floods over the surrounding country, will render its passage very difficult, if not impossible, for three or four weeks to come. Does not this delay afford an opening for another effort in the interests of peace? The position of affairs is this. Russia has succeeded in Asia, and thus she holds a material guarantee for what she may require on behalf of the Christians of Turkey in the shape of a province; in Europe she cannot be said to have yet succeeded, and she will probably have to encounter a desperate resistance, and to make vast sacrifices before she can impose her own terms upon the Porte. Moreover, the longer the war lasts the greater the risk of drawing other Powers in it against her. If hostilities be prolonged Turkey, in her despair, may have recourse to measures to embarrass and injure Russia which may to a certain extent effect that object. Although the rising in the Caucasus may not have the importance that has been attributed to it, and the negotiations between the Porte and revolutionary and national leaders may not lead to serious results, they are undoubtedly a danger to Russia. The real intentions of Russia would also be brought to a test by proposing to her at this moment a mediation. If her real object is, as she asserts, the improvement of the condition of the Christian populations, she has surely now the means of obtaining a satisfactory guarantee for it. The Turkish Government, it must be admitted, has already done a good deal in the direction pointed out by the Powers at the Conference and in the Protocol of London. It is prepared to do more, and would do more, if the war waged against Turkey by Russia permitted it. The lesson which the Porte has received has, no doubt, made it see the absolute necessity of complying with the demands of Europe, without even the material guarantee which Russia may require. If, on the other hand, Russia has the ambitious designs generally attributed to her, and has entered upon this war for the purposes of territorial aggrandisement, her professions of humanity and disinterestedness can now be gauged, and her Majesty's Government will be able, at least, to judge what her real objects and intentions are, and how far the interests of the British Empire may be affected or endangered by them. It must not, however, be inferred that the Porte will be so easily induced to make peace, even were it in extreme peril. There are some Turkish statesmen who see the dangers which threaten their country, and who would feel the absolute necessity of bringing the war to an end almost at any sacrifice. Whilst Russia might desire to exact much, no Turkish Ministers could accept very hard or humiliating conditions without risking their own lives, and even that of the Sultan, and without exposing the Christian populations to a massacre. I may be excused for pointing out the dangers to England of a prolongation of the war, and of a complete subjugation of a large part of the empire by Russia. Should Russia desire to annex at this time any of the European provinces of Turkey, European interests would probably be called into play, and she would be prevented from carrying out her intentions. The influence, however, which she would inevitably establish over these populations would be almost tantamount to absolute possession, and would enable her to annex them, sooner or later, when she could do so with impunity; but as regards the acquisition by her of territory in Asia Minor the case is different. The interests of England would then be alone concerned. IT WOULD PROBABLY SIGNIFY LITTLE TO THE REST OF EUROPE WHETHER

RUSSIA RETAINED ARMENIA OR NOT. BUT ENGLAND HAS TO CONSIDER THE EFFECT OF THE ANNEXATION TO RUSSIA of this IMPORTANT PROVINCE UPON THE BRITISH POSSESSIONS IN INDIA. RUSSIA WOULD THEN COMMAND the WHOLE OF ASIA MINOR and THE GREAT VALLEY OF THE EUPHRATES AND TIGRIS, WHICH WOULD INEVITABLY FALL INTO HER HANDS IN THE COURSE OF TIME. Persia, moreover, would be placed entirely at her mercy. The suspicion that Russia has already made secret offers to Persia to assist her in acquiring the province of Bagdad in exchange for Ghilan and Mazanderan may be unfounded ; but the fact that it exists, and has been entertained by persons not generally ill-informed, proves that this consideration is not one to be altogether lost sight of. In most cases, when the evident interests of two parties are concerned in effecting an exchange, the exchange is sooner or later effected. The desire of Persia to possess the province of Bagdad and the holy shrines of their prophets and martyrs is of very ancient date, and is shared by the whole Persian nation. On the other hand, THE POSSESSION OF THE ENTIRE COAST OF THE CASPIAN SEA AND THE DIRECT ROAD through a rich and well-inhabited country TO HERAT AND AFFGHANISTAN, AND ULTIMATELY TO INDIA, is a matter of VAST POLITICAL IMPORTANCE TO RUSSIA. Such being the case, there is every reason to believe that, when Persia finds that the Turkish empire is threatened with dismemberment, her own interests will get the better of any sympathy for it founded upon community of faith, and that, completely under the control of Russia, she will not be indisposed to agree to an arrangement which would be acceptable to the religious feelings and to the ambition of the Persian people. The possession by Persia of the province of Bagdad would be, as far as England is concerned, its possession by Russia. It must not be forgotten that the possession of Armenia by Russia, as regards any designs that she may have upon India, supposing her to entertain them, would be very different from that of any part of Turkestan or Central Asia. In Armenia and the north of Persia she would have a hardy and abundant population, affording her excellent materials for a large army, ready at any time to advance upon our Indian frontier, and resting upon a convenient and sure base of operations, in direct communication, by the Caspian Sea and by Batoum, with the heart of the Russian Empire. The moral effect of the conquest of Armenia and the annexation of Ghilan and Mazanderan by Russia upon our Mohammedan subjects and upon the populations of Central Asia cannot be overlooked by a statesman who attaches any value to the retention of India as part of the British Empire. It would be out of place to enter at length in this despatch upon the arguments in support of what has been above stated. The great calamities which the prolongation of the war may entail upon the various populations of this country, Mussulman and non-Mussulman, and the vast importance to the interests of humanity in bringing it to a speedy end, may be briefly mentioned. It is scarcely necessary to refer to the terrible loss of life and desolation which such a war must occasion. If the slaughter of thousands and tens of thousands of Turks is to be justified, even those who profess to be the most humane of men may feel some pity for their innocent women and children, who will be left to perish in utter misery. But the Christians may suffer scarcely less than the Mohammedans; their homes will be rendered desolate ; their lives and property will be sacrificed to Turkish fanaticism, or to the disorder and anarchy which the prolongation of the war will cause. The Porte, believing the very existence of the Empire to be at stake, has already withdrawn from the provinces even the forces absolutely necessary for the maintenance of tranquillity and for personal security.

From all sides come already complaints of fears of disorders. In a country infinitely more civilized than Turkey, such would probably be the case under similar circumstances. An impartial man will be surprised that as yet there have been so few excesses committed. The reports of our consular agents prove that the public peace has been maintained in a very remarkable manner. Such outrages as have occurred have been for the most part committed by Circassians, Kurds, and other wild tribes, over which, even in times of peace, the Government can exercise but small control. In Bulgaria and Roumelia in general, as Mr. Blunt's despatches show, the Mohammedan population are well disposed towards the Christians, and their attitude towards them is, for the present, friendly and peaceful. I am informed that the transport of the new levies of many thousands of men from the remotest part of the empire to the armies in the field has been effected with the greatest order. This fact has been confirmed to me by Englishmen and others connected with railways which have been used for conveying them. In Constantinople, notwithstanding the alarm and panics which normally prevail in Galata and Pera, there is also for the present perfect quiet, and there is no reason, as far as I can judge, to anticipate any hostile movement or demonstration against the Christians. Although the state of things in Turkey as regards the Christians is at this time such as I have described it, yet we must not count upon its lasting. Any serious reverses or disasters experienced by the Turkish army in Europe, and the advance of the Russians upon the capital, or a rising of any part of the Christian population, might be used to provoke an outburst amongst the Mussulmans, founded rather upon a feeling of despair than upon fanaticism, that might have the most fatal consequences. The Emperor of Russia has declared to his people that THIS IS A RELIGIOUS WAR, WAGED IN THE CAUSE OF THE ORTHODOX FAITH and against its infidel enemies. If Mussulmans are once convinced that it is a crusade against them and their religion they may, in their agony, turn upon the Christians, and frightful massacres may ensue. Another motive for desiring peace before Russia can completely crush Turkey and dictate her own terms is the REPUGNANCE UNQUESTIONABLY FELT by the most ENLIGHT- ENED and INTELLIGENT CHRISTIANS of all denominations to being placed under RUSSIAN RULE OR PROTECTION, or even under her predominant influence. I have given your lordship evidence of this fact which I believe to be indisputable. It is shown by the encyclical of the Greek Patriarch, transmitted to your lordship by to-day's messenger. It is further confirmed by the remarkable statement of Dr. Washburne, whose impartiality cannot be doubted, and who is certainly no advocate of Turkish misrule, that of the many hundred Bulgarians who have received an American (equivalent to an English) education at Robert College, not one was implicated in the attempted insurrection in Bulgaria. The English people cannot, perhaps, yet bear to hear the truth of the events of last year; but it is my duty to state it to your lordship. The marvellous ability shown by RUSSIA and HER AGENTS in MISLEADING PUBLIC OPINION in England and elsewhere has been amply rewarded. It will probably be long before that which is true can be separated from that which is false; when history does so it will be too late. The Porte has taken no effective means to place its case before Europe. It neither employs the Press nor competent agents for such purposes. Its appeals to the Powers, and the State papers that it issues, to refute the charges against it, are so prepared that they are more calculated to injure its cause. A great portion of the English public are, probably, still under the impression that the statements upon which the denunciations against Turkey were originally founded are true—the 60,000 Christians outraged and massacred; the cartloads of human heads; the crowd of women burnt in a barn; and other similar horrors.

There are persons, and amongst them, I grieve to say, Englishmen, who boast that they invented these stories with the object of 'writing down' Turkey, to which they were impelled by a well-known hand. People in England will scarcely believe that the most accurate and complete inquiries into the events of last year in Bulgaria now reduce the total number of deaths to about 3500 souls, including the Turks who were, in the first instance, slain by the Christians. No impartial man can now deny that a RISING of the CHRISTIANS, which was intended by its authors to lead to a GENERAL MASSACRE of the MOHAMMEDANS, was in contemplation, and that it was directed by RUSSIAN and PANSLAVIST AGENTS. The panic that it created amongst the Mohammedans was the cause of the frightful vengeance they took. The great mass of the Bulgarians did not join in the movement, but were, on the contrary, opposed to it, and took no part in it. The Porte dealt with the insurgents, and those whom they suspected of being their accomplices, in a foolish and barbarous manner. The agents it employed in putting down the incipient insurrection were, for the most part, ignorant, corrupt, and brutal men. The Turkish Government has justly been held responsible for their acts, especially as it has refused to punish with condign severity those who committed horrible outrages; and whether the number of the killed was 60,000 or 3000 the guilt of the Porte is the same. It must not, however, be assumed that the condition of the Bulgarians under the rule of the Sultan was as bad as the enemies of Turkey desire to make it appear. That the administration was vicious and corrupt, and that the Christians of all denominations were unjustly treated, and were not placed on that equality with their Mussulman fellow-subjects to which they have a right, are admitted facts. But nevertheless they have made great progress of late years in material prosperity, education, and wealth. Englishmen who have been engaged in works of charity amongst them, and who were certainly very far from having any prejudice in favour of the Turks when they first came out to Turkey, have told me that they have seen with surprise the condition of the Bulgarian villages and the general comfort and prosperity of their inhabitants, and have learnt with equal surprise how little they had really to complain of before a secret agency excited the hopes and passions which brought about the lamentable events of last year. The Christian populations of Turkey, or rather it may perhaps be said those who, by their knowledge and intelligence, are capable of representing them, are convinced that under the Turkish rule they have a far better chance of carrying out their national aspirations, of retaining their national faith, and developing their political freedom than under that of Russia. They believe that the pressure recently brought to bear upon the Porte by the European Powers, and the lesson which the Turkish Government has received, will contribute to these objects. They are encouraged by the unexpected success of a Turkish Parliament, in which they find that they can freely express their opinions and expose their grievances. They knew that the unchecked success of Russia would at once lead to the destruction of this germ of future liberty and good government. I believe that they are right. A Russian gentleman observed to me, 'RUSSIA LOOKS UPON THE ESTABLISHMENT OF A CONSTITUTION AND A PARLIAMENT BY THE TURKISH GOVERNMENT AS AN INSULT AND DEFIANCE TO HER. Their existence would alone furnish us with a sufficient reason to make war upon Turkey. We will never consent to be the only Power left in Europe without constitutional institutions, and as we are not yet prepared for them, we cannot, it is evident, allow Turkey to have them.' What I have ventured to write in this despatch is. I can assure your lordship, founded upon no preconceived ideas with regard to this country, but upon the information that I have obtained in free and unrestrained conversation with men of all classes, conditions, and religions. Not a day has passed since I have been here that I have not seen many such persons. Some have come to me of their own accord; others, who may have believed that their views would not be palatable to me and have kept away, I have invited to call upon me. I believe that the considerations which I have ventured to place before your lordship will be of considerable importance in the event of the mediation of her Majesty's Government and other Powers being accepted by Turkey and Russia. I must apologize to your lordship for stating them thus frankly. The vast and vital interests at stake in this war, and the confidence which her Majesty's Government have placed in me could alone justify me in doing so."

In a despatch to the Earl of Derby, dated May 23rd, Mr. Layard says:—

"I have had a visit from the Servian agent, M. Christich, who showed me a telegram which he had just received from the Servian Prime Minister, and had communicated this morning to Safvet Pasha. In it M. Ristics gave the MOST POSITIVE ASSURANCES * that the SERVIAN GOVERNMENT did not contemplate ANY ATTACK upon Turkey; and that, so far from any troops having been concentrated on the Turkish frontier with this object, 'there was not in the whole principality a band of more than five men together.' M. Christich said that the Grand Vizier had informed him that the Porte had received information that Russian troops were beginning to arrive at Turn Severin, opposite Gladova, exactly where the Russian volunteers had crossed last year into Servia, and that there are therefore strong grounds for suspecting that, notwithstanding the assurances given by Russia to Austria, she intended to pass an army into Servia. M. Christich added that he had assured the Grand Vizier that the Servian Government had no reason whatever to believe that Russia intended to cross the Danube into Servia; but that, on the contrary, they were convinced that she had no such intention. I thought the opportunity a good one to speak to M. Christich of the great danger that Prince Milan was running if he were to plunge the Principality again into war; and I hinted to him that his Highness might have to deal with Austria as well as Russia."

In a despatch to Lord Derby, dated from St. Petersburg on the 31st of May, Lord A. Loftus, the British Ambassador, gives an account of an interview he had with Prince Gortschakoff prior to his departure for the seat of war:—

"His Highness," says Lord A. Loftus, "expressed his conviction that the interests of the two countries in the East ought not to clash (*se heurter*), and his hope and expectation that the note of which Count Schouvaloff was the bearer would be satisfactory to her Majesty's Government. I inquired of his Highness in what light the Imperial Government regarded the declaration of independence by Roumania. Prince Gortschakoff replied that he regarded it as a *fait accompli de facto*, but not *de jure*. It was a question which could only be treated later, in conjunction with the European Powers. His Highness believed that the Austrian Cabinet took a similar view of it. In regard to Servia, Prince Gortschakoff stated that Prince Milan and the Servian Government had expressed their readiness in the present conjuncture to act according to the (*volonté*) wish of the Emperor, and that it had been signified to them in very decided terms that the EMPEROR'S WISH* was that SERVIA should remain PERFECTLY PASSIVE. Prince Gortschakoff was unable to say what would be the probable duration of the Emperor's absence, but I am told that in the official and court circles it is expected that his absence will not exceed six weeks."

* This is worth while remembering.—F. B.

THE TURKISH CHAMBER OF DEPUTIES

IN a despatch, bearing the date of June 2nd, and addressed to the Earl of Derby, Mr. Layard gives an account of his visit to the Turkish Chamber of Deputies. He says :—

" At the time of my visit the Chamber was discussing a bill concerning municipal taxation. I may state with confidence, and with some experience of the House of Commons, that I never saw a debate carried on with more order and propriety. Members may either speak from their seats or from a tribune, after the French fashion. With the exception of one individual, a Greek, they addressed the speaker or president from their places. Their speeches were short and to the point. Each article of the bill before them was discussed, explanations were demanded of the representatives of the department of the Government that had submitted the law to the Parliament, and were at once given. It was then put to the vote and was passed without a division. Each deputy had a copy of the bill before him, and followed with the greatest interest and attention the discussion. I did not observe one exception. Once, during my presence, there was a little expression of dissatisfaction in the house. The exceptional Greek, to whom I have alluded, went into the tribune with a bundle of papers, and began to read a speech which threatened to last for an indefinite time. It related to the history of Turkey in general, and especially to the grievances of the Christians. The president once or twice represented to him that, although his speech might properly be delivered on a suitable occasion, it had nothing to do with the question in discussion, which referred to a matter of detail of local administration. The deputy, however, persisted, and at last the house, becoming impatient called upon him to comply with the regulations, to obey the president, and to come down. This he was at last obliged to do. In the English House of Commons the speaker would certainly not have allowed him to go on as long as he did. No public assembly of the kind in Europe could perhaps show a more respectable, intelligent, and dignified body of men than the present Turkish Parliament. Christians and Mussulmans from all parts of the empire, even an Arab with his half-Bedouin dress, are seated without distinction together. Among the Mohammedans there are many mollahs, or teachers of the Koran, in their white turbans. The Christian speakers, who predominated the day that I was present, were listened to without any sign of impatience. They spoke with the most complete freedom, and without any restraint. The president rarely interfered, except to point out to a deputy that he was wandering from the question in debate. It must be borne in mind that this was the first attempt to bring together in a popular assembly men from all parts of the empire, Mussulmans and Christians, who were entirely ignorant of the duties they had to perform, and of the way to perform them. Had they not been directed and controlled at first by a strong hand there would have been general confusion, and the experiment would probably have failed. I know no man in Turkey so competent to be their president as Achmet Vefyk Pasha, from his knowledge, his honesty, and his determination and vigour of character. It is surprising, considering the materials with which he had to deal, that he has succeeded so soon in bringing the house into an orderly and business-like assembly. For some months there have been no complaints, even on the part of those who have done their best to discredit the Turkish Parliament, that the president has unnecessarily interfered in its discussions, or has in any way restrained the perfect freedom of debate. If there be any cause of complaint it is perhaps in the opposite direction."

APPENDIX V

STABBING UNDER THE GUISE OF FRIENDSHIP

RUSSIAN GOVERNMENT OFFICALS ENCOURAGING THE INSURGENTS AGAINST THE PORTE, WHILST GENERAL IGNATIEFF WAS THE RUSSIAN AMBASSADOR AT CONSTANTINOPLE, AND TURKEY AND RUSSIA WERE AT PEACE TOGETHER.

THE following is a despatch from Sir H. ELLIOTT to the Earl of DERBY on this subject:—

Constantinople, February 14th, 1876.

MY LORD,—The account of the encouragement and countenance given to the insurgents at Ragusa greatly exceeds all that I was prepared for.

THE RUSSIAN CONSULATE IS THE OPEN RESORT OF THE INSURGENT CHIEFS. Their correspondence is sent to the CONSUL, who is a PARTY to all their PROJECTS, and ASSOCIATES HIMSELF INTIMATELY WITH THEM.

He does not appear to make an attempt to conceal the part he is playing, for on the occasion of the death of the Chief Maxime, in one of the late encounters, the Russian flag at the consulate was hoisted at half mast, and M. Jonine himself joined the funeral procession.

With such acts as these it is not surprising that the insurgents should suppose their attempt to be fully APPROVED BY THE RUSSIAN GOVERNMENT, for they can hardly be expected to believe that an ACCREDITED AGENT would venture upon them without knowing that it meets with the APPROVAL OF HIS SUPERIOR AUTHORITIES.

Some of the wounded, when asked why they continue to struggle when the Porte is ready to grant all their demands, have answered plainly that THEY ARE BOUND TO GO ON AS LONG AS THEY ARE TOLD BY RUSSIA TO DO SO.

The assurances given at St. Petersburg of the wish of the Imperial Government that the insurgents would lay down their arms must naturally go for nothing as long as its OFFICIAL REPRESENTATIVE, with whom they are in communication, ENCOURAGES THEM TO GO ON.

I have, &c.,

(Signed)　　　HENRY ELLIOTT.

APPENDIX VI

THE RUSSIAN WAY OF CHRISTIANIZING THE TURKS
(Official.)

Consul READE to MR. LAYARD.

Shumla, July 23rd, 1877.

SIR,—Having on my arrival here heard that a number of Mussulman men, women, and children, said to have been attacked and wounded by Russian troops, were lying here, I obtained permission to see them.

I have the honour to enclose a list of those whom I saw, and who were lying in a "teke," a Dervish mosque, and apparently well cared for. I saw most of their wounds, and spoke to them.

Several of the elder ones gave very clear accounts of what had occurred to them (as they all said) by horsemen carrying lances, and many of them stated that they were attacked in the long grass where they were hiding themselves. One poor infant, of about nine months, had two frightful gashes on the head, and had one toe cut off.

Most of them had lance-thrusts about their bodies ; some, sabre-cuts. I saw them one by one, and a more sickening spectacle I seldom witnessed, not only from the nature of the wounds, but also from the youth and simplicity of the younger ones.

As regards the rumour that any of these attacks were committed by Bulgarians, I am able to state that, according to those I saw, not one such case has occurred. I asked all the sufferers one by one, separately, if they had been maltreated by any Bulgarian Christian, or if they had heard of any such case : they one and all said not.

From what all asserted, these cruelties can only be attributed to Cossacks, as the perpetrators were all described as " horsemen with lances."

The number of these victims is increasing, as others are brought in daily ; and from what those I saw said, a considerable number must have been killed on the spot.

I have, &c.

(Signed)   R. Reade.

List of Wounded Women and Children lying in the Teké, or Dervish Mosque, at Shumla, and visited by Consul Reade.

1. Habibe : a woman aged 25 years. Wounded in the back by a lance.

2. Mehemed : a boy aged 7 years. Wounded in the left thigh by a lance. Son of No. 1.

3. Ibrahim : a boy aged 5 years. Wounded on the right thigh by a lance : also son of No. 1.

4. Hava : a woman aged 25 years. Lance-wound on the head.

5. Aishé : a woman aged 30 years. Arm and head wound by a sabre ; a lance-wound on the breast.

6. Mehemet : a boy aged 6 years. Stomach pierced by a lance. Son of No. 5.

7. Anfe : a woman aged 24. Four sabre-cuts on the head, three lance-thrusts on left leg, one on right shoulder, and one on right thigh. Sabre-cut on right hand.

8. Nazifé : a girl aged 15. Sabre-cuts on breast and back ; lance-thrust on right foot and right thigh.

9. Mustapha : an infant of about 9 months of age. Top of head frightfully lacerated by a sabre. Toe of right foot cut off. This was a sickening spectacle.

10. Féridé : a woman aged 55 years. Right shoulder wounded by lance Right hand cut off. Lance-wound on back.

11. Eminé : a girl aged 9 years. Three sabre-cuts on head and one on back.

12. Muzcié : a girl aged 12 years. Trampled upon by a horse and severely wounded.

13. Féridé : a woman aged 40 years. Lance-wound on back.

14. Mustafa : a boy aged 9 years. Lance-wound on left leg. Son of No. 13.

15. Fatmé : a girl aged 12 years. Right thigh wounded by lance. Daughter of No. 13.

16 Gursun : a woman aged 32 years. Lance-wound on back.

17. Aishé : a girl aged 7 years. Lance-wound on head.

18. Abrahim : a boy aged 9 years. Sabre-cut on head. Lance-wounds on forehead and thigh.

(Signed)   R. Reade.

Shumla, July 22nd, 1877.

APPENDIX VII

THE SCHOOLMASTERS IN MASSACRE

Consul DICKSON *to Earl* RUSSELL.—(*Received May* 17*th.*)

(*Extract.*)

Soukoun Kalé, March 17th, 1864.

I FEEL it a painful duty to report a deed that has come to my knowledge, which has so exasperated the Circassians as to excite them to further resistance, however desperate their case may be.

A Russian detachment having captured the village of Toobeh on the Soobashi River, inhabited by about 100 Abadzekhs, and after these had surrendered themselves prisoners, they were all massacred by the Russian troops. AMONG THE VICTIMS WERE TWO WOMEN IN AN ADVANCED STATE OF PREGNANCY, AND FIVE CHILDREN. The detachment in question belongs to Count Evdokimoff's army, and is said to have advanced from the Pshish valley.

As the Russian troops gain ground on the coast, the natives are not allowed to remain there on any terms, but are compelled either to transfer themselves to the plains of the Kouban, or emigrate to Turkey.

APPENDIX VIII

OUGHT WE TO HAVE SAVED THE CIRCASSIANS?

Sir H. BULWER *to Earl* RUSSELL.—(*Received May* 20*th.*)

Extract.

Constantinople. May 3rd, 1864.

YOU are aware of the large and sudden immigration of Circassians into the Ottoman dominions.

The Russian Government has now acquired the territory of that brave and devoted race, who have only prized one thing more than country—liberty, or at least the life which is free from the domination of a foreign foe. They are flying the shores immortalized by their defence and seeking an asylum in a neighbouring Empire. In short, Circassia is gone; what yet remains to SAVE IS THE CIRCASSIANS.

APPENDIX IX

LESSONS IN MASSACRE

A PETITION FROM THE CIRCASSIANS FORWARDED TO EARL RUSSELL BY SIR H. BULWER, DATED CONSTANTINOPLE, APRIL 12TH, 1864.

(*Translation.*)

OUR most humble Petition to Her Magnificent Majesty the Queen and Emperor of England is to the effect that—

It is now more than eighty years since the Russian Government is unlawfully striving to subdue and annex to its dominions Circassia, which since the creation of the world has been our home and our country. It slaughters like sheep the children, helpless women, and old men that fall into its hands. It rolls about their heads with the bayonet like melons, and there is no act of oppression or cruelty which is beyond the pale of civilisation and humanity, and which defies description, that it has not committed. We have not, from father to son, at the cost of our lives and properties, refrained from opposing the tyrannical acts of that Government in defence of our country, which is dearer to us than our lives. But during tho last year or two it has taken advantage of a famine caused by a drought with which the Almighty visited us, as well as by its own ravages, and it has occasioned us great distress by its severe attacks by sea and land. Many are the lives which have been lost in battle, from hunger in the mountains, from destitution on the sea-coast, and from want of skill at sea.

WE THEREFORE INVOKE THE MEDIATION AND PRECIOUS ASSISTANCE OF THE BRITISH GOVERNMENT AND PEOPLE— THE GUARDIAN OF HUMANITY AND CENTRE OF JUSTICE— IN ORDER TO REPEL THE BRUTAL ATTACKS OF THE RUSSIAN GOVERNMENT ON OUR COUNTRY, AND SAVE OUR COUNTRY AND OUR NATION TOGETHER.

But if it is not possible to afford this help for the preservation of our country and race, then we pray to be afforded facilities for removing to a place of safety our helpless and miserable children and women that are perishing by the brutal attacks of the enemy as well as by the effects of famine; and if neither of these two requests are taken into consideration, and if in our helpless condition we are utterly annihilated notwithstanding our appeals to the mercy and grace of the Governments, then we shall not cease to invoke our right in the presence of the Lord of the Universe, of Him who has confided to your Majesty sovereignty, strength, and power for the purpose of protecting the weak.

We beg your Excellency to be the medium of making known to the great British Government and to the glorious British nation our condition of helplessness and misery, and we have therefore ventured to present to your Excellency our most humble petition. A copy of it has been submitted to the Sultan's Government and to the Embassies of the other Powers.

Signed by the people of Circassia.

April 9th, 1864.   29 Sheval, 1280.

APPENDIX X

STATEMENT OF THE CIRCASSIAN DEPUTIES IN REFERENCE TO THE CRIMEAN WAR

WE, the undersigned, having been sent from the people of the Nectouage and Abaseck, and further commissioned on their behalf by the Deputies of the other tribes of Circassia assembled at Constantinople, to carry to the Sovereigns and to the people of England and France the appeal of our nation, and to speak for our nation, and after that appeal has been rejected by the Governments of France and of England, and we have presented ourselves before various assemblies of the English people, from whom we have heard kind words, it has then been told to us that there are, among the English people, some who say that we are subjects of the Emperor of Russia, and others who say that in the time of the war in the Crimea the generals of England and France sent to us to require troops to aid them in the war, and that we refused to give such troops, and therefore it is not proper now for England to help us in our distress, or to resist Russia in her violence and aggressions. Therefore, we now say that the words so spoken against us are not true words, but false ones, and we further declare that any one who charges us with such things privately, and who does not bring them forward in such a manner that all shall hear and all shall judge, commits an act not worthy of an honest man, and ought not to be listened to by honest men.

It is easy for us to declare that we are a free people, over whom no king or emperor, or government, has had any power or authority since the world began, or as far back as the memory of man can reach, but we do not do so; we only ask what proof those can adduce who say to the contrary? Let those persons show who the king is who has conquered our country; let him tell what taxes the Circassian people has paid, or what troops have been raised amongst our tribes for the service of a foreign master. This is what no man can tell.

So also let our accusers bring forth the letters, or repeat the words, by which any request for aid was made to us in the time of the war in the Crimea, and then let him produce the answer given by us, refusing that aid or succour, and when he has done so then he may say that we did refuse to join the Allies, but not till then; but no such letter can be produced, and if such demand and such answer would be produced, it would not on that account follow that the injustice of Russia should become justice, that the danger from Russia should become security, or that the taking possession of the Black Sea by the cruisers of Russia, to interrupt all communication and all traffic, and so to make a war with England as well as Circassia, should become honourable and safe to the British nation.

The Circassians are a very small and weak people; they have no money, they pay no taxes, they have no government, they have no newspapers, they are ignorant; but this they do know, that many years Russia has been fighting against them, and that the thousands of men she loses in fighting every year, and the great treasure she expends every year, is not for the sake of Circassia. All our mountains, from the Black Sea to the Caspian, would not be worth to Russia, if she possessed them, so much as she expends on trying to conquer them in one year of the forty years she has been endeavouring to conquer them.

We therefore know that she is expending her army and her treasure, not because she wants Circassia, but because she wants India and the Ottoman Empire; and, therefore, do we say to ourselves, it is because of Turkey and England that we have to fight night and day, that our cattle are carried off, that our houses are burnt, and that our young men have to die, and our old ones and children and women to perish. Why do the Turks and the English not help us? Why are they the friends of the Russians?

We will now tell that which happened in the Crimean War.

It was in the year of your era 1854 that you drew your sword against Russia; before then that sword was in the scabbard, but our sword has never been in the scabbard; peace there never had been between the Circassians and Russians, and for thirty-three years there had been fierce wars. It was at the end of that time that the great nations of Europe went to make war. When we heard this we were very happy, and thought that the time was come when we might take breath; for we have not only to fight, but also to live; but it is very hard for us to live when we have always to fight. We said to ourselves, The great nations in whose hands Russia, is nothing, are going to stop her and give peace. Now we can plough our fields, and pasture our flocks, and rest from our long sufferings. Yet many amongst us got ready to help, and when the Russian troops that lay all along from Anapa to Soukum Kaleh withdrew and collected together, and retired north, we also on our part followed them; but when they crossed the Kouban they did not retire further, but stopped there, and they were in great force, being tens of thousands on one bank of the river, and we on the other, so that neither ventured across to attack. We could not go across whilst they were so posted, but when they saw us ready, neither could they retire so as to go to the Crimea.

Now, every day we expected that some of the Allies would appear behind them and enable us to do something to destroy them, but none came, nor did they send us any succour by the sea; and then we saw there was no aid for us. So it was at the end as at the beginning, and the Allies went away, and, as before, we remained the only enemies of Russia. But it was not by sending our horsemen into the steppes of Russia or into the Crimea that anything could be done to make Russia less powerful or give to us security after the peace.

The Lesghians on the east held a body of 50,000 men ready to fall on Tiflis, so soon as word should be sent by the generals of the English or French, or from Constantinople. The people of our coast knew very well that what they had to do was to crush the Russian armies in the south of the Caucasus, and to restore the people of Georgia, Gouriel, and Imerettia to independence. This was the help they looked for in the war which England and France was making against Russia.

At various times, to the number of seven or eight, on news arriving of envoys sent to us, assemblies were called among the Shapsug and Nectouage to be ready to hear without delay their proposals, so that if any such envoy had come to concert measures with us, such as that above described, and which should be within our power to attempt and for our benefit to achieve, 25,000 horsemen from these tribes alone would have been ready to take the field in a week. Our assemblies met and waited in vain; no envoys came; and they dispersed with heavy hearts.

Then it was that we considered what we ourselves could do, and as the Turkish commander in Kars sent no word to us, we determined to send word to him; and thereupon an envoy was sent, namely, one of the two undersigned now present in London, Hadji Hassan by name, to offer to Selim Pasha the co-operation of the forces of the Circassians, so that whilst we descended from the north they might march from the south, and thus crush the Russian power in Georgia, rescuing a Christian people from a barbarous yoke.

This envoy could only reach the Turkish camp by passing through the Black Sea in a boat with four oars, and had great difficulty in escaping the Russian cruisers. He reached Batun, and then proceeded to the Turkish quarters at Uzurget, twenty hours from Kars. The Turkish commander was glad to hear his tidings, and the plans were being prepared for the campaign, when a messenger arrived from Constantinople. The Pasha read the despatch which he had received; he did not say what it contained, but with tears in his eyes exclaimed, "We are betrayed!" The Circassian envoy understood that the Governments of France and England would not allow the Russians to be attacked where they could be really injured, so he returned to his own country. After the Russian army had been thus saved from destruction, Kars itself became their prey.

Whilst the war was going on in the Crimea, various Turks came from Constantinople; they called themselves envoys, and every one had a different story; but they never came amongst the Circassians, they all stayed at Anapa and Soukum Kaleh, the posts abandoned by the Russians.

There also came from the English and French, consuls and envoys, and captains of ships, and they also said one thing and another another; one saying that he had authority, and another saying he had authority; and then they talked to the Turks, and the Turks talked to them, but never came to the Circassians, but, like the Turks, remained at Anapa and Soukum Kaleh; whilst we were looking for men to propose to our tribes measures of war, and to bring from their countless hosts troops, artillery, and ammunition, to help in the war we were waging against Russia, and had been waging for generations past.

We have since heard that at Anapa and Soukum Kaleh many conversations took place; we have heard that between the Europeans and the Turks, and some Circassians, men who have no authority to act on behalf of the people, that it was said that the European generals wanted a large army of Circassians to leave their country to embark on the sea, and fight in the Crimea. Such things could never have been spoken in an assembly of Circassians, for the long time which they have resisted Russia shows that they are men who know how war is to be made. If such things had been proposed in an assembly of Circassians, our people would have answered, " That is not the way to injure Russia, that is not the way to protect Circassia, that is the way only to destroy your own armies." But such proposals were never made to us, for we are a free people, and nothing is done in secret. We have no Minister as the people of England have. Our warriors fight, not because they are paid, but because they have hearts, and when anything is proposed to us then a meeting must be held. Messengers go forth, and many thousand people are collected together, sometimes 5000 and sometimes 20,000, and they give ear to what is said to them, and when they have understood it, they appoint twenty or thirty of the wise men and elders who consult apart, and after that tell the people, and it is only when the people say Yes to what is consulted that the answer is given. Then all are willing to do what all have understood and all consented to. But amongst our people there is not one who would have consented to go to the Crimea, while every man would have been ready to march on Tiflis and save Kars. So that it appears to us that no message came from the French and English commanders to attack Tiflis for the same reason that the Russians remained on the Kouban instead of retiring into the Crimea. If our troops had not been detained on the Kouban we ourselves would have attacked Tiflis without the aid of the Allies or the co-operation of the Turks.

We have also learnt that when the envoys of England and France at Anapa and Soukum Kaleh said that we should send our forces to the Crimea, the Turkish envoys and other persons replied to them that such proposals could not be made unless the Allies engaged to secure our independence at a peace, and that this was the first word that had to be spoken on the matter; but these envoys would not allow such a word to be spoken either first or last.

Now what advantage have we gained from this war in the Crimea? That war is over seven years ago, and we have been fighting ever since!

YOU MAKE A TREATY OF PEACE TO OPEN THE SEA. THE SEA IS NOT OPEN. Had the undersigned been taken by the Russian vessels in coming to England, we should have been sent to the mines of Siberia, and we know that we the undersigned, are in all cases devoted to death because we have come here.

YOUR ARMIES HAVE BEEN IN THE CRIMEA, WHAT BENEFIT HAS COME TO THE CRIM TARTARS? DID YOU RESTORE TO THEM THEIR COUNTRY? NO, YOU GAVE IT BACK TO RUSSIA.

WHAT BENEFIT DID THE TURKS GET FROM YOUR WAR? You made your enemy pay none of the expenses, and YOU ONLY DEPRIVED THE TURKS OF THEIR VICTORIES.

THE POLES did go to the Crimea, and WHAT BENEFIT did THEY GET FROM THAT WAR?

Did we too not help you? Did we not keep in check 100,000 men? Is Russia not sore and weak by the many years she has been fighting with us? If we did not prefer independence to slavery, would not 100,000 of our men be in her ranks? If we were not engaged in defending our country, would not the Russian frontiers be at Batun?

WHY DO WE SUFFER FROM THIS WAR? Is is not because RUSSIA WANTS TO BE MISTRESS OF INDIA and MISTRESS OF CONSTANTINOPLE? If you wait till her ends are gained it will be too late to get aid from us. If you do not give us to-day a favourable reply, we must go back to our people and tell them that the English people are joined with Russia, so that what Russia could not effect by her arms some people in England will have effected by their calumnies.

All these things we tell you. If you wish to be sure of the truth, make an assembly, as we do, and we will prove them. If you make no such assembly, you have no right to say them. From Europe or from England no help has come to us. We have heard that if there was justice to be found it was in England; we came then to England, weak and poor, expecting to find justice from you.

(Signed)   HADJI HAYDEN HASSAN.
KUSTAR OGLI ISMAEL.

APPENDIX XI

HOLY RUSSIA AND THE CURSED CRESCENT

By A. CLEVELAND COXE,* *Bishop of the Western Diocese of New York.*

TRUMP of the Lord, I hear it blow;
Forward the cross; the world shall know
Jehovah's arm's against the foe.
Down shall the cursed crescent go.
   To arms! To arms!
      God wills it so.

God help the Russians—God bless the Czar,
Shame on the swords that trade can mar,
Shame on the laggards, faint and far,
That rise not to the holy war.
   To arms! To arms!
      The Cross and Czar.

How long, O Lord, for Thou are just,
Vengeance is Thine, in Thee we trust,
Wake, arm of God, and dash to dust
Those hordes of rapine and of lust.
   To arms! To arms!
      Wake swords that rust.

Forward the Cross. Break, clouds of Ire,
Break with the thunder and the fire,
To new Crusades let Faith inspire,
Down with the Crescent to the mire.
   To arms! To arms!
      To vengeance dire.

The Bishop answered by Mr. W. Croffut.

Thou Man of God, who thus implore
Thy brother's sacred blood to pour
In hateful tides of turbid gore,
From Dardanelles to Danube's shore,
   Be still! Be still!
      Blaspheme no more.

God help the babes, God bless the wives;
Shame on the priests that whet the knives,
Shame on the Church whose altar thrives
By wrecking peaceful peasants' lives.
   Be still! Be still!
      'Tis hell that drives.

How long, O Lord, before Thy shrine
Shall men pray Vengeance, God, is Thine,
Then worship Moloch as divine,
And drink the battle's bloody wine?
   Be still! Be still!
      O heart of mine.

---

* I extract these lines from an American paper, which declares that they were written by the Prelate in question. To the best of my belief the Bishop has not denied the statement nor the sentiments which the verses express.—F. B.

APPENDIX XII

THE CORRUPTION OF ARMENIAN OFFICIALS

REPORT OF MR. TAYLOR TO HER MAJESTY'S GOVERNMENT WITH REFERENCE TO THE CORRUPTION OF ARMENIAN OFFICIALS IN HIS (THE ERZEROUM) DISTRICT.

(Extract.)

Christians.—The different sects into which the Christians are divided in the Erzeroum Vilayet are :—

	Souls.
Gregorian Armenians	287,700
Nestorians	110,000
Armenian Catholics	8,000
Orthodox Greeks	4,000
Protestants (natives)	1,300
Total	411,000

Armenians.—The advice and ostentatious leaning towards Russia of the Armenian clergy in my district, headed by the Catholicas residing at Etchmiazin in Russia, and his bishops in these parts, have naturally enough inclined the more ignorant members of their flocks—rich and poor—to adopt the same views ; and considering also that a whole Christian house of ten souls in Russia pays only, for all taxes, 9 roubles (1*l.* 10*s.*) annually as against three times the sum here, if there has not been a general emigration, it is simply owing to the fact that disposable arable lands in Russian Armenia are scarce, while the reverse prevails in Turkey.

Everywhere throughout these districts I found the Armenians bitter in their complaints against the Turkish Government, at the same time that they were unreserved in their praises of Russia, openly avowing their determination to emigrate. This bias is owing, as already stated, to the constant hostile teaching of their clergy ; at the same time, ample cause for discontent, as has already been shown further back, is afforded by the really wretched system of Turkish provincial administration, the unequal imposition of taxes, scandalous method of levying them and the tithes, persistent denial or miscarriage of justice, and practical disavowal of the Christians' claim to be treated with the same consideration and respect as their equals among Moslems. But experience has taught me that which candour and strict impartiality compel me to state, that the subordinate officers of the local Government are aided and abetted in their disgraceful proceedings or encouraged in persistent indifference to crying wrongs, as well by the criminal assistance as wilful apathy or silence of the Armenian Medjliss members, ostensibly elected by the suffrages of their co-religionists to guard their interests. Unfortunately, then, as the evil lies as much with the Christians as the Turks, under existing regulations there is no remedy for it, and there can be none till the local authorities really see for themselves that the Porte's orders are really carried out and to open the way for the introduction of a higher class of people for such employments. As it is, no man of wealth, influence, or character will accept a seat in any one of the Councils ; he will not waste time in attending to official duties in a place where he has to put up with the contumely and impertinent insults of the Moslem members, all which are patiently borne by the fawning and obsequious Christians whose living depends upon this appointment. And even were a man of character and ability to accept a nomination at the hands of his community, the Pasha, with whom in fact the fate of such elections lie, as he has the power of rejection, would always prefer a needy, pliant member to one whose riches and position would place him beyond the reach of his menaces or influence. The interests of the community are consequently entrusted to speculators accustomed to the atmosphere of the Serai in their capacity of revenue farmers or Seraffs, who in such positions have, in addition to their own disgusting servility, all the chicanery and vices of Turkish officials—acquired a dangerous influence, either as the partners or creditors of the chief provincial officers. Such an influence might be meritorious and useful if exercised in the interests of justice and duty, but it becomes a downright evil when practised, as it always is, for their own benefit or that of their partners in corruption, and scarcely ever for their brethren. The claims of the poor are either neglected or betrayed, and those of the rich depend upon the amount of their presents or degree of their sycophancy. The Armenian clergy and head men, on their part, purposely ignoring the villainous conduct of their Medjliss members representing the repeated failures of justice that inevitably result as due to the fanaticism or imbecility of a Government determined to ignore all just claims, exaggerate actual facts; the more readily to induce their dependents to adopt the disloyal views they propagate. As they pursue such intrigues, apparently unchecked and with the secret approval of Russian agents, wavering members, formerly content with or resigned to their lot, openly express disaffection and traitorous ideas.

APPENDIX XIII

FEMALE BRIGANDAGE

MILLINGEN remarks in "Wild Life amongst the Koords":—Amongst the many acts of brigandage of which the Koords are guilty—a peculiar kind of highway robbery must here be stated, which is probably unparalleled. The culprits, the brigands, are in this case young women, who set out on plundering pursuits in order to turn a dishonest penny. A troop of fair bandits take up a station at the side of a road, there patiently to await for the arrival of the doomed traveller. As soon as the vedettes announce his approach, the fair troop starts off to meet him, welcoming him with dances and with fiery glances of irresistible power. He is compelled to stop, as a matter of course, and the fair maids then politely request him to alight. No sooner has the bewildered victim put his feet on the ground than he finds himself at close quarters with the whole troop. Immediately he is stripped of all he has on his back, and is left in that primitive state in which Adam was at one time. Then begins a series of dances and fascinating gestures in the style of those performed by the maids at the Lupercalian games, the object of which is to make the unfortunate victim lose his self-control. An attempt, however, on the part of the victim to reciprocate the advances of his alluring tyrants, becomes instantly fatal. The troop get hold of him in a summary way, declare him to have made attempts on the virtue of the fair maids, and condemn him to be pricked with thorns upon a very sensitive part of his person. These dances and the flagellations, which serve as entractes, are repeated several times over, till the sufferer, exhausted and bleeding, is nearly in a fainting condition. Then the female troop of bandits drag the wretched traveller before a court of matrons, which holds its sittings somewhere in the neighbourhood. There a charge of attempting a criminal assault is brought against the pretended culprit, who not only receives a good dose of upbraiding, but is also condemned to pay a fine.

APPENDIX XIV

THE ROUTES WHICH TRAVERSE ASIA MINOR, AND THE EUPHRATES AND TIGRIS

THE routes which traverse Asia Minor and cross the Euphrates and Tigris commence at Constantinople on the Bosphorus, or at Smyrna on the Ægean Sea, and meet upon the plateau of Asia Minor.

Of these routes the chief are—The Erzeroum and Tabriz; the Diarbekir and Mosul; the Aleppo and Bagdad. On leaving Constantinople, the Bosphorus is crossed; the road then leads along the coast of the Propontus from Scutari to Gebiseh, the ancient Lybissa, and where the tomb of Hannibal can be seen; then beside the Astacenian Gulf, from Gebiseh to Nicomedia (Ismid). Here the three routes separate.

The Erzeroum road leads eastward, and parallel to the coast of the Black Sea.

The Diarbekir route cuts Asia Minor longitudinally, and descends into the valley of the Euphrates towards Malatia. The Aleppo road cuts it obliquely, and descends upon the shores of the Mediterranean near Tarsus.

The Erzeroum route crosses the Sakaria towards its mouth, between Sabanja and Khanda, leads by the villages of Dusdscheh or Muderli to the town of Boli, situated near the ruins of Hadrianopolis; beyond Boli the road is very hilly; it then traverses the towns of Gerideh and Hamanli, and descends with the waters of the Parthenius to the little town of Tcherkis. Tcherkis is at the junction of the Trebizond and Tokat route. The Trebizond route ascends more to the north, crosses the mountains which separate the basin of the Parthenius from that of the Halys, and descends with an affluent of the Halys to Kastamuni, and from there, by Tach-kupri, to the town of Voyavat.

Tach-kupri is built on the site of Pompeiopolis, and Voyavat in a fertile plain, at the foot of a height crowned by an old citadel. Voyavat is an important position, because it is at the intersection of the Sinope and Trebizond route.

The Sinope route turns to the north, and leads through a very rich and undulating country. This is one of the most fertile districts in Asia Minor.

The Trebizond route leads eastward, passes the Halys near Vizir Kupri, and, after numerous ascents and descents, issues beside a watercourse in a bay surrounded by olive-trees. Here is the town of Samsoun. It then leads along the coast of the Black Sea, crosses the Iris near Tcharchembeh, and the Thermadon near Thermeh; and leaving the little town of Unieh to the left and on the sea-shore, it goes by Fatsa, Ordau, and Kerasun to Tripoli; from there, after turning the bay of Platana, it leads to Trebizond.

The Tokat road bends more to the south after leaving Tcherkis; it crosses the mountains which border the basin of the Parthenius near Karadjcur, and descends by Kodja Hissar to the town of Tusia upon the Halys. It next traverses the river near Hadji Hamzeh or Osmanjik, and, after passing Marsivan, crosses the western affluent of the Iris at Amasia; from here it goes by Turkhal to Tokat. The direct route from Tokat to Erzeroum eastward goes from Tokat or from Turkhal to Niksar, on the Lycus, the eastern affluent of the Iris; and continuing by this affluent to Kara Hissar, it ascends near the villages of Kerkif or Lorri, the mountains which separate the waters of the Black Sea from the Euphrates, and descends into the plain of Erzeroum near Vijan.

There is another road from Constantinople to Sivas. This is the regular Angora track; it leaves the Trebizond route at Nicomedia, crosses the Sakaria near Geiweh; and following the chord of the arc which this river describes as it descends from the plateau of Asia Minor, leads by the little towns of Terekli and Torbali to Nalihan, near the ruins of Gordium; after which it ascends by the little town of Bei Bazar on to the Angora plateau. This plateau is one of the points which dominate Asia Minor; hence the reason why formerly so much importance was attached to the fortress of Gordium. The road then leads by the village of Bei Bazar, or by Tabadji, on to a ridge of mountains which separate the basin of the Sakaria from that of the Halys, and descends by the village of Akscrai to the latter of these rivers. The stream is crossed either at a ford or on a raft, and the route goes by the villages of Sangor and Osman Koi to the town of Yuzgat, the chief seat of the family Tchapan-Oglou,* formerly one of the most powerful in Asia Minor. Yuzgat is an important position, because it is at the junction of the two routes from Tokat and Cæsarea. The first leads to the east; and crossing the mountains which separate the basin of the Halys from that of the Iris, it debouches through a deep ravine on to the lofty plateau of Zela, celebrated for Cæsar's victory over Pharnaces; from here it descends and slopes gently down to the Western Iris, near Tokat. The Cæsarea route turns to the south after leaving Yuzgat, and leading by the villages of Ingourli, Kislan, and Boghazlayan, recrosses the Halys near Emlar; after which it goes by Erkelet (Hiklar) to Cæsarea.

Another route leads by Angora to Cæsarea, and from Cæsarea to Malatia in the valley of the Euphrates. It is the route from Constantinople to Diarbekir and to Mosul. After leaving Nicomedia (Ismid) it turns south, ascends the mountains which separate the Astacenian from the Cianean Gulf, and descends to Lake Ascanius, near Nicea; then turning eastward, and passing alongside Mount Olympus, it crosses the Gallus at Lefke (Louka) near its junction with the Sakaria; then ascending this river along its left bank as far as Zugud (Soghat), it crosses the Thymbrius near Eski-Shehr, the ancient Doryleum, situated in the middle of a vast and bare plain. The road now rises insensibly by Sidi Ghazi and Sever Hissar to the Angora Plateau. This is the easiest route to go from Nicomedia to the plateau of Asia Minor. It follows the watercourses.

Two routes lead from Angora to Cæsarea. One crosses the Halys near the village of Kara Keni, from whence it ascends the river along its right bank to the little town of Mandjour, where its two principal affluents unite. Then crossing the eastern affluent, between the villages of Tchalik and Ambar, the route leads to the foot of Mount Argea towards Cæsarea. The other road borders the eastern plateau of Asia Minor; and ascending the Halys along its right bank, passes the eastern affluent of this river above Mandjour; from here the route goes to Cæsarea, across a vast plain destitute of trees. It is the easiest road, but there are no habitations, and provisions are very scarce in this direction.

Cæsarea is a branching point for all the routes which cross the Euphrates, or which descend from the plateau of Asia Minor to the littoral of Cilicia. One of these routes leads to Sivas, another to Diarbekir, a third to Aintab, and a fourth to Adana and Tarsus. The first leads in a north-easterly direction, and ascends the eastern affluent of the Halys from Emlar to Sivas; this is the easiest route by which to ascend to the plateau of Armenia. The road from Angora by Tokat to Sivas is the shortest. It is best provided with provisions; but the route by Cæsarea is less broken and more accessible for artillery. The route from Cæsarea to Diarbekir leads eastward along the Melas till that river joins the Euphrates below Malatia. The river is then crossed in a ferry-boat at the village of Teis Oglan, and the road continues by the little town of Kharput to a chain of mountains which unite Mount Taurus to Mount Niphates. It descends with the principal affluent of the Tigris to Maïden, and from Maïden goes to the town of Arghana; from here it leads alongside this river to Diarbekir, and from Diarbekir goes by Djesire to Mosul.

* Daravish Bey is the last of that celebrated family. He is nearly ruined owing to some dealings with an Armenian usurer.

The road from Cæsarea to Aintab leads in a south-easterly direction, traverses one of the chains which unite Mount Argea to the southern branch of Mount Taurus, and descends by the village of Garrin into the valley of El Bostan, towards the sources of the Sarus. The valley of El Bostan, although very high, is fertile, and planted with fruit-trees. El Bostan is the branching point of three routes which lead—one to Samozate, another to Aintab, and the third to Marash. The first route turns to the east of Mount Amanus and descends with an affluent of the Euphrates to Samozate; the second crosses the mountain, descends by a profound ravine to Aintab, and leads from Aintab-to Aleppo alongside the Chalus. The third turns Mount Amanus on the west, and descends with the Pyramus to the little town of Marash, and from Marash goes to the village of Messis, on the gulf of Alexandretta.

The most frequented route from Cæsarea to Alexandretta is *viâ* Adana or Tarsus. This route leads to the south, turns Mount Argea towards the west, and goes by Endjazou, the ancient Castabale, and by Kara Hissar, the ancient Cybistra, to Yenji Bar, probably the ancient Nora; from here it ascends to the high plain of Nigdeh, which is watered, like El Bostan, by an affluent of the Sarus. It descends from Nigdeh to Ketch Hissar, called Dana by Xenophon, an important position, because it is at the intersection of the two routes of Cæsarea and Koniah; from there the road leads by the village of Tchikisla into a deep and winding gorge, hollowed out in the slopes of Mount Taurus, and where the different affluents of the Sarus unite together. From here the route debouches by the village of Abi Cheik into the great plain of Cilicia, on one side of which is Tarsus, and on the other Adana. In leaving the defile above mentioned, the road branches to the right for Tarsus, and to the left to Adana, and from Adana goes to Alexandretta. The best-known route from Constantinople to Syria is that of Koniah. It traverses the western border of the plateau of Asia Minor, and cuts the peninsula obliquely from the north-west to the south-east. This route, leaving the road to Angora, at Nicca, and ascending those branches of Mount Olympus which bound Lake Ascanius on the south, descends to the little town of Yeni Cheer, where the two routes from Brusa and Kiutayah cross. The first turns to the west and leads to Brusa; it passes by Mount Olympus, on the north. The second turns southward, and passing by Mount Olympus on the east, goes to the town of Ainegol (Yeni Ghoul), towards the sources of the Gallus, and from Ainegol leads by the village of Turbah to the town of Kiutayah upon the Thymbrius. It then ascends by the Thymbrius to its sources towards the village of Altyn Tash, and finally reaches the plateau of Afiun Kara Hissar, bounded on the west by the western chain of the Taurus, and on the east by a range of little lakes which almost touch each other, and which extend towards the south to the environs of Koniah. This plateau is very high. It is separated from the central plateau of Asia Minor by a series of hills, which are crowned towards the south by the Baba Dagh (mountain). The route passes between two chains of mountains, and leads by Bulwadin, built upon the site of Dynia, and by Izaklou to Ak-Shehr. This little town is situated in a well-watered plain, at the foot of a mountain covered with vegetation, and about six miles from a lake which bounds the plain on the east. The route leaves all the lakes to the left, and goes by Ilgyn and Kadoun Khan to the village of Hi Ladik, built upon the ruins of Laodicea Combusta; from here it is a ten hours' march to Koniah, the road leading there at the foot of the mountains which bound the plateau of Asia Minor on the south, and which rise gradually to the southern chain of Mount Taurus.

The most frequented route from Koniah is that which leads by Tarsus or by Adana to Alexandretta. It is the route from Smyrna and Constantinople to Aleppo and Bagdad. It is the route of Antioch, Palmyra, and Babylon. It is the route of all the conquerors.

This route, when it leaves the plain of Koniah, turns the Kara Dagh (mountain) towards the north, goes by the villages of Ismil, of Geiweh, and Hartan to Erekli ; and after joining with the Cæsarea route and below Ketch Hissar descends with the river Sarus towards the village of Tchikisla, and issues from a deep gorge of Mount Taurus into the great plain of Cilicia.

The Alexandretta route cuts the plain obliquely ; leaving Tarsus to the right, it passes the Sarus at Adana, the Pyramus at the village of Messis, three miles from this village enters a cleft in the mountains which border the gulf of Alexandretta ; from here it debouches into a fertile but desert plain, nine miles long, from three to four wide, and surrounded on all sides by arid mountains. There is an exit towards the east, and after a difficult march for an hour, the route descends to the ruined town of Kartanleh, which is now inhabited in the winter by some Turkoman tribes. Kartanleh is situated at the edge of a plateau, or rather a terrace, about three miles long, and bordered on its eastern extremity by some black rocks. They approach each other very closely. The passage is excessively narrow. The defile gradually becomes wider, and a mile farther it debouches on to a little plain about two miles long and one mile broad, bounded on the south by the Gulf of Alexandretta, on the east by a vast marsh, and on the north by a chain of heights, which rise gradually to Mount Amanus. Ayas is at the foot of these heights, and about one mile from the sea. The road now turns south, leads for some time along a sandy shore, and then crosses a little mountain torrent which flows into the marsh, and which some travellers have taken to be the Carsus of Xenophon ; others, the Pinarus of Arrien. After having passed the torrent and rounded the gulf, the road leaves the shore and rises gradually to Pias, situated like Ayas a little distance from the sea, and at the foot of some heights which keep on ascending till they culminate in Mount Amanus. Pias is twenty-six miles from Ayas, sixteen from Alexandretta, and at the south-eastern angle of a bay. Its shore is more easily approached than that of Ayas ; troops could be easily disembarked here. It is the most vulnerable point of the coast. From Pias, as from Alexandretta, it is only three marches to the plateau of Antioch, a dominating point and the key to Syria.

The Aleppo route leaves the sea at Alexandretta, and turning south-east ascends through a deep gorge to Beylan. From here it leads over some mountains which bound the gulf on the east, and which unite the Taurus to the Syrian chain. The route then descends to the plain of Antioch. The road here branches. One branch leads by some mountains, which are on the north to Killis and Aintab ; it then crosses the Euphrates at Kum Kaleh, the ancient Zeugma. The other branch cuts the plain of Antioch from the north to the south, passes the Orontes beneath the walls of the town, and, turning to the east, crosses the Chalus beneath Aleppo.

Aleppo is at the junction of two roads which cross the Euphrates—the one at Bir, in taking a north-eastern course, the other at Kerkisieh or Anah, in leading towards the south-east. The first is the Mosul, and the second the Bagdad route through Babylonia and the desert. The Mosul route, after leaving Aleppo, ascends to a bare plain, traversed by two affluents of the Sadjour, which fall into the Euphrates near the ruins of Hierapolis. The first station is at the village of Hardaran. The road then leads across two affluents of the Sadjour, and goes through olive-gardens to the Euphrates, which is crossed at a ferry near Bir. It would be very difficult to ford the river at this point. After leaving Bir, the road passes over two chains of calcareous hills, between which is a pretty valley, covered with fruit-trees. It descends from the second chain by a steep path, which is paved with big stones, and is cut in several places out of the rock.

Urfa, the ancient Edessa, is situated in a valley between two hills, which are separated from the Tauric chain and united to a series of other hills which cut like a curtain the vast plain of Mesopotamia.

From Urfa to Mosul there are two routes; one, more to the north than the other, joins the Samozate road towards Severek, and, crossing one of the heights of Mount Masius, descends with an affluent of the Tigris to Diarbekir. It goes from here by Djesireh to Mosul. It is a difficult route, but the only one where provisions can be met with. The other route ascends in the direction of the sources of the Khaboras, follows the chord of the arc which forms the Tauric chain from Severek to Mardin, leads from Mardin to Nisibin through a cultivated plain watered by the Mygdonius, and goes from Nisibe to Mosul through an uncultivated district, which extends from the foot of the Tauric chain to the mountain of Singare. There is nothing to stop an army marching along this route save the scarcity of provisions. It is the best road for cavalry. The other one would be more convenient for infantry. Two roads lead from Mosul to Bagdad. One passes along the right bank of the Tigris, and the other the left. The first passes by Tekrit and across the desert—the second by Arbeles and through ancient Assyria. This last route is the longest. It leaves the river, to avoid some hills which border the left bank; but it is the only road where cultivated lands and provisions can be found. Leaving Mosul, it crosses the Tigris upon a bridge of boats, and passes in succession the Bumadus and the Zabus, six miles apart the one from the other. The plain between the two rivers is elevated, and is undulating towards the north-east; but it sinks and becomes flat towards the south-west, in the direction of the angle where the two rivers meet. From the ford where the road crosses the Zabus, it is only twenty-seven miles to Arbeles, which rises like an island in the midst of the most beautiful plain of Assyria. The road undulates slightly, and the position is a favourable one for manœuvring an army. On leaving Arbeles, the route descends beside a small watercourse to Altyn-Kupri. Here the Caprus is crossed upon a stone bridge. The little town of Scherzour, at the foot of the Median chain, is on the left of the route, and it continues by Kerkut and Daour towards the villages of Kifri and Kara Tepe in the plain of Bagdad.

The direct route from Aleppo to Bagdad leads in a south-easterly direction. After leaving the plain of Aleppo, it passes through a long valley closely bordered by two hills. In the middle of the plain is the town of Taib. The road now debouches upon the Euphrates—on one side towards Racca, the ancient Nicephorium, and on the other towards the ruins of Tapsaque, at the beginning of a bend which the great river makes in its course towards Kerkisieh, the ancient Circesium. It appears that the ancients crossed the Euphrates sometimes at one and sometimes at the other of these points. At the present time the route leads along the right bank to Ana, the ancient Anatho, and to Hit, the ancient Æiopolis. Here the river is crossed in a ferry-boat. The road continues along the left bank to Ambar, the ancient Perisabour, and to Felujah, which is the point where the Euphrates in its windings nearest approaches the Tigris. The Babylon and Bagdad routes now separate. The first leads to the south, along the Euphrates. Fifteen hours' march brings you to Hillah, which is built on the site of Babylon. The other road leads eastward; and, after crossing a bare plain which divides the two rivers, you arrive in eleven hours at Bagdad. To enter this town the river has to be crossed on a bridge of boats. As the crow flies, it is only fifty-four miles from Babylon to Bagdad. The route leads from south to north. It is a difficult one. There are fissures in the ground. They become filled with water during the inundations caused by the two rivers. Caravans going from one town to the other generally go round by Feludjah; this lengthens the road by about twenty-one miles.

The route from Aleppo to Bagdad by the desert and by Babylon has this advantage over the Mosul road. It is shorter, because it follows the cord, the other following the circumference of the bow; but as the ground between Aleppo and Tapsaque is no longer cultivated, and as troops can no longer be accompanied by a flotilla of vessels, it is not practicable for an army. It is only suited for a division of cavalry and for caravans with camels; even then there would be a risk of the force perishing from hunger or thirst. The long zone which the road traverses, and which loses itself in the Arabian desert, is a plain with slight undulations, but they are so slight that a man on horseback could scarcely conceal himself. There are few plants; you find some wells of petroleum, hardly any animals. There are no birds; everywhere you see a white soil impregnated with gypsum or salt.

A few palm and fruit trees announce to the traveller that he has arrived at the environs of Bagdad.

Bagdad is the starting-point of two important roads: they lead, one to the south of Persia, the other to the north. The first leads to the south-east, and passing alongside the foot of the Median chain, crosses the Kerah or river of Kirmanchah, the ancient Eulee, near the ruins of Suza, and the two branches of the Karoon, the ancient Orontes, the one at Dizful, the other at Shuster; from whence the route ascends to the plateau of Media, and to Lourkian. It then passes the Persian Pyles towards the sources of the Bendemir, or of the Persian Araxes, and descends with this river upon the plateau of Persia towards Ispahan.

The second road goes to the north-east, ascends the Diala to Sheraban or Apollonia, from whence it rises by Zar-Zil upon the plateau of Media towards Karmanshah. It then passes the defiles of Mount Orontes towards Kangawar, and descends to Hamadan. This is the ancient route from Ecbatana, the great route from Turkey to Persia; Hamadan is at the intersection of two roads which lead—the one to Ispahan in turning south-east, the other to Teheran in leading north-east.

Such are the different routes, remarks Baron Beaujour, which lead from Asia Minor across the Euphrates and Tigris into Asia proper. From what has been said, it will be seen that they are reduced to three principal ones—to the Erzeroum and Tabriz, which turns the two rivers towards their sources; to the Urfa and Mosul, which crosses the rivers in the middle of their course; and to the Aleppo and Bagdad, which leads along the Euphrates to Babylon, and which passes the Tigris near Bagdad. The first route is impracticable for artillery, the last for infantry. The centre road is the only one available for a large army; for whilst cavalry and artillery could pass by Merdin and Nisibin, infantry penetrating from Urfa through the defiles of Severek, into the valley of the Tigris, could descend with this river from Diarbekir to Mosul, and from Mosul to Bagdad; from here, ascending the Diala, the army might continue by the defiles of Mount Zagros on to the plateau of Media towards Karmanshah, and from the plateau of Media by the defiles of Mount Orontes upon the Persian plateau towards Hamadan. Master of the Persian plateau an army could march towards Teheran as far as the foot of the Tauric chain, continue along this chain to Mount Paropamisus, and descend by Kandahar or Cabul into the valley of the Indus towards Attok.

Although this is a long and difficult route, it is not an impracticable one for an army which has previously conquered the Turks and the Persians.

Means of subsistence can be found everywhere along this road. Troops would only meet with opposition from wandering hordes, or from people like the Afghans. However, the hordes are mere robbers. The Afghans would have no chance of victory unless they were united amongst themselves. To conquer the Afghans, all that would be required would be to fight them in detail.

Alexander formerly marched along this route. In our own times, Napoleon and Paul the First, the two most powerful monarchs in Europe, wished to follow it, to attack the English in India. This project, the boldest which has been conceived in modern times, could only be executed by generous princes, who would like to conquer India, not to keep it, but to civilize the country. In the present state of Europe, India could only be conquered by the Russians, who are very little exposed to attacks from other nations. Masters of Georgia and of the line of the Araxes, the Russians can turn the western side of the Caspian Sea, and penetrate by Casbin upon the plateau of Persia, or penetrate by the east and by Bokhara across the Oxus and Jaxartes, which are by no means insurmountable obstacles.

Baron Beaujour concludes his remarks upon the subject by saying :—

" This enterprise would be justifiable provided that the attacking force had some glorious object in view, such as that of civilizing India. The English, who are already masters of the peninsula, can do this last better than the Russians. THE LATTER OUGHT TO CIVILIZE THEM-SELVES BEFORE THEY THINK OF CIVILIZING OTHER NATIONS."

APPENDIX XV

THE MILITARY IMPORTANCE OF SYRIA

BARON BEAUJOUR, in his " Voyage Militaire dans l'Empire Ottoman," published in 1829, remarks about the military importance of Syria as follows:—

Syria has a great military importance. It is on the route from Asia to Africa. If the Isthmus of Suez were cut through, Syria would acquire a still greater importance. This country is now open, art has not defended it on any side ; but nature has defended it on the east and south by deserts ; on the west by the sea, and on the north by a chain of mountains which surround it like a rampart. Mount Amanus, which forms this rampart, and which extends from the Mediterranean to the Euphrates, dominates Syria; this is the reason why the masters of Aleppo and Antioch have always been the masters of the rest of the country. All the routes were open to them. They could not be arrested on any particular road, because each route could be turned by the others. The road from Antioch to Jerusalem ascends the Orontes, and traverses the two chains. It descends by the Leontes into Cœle Syria, by the Jordan into Judea ; and by the Chrysorrhoas into the plain of Damascus. This route is the only one which opens out all the interior of the country. The others only open out the littoral. An army can always be stopped by a foe who occupies the first-mentioned route. The road from Gaza to Laodicea along the coast is only suitable for an army which is accompanied by a fleet. The transversal routes of Caifa or Acre to Damascus by Nazareth, of Tyre or Sidon to Emesa by Cœle Syria—from Tripoli to Hamah by Akka, and from Laodicea to Schogr by Abdama can only conveniently be used by an army which is mistress of the sea.

Syria can be attacked from two sides—either through Asia Minor or through Egypt. TO ATTACK SYRIA FROM ASIA MINOR, MOUNT AMANUS MUST BE PASSED EITHER AT ITS CENTRE NEAR AINTAB, OR AT ITS TWO EXTREMITIES BY ZEUGMA OR BY ISSUS. THE PASS BY ZEUGMA IS THE EASIEST—TO HOLD THIS PASS IT IS NECESSARY TO BE THE MASTER OF THE EUPHRATES. The passage by Aintab is more difficult, but it can be turned. An army can descend by several roads from Mount Amanus along the watercourses into the plain of Antioch as into the plain of Aleppo.

An attack by the gulf of Alexandretta is more difficult. This gulf is closed by a cordon of mountains which is bent on the seaside like a bow. Even if this bow were pierced from one side, it would be necessary to pierce it from the other and penetrate into Syria by the defile of Beilan, after having entered by that of Issus. Syria is defended on the Egyptian side by a desert—here there is neither water nor grass; but so soon as an army has crossed this desert and taken Gaza, it can ascend the coast to Carmel, and if it is mistress of the sea, can ascend at pleasure by the transversal valley of Esdrelon upon the plain of Damascus, or by the transversal valley of Balbek upon the plain of Emesa, which commands the entire valley of the Orontes. An army could even ascend the coast to Laodicea, its right supported on the Lebanon, its left on the sea, and sweep before it the Turks dispersed amidst the towns of the littoral, as the wind drives before it the dust. If the Turks were to rally in the valley of Cœle Syria, or in the plain of Damascus, a defeat here would drive them into the desert. The Mutualis, Druses, Maronites, Ansares are not united—to conquer them it is sufficient to sow dissension in their ranks; even if they were to fight beneath the same standards they could never arrest an army in its march. These people know nothing about tactics, they are only acquainted with mountain warfare. They would never dare to risk themselves in the plain or to sustain the shock of a European battalion. All these people are like Arabs; they are only fit to rob caravans or to follow an army with the object of pillage.

An attack upon Syria by the littoral of Palestine and Phœnicia could only succeed so long as you were mistress of the sea. It would be better to attack Syria by sea than from Egypt; but to attack Syria by sea, one must begin by establishing oneself in the island of Cyprus. Cyprus is to Syria what Zante is to the Morea; it would serve as a depôt for the army and a harbour for the fleet. Larnaca and Famagusta are the most favourable points for naval stations. The Syrian coast is too straight, it possesses no good port, nor even any good roads. The ports of Laodicea, Tripoli, Beyrout, and Sidon are too small. The anchoring roads of Acre, Jaffa, and Gaza are too exposed. Alexandretta and Tyre are the sole points where an army can be disembarked without danger. This is the reason why these two places have always been considered the two keys of Syria, on the side of the sea. An attack by Alexandretta has this advantage, it separates Syria at once from the rest of Turkey. It also has its disadvantages. Depôts must be formed on a very unhealthy shore. The defiles of Mount Rhosus must be passed; here there are difficult gorges where a handful of soldiers could resist an army.

An attack by Tyre would be the easiest and the least dangerous, The peninsula on which this town is built is now no longer defended. This peninsula facilitates a descent upon the neighbouring coast. The surrounding plain is fertile. An army would be thoroughly protected by guarding on one side the defile of Cape Blanc, and on the other that of the valley of the Leontes or of Cœle Syria. From this valley an army could ascend by Balbek to the highest point of the Syrian chain. It could dominate the whole country as if from the summit of an enormous citadel. This point surmounts all the passes, and an army could descend by the Jordan to Jerusalem by the Chrysorrhoas to Damascus, and by the Orontes to Antioch.

Tyre and Alexandretta are the two most vulnerable points in Syria. If history does not recall to the Turks the importance of these two towns, Europeans have not forgotten it. Acre and Laodicea are the next most important points. In summer an army could easily disembark there, and, like Tyre and Alexandretta, they give access to the entire country. The Turks, then, ought to fortify these places better, and especially Alexandretta and Tyre, so as to make them the principal fortresses in Syria: and not to think so much of Aleppo and Damascus, which can be easily defended against the Arabs of the desert.

If Syria is easy to attack—she is equally difficult to conquer. Her territory is mountainous. A small army could defend itself for a long time against a large force. In Mesopotamia and in Egypt a single battle won would be sufficient to reduce the entire country. In Syria it would only enable the foe to occupy a more advanced position, and to march from one valley to another, as from the valley of the Orontes to the valley of the Jordan, or from the littoral of Phœnicia to Palestine ; but to march from one of these positions to the other, it is necessary to pass defiles. If the defenders were masters of the transversal valleys which unite the littoral with the interior of the country—and in particular of the valley of Balbek—no enemy could advance a step without encountering obstacles. This would protract the war, and give the defenders a great advantage. Syria, then, is difficult to conquer, but, once conquered, is easy to defend. This is the reason why it is so important from a military point of view.

APPENDIX B. (XVI.)

SIR JOHN BURGOYNE ON THE DEFENCES OF CONSTANTINOPLE

The following remarks made by Sir John Burgoyne in his work, " Military Opinions," and published in 1859, may not be uninteresting to the reader. Alluding to the events preceding the Crimean War, the author observes :—

There can be but little doubt that the Turkish force on the frontier will be numerically very inferior to that of the Russians. It may be stated at about 120,000, while their enemy must be able to dispose of at least 200,000 serviceable forces. Under such a state of things it is manifest that the best policy for Russia would be to use every effort to strike a heavy blow at once, to force the Danube in mass, and by rapid and vigorous movements to cut off, or thoroughly defeat the divided hordes of the Turks. In the event of success they would push on, so far as their arrangements would allow, towards the Balkan.

When once the Russians are firmly established on the right bank of the Danube, the Turks must necessarily retire to Shumla and the Balkan, and it is to be hoped that this will be effected before the detached corps or the flanks shall be too much compromised. The first real defence, then, that it would appear could be prudently made, would be on the Balkan passes. On the Balkan it is to be hoped that the Turkish armies would, by due arrangements, be under such great advantages of position as to enable them to make an obstinate stand.

Still, the line is long, the passes must be many, and the enemy, still numerous, would probably at length establish himself across it ; but by this time, feeling the effects of the campaign and forward movement in such a country, he would find a difficulty in keeping together such large bodies, in maintaining their efficiency, and obtaining supplies for them. These difficulties would increase as he prolonged the advance.

It may be considered that at such a period a well-prepared field of battle lay along the line of the Carasu river—from its mouth in the Lake of Bujuk Checkmedge, on the Sea of Marmora, to Kara Bournu on the Black Sea. The length of this line, from sea to sea, is twenty-four or twenty-five miles, but each flank, being covered by lakes and rivers, would be easily watched and secured, and the extent of the real fighting-ground would be, by these features, reduced to nine or ten miles of plain, but with favourable undulations affording a good command over the front, and which might be improved in strength in a most powerful degree by a great development of respectable field-works. One most important advantage to be obtained from the occupation of this position would be that it covers the entire Bosphorus, and would therefore enable our fleets to remain masters of the Black Sea to the last, and preclude the enemy from the use of it.

To apply the resources of this position with effect, two ingredients must be available ; first, early and energetic measures for entrenching so great an extent, so as to give it the greatest possible strength : and the other, that an adequate force should remain available for its occupation and defence. The first would require the application of several thousand workmen for several months, and could only be effected by the employment of troops, but with an understanding that a degree of benefit would be derived from their very first labours, which could be progressively improved to the very last moment. The second would require 50,000 good troops, or a proportionate increase in number of such as might be inferior.

These may appear to be heavy demands, but can scarcely be considered so, as the main and last stand to prevent the fall of an empire. The situation of the Dardanelles is detached, but presents far greater facilities for its protection, though still requiring considerable means. This is to be effected by occupying powerfully the neck of land which connects the great European Peninsula (the old Chersonese of Thrace) with the main land. At about seven miles in front of Gallipoli, and near the village of Boulaher, this neck is only three miles wide, being the narrowest part, and presents at that identical part a position that, duly fortified and garrisoned, may be given enormous strength. The whole extent of coast round the peninsula in rear of that line would be protected by the naval forces. Large means would be required to be applied to the preparation of this position within a short time ; 4000 workmen would do it in three months, and a garrison of 12,000 good troops would be necessary for its defence if properly attached.

The use of this position, however, would not be solely confined to securing the retreat of the fleet, but would be very threatening for offensive measures also ; it would cover a very extensive district, within which might be rapidly collected by sea any force that it might be thought advisable at any time to advance, either to the front or flank of the invader, with a comparatively short communication and secure depôts and retreats. It is, in fact, the point that would form the best line of operations for any forces acting in alliance with Turkey, excepting those which would be applied to the immediate protection of Constantinople ; although the water communication would be open to the Gulf of Enos, and perhaps up the Maritza, the depôts, hospitals, reserves, &c., should be established on this peninsula.

To return to the consideration of the defences for Constantinople. A second line has been designed round the city, at only a mile or two in advance ; the ground is extremely favourable. It would cover the whole space from the Sea of Marmora to the Bosphorus and, well entrenched, would be capable of considerable resistance, but it has several defects. 1. It can hardly be deemed sufficiently extensive and influential for the last resort of a great army. 2. It would be too near to the city, and the proceedings and feelings of the forces would be greatly influenced by the tumults, panics, insurrections, treacheries, and confusion of the place ; so much so, that no vigorous defence could be expected from it. 3. It would be considered as a last hold, and merely as a point for surrender. 4. It would not cover the whole of the Bosphorus, and consequently it would necessitate the evacuation of the Black Sea by our fleet.

On these accounts I attach no value to it, provided the Carasu frontier be taken up. If the disposable force was only from 5000 to 12,000 strong, I would recommend its services being exclusively engaged to secure the Dardanelles ; an additional force of 25,000 might form a valuable nucleus for the preparation and defence of the frontier of the Carasu. If a larger army could be collected it would join and act in conjunction with the Turkish forces in the Balkan, for which purpose their best landing-place would be the Gulf of Enos, proceeding to Adrianople up the Maritza river ; or they might act elsewhere, according to the circumstances of the times. An idea is suggested that the Russians, on the understanding of the preparation by the allies, may content themselves with remaining in quiet possession of the

Principalities, and thus gain an absolute advantage. It is not for me, taking in view military operations only, to judge of the effect of such a course, further than to give an opinion that I am not aware of any military measures that it would be desirable to attempt to drive them out without the co-operation of Austria.

The question is rather political than military, but it would appear to me that by so doing they would certainly abandon their cause for war, and would suffer more in prestige than they would gain in substance.

APPENDIX B. (XVII.)

THE CHEKMAGEE LINES

MAJOR-GENERAL MACINTOSH in his work, " A Military Tour in European Turkey," remarks on the possibility of a winter campaign, and on the defences of Constantinople as follows:—

" About the time that I visited the Dardanelles I made an excursion from Constantinople into Bulgaria, noting as I rode along all that appeared of professional interest in the country through which I passed. It was the beginning of November when I set out, but I found the passes of the Balkan quite practicable as regarded snow, though this is not always the case at that season. Excepting an occasional rainy day, I travelled agreeably enough over the plains on both sides of the mountains." " On leaving Constantinople, the Adrianople road carried me over a bleak tract of undulating country resembling our downs, but deeply furrowed in many places with steep ravines, and showing few vestiges of habitation beyond an occasional farm-yard enclosed by a solid wall, and generally containing several dwellings and sheds for cattle. These enclosures might often serve for posts, but they could hardly resist artillery ; although there is a method employed in the East of digging outside the wall a deep ditch, and throwing the earth up to a certain height against it, which would in some degree deaden the fire, at the same time that the ditch formed by the excavation adds an obstacle compensating for the facility which the earth thrown up within would otherwise give to an escalade.

" The road passes at no great distance from the shore of the Sea of Marmora, about ten miles from the city walls. I reached the crest of one of the elevated downs commanding a view of an extensive lake, about seven miles in length, and two in breadth, bordered with marshy land, and stretching from the sea into the country, and in the direction of the ridge called the Lesser Balkan, which lies to the north. The lake is separated from the sea at its south-western extremity by a low ledge, not many yards in breadth, traversed by the ancient highway, now in a ruinous state, and supported in some places on low arches, through which the brackish water passes and repasses, according to the direction of the wind between the sea and the lake. The causeway could be easily closed artificially, when seven miles of country would be rendered unassailable by an enemy ; for, although boats might navigate these lakes to a certain extent, its marshy shores must always render navigation difficult, even if such vessels were at hand, which, hitherto, has not been the case.

" The spot which the Turks call Kuchuk Chekmagee is designated by the Franks Ponte Piccolo, to distinguish it from the greater bridge crossing the isthmus at Buyuk Chekmagee, or Ponte Grande, the second lake, about six miles and a half further on towards Adrianople.

" The ledge at Ponte Piccolo is about three quarters of a mile in length, but the lake expands very considerably further up, and at the distance of four miles is broken into a fork, each branch being fed by a stream which flows from the highlands to the north. Proceeding over the ledge, a country of heights and valleys becoming bolder to the northward extends for about six or seven miles, when the second lake of equal length, but somewhat narrower than the first, presents itself, divided like the other from the sea by a narrow ledge, supporting a bad causeway, the centre of which rests on the large bridge above mentioned. From the brow or crest of the heights above, which are lower than those at Kuchuk Chekmagee, but which command the ledge at a very short distance, a zigzag path leads down to the village of Buyuk Chekmagee. Standing at this point, the spectator is immediately impressed with the conviction of the great strength of such a pass, and of its immense utility to Turkey, if turned to proper account; being, as it were, the abutment on which the left flank of a fine position rests, covering the capital from an enemy in this direction, a capital which, once attained by an hostile army, would mark, most probably, in its own ruin, the fall of the Ottoman Empire in Europe."

"A recent writer has described the locality as 'that formidable position about twenty miles from the capital so celebrated in history, where, owing to the nature of the ground, Attila was stayed in his march to conquer the Eastern Empire, and where at a later period the Huns* were signally defeated by Belisarius.' In reference to this statement, however, it must be observed that, as regards the advance of Attila, Gibbon especially mentions that he was only arrested by the city walls of Constantinople, without alluding to any position whatever. The following is the passage from Gibbon: 'The armies of the Eastern Empire were vanquished in three successive engagements, and the progress of Attila may be traced by the fields of battle. The two first on the banks of the Utus, and under the walls of Marcianopolis, were fought on the extensive plains between the Danube and Mount Hæmus. As the Romans were pressed by a victorious enemy, they gradually and unskilfully retired towards the Chersonesus of Thrace (the peninsula of the Dardanelles), and that narrow peninsula, the last extremity of the land, was marked by their third and irreparable defeat. By the destruction of their army, Attila acquired the indisputable possession of the field. From the Hellespont to Thermopylæ and the suburbs of Constantinople he ravaged without resistance and without mercy the provinces of Thrace and Macedonia. Heraclia† and Constantinople might perhaps escape this dreadful irruption of the Huns.' . . . Belisarius is said by the historian to have intrenched himself at Melanthius, about twenty miles from Constantinople, and there repulsed seven thousand Bulgarians, by whom he was attacked."

Major-General Macintosh, after having described the shore road from Constantinople to the lakes, describes the inland road as follows:—

"Quitting the city by the gate of Adrianople, and leaving on the right the River Sydaris, vulgarly called the Alibey, which flows through a ravine into the Golden Horn, not far from where it receives the Barbysis (now called the Kheat-Khaneh-soo), the road passes between the two great barracks of Ramish Chiflik and Daoud Pasha, situated about two miles from the walls where the Turks, looking much too near the city for its strongest defences, formerly erected field-works, which, though fallen into decay, might, if repaired, serve as the scene of a last struggle with the enemy. This neighbourhood is intersected by the subterranean conduits and lofty aqueducts which convey water from Kalfas, Kavas-Kioi, and other great reservoirs to Constantinople; and though when I visited them they were quite undefended, the Chekmagee lines if erected would effectually protect these works. The vast importance of preserving them will be understood when it is recollected that Constantinople is situated on the extremity of a wedge of land ill supplied with springs or running streams, and in a climate where, at certain seasons,

---

* Bulgarians.

† Situated at the modern Erakler, forty miles beyond Busuk Chekmagee.

there is but little rain for months. Leaving the aqueducts behind, a country is now traversed resembling that on the parallel route already described, but in which the heights are bolder, and the valleys more abrupt, while small towns and farm-houses are of more frequent occurrence, and the supply of water near the road is, by means of copious artificial fountains and occasional rivers by which it is crossed, considerably more abundant. This highly defensible track extends as far as the Chekmagee lines, which may be said to run from the two lakes on the Sea of Marmora, nearly to the fort of Kara-bornoo, on the Black Sea, where it has in its front the salt lake of Derkos, and the narrow ledge dividing it from the sea, which, no doubt, might be easily cut through so as to admit the waters of the Euxine. Our approach to the first of these lines, or that nearest Constantinople, is marked, after passing a khan and fountain, by the summit of a bold position on the Constantinople side of a river flowing through a deep ravine towards the lesser lake, and hence a view is obtained of Kuchuk Chekmagee and the neighbouring sea. Descending into the ravine, the road, which is generally good, crosses the river by a substantial stone bridge, close to which is a fountain, and ascending the steep bank on the opposite side passes a large walled farm, where another position commences.

" From this point we come on a succession of inferior slopes, dipping towards the lakes and marshes, each affording a position.

" One of these about two miles from the Chatsalda marsh in its front, to which it extends, has, in its course, a little to the west of the road, a small isolated height, well suited for a fort or telegraph. From this eminence there is an extensive view, embracing the second lake, with its town and isthmus ; and several villages occur on both sides of the road. This locality is well suited for the encampment of troops, being elevated above the marshes, and at the same time not far distant from water.

" Descending the height the road commences the passage of the marsh, by a narrow ancient causeway composed of square blocks of stone, often much displaced, and frequently intersected by the Kara-soo and other streams, over which long stone slabs are placed, forming a species of bridge removable at pleasure, thus adding to the other means available here for preventing the advance of an enemy. A similar road leads also from Chatsalda towards Derkos, on the Black Sea, a distance of about ten miles, where the right of the lines described would rest near the Cape and Fort of Kara-bornoo. Chatsalda is also about ten miles from the greater bridge, and fifteen or sixteen from the lesser ; and, unfortunately, is in front of the lines, or it would have formed a good station for a depôt, or might have been the head-quarters of a force during the healthy season of the year. . . . The country extending from the Sea of Marmora to the right of the Chatsalda road is very well secured. Thence to the Black Sea the heights become still bolder, and the valley deeper, till the road crosses the Lesser Balkan. The course of the River Kara-soo lies through one of the ravines peculiar to the country, which look like abrupt cracks across the mountain ranges, and of this peculiar formation the Bosphorus itself affords the most striking example.

" A third pass to the right leads through the lines by the village of Kastana-Kioi, and a fourth across the heights of the Lesser Balkan transversely by a road which leads from it along the shore to Midia, joining one from the mouth of the Bosphorus. The three last-mentioned roads, as well as the Chekmagees, could, if strengthened by defensive works, be included in a position comparable with any existing."

INDEX